Christian
Midwifery

Third Edition, 2nd printing
by Betty Peckmann

DISCLAIMER

The medical and health procedures in this book are based on the training, personal experiences, and research of the author and on recommendations of responsible medical sources. But because each person and situation is unique, the author and publisher urge the reader to check with a qualified health professional before using any procedure where there is any question as to its appropriateness.

The author and publisher are not responsible for any adverse effects or consequences resulting from the use of any of the suggestions, preparations, or procedures in this book. Please do not use this book if you are unwilling to assume that risk. Feel free to consult a physician or otherwise qualified professional. It is a sign of wisdom, not cowardice, to seek a second or third opinion.

Jenny Lucchesi

Christian Midwifery

Written by
Betty A. Peckmann

Illustrated by
Marti Geisel and Karen Daker
Logo by Kim Kaufman

Third Edition, 2nd Printing
Revised & Enlarged
2002

Third Edition, 2nd Printing, 2002
Revised and Enlarged
Copyright © 1997 by Betty Peckmann
Normal, Illinois
(First Edition 1990)

ISBN 0-934426-35-X
LCCN: 97-75393

Available from:
NAPSAC INTERNATIONAL
RT. 4, Box 646
Marble Hill, MO 63764
(573) 238-2010
Price $39.95 plus $3 shipping

Printed in the USA by
NAPSAC Reproductions
Marble Hill, Missouri
(573) 238-4846

Publisher's Cataloging-in-Publication
(Provided by Quality Books, Inc.)

Peckmann, Betty A.   Sept. 8, 1934 -
     Christian midwifery / written by Betty A. Peckmann ;
Illustrated by Mari Geisel and Karen Daker ; logo by Kim
Kaufman. -- 3rd ed., rev. and enlarged.
     p. cm.
     Includes bibliographical references and index.
     Preassigned LCCN: 97-75393
     ISBN: 0-934426-35-X

     1. Midwifery. 2. Childbirth--Religious aspects--Christianity.
3. Childbirth at home. I. Title

RG950.P43 1998   618.2'088204
                                  QBI97-41224

ACKNOWLEDGMENTS FOR SECOND EDITION

I wish to give special thanks to my family, especially my husband Jim who prayed fervently for this project to come to completion. Thank you to the rest of my family, daughter Gwen and her husband Dave, sons Steve and Mike, and Amy, for their prayers, and encouragement when I became discouraged.

The beautiful drawings were done by the talented Marti Giesel, with assistance from budding artist Karen Daker, who did the breech drawings. Thank you.

The second edition hopefully is filling in the gaps of the first edition. I have taken my time with this edition, hoping to eliminate most of the typos that were inevitable because of our time crunch in the first edition. I have tried to give more attention to detail this time, in an attempt to fill the need in Christian Midwifery for skills and technical knowledge and how the Word of God applies to the circumstances common to the child bearing years. And yet, as publishing dates have come and gone and additions and corrections have been made, I still find the book lacking in some areas. For the sake of "finally" publishing, I am putting this "baby" to bed and letting it rest. Please forgive the weak areas. Hopefully they are not major and can be covered in workshops.

Many thanks to Dave and Kathy Arns for their encouragement to get this second edition out. Dave, thank you for the miracles you performed converting my antique MS-DOS 1.5 EasyWriter to a form compatible to your Macintosh to "pretty it up," check for spelling and grammatical errors and get it ready for the printer. Thank you for your help, love and "prodding" to finish the project. Jane, Holly, Jill, Julie, Marti, Annette, Kim, Pat, Ellen, you guys are the greatest. Thank you for all your help in my hours of need. I couldn't have finished it without you.

To Renée Stein, my sister. Thank you for encouraging me when I was discouraged. You reached out to me in the midst of your pain, and ministered to me, when your own need was so very great. You are Jesus' faithful servant. You live the talk. That is what Jesus wants us to do. It is an honor to know you.

Thanks Jim, for reminding me that this needs to be finished, when I was ready to quit. Thank you for praying with and for me, when the discouragement was almost overwhelming. You are the tower of strength God knows I need. Thank you for being there, and reminding me that God is there too.

To the Body of Christ; thank you for living proof that you are functioning and alive to the moving of the Holy Spirit, sensitive to bringing deliverance to the captives of the world through the Blood of Jesus and by the Word of the Father, as citizens and ministers of the Kingdom of God.

Above all, I thank the Lord for helping me get this finished. For teaching me the things I needed to learn so I could correct the errors (from lack of knowledge) of the first edition. I especially thank Him for His salvation and deliverance when my hands were slipping on the rope.

May all who study and read this book be blest by our Heavenly Father, and hold fast to the standards of Shiphra and Puah.

ᏟABLE OF ᏟONTENTS

ꟼNTRODUCTION

Congratulations! So—you are going to be parents. Yes, that's what all your friends and family say when you give them the happy news of your pregnancy and expectant birth of your baby. But God and your baby say that you *already* are parents. Yes, that's right, your baby says that he/she is a person, and you already are parents. It is very difficult to think of yourself as parents, when the reality of your baby appears to be so abstract in the first few months of life.

By the time you suspected that you were pregnant, many of your baby's major organs were already formed, and baby was aware of you, your moods and your feelings toward him. (For simplicity's sake, I will use the generic term "him" when speaking of the baby—whether male or female—because a baby is a person, not an "it.") He is aware of God who has spoken life into the fertilized egg, and is forming his bones and all of his innermost parts. Isaiah 44:2–4, 24; Job 31:15, 33:4; Psalm 119:73; 68:5, 139:13–16 and Ecclesiastes 11:5.

Seven days after conception has taken place, your baby has attached himself to the uterine wall and has begun to feed himself through the developing placenta. By the 14th day, the brain stem, blood and skin cells have formed, and by three weeks of age, the spinal cord is growing, the shape of the baby is longer than wide, and is described as being tubular in shape. His nervous system, eyes and ears and the brain can all be differentiated.

At the end of the first month, at the ripe old age of four weeks, your baby's heart is pumping blood through his microscopic circulatory system. His digestive system is formed, his arms and legs are discernable and he is all of $\frac{1}{4}$ inch long! All of this miracle began when an egg, the size of this dot (.), met with a sperm not more than $\frac{1}{100}$ of this dot (.), and God said "Let there be life." How does this fit with what you have experienced as parents? Your baby is already four weeks old when you are wondering, "Did I miss my period, or am I just late"?

In two weeks you will miss your second period, and at this time you may want to get a pregnancy test—just to make sure—or you can pray and ask the Lord for confirmation. The over-the-counter pregnancy tests are pretty accurate, and run about $10.00 to $20.00, depending on brand. Now is the time to think seriously about the birth options available where you live.

Christian Childbirth Education is dedicated to helping the Christian family have a joyous, safe, Christ-centered birth. We facilitate this by applying Biblical principles to the physical experiences of pregnancy, birth and family spacing.

God's Word is three-dimensional, and addresses the needs of man's spirit, soul and body (I Thessalonians 5:23). God says in II Timothy 2:15 that we are to study and be skilled in what we do. As parents we need to be spiritually ready for birth, by learning what God has to say about birth. We do this by studying the Holy Scriptures, meditating on them, and applying them to our lives; in all areas, coming closer to God, and letting Him lead us into a closer relationship with Him. In other words, we need to be diligent about the normal Christian life. See Mark 16:16 and *The Normal Christian Life* by Watchman Nee.

The soul is the mind, will and emotions. The Word of God will bring peace and joy to your emotions, will dispel fear, and will renew your mind to line up with His. This brings you confidence that birth is a normal function of the female body, and is God's will for women.

Sometimes well-meaning friends can frighten you with their "horror" stories of birth, and you may have to separate yourself from them until after your birth, so you can maintain a positive viewpoint for your birth. Perhaps your own memories of a previous birth are not good, and you worry about history repeating itself.

This is a time to be quiet before the Lord. Pour out your heart to Him, and tell Him of your fears. Then, put those fears at the foot of the cross and ask Jesus to replace them with His peace, joy and love. That doesn't mean you will forget, but you will no longer be plagued with paralyzing fear (II Timothy 1:7, Amplified).

Jesus is in the business of giving peace and love. Perfect love casts out fear (I John 4:16). When those old fears come to haunt you, and you feel your supply of peace not as adequate as you need, ask Jesus to give you more. Childbirth preparation classes reinforce a positive attitude for birthing and can facilitate informed consent by accumulating facts and general knowledge of birth. Fear is fed by the unknown. Knowledge will dispel fear and folly (Proverbs 14:18).

Every Christian has a responsibility to his body because it is the temple of God (I Corinthians 3:16). In pregnancy, you have an added responsibility to your baby.

You must exercise and eat properly, and get enough rest, so you will be physically ready for birth and parenting, and the baby can grow with all the potential God intended him to have. In the mean time, don't let another precious moment pass without evaluating your environment, and your baby's environment.

CHAPTER 1

ꟼUTRITION. . .
ꟼHE ꟼEGINNING

Are you eating the kinds of foods that your baby needs to grow? Some of the foods you eat during pregnancy will help her have good development. Some "foods" do not give her optimum nourishment. Hamburger, fries and a soft drink may be quick for lunch when part of that lunch time is spent shopping for baby things, but will not give your baby all the nourishment she needs. Adding a fresh salad and milk to the burger and eliminating the fries and soda will.

Nutrition, God's way, is to eat every herb and vegetable that bears seed and every fruit that bears seed (Genesis 1:29; Leviticus 11:3, 9, 21–22; Deuteronomy 14:1–20), the meat of the animal that chews its cud and has a split hoof (sheep, beef, goat), fish that have scales, and birds that eat grain or seeds (non-predatory). The meats should be cooked at least medium rare so the blood is no longer running, because the life is in the blood. So here you have the list of whole grains, fresh vegetables and fruit, dairy products, and meats. The trick is preparing these foods in appetizing ways so we can enjoy them instead of eating something that has been pre-cooked, packaged, refined, and artificially "fortified."

Take time out to read a few good books on nutrition, e.g., *What Every Pregnant Woman Should Know About Drugs and Nutrition* by Gail and Tom Brewer, M.D., *Let's Have Healthy Children* by Adelle Davis, and *Nourishing Your Unborn Child* by

Phyllis Williams, R.N. Then, to help you find you way through the supermarket to buy all these wonder-"full" foods, read *The Super Market Handbook* by Nikki and David Goldbeck.

In the meantime, you will want to eat 100 grams of protein every day, fresh (raw) and cooked vegetables, and fruit. Your bread should be whole grain; check your label to see if that beautiful brown color is from molasses to cover up the "enriched" flour, or if real whole grain flour was used.

You may find this the opportunity you need to make your own breads. Whole grain flours are best because they have all the nutrients that God put into them. The white "enriched" flours have had most of the nutrients processed out. The "enriched" label means they have replaced some of the natural nutrients with synthetic vitamins. Unfortunately, man has not been able to devise a way for the synthetics to be assimilated by the human body as efficiently as the natural ones God made in the original grains. Only those vitamins man can duplicate fairly well are put back in the flours. These synthetics are usually made from petroleum products. The fiber in the natural grain flour adds bulk to the diet and helps the bowels to do their job efficiently. Fiber also helps prevent varicose veins and hemorrhoids by keeping the stools soft.

On the "Complementary Proteins" chart on the following page you will see thick arrows and thin arrows going from the circles presenting alternative protein sources. The wide arrows connect foods that will give you complete proteins because they complement each other. The narrow arrows are incomplete proteins because they have the same weaknesses in the protein molecules, or lack the same amino acid.

When a protein is matched with another protein with the same amino acid structure, you will only reap the benefits of the least amount of protein in the poorest amino acid present. You will lose the rest of the protein molecule as though it wasn't there, even though the other amino acids were very high quality. Study Adelle Davis' books on nutrition and Francis Lappe's *Diet For A Small Planet* to understand how this principle of nutrition works.

There are many meat substitutes available to 90% of the American public. Legumes, whole grains, and dairy products in the proper combinations make good meat substitutes. Look at the complimentary protein chart. Copy it and stick it on the

Complementary Proteins

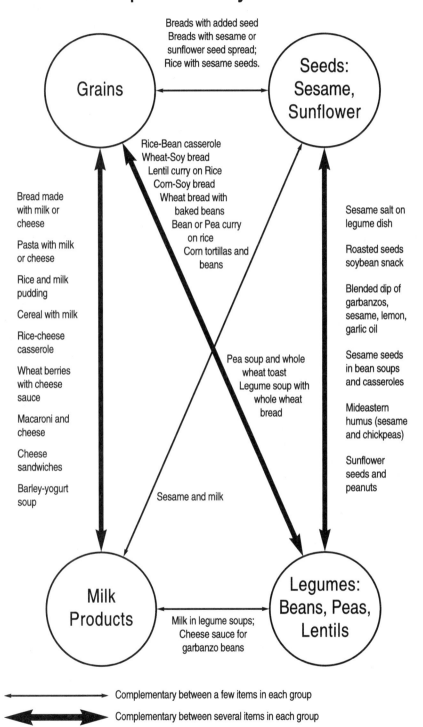

Breads with added seed
Breads with sesame or
sunflower seed spread;
Rice with sesame seeds.

Grains

Seeds:
Sesame,
Sunflower

Bread made
with milk or
cheese

Pasta with milk
or cheese

Rice and milk
pudding

Cereal with milk

Rice-cheese
casserole

Wheat berries
with cheese
sauce

Macaroni and
cheese

Cheese
sandwiches

Barley-yogurt
soup

Rice-Bean casserole
Wheat-Soy bread
Lentil curry on Rice
Corn-Soy bread
Wheat bread with
baked beans
Bean or Pea curry
on rice
Corn tortillas and
beans

Sesame salt on
legume dish

Roasted seeds
soybean snack

Blended dip of
garbanzos,
sesame, lemon,
garlic oil

Sesame seeds
in bean soups
and casseroles

Mideastern
humus (sesame
and chickpeas)

Sunflower
seeds and
peanuts

Pea soup and whole
wheat toast
Legume soup with
whole wheat
bread

Sesame and milk

Milk
Products

Legumes:
Beans, Peas,
Lentils

Milk in legume soups;
Cheese sauce for
garbanzo beans

Complementary between a few items in each group

Complementary between several items in each group

refrigerator. Look at the diet cards that are available through Christian Childbirth Education for $9.00 plus postage. These cards simplify the Brewer Diet, so anyone can get the right foods every day without counting calories and vitamin/mineral equivalents. They also help with menu planning. Please state your preference for general or vegetarian diet cards.

When you eat, eat nourishing foods. *Avoid empty calories!*

You will be surprised with how hungry you are. So eat some yogurt, or an apple with a slice of cheese as a snack. Not that hungry? Then have some fresh fruit, or a small salad or fresh veggies, or a cup of soup. If you are craving sweets, your body really wants protein. If you crave chocolate, then you want calcium. You say a nice big pickle is more your style? Then you probably need more salt and Vitamin C which you will get if you "eat" enough vinegar and brine from your pickles. Oranges and grapefruit, the cabbage family and spinach will also help you get your C. See the list of fruits and vegetables on your cards for your best vitamin and mineral sources.

Weight gain should be consistent. You are aiming for a gain of 30–35 pounds by birth day. According to a study done by both Dr. Tom Brewer some 20 years ago and a recently reported study found in Vol. 105, No. 1 (January–February 1990) of the *Public Health Reports* (Journal of the U.S. Public Health Service), women who gain 30–35 pounds during their pregnancies actually have healthier babies than if they gain less. These women also return to their pre-pregnant weight by six weeks. The Public Health report also looked for increased complications due to the increased weight gain and found none related to weight. In the obese woman, Dr. Brewer found—and my experience in my practice concurs—that she will not gain more than 20–25 pounds (*if* she follows the diet diligently and doesn't have too many fast-food treats). Raw fruits and veggies add fewer calories, but are packed with nutrition for mom and the baby. . . and don't forget fiber. Sometimes extra weight interferes with good elimination. The body is so used to "dieting" that it hoards "food," causing elimination to be sluggish. The fiber in the raw fruits and veggies encourage the bowel to work properly without the use of laxatives (which, by the way, work on the baby, too). Thus you have more energy and feel a lot better.

If you are tired beyond your first trimester, you may be slightly anemic. Some of the best sources of iron are dark green leafy veggies like collard greens, spinach, beet greens, and swiss chard, dates, pumpkin and squash seeds, kelp, nutritional yeast (get the large-flake variety for best flavor), blackstrap molasses, lean beef, and beef liver. Be sure to eat lots of these foods.

Be diligent in getting enough good exercise. Walking is the easiest to do, especially if you are not used to regular "programmed" exercise. One mile a day will do it. If you don't like walking by yourself, maybe your hubby will join you, or take the kids along. They can ride their Big Wheels or tricycles. Remember they need exercise too, and you are interested in getting your circulation moving, and getting the kinks out, not in how fast you can do your mile.

In bad weather, sidewalks are at a premium, or you live on a busy road, check with the local mall. Most malls open early in the morning and are veritable hives of activity before the stores open. You'd be surprised with how many joggers and walkers use the malls to start their day. If you need to bring the kids along, they will enjoy being able to play and even run while you are serious about your walking. With the stores closed, you can keep an eye on them. In many cities, exercise classes are available for pregnant and postpartum moms. Most such classes want a note from your midwife or physician stating that you are healthy and able to participate.

The advantage of exercise, besides becoming flexible and strengthening muscles you forgot you had since you were a small child, is, as you require more oxygen and breathe heavier, your brain sends out the order for more red blood cells to carry the extra oxygen you need to these exercising muscles. Your bone marrow and spleen answer the call and red blood cells are supplied from the nutrients you have supplied your body from this super diet that you are eating. The result is: no more anemia. Usually anemia in pregnancy is simply a low red blood cell count. Now, isn't that simple? If it is caused by lack of Vitamin B, your good diet will take care of that too!

Good nutrition is that simple. The hard part is being diligent in it and following the Lord's admonition in Genesis 1:29, "Behold, I have given you every herb bearing seed, which is upon the face of all the earth, and every tree in which is the fruit of a tree yielding seed; to you it shall be for meat." So, if you can plant its seed and it comes up and reproduces itself, you can eat it. Apple seeds make apple trees which make apples, etc. Plant wheat seed or corn, and you get wheat or corn. Then you grind it and make apple sauce or flour, or grits or whatever. But, you still have the basic food God is speaking of.

In Genesis 9:2–4, God told Noah that he could eat meat. "Every moving thing that liveth shall be meat for you even as the green herb have I given you all things, but flesh with the life thereof, which is the blood thereof, shall ye not eat." In other words, enjoy the steak, but cook it long enough that the blood no longer runs when you cut it with the knife. Pink is fine, red and running is a no-no.

In the book of Acts, chapter 10, verse 15, the Lord tells Peter, "What God has cleansed, that call thou not common, [or unclean]." A lesson in blessing what we eat. This is especially true for those of us that depend on supermarket foods. We never know what has been put in the diet of the animals or what sprays have been used on the fruits and veggies to make the foods more appealing to the consumer. Worrying about it can give you anxiety and ulcers. So pray over the food when you prepare it and before you eat it, thanking God for His provision.

A very good drink to have every day, especially if you are in stress, have a busy schedule, large family, or starting your pregnancy quite underweight is:

Pep-Up Milkshake
From *Let's Have Healthy Children* by Adelle Davis

Mix in blender or whip very fast with a rotary blender:

2	Eggs
1 tbsp	Lecithin Granules
$1\frac{1}{2}$ tbsp	Liquid Calcium and Magnesium
$1\frac{1}{2}$ c	Milk
$1\frac{1}{3}$ c	Nutritional (big flake) Yeast
$1\frac{1}{2}$ c	Non-instant Dry Milk
$1\frac{1}{4}$ c	Soy Flour
1 tsp	Vanilla
$\frac{1}{2}$ can	Frozen undiluted fruit juice (any flavor is fine; choose your favorite, as the drink takes on the flavor of the juice).

Divide contents of blender and drink it as a snack, or with your meals in addition to your regular diet. Keep cool in refrigerator. When using a rotary mixer, beat fast as with egg whites, because the more air you incorporate and the faster you go, the better it will taste.

When you sit down at the table, thank the Lord for His provision, and His merciful kindnesses toward you. Bless the food and drink in His Name and ask Him to cause the nutrition in this food to be exactly what you all need. Ask that the baby and his parents will be nourished and your bodies will be replenished, so your health will be maintained and the baby will grow to maturity as you grow spiritually into the mature Christian that God intended you to be.

Remember, the nutritional qualities in food are: fresh is best, then frozen, then canned. Use salt to taste. Sea salt is good because it has lots of trace elements in it. If you don't use sea salt, use iodized salt for a healthy thyroid gland. Salt is needed for good tissue formation in the baby, and for the making of the amniotic waters that surround and protect the baby. If you use frozen and fresh foods in the preparation of your meals, you will not get too much salt.

Please, for your baby's sake, plan on gaining about 30 to 35 pounds. Following the Brewer Medical Diet; C.C.E.'s Diet Cards will help you meet this goal. We have found that women following this diet will not put excess weight on themselves. Ladies that are quite overweight at the start of their pregnancy, find themselves weighing less after their healthy eight-pounder is born, because they are eating quality food on this diet.

Be sure your supplements have at least 75 mg of all the B vitamins (1 through 17); folacin, 4 mg.; and a non-sulfated iron. Iron glutamate or chelated iron is best. The sulfated irons, as ferrous sulfate, will often cause constipation. The glutamate or chelated kind will not, and will bind well for optimum absorption. Vitamin C helps the absorption of iron but calcium binds the iron, thus preventing absorption.

Here are some other hints of value. Lowering fat in your diet is less important than reducing sugar intake. Fats have Vitamin E and many essential fats our body needs. Sugar is empty calories and will simply add pounds, not nutrition. Stone ground whole grain flours are best. Add wheat germ to your pancake or waffle batters, sprinkle it on your salads, cereal, meat loaf, and casseroles, and you will increase the B Vitamins in your diet. Substitute honey for sugar, ($^2/_3$ cup of honey for one cup of sugar). Honey has trace nutrients plus Vitamin B and is sweeter than sugar. You will have to adjust liquids in recipes when using honey.

Drinking four cups of milk a day, or the equivalent in yogurt or buttermilk, supplies your daily need of 400 I.U. of Vitamin D. A one-inch cube of pure cheddar cheese equals one cup of milk. Hard and soft cheese contain the same amount of Vitamin D. Goat or soybean milk can be substituted for cow's milk but does not have Vitamin B_{12}. You will have to find a good source somewhere else such as lamb, beef, calf or chicken liver, beef kidneys, trout, salmon, tuna, egg yolks, cheddar, Edam, cottage, Swiss, Brie, gruyère, blue and mozzarella cheeses.

Potatoes have three grams of protein, more calcium, twice as much iron, thiamine, riboflavin, much more niacin, and seven times the Vitamin C as one apple. Do not eat potatoes in any form away from home during the first trimester unless you can trust the cook to not include potatoes with blight or sun scorch. Blight is the brown or black "bruise" in the white of the potato, and has been linked with causing spina bifida (part of the spinal cord showing outside the back) and anencephaly, (very small head, with little brain matter developed beyond the brain stem). Sun scorch is the green spots on the potato skin. Scorch can cause cramping, with possible miscarriage, and has been known to dry up a lactating (nursing) mother.

If you are taking megadoses of Vitamin C (1500 or more milligrams per day) because of cold or flu symptoms, for example, the Vitamin B_{12} and folic acid can be flushed out of your system. If you are taking supplements, this is not a problem, as your supplements will compensate for the loss of the B vitamins.

Synthetic Vitamins A and D are the only vitamins that can be toxic from overdose, because they are stored in fat cells. *Natural* Vitamin A and D (from vegetable sources) are never toxic in megadoses. Natural vitamins can be purchased at most natural food stores. Read *The Vitamin Bible* by Earl Mindell, to understand the differences in natural and synthetic vitamins, and any of Roger Williams' books on nutrition for greater details on this subject.

Carob is an excellent substitute for chocolate. It grows on trees that are naturally resistant to disease and insects, so they never need spraying. Carob powder is processed from the pods. The seeds are the source of the carob extract. Carob is low in calories: $3\frac{1}{2}$ oz. has only 180, while chocolate has 528. Carob is low in fat, only 2%, while chocolate is about 75%. Carob has no caffeine or other stimulants, but does contain Vitamins A, B complex, and three times the calcium of milk and traces of magnesium, potassium, phosphorus, sodium, silicon, aluminum, manganese, boron, chromium, copper and nickel. Carob is rich in iron and pectin. Pectin helps regulate digestion in the body and prevents diarrhea in children.

Chocolate, in addition to giving a stimulated high, contains oxalic acid, which combines with calcium and prevents calcium from being absorbed in the human body. Chocolate is of little nutritional value. It is fattening, contains addictive stimulants, and is commonly an allergen for many people (headache, phlegm, etc.). So don't drink chocolate milk and expect to reap the benefits of the calcium in the milk.

Some ladies experience heartburn, nausea, and/or "burpy" feelings during pregnancy. Your first line of attack is to submit to God (James 4:7), that is, check out what you ate. Did you overindulge in some "deceitful dainties?" Then resist the devil, and tell him to get moving. He has no right to put this on you because this in not part of being pregnant. Pregnancy is *normal*. It is God's blessing to women to give birth. It is a very special task that God has given us to nourish children before and after birth. Since this is a normal function of the uterus, just as breathing is normal to the lungs, God has made the woman's body to adjust to pregnancy without distressing her. Until you get your victory in this area, eat small, frequent meals—up to six or eight per day. Spread your daily nutritional requirements over these meals and you will do fine.

Something that has helped many ladies and their husbands is papaya tablets. Papaya fruit has an enzyme (papain) that helps digestion. The tablets are dry, compressed papaya fruit with no additives. They can be purchased in a health food store. They are very helpful for any minor digestive upset. You can eat them in any quantity, and children love them, as they are very pleasant tasting.

Unless your life and future good health depend upon it, please try to refrain from taking all medications (prescription and over-the-counter remedies), during your pregnancy. Obviously, if you are taking certain life-saving medications, e.g., heart medication or insulin, do check frequently with your doctor on the dosage and brand of your medication. Sometimes prescriptions need to be changed or adjusted temporarily. If you are taking a prescription, go to your specialist and your obstetrician on behalf of the safety of your baby. Drugs or medications, herbicides, aerosols, artificial fertilizers, pesticides, lead in water, certain antibiotics, noxious fumes from shellac, varnish, paints, exhausts from automobiles in traffic jams, noxious fumes, living over or near closed dumps that were open before EPA regulations were initiated, may cause at least one of the following problems, malformations, or defects in your baby:

- Interference with major organ development: brain, kidney, liver, heart, spine, digestive system.
- Some authors question the increase of PKU as possibly caused by drugs.
- Blood formation defects (i.e., deformed cells).
- Jaundice, causing brain defects/damages.
- Early separation of the placenta.
- Premature labor, miscarriage (spontaneous abortion).
- Interference with placental development.
- Goiters.
- Reduced oxygen to baby.
- Genital defects, masculinization of female babies, feminization of male babies.
- Delayed cancer development (may have a 20-year delay, for example, DES daughters and sons).
- Physical defects: arms, legs, ears, eyes, nose, mouth structure, deafness, blindness.
- Defective muscle development.
- Permanent teeth discoloration or malformation (pitting, green teeth from erythromycin, etc.).
- Addiction to drugs, alcohol, nicotine.
- Abnormal hardening of bones.

Scurvy-like symptoms have been seen in babies whose mothers took megadoses of Vitamin C during pregnancy (in excess of 3000 mg/day), with a sudden drop in C after birth.

To prevent this, gradually lower the dose before and after giving birth. Should you need medication during pregnancy, ask your physician or midwife the following questions:

- "What are the risks to my baby and me if I do not take this medication?"
- "What are the alternatives to taking this medication?"
- "Is there something I can do to postpone taking this medication?"

Diuretics are usually not good to take during pregnancy. As an alternative, you could try concentrating on eating the vegetables and fruits that are natural diuretics, such as green beans and asparagus, among others. If you have water retention due to pathology, the diuretic action of foods are gentile and will not pull fluids from the baby and the bag of waters as some prescription diuretics might. *Back To Eden,* by Jethro Kloss, has an extensive list of such foods.

Remember, whatever you take into your body, your baby will receive it also. If you eat it, the baby will receive it in five minutes. If you breathe it, your baby receives it in three minutes. If it comes by vein, your baby receives it in 30 seconds. The placenta strains very little out of the blood going to the baby. It is best to just assume that the baby will get whatever you have in your system. Aspirin, Bendectin, Tagamet, and Thalidomide have all been linked to congenital defects.

CHAPTER 2

INFANT DEVELOPMENT. . . THE BREATH OF LIFE

The Psalmist said, "We are fearfully and wonderfully made." We know that each of us is a unique creation. No one else has our fingerprints or voiceprints, and we can recognize others by the way they walk. What a mighty, wonderful God and Creator, to be able to do all of this, and not duplicate any of us. You say you look just like your brother or sister? Just exactly? "Well, almost, you see there is this cowlick by the part in my hair, and he has it in a different spot. . ."

When we get down to it, we find that what we really mean is that we resemble a family member quite closely, but there will be something either in personality, or a little of this or that, so we are not *exactly* like someone else. We are a composite of every person in our family. Some things are more prominent than others, like toes, ears, nose or mouth, and because we see them easier, we proclaim that we are the "spitting image" of that family member.

Did you know that God has taken the time to plan what color your eyes and hair would be, your bone structure, your sex, whether you would be skinny or not, how smart you are, your personality, even down to numbering the very hairs on your head before the foundations of the earth were laid? Well, He did. He also laid the blueprint out for your baby. He says so in Psalm 139:13–16. Genesis 1:27 boldly declares that God created us in His image!

Our soul is our mind, or, in other words, our brain. The brain is like a master computer for the body. It tells our stomach to digest the food, our heart to beat and pump the blood through our bodies, and our lungs to breathe. Those things are some of the involuntary things the brain does every day of our lives without our conscious effort. At the same time, we can consciously (voluntarily) do many other things that we are thinking about, and the brain still sorts everything out without getting mixed up.

As a little exercise, next time you are driving your car, make a list of everything you see and do just in one block, i.e., acceleration, steering, watching the car ahead of you, watching the kids playing in case they run in front of you, monitoring the traffic ahead of you and in the other lanes, listening to the radio or cassette player and talking to others in your car. Yes, our soul knows what a wondrous work our body is, and how wondrously God made it.

Our spirit is that place in us where God dwells when we make Jesus our Savior, and where the Holy Spirit dwells when we receive His indwelling (Romans 8:9–10). It is our spirit that responds to God, and ministers to our conscious mind, causing us to respond with our free will to God. Our spirit will go to heaven when the Father calls us home (Ecclesiastes 12:7) and the redeemed soul will accompany it. The resurrected body will follow on resurrection day (James 2:26). When God fashions a baby, He starts with the brain and the spinal cord and then works His way down the body, from back to front. Let us see how this miracle takes place.

- **Isaiah 44:2–4, 24:** God fashions us in the womb
- **Job 31:15; 33:4:** God forms (shapes) us in the womb, and gives us the breath of life.
- **Psalm 119:73:** God's hands have made me and fashioned me, given me understanding, that I might learn.

Seven days after conception, the fertilized egg has travelled down the fallopian tube, has attached himself to the uterus by spinning into the uterine lining (endometrium), and has begun to feed himself through the developing placenta. Within 14 days after conception (two weeks), the brain, blood and skin cells form. Brain waves can be measured now. By the grand age of 21 days, or three weeks, the spinal cord has grown from the round "mulberry-like" clump of cells when it implanted itself into the endometrium, to the tubular shape of the human body. The brain, nervous system, eyes, and ears can be differentiated. The heart begins to pump the blood through this microscopic circulatory system, and will continue to beat for the rest of this person's life.

By four weeks, the digestive system is formed and the arms and legs are forming, and your baby is $\frac{1}{4}$ inch long. You have noticed that you are approximately two weeks overdue for your menstrual cycle. You may or may not be having some early signs of pregnancy, like having to potty a lot, or maybe tingling in the breasts, or your nipples may be extra tender. Some ladies have what is commonly called "morning sickness."

This does not have to happen in the morning. Sometimes it occurs in the afternoon or at night. Sometimes only after eating a high-fat meal, sometimes only when hungry, or when you have to wait a little past your usual eating time. The cause for this is still being debated. Everyone has his own pet reason for it, and similarly, his own pet cures. I will give you some ideas, and solutions other ladies have had success with. The peculiar thing with "morning sickness" is that no one thing helps everybody, but it usually is over by the 13th week. So, you have to start with one thing and keep trying until you find what is best for you.

The one thing everyone has in common, is a queasy feeling when you are hungry. The cure for hunger, is to eat. During the day, eat some fruit, or a whole-wheat cracker with cheese. If yours begins when you wake up, keep a supply of crackers next to your bed. Eating a high-protein snack just before you go to sleep at night helps. For example, a peanut butter sandwich and a glass of milk. Peanut butter takes a long time to digest, and your blood sugar will not be too low (a suspected cause). Drinking warm water, not cold juice, soothes the tummy first thing in the morning. You may want to postpone your juice until mid-morning or lunch time.

Ginger capsules, purchased at a health food store, and taken three times a day have given relief to ladies with severe nausea. Ginger tea made from nickel-size slice of fresh ginger root (grocery product department) steeped in 2 cups boiling water and then sipped all day. Helps take the piece of root out before drinking. If you can't eat three big meals a day, try six or eight small meals. The problem with lots of small meals is making sure your nutritional requirements are met and that you are not munching on potato chips and cookies. Small meals require planning, but you can do it, because this will pass in a few weeks.

One lady I knew could not stand the smell of food cooking, so her husband fixed the meals, and when the cooking smell was gone, she would eat her meal. This was not easy, but they worked it out. They also had three other children. Early in her pregnancy, she had a difficult time keeping anything down, even after praying about it. So her hubby would bake a large whitefish once a week, and they kept it in the refrigerator for her to nibble off of. This stayed down, gave her good protein for the baby to grow on and many of her vitamins.

Sometimes papaya tablets do the trick. Papaya fruit has an enzyme, **papain**, that helps the digestive process (especially heartburn), so that may be worth trying. Papaya tastes good, and you don't need to limit your intake. Some ladies have found that increasing their Vitamin B_6 helps.

Prayer, of course, should be your first thought. Speak to your body, and tell it "in the name of Jesus, return to divine order, and no longer distress me." Remember, your body is used to obeying your brain, so use your brain to remind your body to behave. This is not a mind-over-matter thing, it is simply causing your body to be in subjection to your will. Who will rule you? Your flesh with its feelings, or your spirit that knows what God's best is for you?

It does not matter if you choose spiritual solutions or physical solutions. What does matter is that you do something if morning sickness is a problem for you. Your baby is growing faster now than he will the rest of his life, and his health and well-being for the rest of his life may depend on your nutrition. This is the only time his major organs will be formed, and that is why he needs all the nutrients he can get.

At two months, baby quadruples his size to one inch long. His internal organs formed, covered with a layer of tissue and transparent skin, and of course, his heart has been beating for three to four weeks. The brain is developing very fast, making the head look very large compared to the body. Baby's arms are developed about one week before the legs. All of the parts of the face (eyes, nose, mouth and palate, eyelids), neck, external ears and urogenitals are well on their way to completion.

The end of the seventh week marks the end of the embryonic period. All internal and external organs are present and only growth and final elaboration is needed. Bone cells also start replacing cartilage during this time. This is a very critical stage of life for your baby: he is very susceptible to **teratogens**.

Teratogens are substances that may cause congenital malformations or even be lethal. Avoid using or inhaling the following teratogens during pregnancy:

- Caffeine (from coffee, some teas, soft drinks, etc.).
- Tannic acid (from over-brewed tea).
- Smoking (toxic inhalants include cyanide, carbon monoxide, nicotine etc.). One cigarette removes 25 milligrams of Vitamin C from your body. This is not good, because Vitamin C helps fight viruses (colds and flus) and helps the body to repair itself and helps maintain cell integrity (good health).
- Marijuana; it builds up in the ovaries and testes of the baby, causing changes in the DNA, possibly damaging future generations.

Other things to avoid contact with, if at all possible, are: drugs, viruses, aerosols, pesticides, herbicides, paint removers, fertilizers, x-rays, glues, cleaning fluids, volatile paints, lacquer thinners, glues, household cleaners, and contact cements. Some researchers include ultrasound, because we have not had enough time/generations to compare human outcomes with the laboratory animal results, and to see if its effects on humans are detrimental.

If your life and/or health depends on your prescription, please talk with your physician. Some medications will hinder your conceiving, or may even abort your baby. Your doctor may want to change your prescription, if he knows you want to get pregnant, or are already pregnant. Then, ask her/him if your medication has been tested for safety for the unborn child. If not, ask for a substitute. Sometimes the substitute is safe for your child, but you will not be as comfortable as you were with the old medication. You will have to make the final decision, so be sure to make the one you are willing to live with.

The last negative thing we will discuss in this area is **toxoplasmosis**. This unfriendly "critter" is transmitted through the dust in your kitty's litter box. The virus causing toxoplasmosis is so tiny it can sit on the edge of a piece of dust floating in the air above the litter box, and you would not see it. If your kitty never goes outside, and never eats raw meat, it is unlikely that you need to be concerned about this. Cats are natural hunters and carriers of this disease, although it does not affect them. They pick up the virus when they kill, injure, or eat birds and/or small rodents. If your cat stays outside, or never uses a litter box, don't worry about it. Just be sure to wash your hands after petting kitty. If you have a litter box, have someone else clean it for you during your pregnancy. Toxoplasmosis can cause abortion, retardation, neurological problems, malformation of the head, blindness, or fatal illness in the baby, *if* mother is actively infected with the disease. Simple exposure giving immunity in the mother, usually will not cause problems in the baby.

At three months, baby has tripled his size to three inches long, and weighs one ounce. He now has fingers, toes, eyelids, and a skeleton of bones. The umbilical cord is longer, and baby is free-floating in the bag of waters, receiving nourishment through the placenta. Sex differences are visible. Sometimes, ladies have felt the baby kick. Well, really, it feels more like butterflies flitting about in the tummy, than a real kick, but it *is* the baby moving. He can frown, make respiratory movements, urinate, move the specific parts of the limbs, squint, open and shut his mouth. He even sucks his thumb on occasion. From now until birth day, baby will be growing and maturing what has already formed.

By four months, baby has grown to six inches long and weighs seven ounces. He's really coming along, isn't he? His weight has increased by a factor of seven in four weeks. Movements are stronger and unmistakable by mother. She no longer wonders if she was feeling gas bubbles. His skin is still very thin, and the capillaries are still visible. He can make a fist, and if something like a straw is placed in his hand, he will try to hold it.

At five months, baby grows to 12 inches, becomes sensitive to sound, his nails become harder, and the nipples on his chest become visible. Heart tones are easily heard with a stethoscope. **Vernix caseosa** (God's cold cream that protects the baby's skin from the watery environment), covers the whole body. He also is covered with lots of hair, called **lanugo**.

In the sixth and seventh months, baby sucks his thumb, occasionally has hiccups, stretches, kicks hard enough to bounce this book off your tummy, and turns somersaults. His skin is still translucent, quite red and wrinkled, making him look like a little old man. Some researchers and mothers report the baby can cry at this age. His grip is stronger now and will hold anything placed in his hand. His organs function independently and he opens and closes his eyes. He will shade his eyes from a bright light shining against his mother's tummy. He weighs $2\frac{1}{2}$ pounds, a five-fold gain from five months. During the seventh month, the baby begins to store fat, giving his body a more contoured look. He is still very lean, old and wrinkled-looking.

- **Psalm 121:7:** Protection and direction from God!

When I was a young nurse, I remember a pregnant lady being admitted to my floor. She had been in a automobile accident, and a fence post had gone through the car and pinned her to the seat. The splintered post had penetrated her uterus, but the bag of waters was unbroken and the baby was not injured. Since she was only 6 months pregnant, and baby's viability was questionable outside the uterus, it was decided to repair the uterus, keep close eye on the situation and hope she could carry the baby to term. She did, and had a vaginal birth with a very healthy baby. The baby was born gripping a wood splinter in his hand. God has made the membranes very strong, and they are the baby's protection. Just as a water balloon takes a lot of punishment to break by poking, so it is with the bag of waters.

- **Ecclesiastes 11:5:** God knows how the bones are formed in the uterus.
- **Isaiah 40:11:** The Lord shall feed me, gather me, carry me, and He gently leads those with child, (spiritually and physically).

In the eighth month, baby is 16 inches long. He is starting a big growth spurt here, and all his organs are completely self-sufficient. He weighs about four pounds. The fat storage continues and the baby loses all of his wrinkles. He no longer has an "old" look about him. Thick vernix casiosa covers the baby. The hair on his head continues to grow and the lanugo is plentiful, except on the face, where it has disappeared. The fingernails have reached the end of the fingers, and the toenails are at the end of the toes. Baby can control rhythmic breathing patterns and body temperature. The eyes are open. Baby boy's left testicle has descended into the scrotum.

At last, you have reached your ninth month. Baby is quieter now; sleeping and "eating" are the only major activities. Some shifting is felt, but not as actively as before, because of the "shrinking" of the available space. Full weight and growth, to 19–22 inches at birth, is achieved this month. The right testicle descends into the scrotum. The vernix caseosa is either absorbed or comes off the skin when the lanugo disappears. The skin varies in color from white to pink to bluish-pink, regardless of race, because the melanin that colors the skin is produced only after exposure to light. The weight will increase to somewhere between $6\frac{1}{2}$ and 10 pounds or even more. Mother supplies baby with special proteins and antibodies to ensure his health when he comes in contact with the world. The last week before birth, baby settles down into the pelvis and rests. Growth is complete until after the birth.

- **Isaiah 49:1, 5, 15:** The Lord calls the child from the uterus on "birthday."

When the Lord calls the baby forth, the baby responds by releasing a hormone, which he has made for this day, and this day only. It will never be in his body again! This hormone goes to the placenta via his blood, and crosses over to the mother's bloodstream. It then travels to her pituitary gland, which "reads" it, sends a message to the uterus: "This baby is ready to be born!", and labor begins. And God planned this!

- **Ezekiel 16:4–6, 9:** The Lord has formed me in the womb, has compassion on child of the womb, and as a mother does not forget her child, neither does God.

CHAPTER 3

PRENATAL CARE. . . PARENTING BEGINS

I hope that by now you have concluded that the responsibility of prenatal care is on the expectant couple's shoulders. Yes, this is contrary from what we have experienced in the past. We have learned from society that the "experts" know best, and if we just do as they say, everything will turn out all right. That would be fine *if* we did not have libraries, book stores, tapes, videos, and records from which to learn. But since there is such a flood of information available, we really have no excuse for *not* learning about pregnancy except our own laziness. God has never given us the authority to turn our lives over to anyone but Him. He admonishes us to learn and apply what we learn. He does warn us against being hearers only and not doers. In James 2:22 and in II Timothy 3:7, God talks about those who are always learning, but never truly learning. They just run from teacher to teacher and say, "Yes, that is right. Thank you for teaching me such wonderful things." And the next day they are saying the same thing to someone who has just said the opposite. Knowledge just never seems to take root in their brain. . . "In one ear and out the other," as my mother used to say.

Just as God wants us to apply the spiritual truths He teaches us in His Word, we must also apply the things in the natural to see if they "work" and line up with God's Word (Daniel 1:17). Eating right and exercising properly, reading, and going to class are what you should do. But you still need to make sure the baby is doing well and everything is progressing as it should, by seeing a trained third party.

Monitoring your prenatal care is what the midwife and/or doctor's role is all about. Your midwife/doctor is not swayed by wishful thinking, or what your dream is. They will be alert to watch for the normal and any variations, and after parents/clients and caregivers discuss options, will take proper precautions before problems become serious. I like to have prenatal visits in my office after the initial interview, every three weeks up to the 28th week of pregnancy. Then, every two weeks until the 36th week of your pregnancy, when we have weekly visits until birth day. One of those weekly visits will be in the home to refresh the midwife's memory on how to find the couple's house without the pressure of the mother being in labor. The Amish usually do not leave the home place the last four to six weeks, so those visits are done in their homes. It is nice for the midwife to know where the parents keep their birth supplies, in case she needs to get them out on birth day because the parents are "too busy." The home visit also lets the midwife know where things like glasses and snacks are kept.

At your initial prenatal visit, your midwife or doctor will take your obstetrical, gynecological, and general health history. This is not to invade your privacy, but is an aid to giving you the best personalized care possible. Sometimes what you may consider a minor, forgotten incident can be important in your care. Like the time you bounced down the stairs hard on your sitting spot and couldn't walk very well for a day or so. You didn't pay any attention to that because it happened when you were a child, and hasn't bothered you. But, when the midwife asked you about any tail bone injuries, you remembered that. This may make a difference in labor. . . especially if your baby is in a posterior position. Knowing about a possible tail bone injury, the midwife can suggest position changes that will take some of the pressure off of it during labor.

In previous chapters, we discovered that before you even realized you were pregnant and could start eating right and doing all the right things, most of the baby's development had already happened. Now, don't just throw this book in the air and say, "It's too late now!" Most of us, by God's grace, have some reserves that the baby has been drawing on. This, of course, cannot continue indefinitely, but will help us get by until we get started doing something positive.

The first thing, of course, is shaping up the old diet. You will read a lot about nutrition in this book; not because I have a fixation on the subject, but because good nutrition prevents 90% of all complications in pregnancy, labor, birth, and post-partum for mother, and developmental problems in the baby. Of course, good nutrition cannot prevent genetic problems, but it can give the baby the edge he needs to get through the early neonatal period until appropriate correction or help is given.

Weight gain should be consistent. You are aiming for a gain of 30–35 pounds by birth day. According to a study done by Dr. Tom Brewer some 20 years ago, as well as a recently reported study found in the January-February 1990 issue of the *Public Health Reports* (Journal of the U.S. Public Health Service, Vol. 105, No. 1), women who gain 30–35 pounds during their pregnancy actually have healthier babies than those who gain less. Also, these women typically return to their pre-pregnant weight by six weeks. The Public Health report also looked for increased complications due to the increased weight gain and found none related to weight.

In the obese woman, Dr. Brewer found—and my experience concurs—that she will probably not gain more than 20–25 pounds *if* she follows the diet diligently and doesn't have too many fast-food treats. Raw fruits and vegies add fewer calories, but are packed with nutrition for mom and the baby. . . and don't forget fiber. Sometimes extra weight interferes with good elimination. The body is so used to "dieting", that it hoards "food," causing elimination to be sluggish. The fiber in the raw fruits and veggies encourages the bowel to work properly without the use of laxatives, which, by the way, work on the baby too. Thus, you have more energy and feel a lot better. A gentle herbal laxative is Psyllium.

You might want to ask if there are any exercises you should be doing to prepare you for childbirth. Some communities have hospital- and doctor-sponsored classes that are free. Other communities charge a nominal amount. Among the best known is *Expectorcise*. There are several videos for pregnant women available at your local retailer. The low-impact and gentle stretch styles are the best. High-impact is not recommended during pregnancy.

Elizabeth Noble's *Essential Exercises for the Childbearing Year* is an excellent book. After describing how to do the exercises, she also explains what the exercise does for your muscles, and also when *not* to do the exercise. Walking a mile every day is very effective exercise. When done briskly, walking will give your cardiovascular system a good workout as well as your abdominals, legs, and arms. When you swing your arms, your chest and back also get exercised.

When you see your caregiver, she usually wants a urine specimen to test for several things, using a urine test strip (also called a "reagent strip," or simply a "dipstick"). I usually use the **Chemstrip 9-G** (from Biodynamics) or **Multistix 9-G** (from the Ames Company) which test for leukocytes, protein, glucose, nitrite, urobilinogen, bilirubin, ketones, blood, specific gravity, and pH. The color shadings reveal how the liver, kidneys, gall bladder and digestive system are functioning before clinical disease is manifested, so simple measures such as increasing liquid intake can be taken to maintain good health. The following are merely generalizations to acquaint you with some of the information that little dipstick can give you.

Leukocytes are white blood cells and are present in mucus, which is normal for the pregnant woman. However, if she has any pus in her body, from cystitis, a cold or the flu, or if the mucus plug is melting, or there is semen present, the leukocyte reading will show a 2 plus.

The **pH** is a reflection of how well the acid-base balance is being regulated by the kidneys and the lungs. In the urine, the pH is an important indicator of certain metabolic, kidney, gastrointestinal and respiratory factors. In my practice, I have noticed that most vegetarians have pH readings of 7 or 8 (alkaline), while meat eaters will have a more acid pH of 5 or 6. However, if chronic cystitis, pyloric stenosis, or acute/chronic kidney failure are present, the urine may be very alkaline over a long period of time. It may also indicate bacterial infection and/or dehydration, uncontrolled diabetes mellitus or pulmonary emphysema.

If you are not eating enough **protein**, your body will read what protein you are eating as incomplete and will throw it off in the urine. Should you not correct this by increasing your protein intake you will run the risk of developing Metabolic Toxemia of Late Pregnancy (MTLP, or simply "toxemia"). Toxemia can result in convulsions which are hazardous to your health and your baby's life. Dr. Brewer proved that eclampsia/ toxemia is due to poor nutrition (read books by Tom Brewer, Gail Sforza Brewer and Adelle Davis.) Following CCE's nutrition cards will prevent this disease of malnutrition. Certain bacteria may also throw off protein, so if the diet is good, look at this as a possibility.

Most pregnant women will throw sugar (**glucose**) in their urine a lot quicker than the non-pregnant woman. A by-product of "used" protein is sugar. In other words as the baby uses the protein to make new cells, a waste product is glucogen. This is passed back to mom and she stores this in her liver. When mom indulges in a treat, like a soda or piece of candy on her way to the midwife for her check up. . . guess what? You got it: a $\frac{1}{2}$ gram or more glucose shows up. Ordinarily, that would not get spilled, but because of her pregnancy it does. Some women spill sugar more readily than others. No one seems to know why, but it does alert doctors to a "new" thing called **gestational diabetes**. Some doctors find gestational diabetes "behind every tree," so to speak. In reality, it really does not occur that often, so it is wise to confess when you have binged, or had candy, etc., within a few hours (for some women, 12 hours) of your appointment. We will discuss gestational diabetes at some length in Chapter 4, so we won't go into it now. Usually, gestational diabetes is not suspected unless you have had at least two unexplained incidences of one-gram (each) sugar spills. Uncontrolled diabetics will also spill sugar/glucose.

In the context of a dipstick, "**blood**" really means "free hemoglobin." Hemoglobin is released when red blood cells are broken down somewhere in the body. Large amounts usually mean a disease process in the body. It can also be caused by unaccustomed, strenuous exercise. I have also occasionally seen it when a couple starts the prenatal vaginal massage exercise to prevent lacerations at birth, a scratch from harsh toilet paper or slight irritation from sexual intercourse. Often during pregnancy, the vaginal mucosa does not provide enough lubrication, and the dryness causes an irritation. Late in pregnancy, it could be a sign that the mucus plug is beginning to melt away. It is always wise to find the reasons for the blood, and head off a nasty bladder infection, or stop a vaginal infection before it becomes a serious problem. A mucus discharge and blood could signal a yeast or trichonomas infection, both of which are easily treated in the early stages. If allowed to continue, a prescription from the doctor may be necessary.

Ketones are easily eliminated. Throwing ketones in your urine means you are not eating enough calories, and you are burning up your reserves. These reserves are what you will need to make milk and keep you going during the first six weeks postpartum when you are up half the night and all day caring for your baby and the family. They keep you and baby going when meals are little late during the pregnancy. Diabetics also spill ketones if they are not taking enough insulin. If you have a "good case" of the flu, or severe morning sickness, or working too hard for your food intake, you are likely to spill ketones. You need to increase your food intake.

Nitrites are produced by 95% of common urinary bacteria. Generally, four hours in the bladder is required to incubate the bacteria. Any pink on the stick will reveal urinary tract infection, i.e., kidneys, ureters, bladder or urethra. You do not need symptoms of fever, burning, or pain for the infection to show on the stick. By the time symptoms appear, damage can be done. Usually flushing the urinary system with lots of water, cranberry juice (the unsweetened kind, not cranberry juice cocktail) and some Vitamin C will stop these bacteria in their tracks.

Do not confuse this with the nitrates that are in surface and shallow well water, or in foods. Nitrates/nitrites get into the drinking water from the run off of fertilized fields. Nitrates in foods and drinking water are changed into nitrosamines by our body's metabolism. Nitrosamines are carcinogenic in babies and children under five, because they are growing so fast. Usually, the body "sees" a cell growing rapidly and sends out the "army" from the immune system to destroy the invaders. However, because the child under five years of age is normally in a fast growing state, the body does not see fast growing cells as a danger and misses the young cancer cell. This is another reason why you should limit meats with nitrates in them during pregnancy. This additive is present in bacon, lunch meats, hot dogs, sausages, etc. Read the label.

There are deli foods without nitrate added, but usually you have to pay a premium price. . . but what price is health? Check at your local health-food store if you can not find nitrate-free meats at your grocer. You might talk to the manager and request nitrate-free meats. Your request may be the one that moves him/her to order them.

Bilirubin is formed in the spleen and bone marrow from the breakdown of old or damaged red blood cells. It comes from the heme part of the hemoglobin within the red cells. Red blood cells live about 120 days. When they die, your body recycles the **heme** (iron stores) and the **globin** (protein) and places them in the "new" red cells. The waste part, bilirubin, is sent to the liver. Usually it is excreted into the intestines via the common bile duct. The bilirubin gives the bile its distinctive color, and also helps emulsify and digest fats. In the intestine, bacteria convert bilirubin to urobilinogens. Bacteria also produce Vitamins K and B_6 in the intestine. Remember this when taking antibiotics; you will want to replace what the medication "kills."

Urobilinogen is usually found in the intestines. However, if excessive amounts of red cells are being destroyed as in pernicious anemia, hemolytic anemia or sickle cell disease, urobilinogen will be found in the urine. It also signals hemolytic (or pre-hepatic) jaundice. Hemolytic jaundice indicates excessive amounts of red blood cells are being destroyed in the bone marrow, liver or spleen. Tranquilizers can give "false positive" bilirubin results and antibiotics can reduce urobilinogen levels.

The **specific gravity** measures the concentration (or lack thereof) of dissolved salts and other wastes. Dehydration can cause high concentrations of salts, while large intake of water can dilute them greatly. The normal values are between 1.001 and 1.135. Extremely high or low values are cause for further investigation.

After your urine has passed scrutiny, your blood pressure is "on the block," so to speak. Most midwives spend time chatting with you about how things are going with your pregnancy, and if anything exciting is occurring in your life, before starting the exam. This gives you a little time to relax after fighting traffic, and refereeing the kids in the back seat. Do your kids always take ten times longer to get ready to go anywhere, especially if you're a little late getting started, or were mine "the only ones?" That can raise the blood pressure at least five millimeters. Sometimes getting to the midwife or doctor's office is as hectic as Sunday morning. Worries about ailing family members or that long list of "must dos" can get the blood pressure a-pounding. If your diet is good but your blood pressure is up, and you know it is because of worry and anxiety, learn to sit down and relax. Taking time out every day to meditate on the Word of God, praying and "casting all your cares on Him, because He cares for you" (I Peter 5:7) will do more for lowering that blood pressure than all the pills in a bottle. Learn to be content with what God has given you, and with the place God has planted and called you to. I Thessalonians 5:18 reminds us to give thanks in everything. A reading of 140/90 more than three times in a row is a signal to investigate more thoroughly. It is best to get rid of what is eating at you before you get chewed up. Read Dr. McMillan's *None of These Diseases*.

The blood pressure norm is about 100/60 to 120/80. The top number (systolic) is the amount of pressure, expressed in millimeters of mercury, exerted by the blood against the wall of the artery during the heart/pulse beat. The bottom number (diastolic) is the amount of pressure, also expressed in millimeters of mercury, of the blood in the artery during the period of rest between heart/pulse beats. Rising blood pressure may indicate tension, anxiety, or possible toxemia. If due to tension and anxiety, taking time to be quiet before the Lord and giving Him those tensions and anxieties will bring that pressure down very quickly.

Tension and anxiety are usually caused by doing more than we can comfortably handle, and then taking responsibility for what we can't do. Reviewing priorities and learning to say "No!" will help a great deal. Taking time out to talk with Jesus in prayer and meditating on His Word will help take the "kinks" out and relax you. Praying in the Spirit and praising the Lord will relax you faster than anything I know. It is physiologically impossible to be tense and say "I love you, Jesus. Praise your Holy Name."

I heard a testimony on Christian radio by a scientist who was a Christian, and had participated in a scientific research team that was studying the brain waves of persons dying of brain tumors. The simplified results reported Christians praying or having a vision of Jesus at death, registered pleasure or had very restful brain waves. Those who were not believers manifested very stressed brain waves. This was confirmed scientifically and all the scientists involved agreed with the results. The nonbelievers reported seeing a very frightening scene and were struggling against death. This study is what converted this scientist. Praise the Lord! Prayer has many benefits besides "letting the Lord know what we need or want." It has also been proven that it is impossible to hypnotize or "brainwash" anyone who is praying in the Spirit, whether he is vocalizing or thinking the prayer. Thank you, Jesus, for such provision.

At about the 28th week, a **roll-over** test can be done. This is a non-invasive screening test for toxemia. The blood pressure is taken while you sit on the side of the table or bed, then again immediately after you lie down. If there is a rise of 10 in the numbers, you are at risk of eclampsia. Special care that you eat enough protein will usually take care of this. Sometimes a lady will need more protein, so extra protein snacks or protein drinks (shakes) made with milk will fill the need. Some ladies have sprinkled protein powder on their cereal and other foods. This fulfills the increased need of protein without adding volume, which can be a problem in the last trimester.

The **hemoglobin** or **hematocrit** should be monitored about three times during the pregnancy. I usually check it first at three months, then six months and again about eight months. By waiting until three months, the blood volume has increased as much as it is going to, and I can see if the dilution of red cells is critical. At six months, mom's iron stores are going to begin to be depleted if her diet is low, or if she is not able to glean what she needs from her foods and supplements. At eight months, we will see if the baby is getting enough iron from mom and depleting her stores. During the last month, baby is storing up the iron he will need until he is able to get his own supply from his foods at about six months. If the hemoglobin is below 11 or the hematocrit below 32 at eight months, dandelion root tincture will bring it up in seven days. At any other time, we will rely on diet and supplements. Be sure not to take your iron supplement/ foods when you are taking calcium. Calcium will bind with iron and make it impossible for your body to absorb it efficiently. Vitamin C, on the other hand, helps your body to absorb iron. Reading the previously mentioned nutrition books will give you additional hints. Earl Mindell's *Vitamin Bible* also gives practical advice on how to get maximum benefit from your supplements.

At your initial prenatal visit, your midwife or doctor may also want to do a physical exam, especially if it has been a while since you had one. A physical exam involves listening to your heart, checking for tenderness about the kidneys, looking for scoliosis (curvature of the spine), varicosities and taking blood samples for laboratory analysis. The lab will do state-mandated tests for pregnant women, in addition to the liver and kidney profiles, a complete blood count (CBC), hemoglobin and/or hematocrit, and antibody count. If you are Rh negative, the lab will look for sensitization to Rh positive blood. If you are sensitized, you will need RhoGam for the baby's protection. There is some risk of receiving blood transmitted disease through RhoGam, because it is a human blood derivative. If you have a lab nearby that can make RhoGam with your donated blood, do so before pregnancy. If you can get a family member or friend that you know well to donate blood for the lab to make your RhoGam for you, great. Otherwise, pray over the RhoGam that it will not harbor evil, but will be a blessing for your baby. Synthetic RhoGam will be available by 1999.

The growth of the baby is monitored by measuring the height of the **fundus** (the top of the uterus). This measurement, expressed in centimeters, usually corresponds with the number of weeks you are pregnant. It is especially true after the 20th week, and can be helpful in determining your due date if your last menstrual date is unclear. Because of the vast variance in growth patterns the first 20 weeks, it is not accurate to compare growth with weeks pregnant then. You can get an idea of whether the baby is growing, by the steady increase in size.

Intra-uterine growth retardation is very difficult to determine before 16 to 18 weeks, but you may begin to suspect it before then. As the pregnancy progresses, "Pat" will be constantly spilling protein and ketones to varying degrees, and will not be gaining her average pound a week, after 13 weeks. If the baby is truly IUGR, serious problems can result on birth day. This is due to malnutrition in the developing baby. The problems can be anything from malformation of the body to severe brain growth problems. If growth has been retarded sufficiently, you may have a very sick baby requiring life support systems. Usually IUGR will be risked out of home birth. So pay close attention to the size of the baby on palpation and fundal measurement.

After the twentieth week, the halfway mark of the average 40-week pregnancy, baby should grow 1 cm per week. Please see the drawing for the usual fundal height in relation to week of pregnancy. Not all women will reach 40 cm, but most will reach 38–39 cm before they "drop." The medical term is "lightening," a more descriptive word to me.

At lightening, the baby settles into the pelvis, giving mother a sense of feeling lighter or less heavy in the belly. Her profile resembles a lady carrying a watermelon, because the baby sticks out at a greater angle than before. It is a lot easier to breathe, but not as easy to bend over or walk for any distance. The leg and hip joints and pubic bone feel like they are turning to Jello, and care must be taken when pivoting. Slow and easy is the lady's gait now. Some ladies develop a kind of waddle because the baby's head is deep in the pelvis and putting pressure on the leg socket. Waddling eases that pressure, so try to resist the urge to comment, husband and friends, except to encourage her that it can't be long before birth day.

Sometimes baby does not read the calendar to find out that he is supposed to come on Uncle John's birthday, and has passed that date by three weeks. As long as Pat can count ten major movements a day, the heart tones are okay, and baby is not growing too big, the baby just might need extra time to mature. This may be when the midwife may want to do a nonstress test at your weekly visits, if there is some question about baby's movements. Occasionally, baby needs ten months to mature on the inside. If you have concern, and depending on your backup situation, you may want a second opinion from another midwife or from your backup.

If the lady is carrying the baby very low all the way through the pregnancy, she will have a waddle early, and her fundal height will be consistently less than her weeks pregnant. If Pat experiences pressure earlier than her last month, it is a sign that her "kegel" (pubococcygeal) muscles are not very strong. So, Pat, *kegel, kegel, kegel, kegel,* at every stop sign and light, every commercial on radio or TV, when you change your toddler's diapers, wash dishes, sort clothes, fold clothes, during the sermon and during the announcements at church, during "coffee" break, when the phone rings and while you talk on the phone, while you stir the gravy, etc. Do at least ten series of ten kegels every day for the rest of your life. You will reap benefits in the bedroom and at your birth. The last month of your pregnancy, occasionally relax those muscles instead of tightening them. Then do your kegel again. This will help you relax during the perineal massage exercise, and when baby is born.

To do the kegel exercise properly, you tighten those muscles around the vagina, rectum and urethra. Now count to ten, one number per second, still holding the muscles tight. Use all the muscles you need to keep it tight while you count to ten. Start off doing a series of five, and gradually work up to ten in each series. You know that your are doing it right if you can stop a stream of urine and then let the urine out in spurts, not drops. If you are doing a kegel and the urine comes anyway, you know that you have to practice to strengthen that muscle. After one day of doing ten series, you will notice a difference.

Another benefit is that when you are about 45 years old (I know, you will not be that old for another 60 years) and you are shopping by the freezers at the supermarket, you won't be embarrassed by a sudden exit of urine. The reason for the adult diaper ads, is not for the senile nursing home resident, but for the active middle age female who has never exercised her kegels after her first child was born. This is especially necessary if you have had an episiotomy or had a laceration at birth.

Those muscles were injured and need therapy. Exercise that muscle, so it can stretch, contract and hold your bladder, uterus and rectum in place. The **broad ligament** that supports the uterus gets its strength from the Kegel muscle, which acts as a foundation for the broad ligament. If the kegel muscle is soft and flabby, the broad ligament has nothing to "stand on." The fundus, or top of the uterus "hangs" from the top of the broad ligament, which divides and arches down on each side of the uterus until it reaches or "stands" on the kegel muscle.

We must make sure the foundation is strong for this important ligament. Sometimes in early pregnancy, some ladies will experience a "catch" in their lower abdomen. If you do, just relax and breathe deeply. When the pain is gone, work on that kegel! You have just received a message from the broad ligament saying, "Strengthen this Kegel muscle up, my foundation is slipping."

Another part of regular care is palpating the baby. Palpation is feeling the baby between both hands through the mother's abdomen. You start by putting the fingers of both hands at the pubic bones and using the flat palm side of the whole hand sliding them upward towards the ribs, and lightly "bouncing" the baby back and forth between the hands, until you get to the top of the uterus. "Walk" your fingers along that long, smooth firm surface that you felt. . . it's the back. Compare that with the other side. See how bumpy and lumpy it is? Those are the arms and maybe the legs, depending on how tightly he is curled up. As you feel the uterus between your hands, pay attention to how quickly your hands seem to spread apart. If the seem to spread far apart quickly, the baby is probably in a transverse lie, or lying crosswise. If the uterus is in a pear shape, the baby is vertical, either head down or sitting head up in a breech position.

Next you palpate for the head. You know where the back is from the first "pass across the tummy". Now go to the ends of the baby, and try to find the end that is the hardest and the roundest. Grasp it between the thumb and first finger and try to wiggle it from side to side. If the hard round part is the only thing that moves from side to side, it is the head. If the whole body moves, you probably have the bottom end.

While palpating, also estimate the size of the baby you are feeling and mentally compare him with the size of a baby at this stage of pregnancy and development. This is how you determine if the baby is growing according to date. If this baby feels small, recheck the dates. Occasionally you have to check with mother away from her husband and friends, because she may not want to admit "confusion" about dates "publicly". She would rather claim carrying an 11-month or a 7-month baby, or "accuse" the care giver of confusing dates.

The baby can lie in a transverse (crosswise) position with no problem to baby or mother for the first 6–8 months of pregnancy. There is still time left to turn. We would like the baby to turn to head down by the end of the eighth month, while there is still room and water space for such grand movements. The last four weeks, the baby is growing so fast, that his quarters get a little cramped and it is hard to change positions. It's like curling up in a clothes basket and trying to change your position, without getting out of the basket.

Babies can be born vaginally in a breech position, but there are added risks which we will talk about later, in Chapter 8. The best idea is turn the baby before birth day. If the baby is lying in the transverse position, and you want him to turn, sometimes doing pelvic rocks will help him slip off the pelvic bone and into the pelvis. You want gravity to help you, and the head is the heaviest part of the baby. So get into a position where gravity can "pull" the head out of the pelvis, such as the **breech tilt**. You may not feel confident doing all of this without someone to help you, so save this for when hubby is home in the evening, or before he goes to work in the morning.

If the pelvic rock has not helped the head to slip off the pelvic (hip) bone, then get out the ironing board, and prop it against the sofa. You want an 18 inch rise. If you have enough pillows, you can use them, instead of the board, but keep your back in a straight line, don't be sagging in the middle. Then you "climb on" the ironing board/tilt board and lie with your head lower than your hips and feet for 15 minutes. Getting off is easier than getting on. Roll off to the left side, or to the side the baby is facing. Lie on your side until you get your bearings, then roll over onto all fours. Get up by going into a squat position, and then stand up and walk around for 30 minutes.

The walking will help the baby to settle down into your pelvis. You should feel a difference in walking after the first try. Going into the knee-chest position and pelvic rocks on all fours also help, and have the advantage of not needing help to do them. The disadvantage is that you need to have enough water, so the baby can move easily into the proper position. Palpation and feeling kicks in the ribs will confirm the baby's position change.

Locating the heart tones also tells a lot about the position of the baby. If the heart tones are above the umbilicus (belly button) in the last trimester, the baby is in the breech position. If they are just below the umbilicus and to the right, the baby is in the right transverse position. If the heart tones are on the right side, but close to the middle line, and below the umbilicus but closer to the pubic bone, the baby is in the right occiput anterior. A right posterior baby will be way to the mother's right, near her side. If the FHTs are in the corresponding places but on the left, you change to left anterior, etc. Remember the right or left is "Pat's" right or left, not the attendant's. Most babies are born Right Occiput Anterior (ROA) or Left Occiput Anterior (LOA), rather than posterior (looking towards the pubic bone). Usually there is no problem with a posterior baby other than the labor is more in the back and might be a little longer, because the posterior baby's head must mold more than the anterior baby's.

More babies are born Right Occiput Anterior than Left Occiput Anterior. Occiput Anterior means baby is facing your spine. Posterior babies can usually be turned either before or during labor by lying on the left side. The homeopathic remedy, Pulsatilla, also will change malpresentations to more advantageous presentations. Many times posterior babies turn to anterior during the second stage of labor. "Leaning" into the contraction with a catch in your breath—not a push—will often turn the baby during the transitional phase.

The following factors may increase the difficulty of palpating the baby easily:

- Lots of extra water (**hydramnios**). The bag of waters is like a water balloon, and if there is excess, the waters have stretched the uterus, giving the baby lots of room to move, and "hide" from the palpating hands. Because of the extra water, the muscles and uterus are stretched tight and will not "give" to the palpating hands.
- A very strong abdominal wall. If "Pat" is athletic or very active, is very hard to palpate, so it is important for her to be relaxed.
- A thick layer of fat on the abdominal wall is softer than the strong wall, but is confusing because of the knobby nature of fatty tissue. It makes it very hard to determine the soft parts, and cushions the hardness of the head.
- Tenseness of the mother. This could be because of the attendants cold hands, or Pat's nervousness will cause the abdominal muscles to harden, and you can't press well enough to feel.
- Not pressing firmly enough. You want to press firmly enough to feel the baby, without being rough.

- Lack of a good visual image of what you are feeling. It helps to mentally draw a picture in your mind with what you feel. Don't expect your fingers to fill in the details of eye color and shape of the nose. Be thankful for finding the head and back. After practice, you will develop "eyes" on your finger tips. Pat will tell you where the feet are, to confirm what you feel.
- Jumping to conclusions with insufficient data, caused by poor examination techniques and/or wishful thinking contribute to errors in judgment.

Now, when Pat is palpating, she has the advantage, because she can feel the reaction of the baby, and that helps her isolate the various parts of her baby. Knowing where the baby has been kicking lately will tell you where to look for the back. The baby will kick away from the back, because the feet point to the front, same with the hands. During the last trimester of the pregnancy, the baby will fill the uterus, and you can see the shape of the baby, by looking at the shape of the abdomen, if there is not too much water.

The **fetal heart tones** (FHTs) give us an indication of the overall health of the baby, especially of the nervous system. The normal rate is between 120 and 160. As with Pat's heart, you want to hear a regular pattern. The FHT rate is supposed to vary some depending on the baby's activity. If the baby moves, we expect the heart rate to increase; when the baby is resting, the rate should be slower. Palpation often will wake the baby up and cause him to move. If the heart rate does not increase with movement, we will want to find out why. Ask Pat how often the baby moves, and for how long a period of time. Be sure you are listening at the best place to hear, i.e., upper back of the baby, where the FHT is loudest, before getting concerned. Irregular FHTs, a rate below 120 or above 160, and lack of variance point to a baby with either anomalies or distress, and should be checked out by a doctor.

Variability of the heart rate is determined by counting in six-second intervals. If the pattern is 12, 13, 12, 16, 15, 12, 13, etc., it would be easy to guess that the increase was a result of a kick. Some times the FHTs increase gradually and get very fast, then slow down to the original speed. This indicates a large movement, such as a roll. Usually you can see these movements or in case of a kick, you will hear it in the fetoscope. To know what the one-minute count for the FHT is, you multiply the six-second count by 10, since you counted that many in six seconds and there are 60 (10×6) seconds in one minute. Since there were more 12s and 13s than 16s, you know that the base line is between 120 and 130. If you need to know exactly what that base is, you count for a full minute.

I usually count for a full minute at prenatal visits. During labor, I like to take six-second intervals for a full minute or two. In other words, I count every six seconds during the minute to get a better idea of the variables in the heart beat. This gives me a more accurate indication of the baby's tolerance to labor.

Unless your life and future good health depend upon it, please try to refrain from taking all medications, (prescription and over-the-counter remedies) during your pregnancy. If you are taking a prescription, go to your specialist and your obstetrician on behalf of the safety of your baby. At this printing, *no* medication has been declared absolutely safe for a pregnant woman and her baby. However, some, such as insulin, etc., are necessary. Some prescriptions seem to be safer than others, so perhaps your prescription *may* have to be temporarily changed until your baby is born.

Drugs, medications, x-rays or ultrasound may cause at least one of the following malformations or defects in your baby: interference with major organ development (brain, kidney, liver, heart, spine, digestive system). Some authors attribute the increase of PKU as possibly caused by drugs or ultrasound. Other problems include blood formation defects, (deformed cells), jaundice (causing brain defects/damage), early separation of placenta, premature labor, miscarriage/abortion, interference with placental development, goiters, reduced oxygen and nutrient exchange to infant, genital defects in girls and boys at birth, delayed cancer development (with up to a 20-year delay, as in the case of the DES daughters and sons), physical defects of arms, legs, ears, eyes, nose, and mouth structure, defective muscle development, permanent tooth discoloration or malformation (for example, pitting and green teeth from erythromycin), deafness, blindness, addiction to drugs, alcohol, nicotine, masculinization of female baby, feminization of male babies, stillbirth, and abnormal hardening of the bones. All these problems have been linked with medication taken during pregnancy. Scurvy-like symptoms have been seen in babies whose mothers took megadoses of Vitamin C during pregnancy (in excess of 3000 mg/day), with a sudden drop in C after the birth.

Should you need medication during pregnancy, ask your physician or midwife the following questions: "What are the risks to my baby and me if I do not take this medication?" "What are the alternatives to taking this medication?" "Is there something I can do to postpone taking this medication?" Obviously, heart medicine and insulin are life-saving medications, and you must take it, but do check frequently with your doctor on dosage and brand of your medication. Sometimes prescriptions need to be changed temporarily.

Diuretics are usually not good to take during pregnancy, so maybe you could try concentrating on the vegetables and fruits that are natural diuretics, such as green beans and asparagus, among others, if water retention is a problem for you. The diuretic action of foods are gentle and will not pull fluids from the baby and the bag of waters as some prescription diuretics might. *Back To Eden* by Jethro Kloss has an extensive list of such foods.

As mentioned in Chapter 2, some other things you will want to avoid are: aerosol sprays, alcohol, caffeine, tannic acid (from over-brewed tea), carbon monoxide (prolonged traffic jams), using lead-containing paints, smoking (toxic inhalants are cyanide, carbon monoxide, nicotine, etc.), marijuana, cleaning fluids, contact cements, volatile paints, lacquer thinners, some glues, household cleaners, herbicides and insecticides.

If you live in a rural area, you might contact the farmer upwind from your place and get his planned schedule to spray any fields that could have possible wind drift toward your house. Explain to him your concern, and he will usually be glad to give you names of his planned brands, strength of applications etc. Farmers are all aware of the toxicity of the products they use, so be kind and friendly when you talk to him and he will likely be very cooperative. No one wants to deliberately hurt his neighbor.

Because there are so many things that can hinder a normal pregnancy or interfere with baby's development, "John" and "Pat," as parents, need to pray the Lord's protection over and around Baby every day. Together, you need to pray that nothing and no one is allowed to interfere with Baby's growth and development in the Name of Jesus! God drew a blueprint of your baby before the foundations of the world were laid. Pray that those plans are being followed. Put the whole armor of God (Ephesians 6:11–17) on yourselves, your children, and on your baby every day. Pray a hedge of protection around her and yours. Now, leave your worries and concerns for your baby and Pat at the Cross, because this baby will be formed as God desires, and the pregnancy will follow God's perfect plan.

CHAPTER

4

TESTS AND TECHNOLOGY. . . THE WONDERS OF MODERN MEDICINE

Americans have a love affair with technology. We have learned that machines can do many tasks quicker and better than man, and when set properly, can work almost indefinitely without tiring. All they need is a squirt of oil, or access to electricity and they will work around the clock for us, without a lunch break, time off for vacations, and the like. In this age of electronics, the computer has been given tasks that traditionally have been difficult, or too inefficient timewise to be worthwhile. Now we have answers to mathematical equations in seconds that once took weeks to compute. Electronics has also entered the field of medicine, and man has had a heyday inventing many wonderful new tools for the "improvement of mankind".

When used as an adjunct to diagnostic skill and knowledge, these new tools can be lifesavers; for example, cardiac monitors, pacemakers, kidney dialysis, and prostheses that function by the electric signals sent out by adjacent muscles. These and many other medical wonders have given countless people new leases on life and are wonderful, albeit man-made, blessings. Some of the new tools however, have taken the place of the cool hand of the nurse, or the comfort of someone with a compassionate heart at the bedside. It wasn't meant to be that way. When the hospital is understaffed and overworked, these electronic marvels have saved lives by signalling a warning, bringing the nurses into the room and checking everything out with the baby and mom. And then we are thankful for them.

Technology: For Better or Worse?

Historically, the maternity department and its staff had the leftovers from other departments, because having babies wasn't as dramatic as a coronary, or brain surgery or even a gall bladder attack. Pregnancy and birth were always considered normal functions of life. Those who devoted their lives to caring for the newborn and their mothers, often were looked on as persons not as skilled as their peers in the rest of the hospital. This prejudice led to unconscious rivalry to prove their skills and professionalism. And in years past, in the name of "doing what is best for those entrusted to our care," restrictions on visiting hours, visitors, and who could work in the department were developed.

Soon, the maternity department was looked upon as a public relations tool, and the well-decorated rooms, the smiling, personable staff, modernized birthing rooms and nurseries became the norm. Along with this "new look," the medical supply companies developed the sonogram and electronic fetal monitors, dopplers and all the other trappings to keep up with the demand for equal technology in obstetrics as in the other branches of medicine.

Yes, these devices have saved the lives of many babies and mothers. Women with high-risk pregnancies have much better chances of going to term with healthier babies than they had 10 years ago. High-risk infants and sick newborns have a much better chance of survival than they had just five years ago, and for that we praise the Lord for giving man the ability to invent and develop such marvelous tools. Man's brain is a wondrous thing. When man sees success with something, he tends to use it more and more, and soon it becomes so routine, he has forgotten the risks involved in using the tool. More and more, physicians are considering pregnancy as a disease with the only known cure to be delivery as soon as possible and as quickly as possible by whatever means. (And we wonder at the increase of caesarean births?)

This routine use of technology, applied across the board to all women and unborn infants, is what we want to address here. Remember, we have no quarrel with the use of these tests and monitors when *medically indicated,* but we do question their use as routine in the low-risk mother and infant. There is reason to suspect that they may increase the risk to the low-risk mother and low-risk infant when used routinely. The more common tests and technology will be discussed next, giving you, the consumer, the reasons for them and the known risks. Some are so new that the risks are not yet defined, but I will try to give you the suspicions of yet-to-be-completed studies. I will try to identify what is known for sure as well as what is not known for sure, but highly suspected. You then will have to make your own decision based on the facts you have. As of this writing, no medication, whether prescription or over-the-counter, has been proven safe for the unborn child. The same warning goes for the following tests and procedures.

Try to postpone x-rays until after your baby is born, since your baby will be irradiated with an adult dose when you are x-rayed. Do not get abdominal x-rays unless it is a life-threatening situation. If you need dental x-rays because of extreme pain, wear a lead apron, but don't get routine x-rays during pregnancy. X-rays increase the incidence of bone cancer in your child in his pre-adolescent or adolescent years.

God's Part

Because we live in an environment that is compromised, ecologically speaking, we need some positive reinforcement. If we could claim our environment to be as clean as when Daniel Boone walked the earth, that would be a real "Praise the Lord!", but most of us have acid rain, smog, herbicides, etc., all about us. Scripture gives us a lot of comfort. Even though we don't always know what residues (to make it grow faster and better) are "lurking" in our food, in our air, or in the water that we drink, God does, and He promises to answer our prayers, as we ask of Him. Jesus said, "whatsoever ye shall ask in My name, that will I do, that the Father may be glorified in the Son. If ye ask anything in My name, I will do it." (John 14:13–14). Our heavenly Father has given us some spiritual principles that He is bound by His Word to abide by. "God is not a man that He should lie, neither the son of man, that He should repent: hath He said and shall He not do it? or hath He spoken, and shall He not make it good? Behold I have received commandment to bless; and He hath blessed, and I cannot reverse it." (Numbers 23:19–20).

God promises: to preserve us (Psalm 36:6); to give us healing (I Peter 2:24); to form the hands and the arms (Genesis 49:24), the bones (Psalm 34:20), the mouth and lips (Psalm 63:5), the heart (Psalm 31:24), and the face (Psalm 42:11); to form and protect us (Isaiah 44:2–4); to give the breath of life (Genesis 2:7). In Acts 10:15, God told Peter that what He cleanses is cleansed and no longer unclean. Use these scriptures and those the Lord shows you in your daily prayers over your baby. Write them out and you and your husband agree together that God's perfect will and plan will be done concerning the growth and development of this baby. In Jesus' name, everything will be in its proper place, and will function exactly as it was ordained since the foundation of the earth. Read Scripture to your baby, meditate on the Lord, sing and play music that glorifies God in your home and in your car, and the enemy will have a hard time surprising you and taking advantage of you.

In Psalm 37:4 and I Samuel 1:18–21, we learn that if we delight ourselves in the Lord, He will grant us the desires of our heart. Delighting in the Lord is putting Him first in everything that we do or think or say. Remember, God looks at your attitude and motives more than your deeds. The above suggestions are not magical talismans that will produce certain wonderful results. No indeed. But, if you do these things because you love God and desire to know Him and praise Him, then "all these things shall be added unto you (Matthew 6:33, Psalm 84:11–12).

Common Tests

Some tests that are commonly used to determine the well-being of the baby and mother are:

Endoscope

The endoscope is an instrument with a flexible, very thin, light-bearing tube. This thin tube is inserted vaginally through the cervix, to see the color of the amniotic fluid. It is usually not done before the eighth month, and is a simple, quick way to determine fetal distress. Dr. Michael Odent states that he uses it only when mother is postdue, 43 weeks or more, and the baby is presenting in breech position. If the amniotic fluid is clear, there is no distress and baby is doing well. If the fluid is greenish-yellow, there is meconium present and the baby is in distress. This could be done at any time after the eighth month when fetal distress is a possibility, and caesarean or other intervention is being discussed.

Ultrasound

Ultrasound is usually described as "high frequency sound," making it seem harmless. It is *not* harmless. Sound that is audible to humans is between 20 hertz and 20 kilohertz (one hertz is one cycle per second). Ultrasound is between two and four megahertz, and has been classified as radiation by the Bureau of Radiological Health (a branch of the Food and Drug Administration). Ultrasound is not ionizing radiation like x-rays, but it is sound radiation.

Three types of ultrasound diagnostic devices in use in obstetrics are ultrasound scanning devices, dopplers, and fetal monitors. The scan uses pulsed radiation and is usually used for short periods of time. Both the doppler and the fetal monitor use a continuous wave and may be used for hours at a time. All testing for safety so far seems to be limited to the scan, ignoring the doppler and monitor and their possible effects. Not only that, but the so-called "control groups" in the tests are not being controlled for use of the doppler or monitor, only the scan. This may be producing "control groups" which actually have higher exposure rates than the study groups. In other words, so many women and their unborn babies are being exposed to so much ultrasound that it will not be easy to find pregnant women who are not being exposed in order that the two groups can be compared.

Ultrasonography is done for many reasons. The most frequent use is: confirmation of due date, verifying alpha fetal protein (AFP) test for neural tube anomalies, verifying multiple pregnancy, positions and development of the baby, and during infant viability tests, such as amniocentesis, or in the form of the fetal monitor during non-stress tests or the Oxytocin Challenge Test (OCT). Each time the ultrasound scan is done, measurements are taken of the length of the baby's femur (thigh bone) and the bi-parietal diameter (width) of the head. At 18 weeks these measurements can predict within three days your baby's birth day. If done in the last trimester, the birth day can not be determined to within three weeks because of genetic variances. Apparent maturity, size, external anomalies and position of the baby can be determined. In non-pregnant use, ultrasonography is useful to visualize soft tissue that x-ray does not define well.

Demonstrated ill effects on the human fetus from ultrasound are: an increase (30–60%) in low-birth-weight babies; an increase (33–120%) in dyslexia; blood stasis; increased neonatal jaundice; adverse effects on the immune system; and there is evidence that children exposed *in utero* (in the womb) to ultrasound appear to be developing leukemia and other cancers in higher numbers than unexposed children. Women seem to ovulate prematurely after ovarian ultrasonography (this brings up questions about the ova of the unborn female fetus—the ultrasound beam certainly irradiates the genetic material of both mother and child). Demonstrated effects on human cells *in vitro* (in a laboratory dish) include: growth alterations; changes in cell motility (could have significant implications for fetal central nervous system development); and DNA changes (may lead to cancer in 15–20 years as well as I.Q. deficits and learning disabilities). Also, changes in cell growth and behavior that may persist for many, many generations; inner and middle ear aches and "infections" with occasional malformation of the ear structures leading to hearing disabilities have been linked to sonography.

Animal studies have shown that even *ten generations* after exposure, the following ill effects are still present: chromosome damage and breakdown in DNA; cranial (head bones) and facial malformations; smaller offspring and reduction in litter size; blood stasis; liver cell changes; jaundice; brain enzyme changes; EEG (electroencephalogram, or brain wave) changes; delayed postnatal grasp reflex; increased emotional reactivity; neuromuscular development delay; reduction of immunoglobin antibodies; abnormal heart development; and increases in skeletal abnormalities.

Animal or human, these studies do show that we need to pray and think twice before having a sonogram. Just to see the baby or to decide if the nursery should be painted pink or blue, are not good enough reasons. God tells you the sex when He gives you the child's name. More about that later. Bonding can be started by patting baby's feet when he kicks, talking to him, etc. The cost of a sonogram is between $100 and $800.

Amniocentesis

Amniocentesis is the withdrawal of amniotic fluid from the uterus by inserting a long needle attached to a syringe through the mother's umbilicus (belly button), uterine wall and into the amniotic sac (bag of waters). This test should be done before 36 weeks (the average pregnancy is 40 weeks), as the amniotic fluid decreases after that. A sonogram scan should be in progress during insertion of the needle, to avoid sticking the baby. Mother's skin may be anesthetized (local), but many doctors think the injection is not worth it in terms of maternal comfort, that is, the local anesthetic does not add that much relief.

There is a popping sensation when the needle enters the uterus, and some women experience a sensation of pressure when the fluid is withdrawn. Uterine contractions may be felt for a day or two after the test. Reasons for this test are to determine genetic anomalies (in the second trimester) and to see if the baby is mature enough to be born (in the third trimester). Maturity of baby's lungs is required before elective induction or elective caesarean to prevent Respiratory Distress Syndrome (RDS) in the newborn. RDS, formerly called Hyaline Membrane Disease, is a major contributor to newborn mortality. Cost for amniocentesis and generic counselling, if needed, ranges from $300 to $800.

Tests for Fetal Maturity

The **shake test** or **surfactant test** is performed by taking the amniotic fluid removed during the amniocentesis, diluting it with chemicals and shaking the test tube for 15 seconds.

The test tube is rested on a rack for 15 minutes, then held up to light to see if small bubbles are present. When a complete ring of bubbles is seen at the rounded top (meniscus) of the solution, then the test is positive, a desirable reading, because it indicates enough phospholipid is present in the surfactant to form a film in the test tube which can support foam. The shake test is about 70% accurate, takes 30 minutes, and costs about $25. It is often done in conjunction with the more accurate L/S ratio (discussed next).

The **L/S ratio** measures the amount of one of the phospholipids in the surfactant, lecithin, as it appears in relationship to sphingomyclin in the lung cells. When the ratio of lecithin to sphingomyclin is 2:1 or greater, the test is positive, meaning the lungs are mature. The cost is about $40, takes at least four hours and is about 80% accurate and its accuracy is increased when done with the PG test.

The **PG test** measures another phospholipid in amniotic fluid, **phosphotidyl glycerol**, which stabilizes the lecithin in the surfactant. Phosphotidyl glycerol also rises in a characteristic ratio when the lungs mature, so its presence in the right amounts is further assurance that the surfactant is present. The PG test takes about four hours like the L/S ratio, costs about $35, and is considered 100% accurate when done with the L/S. These tests are often done to compare the ultrasound to measurement of the bi-parietal diameter of the fetal head.

The **Fetal Lung Profile** is a more complete evaluation of lung maturity. It tests for the L/S ratio, for a rise in phosphotidyl inositol, and also for phosphotidyl glycerol as well as acetone precipitation. From these readings, a profile is given of the immature, premature, transitional, mature, post-term and postmature fetus. The fetal lung profile is fairly new and not always available in every community. It is particularly useful for assessing maturity in the fetus of a diabetic mother. It costs about $75.

Tests for Maternal Health

The **rollover test** is an easy non-invasive way to help determine which women will develop hypertension. It is done in the doctor's or midwife's office between the 28th and 32nd weeks. Its use is based on the rationale that supine hypertension (high blood pressure when a woman is lying on her back) is present

8–10 weeks before the onset of pre-eclampsia, and early detection can cut down on problems.

The woman sits on the bed or examining table while her blood pressure is checked. She then lies down on her back (supine position) and blood pressure is taken again immediately and again in five minutes. If there is no increase, then the test is negative, a desirable reading. If it goes up, and the diastolic pressure increases 10 mm of Hg or more the test is positive. Advantages include its simplicity and safety, and there is no additional cost. It is possible that its use with such clients as teenagers or those whose poor diets place them at risk for hypertension could improve the course of their pregnancy. Disadvantages lie in its high false-positive rate which can lead to unnecessary concern in women who, in the end, do not develop high blood pressure despite a positive rollover test. The "white coat syndrome" or "doctor's/midwife's office syndrome"—an increase in blood pressure produced by a fear of medical personnel or equipment— can be proven by taking her blood pressure in her home. If it is normal, it is "White Coat Syndrome" and can be overlooked by raising her normal baseline for the office.

The other question is whether such measures as bedrest will actually improve the health of a mother with hypertension, since at least one study says it will not. Hypertension is so well associated with maternal stress and anxiety, it is worth considering the impact of routine testing on a woman's blood pressure. And whether the bedrest will add emotional strain including anxiety and depression, feelings that can promote complications. Many women have found that a daily quiet time with the Lord, meditating on God's Word, and following the admonishment in Philippians 4:8–9, brings the blood pressure down to normal very quickly. Increasing the mother's protein intake will prevent eclampsia and lower the blood pressure also.

Estriol is a hormone produced by the placenta in response to the stimulation of substances in the maternal blood. Estriol is the placental form of estrogen (which is produced in the non-pregnant woman's ovary), and is produced in larger amounts as the pregnancy advances. The test is made serially (either weekly or more frequently), by measuring the estriol in a 24-hour urine sample or in a blood sample from the mother. Daily fluctuations are common, so a gradual and continued fall or an abrupt drop in values is a danger signal. More tests will be ordered to see if the pregnancy should be terminated. One test costs about $35 and since two will be ordered, the total cost will be a minimum of $70. Estriol counts are not considered accurate enough to be the sole basis of a decision to perform a caesarean delivery.

The **Oxytocin Challenge Test (OCT)**, also called **stress test**, gives the physician an indication of how well the baby will withstand the stress of labor. OCTs are ordered when estriol determinations are ominous; or in high-risk pregnancies; and when there are pregnancy complications such as pre-eclampsia and hypertension. In an OCT, an external fetal monitor is applied. The fetal heart rate (FHR) is observed to establish a "baseline" and then labor contractions are induced, with an intravenous drip of 1 amp. Pitocin® in 1000 cc Ringers solution. Once contractions begin, the baseline is carefully observed for ominous decelerations.

In a healthy baby, the heart rate remains between 120 and 160 beats per minute, although there may be periodic changes during a contraction. If the baby is compromised by either its poor condition or an insufficiently functioning placenta, late decelerations or dips of the fetal heart tones may show up repeatedly on the monitor graph. When this happens, the mother may have her labor induced, or, if the baby's condition appears quite serious, may have a caesarean delivery to spare the baby the rigors of labor. Women with serious health problems may be hospitalized in their last months of pregnancy and be given an OCT weekly.

To have this test, the woman goes to the hospital where she will spend one to two hours for the test. She should know, so she can be prepared, whether or not she will remain in the hospital for induction or surgery if the test is positive. Because of this possibility and also because sometimes the test induces labor, she is not to eat or drink for eight hours prior to the test. (If a caesarean is a possibility, she should make arrangements with her primary physician to have the anesthesiologist of her choice on standby, so she can have a non-general anesthetic. See the Caesarean section for details.)

When she arrives at the hospital, she will be asked to urinate, and then lie on a bed. She should lie on her left side, with pillows to support her tummy and between her legs. If the staff insists that she be on her back, she should insist on the bed being cranked up at least 45°, or to remain on her left side, to avoid supine hypotension. Supine hypotension is caused by the woman lying on her back, with the weight of her uterus resting on the major vein (vena cava) and the major artery (aorta), thus partially occluding them (the vena cava returns the blood from the mother's body and the placenta back to her heart, and the aorta brings oxygenated blood to the lower body, including the placenta). This causes a drop in the mother's blood pressure, due to the decrease of blood returning to the mother's heart, and therefore a decrease in the oxygen supply to the baby. The baby responds with a decrease in heart rate, and gives the appearance of a baby in distress.

Once the baseline has been established, the "Pit drip" is begun and continued until three contractions occur within ten minutes, about three minutes apart. When this happens, the fetal monitor is watched for any decelerations in the FHR. If not, then the test is negative, which is desirable. If late decelerations appear in response to three successive contractions, then the OCT is positive and intervention is planned. A "suspicious" OCT shows some slowing or dip in the fetal heart rate but not in three successive contractions. An "unsatisfactory" OCT reflects an equipment problem or a situation where regular contractions did not occur.

The OCT will show you most fetal problems before labor begins, and is sometimes used to continue a high risk pregnancy past the time intervention might have been used. Disadvantages include the need to impose a stimulated labor on both mother and baby, with the high false positive rate that can lead to unnecessary surgery, and the fact it cannot be used in women with placenta previa or with a history of prior caesarean section if a vertical uterine incision was used. Since induction itself is a form of stress, some believe the test causes some ominous decelerations that might otherwise never have appeared, if labor were allowed to start spontaneously. Should you decide for health reasons that this test is necessary, please take your labor coach to the hospital with you, to help you relax with the contractions. If the OCT is negative, then the pregnancy is allowed to continue. If it is suspicious or unsatisfactory, it is repeated or rescheduled. This will cost you about $100 and is accurate about 75% of the time.

The **non-stress test** is stimulation by auditory stimulus (sound) at 2,000 cycles per second of pure tone by speaker to the mother's abdomen. It is applied as a five-second pulse starting at 105 decibels repeated three times, at least one minute apart, and at least one minute after a significant event, such as a kick, contraction, or FHR acceleration. Sound is increased until response is made: 15-beat acceleration is positive. Less than 15, but more than a five-beat acceleration is vague, and no response at 115 and 120 decibels is negative. This test eliminates the OCT in the normal child, but does not answer the question about the hearing impaired child. Non-stress test can be used when the OCT is contraindicated, such as a woman trying for a VBAC. Distressed baby is referred to the OCT test (vague or no response).

A variation of the non-stress test can be done in the midwife's office. Have Pat lie on her back on a firm bed with a very small pillow under her head. Listen to the FHTs continuously for one hour, calling out the six-second counts. Each time the baby moves, Pat is to say so, and it is noted next to the corresponding count. Ten major movements and corresponding increased FHR indicate a healthy baby. The baby should have an accelerated FHR even without movement due to Pat's position. When the test is over, help Pat roll to her left side. She should stay there for a few minutes before sitting up, to allow her circulation to get back to normal.

The **postprandial** test for glucose has gone out of fashion with the allopaths. They feel it is not as accurate as the one- or two-hour glucose load challenge tests combined with the eight-hour fasting blood sugar. The postprandial test is a blood test taken two hours after a high-carbohydrate meal, usually breakfast. If your blood glucose level is 180 milligrams or more glucose per 100 milliliters of blood, you are diabetic. You are considered at risk of developing diabetes if your blood glucose ranges between 140 and 180 milligrams. During pregnancy your metabolism changes drastically so these "normal" values are not always accurate.

The one-hour glucose challenge screen (when done alone) has an exceptionally high incidence of false-positive outcomes, requiring more unnecessary three-hour glucose tolerance tests.

But, no woman with diabetes will be missed. The two-hour glucose challenge screening test has a lower rate of false positives. Some women with diabetes may be missed. Thus, the combination of fasting blood sugar and the two-hour glucose challenge has become a more accurate screening and is more cost-effective, as today's fashion dictates. The woman is required to eat and drink nothing after midnight. At the lab, after her first blood test, she drinks the entire glucose flavored mixture in 10 minutes. Then she waits one to two hours for the second blood test. During this waiting period, she can not eat, exercise (don't chase Junior around the waiting room) or smoke. She can drink water, but *only* water.

Norms vary from laboratory to laboratory. Most labs have based their values on 100 grams of glucose, but new norms have been established for 50 or 75 grams. The normal range of blood glucose levels depend on what norm your lab uses, so please find out so you know what to expect on your reports. Most labs have the normal ranges printed on the reports so you can see if the values are high, low or in the middle (normal) range. It is good to know, or at least have normal values posted for your own information, and not depend solely on someone else. A fasting plasma blood sugar of 105 milligrams or greater per 100 milliliters of blood, a one-hour 50-gram glucose challenge plasma blood sugar of 135 milligrams or greater per 100 milliliters of blood, and a two-hour 75-gram glucose challenge plasma of 120 milligrams or greater per 100 milliliters of blood are abnormal values. If the woman fails the fasting and the challenge test, she will need. . .

The **glucose tolerance test**. The oral GTT involves drinking 100 grams of a glucose mixture that is usually poorly tolerated during pregnancy and causes nausea and vomiting in most women, causing a variable rate of absorption in the intestines. The intravenous GTT has a high incidence of false-negative outcomes in the pregnant woman. . . up to a third again as many as for the oral GTT.

If two or more of the following glucose values are met or exceeded, the Oral GTT is considered abnormal.

Chart for Progression of Diabetic Screening

Fasting Blood Sugar	+	One- or Two-hour Glucose Challenge	=	Indicated Action
Positive		Negative		Do GTT
Negative		Positive		Do GTT
Positive		Positive		Do *not* do GTT; woman is diabetic. Refer to physician.
Negative		Negative		Rescreen at 34–36 weeks gestation, if has risk factors; if no risk factors, not necessary to screen again.

Reference Chart Based on Laboratory Tests

Fasting Blood Sugar	+	One- or Two-Hour Glucose Challenge	+	Glucose Tolerance Test	=	Diagnosis
Positive		Negative		Two abnormal values		Diabetic
Negative		Positive		Two abnormal values		Gestational Diabetic
Positive		Positive		Not Done		Diabetic
Negative		Negative		Not Done		Not Diabetic

Gestational diabetes is an allopathic term applied to the woman with irregularities in glucose levels only during pregnancy. This phenomenon was seen shortly after the National Diabetes Data Group redefined what constituted diabetes in 1979. Prior to that time, a blood glucose level of 140-150 milligrams per milliliters of plasma after fasting for 12 hours was used as the range of normal in pregnant and non-pregnant adults. After new research was done, a new but *lower value* of 105 milligrams per milliliter was recommended as the upper limit of safety during pregnancy. This research was done with no consideration of what the normal levels are in well-nourished subjects! Large numbers of poorly nourished women who had not been instructed in good prenatal nutrition and who were not monitored for nutritional problems became the standard by which all women are measured, regardless of their nutritional status.

The average for these women was 105; much too low for a well-nourished pregnant woman. Well-nourished pregnant women who have adequate protein, calories, vitamins and minerals keep their blood glucose levels normal and even maintain an energy supply reserve (glycogen) stored in their livers. Glycogen stores are good for about 12 hours in the well-nourished pregnant woman. In the under-nourished pregnant woman there are no glycogen stores; thus, her blood level of glucose falls soon after eating and then scrapes along until the next meal. The usual allopathic treatment is restricting carbohydrates, insulin therapy, and monitoring glucose levels at home *every hour* with instructions to keep it between 100 and 105.

The allopathic criteria to determine if you are a high-risk gestational diabetic is answering "yes" to any one of the following:

- A family history of diabetes alerts your physician to the possibility that you, too, may be developing the disease, even though you are not spilling glucose in your urine.
- You have birthed a baby weighing more than 9 pounds due to your excellent diet and/or baby's genetic makeup.
- You are gaining more than the outdated 20 pounds per baby/pregnancy (the thinking of 30 years ago). . . no matter what is going on (twins, good diet, etc.)
- Your sonogram says that your baby is bigger than the charts say it should be for the length of your pregnancy (no account is taken of the fact that those charts are heavily weighted with babies from undernourished mothers).
- You have a normal (by the old standard) blood glucose level of 140–150 mg per ml when you take tests at your doctors insistence.
- You spill some glucose in your urine, but upon further evaluation show no other sign of diabetes. (Some women have a low renal threshold for glucose which is in no way related to diabetes. Low renal threshold for glucose is harmless).
- History of unexplained stillbirth.
- Poor obstetrical history (for example, spontaneous abortions, congenital anomalies).

- Non-pregnant weight greater than 180 pounds (may vary depending on body build and height).
- Recurrent monilial infections (if this alone, screen only at 28 weeks).
- Recurrent (two positive tests) glycosuria clean-catch specimens not explained by dietary intake.
- Pre-eclampsia or chronic hypertension.
- Hydramnios.
- Age 26 or older.
- Gestational diabetes in a previous pregnancy.

If you are diabetic, do abide by the Brewer Diet as described briefly in this book with the addition of more protein intake in the form of between-meal snacks to achieve the one-gram-per-pound ratio that the best research advises. Better yet, get a copy of Dr. Brewer's book *The Brewer Medical Diet For Normal and High-Risk Pregnancy*. Study it and follow the golden advice it contains.

Allopathic Care and Diagnostic Screens for Gestational Diabetes

The fasting blood sugar is not to be used alone because it is normal in the woman with "gestational diabetes." Post-prandial screening has been replaced with glucose load challenge screening tests. The one-hour glucose challenge screen has an exceptionally high incidence of false-positive outcomes, which means that a larger number of unnecessary three-hour glucose tolerance tests (GTTs) will be done; but, the "real" diabetic will not be missed. The two-hour glucose challenge screen has a lower rate of false-positives, but also misses some "real" diabetics. So, allopaths suggest a combination of a fasting blood sugar and the one-hour or two-hour post-glucose challenge for accuracy and cost-effectiveness.

Oral GTT is considered abnormal, or diagnostic for diabetes if two or more of the following glucose values are met or exceeded:

- Fasting: 90 milligrams of glucose per 100 milliliters of whole blood;
- 1 hour: 165 milligrams of glucose per 100 milliliters of whole blood;
- 2 hour: 145 milligrams of glucose per 100 milliliters of whole blood;
- 3 hour: 125 milligrams of glucose per 100 milliliters of whole blood.

If plasma, rather than whole blood, is analyzed for glucose, then the values are approximately 15% higher, as follows:

- Fasting: 105 milligrams of glucose per 100 milliliters of plasma;
- 1 hour: 190 milligrams of glucose per 100 milliliters of plasma;
- 2 hour: 165 milligrams of glucose per 100 milliliters of plasma;
- 3 hour: 145 milligrams of glucose per 100 milliliters of plasma.

If you and/or your client have objections to the letting of innocent blood and you are concerned about frequent sugar spills in the urine, and she assures you that she has not had a soda or cough drop or other source of "pure" sugar, you need to seriously consider some herbal teas to normalize her blood sugar. Some foods and herbs that normalize blood sugar are:

Artichoke	Goat's Rue	Chicory
Bilberry	Juniper	Milfoil
Blue Cohosh	Kidney Bean	Dandelion
Common Lettuce	Nettle	Onion
Dwarf Nettle	Queen of the Meadow	Sumac
Elecampane	Saw Palmetto	Flax
European Centaury	Spotted Cranebill	Fenugreek
European Solomon's Seal	Wild Red Raspberry	Wintergreen

There are others, so get a good herbal reference book such as *The Herb Book* by John Lust, *Back to Eden* by Jethro Klaus or *Herbally Yours* by Penny C. Royal. Herbs require careful monitoring and research as the dosage varies depending on growing conditions. When used carefully, they do very well with the purpose required of them.

CHAPTER 5

RISK FACTORS, EMOTIONAL ISSUES AND GUIDELINES

It does not matter *how* you deal with a problem in your pregnancy, or at your birth. You can handle it spiritually or physically. The important thing is that you deal with it. It will not go away, if you ignore it. In fact, it probably will get worse. There is no condemnation, when you act on what you know, spiritually or physically. The condemnation comes when we turn our back on what we know to do and do nothing (James 4:17).

"Fear" is defined by Webster as "anxiety and agitation, caused by presence of danger, evil, or pain." God tells us to "not be anxious then. . . for your heavenly Father knows that you need all these things" (Matthew 6:30–34). In II Timothy 1:17 we read that "God did not give us a spirit of timidity—of cowardice, of craven and cringing and fawning fear—but [He has given us a spirit] of power and love and of calm and well-balanced mind and discipline and self-control." (Amplified).

We have "good" fears (or you could call it "being cautious")—the kind that tells us to walk on the sidewalk and not down the middle of the road, or the kind that puts us on the alert for potential danger, or when we have pain, our body is telling us to pay attention to it. Pain can again be differentiated to "good" and "bad." Sometimes labor can be categorized as "good" pain. It is pain because it hurts, but it is good, because the body is working and doing a normal function. It will pass—after a while. Bad pain is like a gall bladder attack. It hurts, but the body is alerting you that something is wrong and needs attention. The pain will not go away until that particular pathology is cured.

Sometimes pain is not that simple. Sometimes it is based on vagaries like: "Is the baby all right? I haven't felt it move for ten minutes," or "What if I can't stand the pain. . . how much does it hurt?" "What if I tear?" "Does my body know how to have this baby?" "What if my body quits?" Worry, anxiety, and fear are desperate taskmasters. They are never satisfied, but heap more fear, worry, and anxiety upon you until everything is out of proportion, and the old adage about a mountain being created out of the molehill is fulfilled.

Think about "whatsoever things are true, whatsoever things are honest, whatsoever things are just, whatsoever things are pure, whatsoever things are lovely, whatsoever things are of good report; if there be any virtue, and if there be any praise, think on these things. Those things, which ye have both learned, and received, and heard, and seen in me, do: and the God of peace shall be with you." (Philippians 4:8–9).

Jesus reminds us that He takes care of the birds, and we are of more value than they, and our worry does not change anything. Therefore seek His kingdom first and He will take care of all those things. (Matthew 6:25–34). This is not easy to do, but once we grasp the principle, we enjoy great peace and the liberty that is ours in Christ Jesus. It keeps the blood pressure down, prevents colitis, ulcers, and heart trouble, not to mention sleepless nights. Our Lord enlarges on this theme in I Thessalonians 5:16–18, 24, Ephesians 3:14–21, and Colossians 3:12–17.

Our parents and teachers spoke about and tried to teach us what responsibility was as we grew up, and as adults, we like to think of ourselves as being responsible. Being responsible means that I am ready to take the consequences of my actions, and the words that I say. Now that you are parents, you are also responsible for that new life that is incapable of being accountable for himself. Your decision, or lack of decision can be very important to this baby. Your example will either reinforce your words, or invalidate them. This can be very frightening, but it can be very stimulating also. It all depends on your attitude towards responsibility.

Your responsibility in pregnancy and childbirth is to do everything possible, both physically and spiritually, to ensure that everything will go right. That means that you are in right-standing with God, in spiritual order within the expression of Christ's body where you worship and fellowship. Your household is in order, by God's standards, and you have studied and prepared physically for the birth with good prenatal care, and have chosen your attendants, doctor, or midwife with prayer and care. You have done everything you were to do, such as gathering supplies, everything is well-planned and organized, and prepared.

All should go well. But what if it doesn't? We seldom think of birth as being sad. Birth is thought of as a happy time, and it is, most of the time. Sometimes, birth is less than what we expected or dreamed it would be. The baby may have a physical or mental disability, or something happens unexpectedly and the baby dies. Sometimes, no matter how hard you pray, work skillfully and use the latest available emergency equipment, things do not go right. What then? Do you blame God? Do you blame the attendant, and get your "pound of flesh" through the courts? Or do you accept what God has allowed as Job did, and say, "The Lord gave and the Lord hath taken away, blessed be the name of the Lord." (Job 1: 21–22). God is in control of this universe and all within it. We like to control our own destiny, and God many times allows us to think we do. When we come face to face with tragedy, be it death or a congenital malformation, we don't want to acknowledge it, and try to find a way out.

Even though we have planned, studied, prayed, and worked for the best possible birth, we need to decide what we will do when it doesn't turn out that way. Can we get on our knees and ask God to give us grace and understanding? Or do we need a scapegoat? This is a new form of responsibility that we are not used to taking. Our culture is so used to someone else "taking care of it" for us. So much of our life is covered by the State in one form or another, and we have so many people suing for damages for this or that wrong, it seems right to blame others for what could very well be out of their control.

God never meant for man to surrender himself to the total control of another man. God considers that to be idolatry. We are to surrender ourselves to God (James 4:7–10). When we demand perfect outcomes and perfect babies, because our attendants have certain qualifications that give them special skills we do not have, we are asking them to act in the place of God. When we participate in that kind of sin, we are setting ourselves up for disaster. Our trust should be in God. Yes, we can receive advice and accept care from those that have the anointing to help us, but they are mere mortals, subject to the faults that are common to man. Please, do not expect more from people than what mere people can give you. To do otherwise, is to compound tragedy upon tragedy.

Discuss with your caregiver, especially if you are planning a home birth, what procedures are required when a less-than-perfect outcome occurs. What do you do in your area if the child has a deformity? What if the baby dies just before birth? What if shortly after birth? In many states, *if* the birth takes place in the hospital, it is considered an "act of God" should a baby die during or shortly after birth. If the same circumstances occur at home, the attendant may be subject to charges of murder. These charges often are pressed by a third party that is not involved with the situation. You need good communication between yourself and your attendant. Openly discuss what is concerning you, so everybody will be working together. If you follow these suggestions, you will have mutual support, and you will know that everyone did all they knew to do. With that knowledge, you will not waste time and energy with "what might have been," and you can get on with what must be done. This will give you a more positive direction for your grief, and the roots of bitterness, resentment, anger, and hate will not have a place to grow. Love can reach out to heal the disappointment and ease the pain. The attendants hurt too, and they also need to reach out to the parents, if only to let the parents know how much they care. To be vengeful cuts you off from that support.

There are many organizations that have been formed to support parents and attendants in the event that birth did not fulfill your dreams. One such organization, *Compassionate Friends*, has chapters all over the United States. Contact their home office for the chapter nearest you. Most "fetal anomalies" have their own local support groups that usually are more aware of the latest research and help than the doctors or nurses, because they concentrate in that area. Most local hospitals, health departments or funeral homes can direct you to local support groups that are very helpful and can help you through all the unfamiliar details that must be handled at this time. Usually there is someone in that group that has endured the same heartbreak you are experiencing, and can give you the comfort and understanding that no one else can.

In the rare event that circumstances were such, that definite poor judgement was used leading to other events that caused the death of the child, what was your role in this? Did you protest the poor judgement that led to the irreversible tragedy? Did you try to find a replacement attendant? It is never too late to fire your attendant. You can fire and hire until you find someone that agrees with your philosophy. The only problem with this, is you may run out of time and local people, if you start firing and hiring late in the pregnancy. That is why you need frank, open communication with your attendant, and really listen to what your attendant is saying. You also need to know that she/he is truly understanding what it is you are saying, too. Your midwife should also feel free to resign from the birth team, if you are too high a risk for his or her skills, if you insist on birthing at home.

Continuing on beyond your attendant's skills is foolish and presumptuous. Both are situations God says to turn away from, for they are sin. Endangering your wife's life or the life of the baby by insisting your attendant to help you in a situation beyond her skills is immature and inconsiderate of your family, and the families of your birth team. Unnecessary tragedy usually follows such actions. Remember, you have to live with your decisions. Your decision could put your attendant in jail, leaving his or her children without a parent, thus heaping tragedy upon tragedy. Make the best possible choices you can, with prayer, and God will honor your heart and give you peace in your decisions.

One way to study your attendant's skill and education is to ask for an Informed Consent Agreement (ICA). Most midwives have one written up, listing his or her formal and informal education, current memberships in professional organizations and unusual circumstances that she/he has handled successfully. Also inquire about back-up arrangements. She should be glad to give this information to you, as it gives you a better way to assess her abilities and match them with your needs. Most

ICAs have a consent/contract form to sign, stating you understand the risks of home birth and the skill level of your attendant and your own responsibility for this birth. I recommend that you sign it. That way no one can say anyone was "fooled", but that everyone involved acted as responsible, informed adults, and understood what was expected of them.

Pain

The one concern that every woman has talked about with me at least one time in her pregnancy, was how she would handle the pain of birth. I truly wish that I could tell her exactly what to expect, and for how long. Every woman accepts birth differently than her sisters, and each labor is a unique experience. The general pattern will be the same, but still different enough that afterwards, you will be able to pinpoint slight differences. Sometimes these differences are quite large: for example, one birth is much quicker than the other, or harder, or easier, or the lady was more "relaxed and it seemed so easy" even though the attendants all thought it was a rather difficult labor. How can such a variance of conception exist? Is it the vitamins or the diet or God's grace?

The answer to that is basically the same for everyone, God's grace. How do you react to labor? What is your concept of it? Is labor a temporary period of excruciating torture that God puts us through because of Eve? Or do you look at it as a way to get the baby out? If labor is something you dread, you will probably go into it ready to "fight." If labor is a means to get the baby "out of your belly" and into your arms, you will accept it, and flow with it. This is the lady that will probably have a "good" and "easy" time of it. Her labor may not hurt less, but she will yield to it with a good attitude, and it will *feel* like it hurts less. No, I am not talking in riddles. The lady who is going to "fight" this labor and conquer it, will not allow her contractions to do their maximum job, because she will not yield to them. Thus, each contraction will have to repeat itself until it gets its job done. After a while, the lady will be exhausted and each contraction will hurt much more than if she were less tired.

The conception of pain has been diagrammed like a wheel. At the top of the wheel is *fear*, then comes *tension* at 3 o'clock, *weariness* at 6 o'clock and *pain* at 9 o'clock, and back to *fear* at

12 o'clock. When all of these factors are present, the lady can not relax either between or with contractions. So each cycle of the wheel becomes more intense, and soon she is out of control, and panic has set in. We must conquer fear as soon in our pregnancy as we can, if not before (II Timothy 1:7). Most fear comes from lack of understanding and understanding comes from knowledge. Once you know, and understand, there is no fear of the unknown to torment you. That is why you are reading this book, taking childbirth classes from an independent childbirth educator, and reading every book you can get your hands on about birth. Along with all that reading, you do want to be careful that you "spit out the sticks as you chew the hay," as Joy Young said in her book *Christian Home Birth.*

Childbirth books are not written to elevate you into great spiritual realms. They are written to give you information about birth and are liberally sprinkled with the authors convictions and beliefs. Many have been influenced by the New Age Movement and Eastern Philosophy, but may also have a nugget of gold about birth. Educators agree that what ever is planted in the brain through the eye or the ear remains, and will be recalled sometime in the future to influence decisions. Thus, you must pray and ask the Holy Spirit to guide you, and help you chew the hay and spit out the sticks, like a good cud-chewing cow. Cows chew their cuds so they can get the maximum nourishment out of what they eat. We need to "chew" all that we read, and measure it next to God's Word so we can get proper nourishment. Should you read something that does not measure up to the Word of God, then ask Jesus to wash it out of your mind.

Some natural tools for the labor coach to use during labor are:

1. Maintaining eye-to-eye contact with Pat;
2. Aiding Pat to handle contractions by breathing with her at a natural pace, sometimes facilitated by:
   a. Deep abdominal breathing by holding the abdomen up and taking short "shelf breaths," as described by Helen Wessel in *Childbirth Without Fear* by Grantly Dick-Read;
   b. Breathing like you do when you're asleep, as Dr. Robert Bradley suggests in *Husband Coached Childbirth;*

3. Keeping the mother relaxed and calm and maintaining positive attitudes by saying such statements as: "Very good, you are relaxing so nicely," "Such a good mom, you are loving your baby already by being so relaxed," or "You are doing such a wonderful job," and so forth;
4. Maintaining hydration, by encouraging Pat to drink juices, water, cool raspberry tea, and eating easily digested foods, like clear soups, yogurt, finger jello cubes, juice cubes;
5. Placing cool cloths on Pat's forehead;
6. Giving her a massage;

. . .and in general, paying lots of loving attention to her will help her along.

Maybe she needs to be alone with her husband and midwife close by. Some ladies need lots of space to themselves without lots of talking or touching. Other ladies want conversation going in the room, just don't make her participate in it. Whatever works for her is what is needful and she will bless you by relaxing and having her baby in record time.

Changing her position frequently, like every two hours and going to the bathroom to urinate helps a lot. It helps the baby to move into the pelvis when mom moves about, and that facilitates the labor. Sometimes "hula hooping" your hips or doing a standing pelvic rock will help a baby in a posterior position move into an anterior position, or facilitate the descent for a big baby.

Sometimes we get so excited when labor starts, that we forget that the contractions will get harder, longer and usually closer together, and we start working real hard too soon. Remember to use the least amount of energy with each contraction, so you don't get tired prematurely. In early labor, sometimes it is helpful to bake cookies, or do something easy that will help keep your mind busy, like a walk in the park, or around the block.

In the later stages of labor, keep your breathing deep and slow and you won't hyperventilate. When the urge to push comes, that is always such a relief, because now you can participate in the birth actively, instead of having labor happen to you. This still requires control. You want to breathe your baby out over the perineum, so *please*, do not hold your breath and push with all your might! There are very few time-crunch emergencies that would justify such pushing. It is so much better for your baby and you if you take a breath and let it out as you push from your diaphragm, much like singing. Don't let the air out too soon. You need the air for your diaphragm to put pressure on your abdomen. Let the air out a little at a time. You will need to take at least two deep breaths and maybe three for each pushing contraction. Pay attention to your breathing as you sing, then push the same way. I heard a lady sing the most beautiful song to the Lord and her baby during second stage "pushing". You could really sense the presence of God during that birth. After the birth she was so amazed that she did not have a single scratch or tear. (Her doctor had given her episiotomies for each of her other three babies and told her she was too small to birth without one.) Her baby came out so gently that her perineum was able to stretch as much as it needed, and went right back to normal, as God intended it to be. Oh yes: her baby was one pound larger than her others were.

Some hindrances to labor are trauma, depression, and attitudes of sexuality. Trauma has its roots in injury and hurt. This can be physical, from abuse or attack resulting in defrauding you physically and emotionally, leaving you feeling inferior and lacking worth. Sometimes the physical and emotional trauma are so intertwined that it is hard to separate them. Picking it all apart and looking for the very minute in your past that such injury first happened is non-productive. It is much better to lay it at the cross of Jesus, and accept that He died for that hurt, brokenheartedness, pain and injury. Only Jesus can take the pain, bitterness, resentment, hate and all the other demons that came along with those "prince spirits," and send them back to the pit from whence they came. Pour your heart out to Him, and ask Jesus to heal the hurts and let you feel His love.

I am so thankful that Jesus never puts degrees on suffering and sin. It is all alike to Him, and He is so willing to bear it for you. That is why He cried "It is finished!" on the cross. The debt was paid for all eternity, so we can live redeemed, fully ransomed and free in the liberty of Christ Jesus (see Galatians 3:13–14 and 5:1). Now, thank Him for setting you free from that terrible yoke that had you so bound up. Do not let the enemy say that anything was left undone. "No, no, Satan go away, Jesus came here to stay." That is a cheer my grandchildren say when they feel compassed about and under attack by the devil. It may seem silly, but you sure feel better when you say it, and it builds up your faith, to know that our Heavenly Father will not let anything take us out of His hand! (John 10:28–29).

Now we will address some other causes of psychological trauma. Moving you from room to room, just as you have gotten used to where you are, can be enough of a disturbance to slow labor down or even stop it. This is not caused by walking around your house, but going from your house to the hospital admitting room, to the labor room, to the delivery room. Each move requires a time of settling in and "getting acquainted" with personnel, and place. Niles Newton did a study on laboring mice, and found the mortality rate went up in the pups whose mother was moved during labor. Other studies have shown that hemorrhage increases 5% in mothers who were moved about during labor from room to room, as above.

In addition to reacclimating yourself to new places as you go from labor stage to labor stage, you may find yourself in conflict with another person's personality. That person may be the one who is assigned to care for you in labor or delivery. At your first opportunity, let your husband/support person or monitrice know, so they can ask the supervisor for reassignment if attitudes are not changed. Hopefully, your support people will see this and be taking corrective steps already. Now if you are birthing at home, you may feel a little intimidated about asking your best friend or your midwife to "either cool it or move it out." Please don't feel that way. They may not realize they brought some unnecessary baggage along with them. Give them a chance to change their attitudes (maybe they had an encounter with a rude driver in traffic), before you ask them to go. But, you must tell them what is bothering you, so they can change their attitudes. Maybe they are chatting, and you want it to be quieter. Or, it is *too* quiet. That is easy to accommodate. Remember this is *your* birth, and it should be according to *your* birth plan.

There have been many studies done on prison populations, but one very interesting study was looking for the root cause of anti-social behavior and child abuse (a common denominator with many criminals). The one thing that was common to all was a lack of/or delayed bonding with their mothers at birth. Many times delayed bonding was due to traumatic birth, complications of the birth, sick baby, or anesthesia and the baby was not given to mother for 12 to 24 hours or more. Perhaps the baby was a premie and mother could not see the baby for weeks or months because of lack of transportation to the regional neonatal unit. Often on the fifth day, mother will have post-partum depression because of the trauma and separation, leading to more separation because of mother's unstable mental state, and on and on it goes. The longer the mother is separated from her baby, the more baby seems like a dream. Then suddenly the baby is home, and we have two strangers "forced" upon each other. One demands and needs a lot of care. The other is insecure with such a tiny baby needing special care and not sure of her ability to give it.

Then depression is triggered by a feeling of guilt that she isn't the mother she always wanted to be, or her baby would be with her. Or maybe, she feels like a bad mother because the birth was traumatic, and she convinces herself the baby is ruined for life because the birth was traumatic. The root of all depression is lies from the pit. Satan can make mountains out of molehills that were never there. Because you are at a vulnerable time in your life, he takes advantage of you and tells you all sorts of half-truths. Resist the devil! Submit yourself to God! (James 4:7–8).

Sometimes depression is caused by being overwhelmed by the pressures of parenting active preschoolers and a new baby, and being her version of the perfect wife and mother. The scenario is similar to this: The date is about 10 days after baby's birth. Mom has seen her house "deteriorate" from her usual neat-as-a-pin-everything-on-schedule-and-everything-in-its-place home, to a noisy, cluttered place desperately in need of a firm hand. So she determines to do something about it. She starts early in the morning, after husband and the older children are off to school. All day long it has been a challenge to get something done before the baby needed to be fed or diapered, or the toddler has "discumboomerated" same. It is now five o'clock. The children are home from school and all talking at once about the day's activities. The baby is crying, and the toddler is emptying the garbage all over the clean rug in the living room. Husband is due home any minute, wanting his supper. Mom has missed her nap, which she desperately needed, and supper is not started. At this moment, she would trade the whole bunch for one day of the peace and quiet she remembers from her single days.

You, the husband, come in the door, remembering how well-run your home usually is. Totally oblivious to the din, you ask your dear wife, "What's for supper?" There is not one thing wrong with that question, for you have asked that question daily since the day you were married. Today is the exception, and your wife:

    a. Dissolves in tears,

    b. Runs out of the room into the bedroom and slams the door,

    c. Takes a deep breath and tells you that if you are so insensitive "you can just cook your own whatever," which leads to a long list of real or imagined slights/sins you have committed against her and ends with her grabbing the baby and stomping out of the room or house.

This, of course, is very upsetting to you, and you react with:

    a. Righteous indignation and tell her a few things, or

    b. You rock back on your heels with your mouth open wide in disbelief and shock at the disappearance of the sweet, calm, considerate, loving woman you married.

Then something rises up inside of you and the thought occurs: "Why should I have to take that? *I* didn't do anything to deserve that kind of treatment!" *Do not yield* to such garbage. That thought is straight out of the pit, and if you yield to it, it will cripple your marriage. Instead, get the peanut butter and bread out, put the kids at the table with the oldest in charge of making peanut butter sandwiches, or send the children outside or downstairs in the basement to play.

Now, go to your wife—cautiously, if she is tempestuous—and take her in your arms and tell her you love her. After she cries, yells and blames everybody and everything for her moment of panic, get her calmed down. Then you ask her what happened that got her so upset (if you haven't figured it out from her ranting and raving), and what can you do to help. Please be convincing about how you perceive her as a very organized person, and how she is truly the "Proverbs 31 woman," and how much you love her. No matter how silly it sounds to you, don't laugh, or she may never trust you with her heart's thoughts again. Your wife has to feel that she is a person of great worth to you, or she will never again feel 100% confident of her worthiness as a wife. That can have very serious ramifications as to how she perceives herself as a woman, wife and mother. If she loses confidence in herself at this particular time, you both are in for a hard time in your marriage. Now you are applying I Thessalonians 5:8–11, 14–15 and Philippians 1:6, 4:8–9. Your wife has been confessing these Scriptures all day along with how her children are taught of the Lord, and great is their peace and undisturbed composure (Isaiah 54:13, Amplified). She's believing, but she hasn't seen the manifestation to be complete, so support her, and let her know that she is doing a great job.

Now is the time for you to take leadership, and let mom get on with cooking, etc., while you handle the children. Maybe daddy and the children can go in the kitchen and warm up some leftovers, make some sandwiches and open a can of soup, while mom takes a nice bubble bath, and feeds the baby. Children always behave better for daddy, because they recognize the *authority* that God *has given him*—and never forget that. It is demoralizing for a husband to say to his wife, "They always mind me better than you." (She already knows that. You need to let the children know that they must mind her as well as they do you.) "Go with the flow," as the saying goes; whatever is the most needed at the time, do it.

Okay, the children are all tucked in their beds, and now it is you and your wife, all alone, enjoying that peaceful time of the day, just the two of you. If you are uncomfortable demonstrating your love in front of the children with a hug or kiss, now is the time to do it. Not with any "strings attached," just to let her know how much she means to you. Women usually have a hard time feeling "lovey dovey" after a day like I just described. She is too tired to be romantic, and it is too soon after pregnancy for her to even deal with the thought of being fertile, etc. A nice cuddling on the couch, or in bed, telling her sweet, wonderful things about how much she means to you, giving her a back rub or gentle massage, will get her back in the mood faster than anything. The art of loving your spouse is more than bedtime sex, and once you have mastered the art, your marriage will blossom and bear the most wonderful fruit: a happy, secure wife, and happy secure children. Truly your house will be the home of the blessed of the Lord (Isaiah 63:9, 65:22–23).

Curses

Satan is waging war against the church and family more openly every day. He gets lots of help from the world and the "eat, drink and be merry" mindset that is so prevalent now. He knows that his time is short, and is waging a blitzkrieg-type war on God's people and God's church. Satan is just waiting for you to allow your armor (Ephesians 6:10–18) to slip, or get lazy in your Christian life and stray off to the shoulder instead of the middle of God's road.

God has promised full protection and provision *if* we obey Him and follow His direction (Deuteronomy 11:26–28 and 7:7–19). We know that the devil is a liar and murderer from the beginning (John 8:44). Put your armor on daily. Read your Bible daily. Meditate on God's Word. Pray with out ceasing (I Thessalonians 5:17). Be in communion with the all-knowing, ever-present, all-powerful God. Satan can not harm you if you obey God in all areas of your life.

But Satan does not play fair. He's a cheat, and cheats don't give up easily. If he can't attack you directly in your person, he will work on your marriage, your children, your house, car, cows, horses, chickens—anything that is "yours." Ministries are his favorite target, especially pastors and midwives. Midwives are in the same battle today as the Hebrew midwives were in in Exodus 1:15–22. Satan wanted to keep Israel in slavery and prevent God's man, Moses, from leading Israel out of Egypt. Today, Satan wants to keep the Church in bondage to the systems of this world, and eliminate the ministries that preach the uncompromising Word of God, and midwives who are helping families raise up a Godly seed unto the Lord.

Curses spoken against people or groups are very common and carry great power and it does not have to be by someone in witchcraft. The scripture tells us "we can have whatsoever we say" (Mark 11:23). This is a law of God and is true in the Christian and in the non-Christian world. We are told not to speak evil against anyone (James 4:11) because the power of life and death is in the tongue (Proverbs 18:21). Those in witchcraft know this and practice it. Christians need to understand this and weigh every word they say. This is why the scripture tells us that we will give an account for every word we say (Matthew 12:36–37). That is sobering, and if we remember it, we will put aside foolish jesting. It is alright to tell jokes and have fun; just be careful that what you say is not at someone else's expense.

It is possible for people to bind themselves under a curse and conspire to tear up a church, try to kill a person or get rid of a pastor. In Acts 23:12–14, forty men conspired and bound themselves under a curse to kill Paul. God made a way of escape.

The local church, or even part of the congregation needs to gather together regularly: to pray, bind up and pull down all the strongholds of Satan in their city, homes, churches, county, and state, and send back all curses being spoken against the group. Then the power of the Holy Ghost will be manifested in the local church and things will start happening! If your church, corporately, does not want to do this, then get a few friends together and start waging spiritual warfare. Pray blessings and spiritual understanding on your leaders, and if their heart is toward God, God will move and soon the whole church will be praying with you.

Sometimes we put curses on ourselves out of ignorance. We can get a curse by refusing to fight in the battle. The church is in a battle with Satan. Satan is pulling out his big guns against the church, and we either fight with God or we are against him (Matthew 12:30, Luke 9:50). Judges 5:23 and Jeremiah 48:10 includes "deceitful workers." These are those that do not speak or live the full revelation of truth that God has given them, because they wish to be popular.

Anything that robs you of the promises of God and His abundance is a curse. Deuteronomy 28:15–68 lists the curses that follow sin. Rh negative blood that has been sensitized to Rh positive blood causes miscarriages and death in the unborn. It is a curse. Many testimonies have been told of God changing blood types to positive, in answer to prayer. James 5:16 promises that the fervent prayer of a righteous man avails much. Deuteronomy 28:1–14 lists all the blessings for God's people if they obey His commandments and follow His laws. God so loved the world, that He gave His only begotten Son, that whosoever believeth in Him shall be saved (John 3:16). Jesus came to save the world, but not all the world is saved. He redeemed us from the curse of the law. He became that curse for us (Galatians 3:13). He has broken the power of the curse, but it isn't automatic, just as salvation isn't automatic.

Give up your idols. That includes your children, the ministry (pastors, evangelists, teachers, prophets, and apostles), especially your own ministry. That also includes your idea to only listen to one or two speakers, and their teachings, or only listen to one kind of teaching—for example, healing, visions, prophecy, and so forth—and be out of balance (Galatians 5:9 and Proverbs 11:1). You can read too many books and listen to too many tapes, also. A spirit of idolatry can come in and soon you will be just a parrot, parroting what that speaker says. It is hard to believe that a parrot has any anointing to break the yokes off of God's people. You will be cursed by God because of this dreadful sin of leaning on the arm of flesh—*He will curse you* (Jeremiah 17:5).

When those in witchcraft send a curse, they also send an alternate curse with it. As an example : A curse of sickness is spoken against you, and to make sure you are not able to reject it, they also speak it against your dog, cow or car or some other item that belongs to you. Because Jesus took the curse upon himself for us, we are free from the curse! (Galatians 3:13). In your prayer against curses spoken against you by a reprobate (reprobates refuse to have anything to do with God, and refuse to accept anything connected with Jesus, His Blood or the Holy Spirit), also say: "Satan, I stand against any curse or alternate curse against me and break its power in the Name of Jesus and send it back to the sender according to Psalm 109:17–19: "As he loved cursing, so let it come unto him: as he delighted not in blessing, so let it be far from him. As he clothed himself with cursing like as with his garment, so let it come into his bowels like water, and like oil into his bones. Let this be the reward of mine adversaries from the Lord, and of them that speak evil against my soul".

If you find yourself under any curse, don't beat yourself up about it; confess and repent of your sin, and believe God heard you. If the curse was put on you by someone else, and you determine that it was because of ignorance, and not from a reprobate, bind and break the curse as above, but do not send it back to the sender. We are to pray for them that spitefully use us. Until that one has breathed his last breath, there is a possibility that he will accept Jesus as Savior. Pray blessings on such people and ask God to teach them by giving them understanding and compassion towards you. They may have sent a horrid curse to you that you would not want anyone to suffer. Thank Him for His forgiveness and start walking in victory! Hallelujah! Jesus is alive! His arm is not shortened, neither does He forget his people. He does give deliverance and peace. Remember, another definition of salvation is deliverance! You may have to remind Satan a few more times in the coming days, after all, he's had a pretty free reign around you and he is not going to give that up easily. You don't need to have any conversations with him. If you do, he'll take your victory away from you. The devil sucks life from Christians. That's how he survives.

Guidelines

At Christian Childbirth Education, we have developed seven checkpoints to be reviewed before birth. These are our spiritual guidelines. Violation of these guidelines may be grounds to risk a couple out of home birth with our ministry. We will go to the hospital and labor coach them, if they wish.

I. Salvation

Baptism in the Holy Spirit (preferred). Not all Christian churches teach this. We do expect the couple to be "Blood bought by the Lamb of God." (Ephesians 4:23–32, II Timothy 1:8–9).

II. Consistent Walk

Read Ephesians 5:15–17 and Romans 8:1–9.
- No presumption—no unrepented sin (Acts 3:19).
- Submitted to a local body (I Peter 5:5).
- Adequate prayer life (I Thessalonians 5:17).
- Regular Bible reading, study, and meditation.

III. Understanding Spiritual Warfare

Read Ephesians 6:11–18:
- "Leaven" out of the home
  - Rock music
  - False gods

- Drugs
- Astrology
- Occult
- Out of balance teaching
- Understanding authority of Christians in Christ
- Prayer of authority
- Prayer of binding and loosing
- Deliverance—forgiveness
- Reversal of curses
- Being in a position to receive blessings
- Recognizing enemies—fear, unbelief, negative confession, etc.
- Putting on armor of God

IV. Scriptural Order
- With the local body and its leadership (I Peter 5:5)
- Within family:
  - Priesthood of the husband (Ephesians 5:23–31, 6:4)
  - Submission of the wife and children (Ephesians 5:22–24, 6:1–3)
  - Relationship of love (Colossians.3:18–21)

V. No Doublemindedness (II Peter 1:3–25, 2:1–12)
- Faith in God alone
- Proper motives
- Understanding separation from world systems

VI. Prenatal Care
- Scripture
- Positive confessions
- Spirit-led prayer against specific problems
- Natural preparation:
  - Nutrition
  - Exercise
  - Class and reading independently
  - Healing if necessary
  - List of supplies filled

VII. Birth
- Who should attend
- Phone lists—who will pray, tend to other children etc.
- Decisions about taping, photographs, etc.
- Preparation for new baby:

- Equipment
- Help from family and friends
- Meals, etc. prepared ahead

This is a summary of the things we have found helpful and important for the family to consider and pray about. In the final analysis, the preparation for the childbirth, both spiritual and natural, rests with the family, not with the ministry. We are a ministry of helps, ordained and anointed of God. We will stand with you in faith, as the Lord calls forth your baby. As midwives, we will assist you with the skills God has given us, but we do not usurp or in any way interfere with the ordained function of the family.

What Are "Risk Factors?"

We have referred to "high risk" and "low risk" earlier, but how are risks determined? Why should an apparently normal phase of a woman's life become a high risk, and for whom? The mother? The baby? The attendant? The answer is any one or all—it depends on the situation. The clue lies in the cause of the risk factor, how severe it is, what the local standard of practice is and who sets that standard.

You lower your "risk" the closer you are to "normal," or sometimes what the textbooks say is normal. The low-risk mother can be generally described as one who: is in general good health, eats good nutritious meals regularly by following the Brewer Diet, gets the amount of rest she needs, exercises regularly, is not anemic, her baby "fits" the pelvis with the head down, is born about due date (give or take two weeks, either side of estimated date), and both parents take an active part in the prenatal care, and her factors do not exceed a 2. In addition, since I am talking to Christian couples I expect them to follow the above "Guidelines" with their full armor in place (as described in Ephesians 6:11–18).

The intermediate-risk mother has a risk factor of 3 or 4. This can be brought down to a 2 or even a 1 by Pat assuming responsibility for herself, and aligning her lifestyle with God's Word and following the Brewer Diet.

As a contrast, the high-risk mother will have a life threatening complication, such as placenta abruptio or placenta previa, a chronic health problem requiring constant monitoring or medication, or is a substance abuser. She is not prepared spiritually or physically for the birth, and her home is not in Scriptural order (I Corinthians 7:12–16, I Peter 3:1–12, Ephesians 6:1–4). Her risk factor is a 5 and will need major miracles from the Lord. She needs to start early in her pregnancy to find "Dr. Wonderful" and "Marvelous Hospital". The midwife can help Pat and John to get a workable birth plan with Dr. Wonderful, and even plan to go to the hospital as a support person.

According to *Taber's Cyclopedic Medical Dictionary*, 10th edition, a complication is an "added difficulty; a complex state, a disease or accident superimposed upon another without being specifically related, yet affecting or modifying the prognosis of the original disease, or state of being; e.g., pneumonia is a complication of measles. . ." On the other hand, the same source says that an emergency is a sudden, generally unexpected occurrence or set of circumstances demanding immediate action, e.g., shock, convulsion, asphyxiation, hemorrhage, etc.

There are some situations that would definitely make you too high a risk for home birth. The rationale behind this statement is that either the mother or the baby are more likely to: need emergency care, or develop complications best handled in the hospital, than if these circumstances would not be present. Christian Childbirth Education supports the following risk assessment guidelines to assist the midwife and parents to determine who is a suitable candidate for home birth.

- When the risk factor is 5, the midwife will take the following steps:
  - Discuss the problem with the parents and tell them specifically that they are high risk for home birth and unless the risk factor is lowered, they should plan a hospital birth.
  - If a 5 first develops during or after labor and delivery, and the parents refuse transport to a hospital, the midwife will do her best to convince them to go, and inform them fully of the risks.
  - If a 5 first develops when birth is imminent or birth will occur before arrival at hospital, the midwife must assess the degree of danger to mother and child, relative risks of staying at home or transporting, and her skills and equipment. Discussion of risk with the par-

ents may be limited to emergency instructions, as long as it is fully discussed with them later.
- All births with a risk factor of 5 should be subject to consultation or peer review with the midwives in your group practice, or area depending on the midwife's skills, experience, equipment, political climate and backups.
- With a risk factor of 4, parents must be made aware of the increased risk, and referral may be made to a medical doctor. With a risk factor of 3, parents must be informed of the increased risk, and consultation must be made with another health care practitioner. With a risk factor of 1 or 2, the midwife will evaluate for increased risk on an individual basis. Parents must be informed of any increased risk.
- Risk factor numbers are not additive, though midwives are encouraged to use an additive method to obtain a good overview of the mother's or baby's condition.

Initial History and Physical Risk Evaluation

Risk Factor of 1
- Age less than 17 or over 45 if primipara
- Underweight: more than 20 pounds under ideal weight for height, or less than 90 pounds at the time of conception
- First prenatal visit at more than 20 weeks gestation
- Exposure to x-rays in the first trimester (without protective apron)
- History of infant over 10 pounds
- Small stature (less than 4' 8")
- Use of antibiotics during present pregnancy

Risk Factor of 2
- History of low-birth-weight infant
- Uncertain due dates
- History of venereal disease
- Less than 12 months from last delivery to present due date
- Grand multipara (over 5 children) unless eating the Brewer Diet
- Repeated spontaneous abortions
- Midforceps or difficult delivery in the past

- History of premature baby (less than 37 weeks)
- Previous antepartum hemorrhage
- History of pre-eclampsia or Pregnancy-Induced Hypertension
- Hepatitis within the last two years
- Overweight: over 50 pounds overweight at the time of conception

Risk Factor of 3.

- History of a child with significant genetic congenital anomalies
- Use of Flagyl in first trimester
- Surviving birth-damaged infants. . . determine why they are damaged
- Neonatal deaths—stillborn or during the first 30 days
- Previous caesarean section
- Smoking
- Poor nutrition

Risk Factor of 4.

- Rubella during first trimester of present pregnancy
- Medical history of:
  - Heart disease
  - Thromboembolism
  - Chronic pulmonary disease
  - Renal disease as an adult
  - Diabetes
  - Serious endocrine problems
  - Serious emotional or psychiatric problems
- Use of the following drugs at any time during the present pregnancy:
  - Anticoagulants
  - Anticonvulsants
  - Antidiabetics
  - Antihypertensives
  - Chemotherapeutics
  - Corticosteroids
  - Sex steroids
  - Ergots

Risk Factors: During Prenatal Care

Risk Factor of 1

- Exposure of both parents to environmental hazards
- Emotional stress or physical stress
- Weight gain of over 50 pounds or excessive weight gain

Risk Factor of 2

- Lack of support person
- Marginal anemia (Hgb. less than 11, Hct. less than 32)
- At term—unengaged fetal head in primipara

Risk Factor of 3

- Not assuming responsibility for self-care
- Poor nutrition
- Smoking
- Glucose in urine (1 g/dl on two separate occasions)
- Documented post-term pregnancy (over 43 weeks)
- Malpresentation at 36+ weeks gestation
- Insufficient weight gain
- Active herpes not responding to Herp-Elim Herbal Tincture

Risk Factor of 4

- Suspected pre-eclampsia
- Pregnancy Induced Hypertension (140/90 on two successive visits, after 30 minutes quiet relaxation)
- Pyelonephritis
- Undiagnosed vaginal bleeding
- Threatened labor less than 37 weeks
- Suspected hydramnios or oligodramnios
- Intrauterine Growth Retardation

Risk Factor of 5

- Serious blood disorders
- Severe anemia (hemoglobin less than 10, hematocrit less than 30 at term)
- Diabetes
- Heart Disease
- Pre-eclampsia
- Syphilis
- Hepatitis
- Abruptio placenta

- Placenta previa
- Rh sensitization
- Epilepsy
- Abuse or frequent use of the following:
- Alcohol
- Antidepressants
- Hallucinogens
- Narcotics
- Psychotropic herbs
- Sedatives and/or Hypnotics

Risk Factors: During Labor and Delivery

Risk Factor of 1

- Emotional stress
- Failure to progress
- Hypertension (>140/90)
- Light meconium-stained amniotic fluid—if straw-colored in the presence of excellent FHTs and no solids, it is not a risk factor
- Premature rupture of membranes

Risk Factor of 3

- Temperature over 100.4° F.
- Prolonged rupture of membranes (over 24 hours prior to delivery)
- Prolonged active phase
- Abnormal presentation in multipara (breech, brow, transverse lie)
- Multiple pregnancy in multipara

Risk Factor of 4

- Fetal tachycardia—responding to therapy but recurring
- Fetal bradycardia—responding to therapy but recurring
- Maternal exhaustion
- Maternal dehydration
- Incoordinate contractions

Risk Factor of 5

- Failure to progress in presence of strong contractions
- No prenatal care
- Premature labor (less than 37 weeks—verified due dates)
- Pre-eclampsia

- Suspected placental abruption or abnormal vaginal bleeding
- Suspected placenta previa
- Active primary herpes at time of labor or within two weeks prior to labor
- Uterine rupture
- Prolonged second stage (over three hours of good pushes with little or no progress)
- Abnormal persistent presentation (i.e. breech, brow, transverse lie, in primipara)
- Multiple pregnancy in primipara
- Meconium in amniotic fluid ("pea soup" at any time during first or second stage)
- Prolapsed cord
- Fetal tachycardia (greater than 160, longer than 30 minutes)
- Prolonged deceleration
- Fetal bradycardia (less than 100 beats per minute, not immediately responding to therapy during first stage)
- Severe variable decelerations
- Late decelerations not responding to therapy
- Estimated fetal weight less than $5\frac{1}{2}$ pounds

Risk Factors: Postpartum

Risk Factor of 2

Mother	Baby
Incomplete membranes	Birth weight 10 lbs. or more
Prolapsed cervix	Meconium at birth
Mastitis	Minor fetal anomolies
Hydramnios or oligohydramnios	Jaundice

Risk Factor of 3

Retained placenta—over two hours with no hemorrhage	Less than three vessels in umbilical cord

Risk Factor of 4

Fever over 101° F.
Signs of uterine infection
Perineal lacerations
  (4th degree)

Failure to gain weight
Infant less than $5\frac{1}{2}$ lbs.
High-pitched cries
Jaundice in first 24 hours
Abnormal neurological signs
Inability to nurse
5-minute Apgar less than 6

Risk Factor of 5

Hemorrhage, uncontrolled
Signs of shock
Inverted uterus
Significant portions of
  placenta retained
Thrombophlebitis or
  thromboembolism
Significant rise in BP after
  birth

Asphyxia, anoxia
Trembling, jerky movements,
  spasms
Convulsions
Suspected heart problems;
  cyanosis or pallor
Meconium aspiration
Suspected sepsis
Major fetal anomolies
Inability to nurse after 24
  hours

Most of these situations are due to not taking care of your body, before your pregnancy or during. I Corinthians 6:19–20 tells us that our body is the temple of the Lord, and we are to glorify God in our body and in our spirit, because they belong to God. If our body is the temple of God (remember, we invited Him to live in us when we accepted Jesus as Savior, and when we committed our lives to Him, asking for the Holy Spirit to abide in us), then we must consider what kind of a house do we have for God. Another way of looking at this is; would you drink or smoke if Jesus was standing in front of you in a physical presence? Would you give that cigarette to your newborn baby to smoke, or that alcoholic drink for the baby to drink? Of course not. Remember, whatever you eat or drink takes only five to ten minutes to get to your baby. Whatever goes into your veins takes 30 to 60 seconds, and whatever goes into your muscles takes two to three minutes to get to your baby.

Okay, so you don't smoke, but you work in an office where many others do, and you must breathe that smoky air all day. The Clean Air Act in your state may provide a clause stating what your rights are as a pregnant mother. You might be eligible for placement in a non-smoking area, or the smokers may have to limit their smoking to a designated place. Check at your local library for a copy of the Clean Air Act enforced in your state. An occasional breath of smoke will not harm the baby, but we are talking about prolonged exposure here.

As a Christian sold out to Jesus, the office party can be a challenge to take a stand for righteousness and holiness. Pregnant women should not drink alcoholic beverages. Instead enjoy the ever-present orange juice or tomato juice, if you don't want to order a "Shirley Temple." Your baby will not be harmed by one cocktail or beer a week, but usually if one has one drink, you will have another, and it is the cumulative, not the month's average that counts. A jolt of 12 ounces of cocktails, wine, etc., is quite a lot for a baby that is trying to grow. Doesn't it make more sense to drink some orange juice, or vegetable juice that gives the baby nutrients to grow on, rather than something that she can not use because it acts as a toxin that her immature system has difficulty casting off? Please read Romans 13:13–14, and I Corinthians 6:19–20.

As a Christian, you have the healing power of God available to you for the abnormal hindrances to birth, if you want to appropriate it. Galatians 3:13–14 reminds us that we are redeemed from the curse of the law, because Jesus paid the price in full for us. Hallelujah! Isaiah 65:23 says that we will not labor in vain or have a premature delivery from shock or fear, because we are descendents of the blessed of the Lord, and our offspring are also. Isaiah 53:3–6 and I Peter 2:24 tells us how Jesus accepted all of our sickness, physical and mental, all of our sins (the "big" ones and the "little" ones, too), and gave us healing and salvation and forgiveness in return. It is up to us as individuals before God, what we want to appropriate in our own lives. Be careful how you reject any of it. If any part of the Bible is *not* true, what part of it can we know for sure *is* true? It may be that we in our finite minds do not understand what God is saying in His Word, for His ways are not our ways, and His thoughts are not like our thoughts (Isaiah 55:8–9). Therefore what we do not understand, we need to go to the Lord, and pray for guidance and understanding of His Word, and what He wants us to do.

CHAPTER 6

CHOOSING YOUR MIDWIFE, HELPERS, AND PHYSICIAN

There are lots of consumer and parenting groups being formed. Usually they are an outgrowth of home birth classes, La Leche League, International (LLLI), or the like. NAPSAC has many member groups that support home birth, breastfeeding, midwifery, good nutrition, and natural childbirth. These groups are good resources. Many of them have questionnaires on file that they have sent out to doctors, midwives, and hospitals for their philosophy regarding birth. These files can help limit your search to those attendants (doctor or midwife) that are closest to your beliefs and convictions. You will also find a lot of support and sources of information at their meetings, so get acquainted and participate in their activities. They need you as much as you need them.

Perhaps you live in an area where doctors are not friendly to midwives. Don't give up. You can still have your home birth. Contacts and resources to help you find the local midwives include: Midwives Alliance of North America, La Leche League, Crisis Pregnancy Centers, local parenting support groups such as the local chapter of NAPSAC, local health food stores (talk with the manager), local chiropractor association, other health alternative practitioners or local herbalist.

Selecting a Midwife

Some national organizations that can give you midwifery referrals are Midwives Alliance of North America (MANA), Inter-National Association of Parents and Professionals for Safe Alternatives in Childbirth (NAPSAC), American College of Nurse Midwives (ACNM), International Cesarean Awareness Network (ICAN), and North American Registry of Midwives (NARM).

If political pressure is strong, you may have to leave your name with the contact and the midwife will call you. You should try to locate the midwife before getting the back-up doctor. Sometimes doctors have agreed to back up the home birth in hopes of entrapping the midwife. You want to protect the midwife as much as possible, by contacting only "safe" allopathic backup.

Whether you choose to have a home birth or a hospital birth, you want your attendant to believe that birth is a natural event in the life of a woman and family. Attendants, be they midwives or doctors, who consider birth and pregnancy a dangerous time, will treat you as a high-risk person even when you are not, so it is important to interview them.

Set up an interview with her/him. There are a few male midwives, just as there are a few female doctors. For simplicity's sake, I will yield to the majority in each category and refer to the midwife as "she" and the doctor as "he" in this text. The midwife may wish to conduct the initial interview in your home, her office or in a neutral place such as a restaurant, park, or at a mutual friend's home.

In politically difficult areas, the midwife will want to know some things before the interview: why you want a midwife, how you got her name, and who referred you to her, your philosophy of life and why you believe yourself as a reliable person "worthy" of home birth and her services. If you have your medical records, make them available to her, especially if you had a forceps/vacuum extraction or caesarean birth. Most midwives, unless they are practicing in a clearly legal state, are slightly paranoid because of the "Sword of Damocles" hanging over their heads.

Some questions you will want to ask are:

- What is your stand/philosophy on life? If you are strongly pro-life, you may not be comfortable with a pro-abortionist.

- What is your religious orientation? Are you a Christian? Will you, the client, be comfortable with someone that uses crystals and is into the New Age Movement or Eastern philosophies/religions? Can you adjust your practice of midwifery to comply with our practice of Christianity? This may be your opportunity for evangelism. Perhaps God brought you all together to bring her into His Kingdom. Do pray and seek God's will. The flip side—which is also possible—is that it is *not* His will to cast pearls before reprobates (Matthew 7:6). The ideal, of course, is a midwife that is rooted and grounded in the Word of God, has the anointing and the call to midwifery by the Father, knows the authority of the Word and the Blood, and uses it for God's glory. Her prayer life is active, she is in submission to the local expression of the Body of Christ, and to her husband also, should she be married.
- May you have a copy of her Informed Consent Agreement to read and sign, should you decide to hire her? This is when you discuss her skill level. A Christian midwife is a blessing, but does she have midwifery skills? Does she pray babies out, or does she couple her faith with works? (James 2:17, II Timothy 2:15). Did God teach her her skills or did she go to school? Some State Midwifery Associations have self-certification programs. Is she a member in good standing with them? I have met some precious sisters in the Lord that are practicing midwives and have no equipment, nor skills. Some of them have had problems and ended up transporting unnecessarily because they were not equipped. Midwives are on the front lines in bringing forth the Godly seed and preserving the family. The enemy is launching an all-out war against those values today. We can't go into battle unarmed (Ephesians 6:13–20). Birthing babies is a physical manifestation of important spiritual principles (James 2:18, John 3:16–21).
- What equipment does she bring to the birth and what does she want you to furnish? Is she prepared for common emergencies? Is she able to stabilize the baby/mom for transport?
- What arrangements does she have concerning a back-up physician and hospital, if any?

- Will she bring assistants/apprentices, or are you to furnish the assistants?
- How often and where does she do the prenatal visits? My personal preference is that she should do all of your prenatal care. If a question comes up, all of you can discuss it and resolve it to mutual satisfaction. If you wish to supplement her care with a physician's care, discuss that with the midwife. Perhaps there is someone she can recommend. Often such an arrangement will develop a backup physician for the midwife.
- What vitamins should you be taking, and what exercises does she recommend to prevent lacerations (tears)?
- Fees: it is always nice to know where everyone stands. Some midwives accept barter, others do not.
- Does she teach classes, or are there childbirth classes available that she recommends?

If there are doctors in your area that attend home births, you still need to interview them and see what their attitude and philosophy are. Some doctors treat birth as a midwife would, but the advantage here is the added expertise, should the unexpected happen. You also have the continuity of care in the hospital, should a transport be necessary. Other doctors "bring the hospital" with them, like a portable delivery table, electronic fetal monitors, IVs, etc. Of course, if they went to all the trouble of bringing it, they may want to use it, too.

Midwives come from all levels of education and backgrounds. The most highly trained and skilled is the CNM (Certified Nurse-Midwife). She has a B.S.N. or M.S.N. with about 12 years of specialized training in obstetrics. She knows the obscure complication as well as the normal pregnancy, birth and postpartum experience. She is also skilled in well woman care, and the care of the healthy or mildly sick newborn. She may attend women only in hospital because of local politics, or her medical attitudes. Or she may be a strong home-birth advocate, looking at birth as a natural event. Should you need to transport, she will be able to go into the delivery room with you, and help you birth, or assist her backup physician. Of course, she cannot do a caesarean, nor will she want to use forceps, but she can be with you and your husband during those procedures.

A CNM, in addition to her backup physician, has hospital privileges where she can also attend planned hospital births. Many CNMs operate free-standing birth centers that provide a home-like atmosphere with the advantage of the midwife having emergency equipment handy, and early dismissal. Third party (insurance) payment is usually covered with a CNM.

The next category is the empirical/traditional midwife. I prefer the term "traditional" or "empirical" midwife rather than "lay" midwife. The term "lay" implies she is unskilled and unlearned. A true midwife has a hunger to know about birth, she has studied and applied I Timothy 2:15 to her ministry. This is the midwife that God is calling forth today. In addition to learning traditional skills from midwifery texts and apprenticeship, the Lord has taught her His principles and given her His skills. I have sat in many workshops and had confirmation from "the experts" those things God had taught me during quiet time with Him. On occasion, I have been able to share things with the "experts" what God taught me; for example, easier, less invasive and safer procedures. We will expand on that later.

There is great variety of education and background and skill levels here. Some empirical/traditional midwives are as skilled as CNMs and others are limited in their skills. The services of a traditional midwife may not be covered by insurance, unless she/he is recognized by the state she practices in, either by licensure or registration. Some state midwifery associations have a self-certification program. The state may or may not recognize this certification, but it can give you a guideline as to how she compares with her peers. Be sure to check the fine print, and inquire of your agent if not sure. Some folks have had to push their claim up to the executive level at the insurance company's headquarters to get their midwife paid.

The CPM (certified Professional Midwife) is a direct entry midwife who has met the standards of apprenticeship, academics and skills set forth by MEAC (Midwifery Education Accreditation Council) and NARM and passed the national skills and written exams.

The Midwife's Skill Level

Most empirical/traditional midwives have learned by experience, reading every book she could find about birth, and may have apprenticed with an experienced midwife or doctor. She believes in the natural processes of birth, is empathetic, and has developed techniques to facilitate birth without medication. She often uses herbs or homeopathics, and considers good nutrition necessary for safe birth. She may have pioneered home births in your area. She may or may not have medical or hospital backup. She certainly will have a list of resources available to you in the area.

The Minimum Skill Level of the CPM

She will be able to evaluate the baby by the APGAR scoring, and can tell if your labor is normal or not. She will be able to: examine the placenta and know if it is complete with all the membranes present; care for the healthy newborn and advise you about resources for the newborn needing further evaluation; she knows emergency procedures such as CPR, and can determine dilation of the cervix; does prenatal care and postnatal care; educates the parents for a good safe birth; is wise, cool and calm; and allows the couple to direct their own birth. She knows how to prevent tears, but can repair them should they occur, and can help you and the baby get off to a good start with breastfeeding.

The Medium- to Highly-Skilled CPM

Next is the traditional midwife that has attended a midwifery school, and has a certificate of completion or attendance. She will be skilled from a hands-on training program calculated to give her as much variety in experience as possible. Her attitudes will be formed from her instructors. She will have the same skills and perhaps more technical information than the empirical, and the same attitude to birth. I have listed a few midwifery schools in the "Resources" section in the back of the book. . Please investigate and pray before committing yourself to a formal training situation that is incompatible with your beliefs and principles. There are midwifery schools that are basically clinics that serve the very poor, especially in the border towns of Texas.

Some of the women who come to these clinics will have had little or no prenatal care, and will just walk in during labor for help with birthing, resulting in complicated births, or very quick births because of the time it has taken them to get to the clinic. Thus, the midwifery school student from Texas will have seen many high-risk births with the attendant complications that the average midwife has not seen.

Midwifery Today magazine amd MANA hold annual conferences with wonderful workshops and lectures. MANA also has regional conferences that usually have hands-on workshops as well as great lectures for the beginner to the advanced midwife, and may be closer to where you live.

Some state midwifery associations have developed their own certification programs. These programs have minimum requirements of academic study, apprenticeships, and examinations similar to state boards. There are student, apprentice, as well as fully-certified, senior-midwife categories. These programs have been developed in states that do not recognize midwifery, for the purpose of meeting the public's need for skilled, educated midwives.

The North American Registry of Midwives is an international certification agency established by MANA in 1987 to establish certification for the "Certified Professional Midwife." It encompasses direct entry, self-study, and all levels of midwifery schools. You can be assured that she has the same skills that the midwife has who attended the midwifery school. It has just taken her longer to become a midwife.

Many senior midwives will have "proven" themselves as responsible professionals and have medical backup. This is not easy to get because of the political problems midwives have in "illegal" states. Most midwives go through a period of "proving" themselves to doctors. This is a very unfortunate situation, because it puts the client in the middle. On the positive side, it also gives the client the opportunity to educate the physician about the skills of her midwife.

The "proof of the pudding," so to speak, is the birth. When the baby and the mother are healthy, with no problems during or after the birth, the doctor remembers, and mentally tallies these births. After a period of time, or when the midwife goes to the doctor with the client, acting as a friend, because she suspects something, and asks intelligent (according to the doctor) questions about reversing the difficulty, he remembers this. Sooner or later, the midwife will demonstrate her skills at a difficult birth resulting in a healthy baby and mother, and he will recognize her as a professional. Somewhere during this process an agreement will be made between them. The ideal situation for a midwife is to apprentice to a friendly doctor, who will teach her how to catch a baby with an unusual presentation, how to repair lacerations, and back her up when she has to transport.

This, however, is a rare situation. Most doctors trained since the 1960s have not learned how to do breech or multiple births vaginally, nor have they been instructed in internal or external version. They have been taught caesarean techniques instead. Now you know why the caesarean rate is over 25% and still climbing in this country!

In the meantime, much prayer and wisdom is needed that God will cause the doctor to recognize the midwife as a skilled professional and look on her with favor. Until God has done that work in him or her, the client has to pray for wisdom that she can talk about her midwife without alienating the doctor and not giving out the midwife's name prematurely. This wisdom is needful to protect the midwife from needless harassment and possible legal difficulties.

Duties of the Attendants

The duties of your attendants vary, depending on how big a crowd you want at your birth. Not all have to be in the birth room, and several jobs can be filled by one person. Some jobs are not absolutely necessary, but are listed because some folks have had those options at their births.

The **primary attendant** is the "baby catcher." This person can be the baby's father, with or without coaching from the midwife, or is the midwife. He or she is responsible for the hot compresses and oil massage to prevent the perineum from tearing, and helping the baby have a gentle birth. The primary attendant is also responsible for monitoring the labor and making sure mother and baby remain within normal parameters by checking the FHTs, BP, contractions, hydration and energy level, dilation and descent of the baby as is necessary. She also offers suggestions to help mother labor more comfortably, for example, position changes or massage. After the baby is born, the primary attendant assists the mother to expel the placenta and examines it for completeness, condition and type.

The **secondary attendant** may also spell the primary in taking Fetal Heart Tones (FHTs), supporting "Pat" (the mother), giving massage, etc., during first stage of labor. This will help her recognize the baby's rhythm and reaction to labor, so she can more quickly evaluate the baby's well-being in second stage. She is responsible for listening to the heart tones during the last stage of labor, and taking care of the baby immediately after birth. This includes helping Pat initiate breastfeeding, evaluating baby according to the Apgar scale, and doing any emergency procedures (such as CPR) as are necessary. She will also help labor-coach Pat, if "John" (the husband) is going to catch his baby.

Either the primary or the secondary attendant will keep the labor notes current and get the sterile supplies out and ready for birth at the proper time. If the bed has not been prepared, they will prepare it. Together, they will constantly evaluate the labor, keeping in mind the goal of being the "invisible midwife" (invisible midwives have the ability to get their jobs done, without being intrusive or noticed by the laboring woman). After birth, they will help Pat and baby with the herbal sitz bath, clean up the birth room and do the newborn exam, do the final vital-signs check, fundal height exam and give the postpartum instructions. While the family is bonding, the paperwork is completed, questions are answered, and when the four-hour postpartum "watch" is completed, the midwives go home.

The **gopher/timekeeper** takes notes of events of birth and their times, and the **photographer**, obviously, is the one in charge of taking pictures or videos of the birth. One person can handle this, but could require "relationship" with an octopus. If she is well-organized, she can handle this, but if you want lots of pictures, you may have to have a separate photographer. Videos take the pressure off, and have the advantage of being very private. No one sees the "negative" and you have complete control over who sees your "pictures." Cameras can be borrowed or rented. Check around. You may be surprised how many friends have cameras and would be honored to loan you theirs. After the birth, perhaps she could pop the frozen "birth-day dinner" in the oven, to heat up while the family is bonding. This is especially helpful if there are several small children in the family and the child-care person is swamped keeping up with all the energy the children suddenly have.

Figure 6-1: Siblings at the birth

Other than the primary and secondary attendants, the other absolutely necessary person is the one who is caring for the siblings. You need at least one per child under three, if the children are going to be present in the birth room, during the birth. If the children are going to wait elsewhere until after the baby is born, and then come in, you only need as many as are necessary to care for them, and keep them quietly occupied during labor. Children that are prepared and understand labor often encourage and comfort mom, so you may allow them to come and go during early stages. However, a demanding child is not helpful during labor and should be taken outside to run off some energy, or to someone else's house to play. Children should be allowed to be children, so don't require more of them than they can give.

The child-care person(s) can also answer the phone and or the door, since the children usually race for the door or the phone anyway. It is thus natural for whoever is with the children to do this courtesy. Children are always hungry. Especially if they think they can get extra snacks, because of all the extra people and food in the house. So, while you are getting their juice, pour an extra glass, or make an extra plate of snacks for Pat and the birth team.

While the family is bonding together, the child-care giver could take the birth-day dinner out of the freezer and heat it up for everybody. This is especially wonderful if meal time has been skipped because birth was imminent. Mom does not realize how hungry she is until she tastes the food.

Children at Birth

If the children are to be around for all or part of the labor and or birth, they need to be taught about birth. Maleki's *Mom and Dad and I Are Having a Baby* is an excellent book. *Children at Birth* by Marjie and Jay Hathaway, Penny Simkin's video of her sibling class *Children at Birth*, the video *Andrew's Birth*, available from NAPSAC or AAHCC, also prepare children for the physical process of birth. Children must also know that birth is a Holy event. You should not tell children about birth without sharing God's point of view. As Christians, I believe God is calling us to a higher accountability than the unbeliever. If God intended children to be present at sibling's birth, can we say that it is also His intent for them to be observing the conception of that sibling also? Perhaps we need to ask ourselves a few questions. Why do we want that child at the birth? Is it to participate in the latest fad in birthing? How necessary is it for the child to have experiential knowledge about labor, and birth? Are they interested in sexual intercourse? Are you trying to make a statement concerning their abstinence from sex, "or they will have to go through all of this" as a consequence? Will your 5-, 6-, or 10-year-old be in a situation that probably will require him or her to assist a woman giving birth in the near future? Are you also planning to tell your child the "how tos" of sexual intercourse before entering school, so they have the "correct" views about it?

I realize that many school sex education courses are too explicit, and do tell children more than they really need to know. But if you contribute to that carnal knowledge without emphasizing the Biblical point of view, are you not endorsing such programs? We need to take a stand for righteousness and holiness. Maintaining privacy, modesty and treating birth as a holy event between husband and wife, limiting those in the birth room to the absolute minimum does not promote shame or prudishness. It promotes honor and respect to the laboring woman. Why is it that when a woman is giving birth, our "Christian" culture thinks it is alright to expose her entire body to the "whole world," but not at any other time? How would the man feel if he was stripped naked and women traipsed in and out of the bedroom while he was expelling a kidney stone? An excellent book to read concerning children and sexuality is *Raising Them Chaste* by Rick and Renee Durfield.

When I first began attending births, I thought that children should be at birth. I was so hungry to learn about home birth, that sometimes I forgot to spit out the sticks. Then God sent a young woman to me as an apprentice, by the name of Anna (Fraley) Smith. Anna proceeded to write a book *Birth and the Bonding of the Family.* She used Leviticus 18:1–18 as her basic text. Every Christian midwife needs at least one copy in her library. See the bibliography for the address. Besides Anna's beautiful discourse, I was beginning to see the fruit of children at birth. Families that had children over two years old who sat in "front row center seats" at the birth, were beginning to get out of scriptural order by the time sibling three or four arrived. The first-born boys were beginning to take over the protector role their fathers should stand in.

When a small child wraps himself in mother's skirts as she converses with another adult, one thinks the child is shy. When that same behavior occurs at age five, and only when mother is speaking to someone the child is not familiar with, it is "peculiar." When the child puts enough pressure on mother that she needs to step back it is "interesting." When that child starts to whine like he is tired, or at the slightest break in the conversation requests something of mother that makes her go across the room to get it, is "very peculiar." It is especially "peculiar" when that child shows no interest in mother at all when she is talking with a familiar person. Coupled with a strong open jealousy of the siblings and a sneaky way of trying to get siblings in trouble or hurt them, that bothers me. If I had seen this in just one family, I would blow it away and say that particular child needs help, but I am seeing it in several families.

What is the answer? Send the children to the neighbor's, grandmother's, or aunt's house when the contractions need concentration, not distraction. After the baby is born, and you've had your bath, bring the children home. They can watch the new born exam, gently feel and touch the baby, see that Mother is all right, and they can bond as "much or as little" as they want that first week. This seems to work out the very best. The children see Mom at home, in her bed, or in her favorite chair, with the new baby that Daddy introduces to them. This is normal to the child. Usually the younger children will look at the eyes, nose and fingers, look up at Mother grin and say something, then run off to play. Later they may bring a favorite toy to the baby, or snuggle up to baby and mother to take a nap, depending on the time of day.

Sometimes parents are disappointed with the youngest one's reaction. He doesn't seem to pay much attention to the baby, except to occasionally look to see what Mom is doing. Just give "Johnny" time. About the third day, when everyone else has run out of oohs and aahs, "Johnny" will crawl up on the bed next to Mom and the baby and do his exploring. Perhaps this is when he will bring his "blankey" or sleeping bear and give it to the baby. This is his way of saying, "I'm not the baby anymore, I am a big brother/sister now." The truth is, he has been thinking about this since the baby was born. He has evaluated the things that he can do against what the baby does, and realizes that he is growing up just like his siblings are. If you allow "Johnny" the space to figure this out by himself, and not pressure him to act like a big brother, he will do fine in his own time, usually in the first week or two. Doing it himself will be a complete work, because he will be ready. Telling/making him to "grow up and be a big boy" may cause a certain amount of rebellion or injury to his self-worth that will reap rotten fruit later.

Jealousy is usually not a problem with home birth children, unless the children are very competitive. Then it is the responsibility of the parents to channel that competition into positive ways, i.e., jobs/responsibilities, that will bring out the best in each child. Children need to feel accepted, loved and respected as contributors to the family. They contribute by having a job/responsibility to fulfill that is within their capabilities. Praise them when they do their job. Don't expect expert accomplishment when they are still learning, and they will reward you by becoming good, willing workers.

Competence of Attendants

The ICA (Informed Consent Agreement) covers the attendant's education, competence level, fees, services she provides, what is expected of the pregnant couple, what equipment the midwife will bring to the birth and her usual procedures in normal and unusual birth and pregnancy. The ICA will give: the numbers of births attended as primary and secondary attendant; the unusual births she has attended, their outcome and what she did to facilitate the return to normalcy. Whether she has medical backup; the organizations she is in good standing with; and what continuing education she participates in.

In addition, you want to determine if she will take the time to talk with you, or does she hustle you through like an assembly line. Who will do the monitoring of labor, the primary or her apprentice? If the apprentice is there, when does she call the senior midwife? Does the senior, as a general practice, wait to come to the birth when the head is crowning like some doctors at the hospital, or does she come during first stage? Does she understand, know and respect the family and the family's culture?

The majority of doctors are male, and some doctors consider themselves more midwife than doctor. There are doctors that began as a midwife, then became a certified nurse midwife and finally a doctor, who have remained midwives at heart. To all, I give three cheers; it is not easy to "buck the system." We honor you and thank you for being there for people who want to take responsibility for their decisions. You are the advance guard. Breaking virgin sod is never easy. Thank you for being there. May the Lord keep and bless each and every one of you.

Choosing Your Backup Doctor and Hospital

Choosing your backup can be either a challenge or a "piece of cake," depending on your location. If you have chosen your home birth attendant already, your backup will probably be someone your attendant works with, or can recommend. If not, then start with the recommendations of friends that had natural births in the hospital. Remember, "natural birth" is not just having a vaginal birth, but includes non-interference in the natural processes of birth.

When making your appointment, tell the receptionist that you wish to make an appointment to interview the doctor, and would like about 30–45 minutes in his office. If she insists that you have a regular prenatal appointment, tell her firmly but politely that you prefer to do that after you have determined if you and the doctor have the same philosophy of birth. If the doctor is not available for interviews, thank her and go on to the next. Make appropriate notes, so you are not calling the same doctor more than once, or forget which receptionist was less than friendly or helpful. The office personnel are an extension of the doctor's personality and philosophy. If he is friendly and helpful, the staff will be, too.

The big day has arrived and you and your husband are ushered into the office for the interview. Be cheerful, polite, and introduce yourself as parents that wish to work with their health team. State that you have done a lot of reading, consider yourself in good health, and expect to have a normal, uneventful pregnancy and birth. As reasonably intelligent adults, you desire open communications so that everyone understands each other, and the best experience can be had by all.

You may want to ask some questions to find out his philosophy concerning birth and pregnancy. Or, you may want to make a birth plan list of things that you are very concerned about. Such a list of questions for the doctor might include:

- What are your routine or standing orders for the normal pregnant woman?
- Do you routinely order sonograms? Or do you only order them when medically indicated?
- Will you allow a woman with normal uneventful pregnancy to labor with freedom to move about at will, including:

- Changing position to facilitate her labor including when the desire to push occurs;
- Allowing her to use gentle pushing to avoid the valsalva maneuver (holding the breath while pushing very hard; this causes increased viscosity of the blood, thereby increasing the risk of blood clotting, overloading the cardiovascular system, and leading to cardiac arrest); and
- Eating light snacks and drinking clear liquids as desired.
- Do you do fetoscope monitoring of heart tones every 20–30 minutes and during the contractions once each hour unless labor is progressing very quickly or bag of waters has broken spontaneously, then every 15 minutes or less?
- Do you permit unlimited bonding in the birthing room, with the newborn exam done on mother's bed?
- What is your caesarean rate? What percentage of that is referral?
- What percentage of your clients have episiotomies? Will you do perineal massage and support to prevent the episiotomy and tearing?
- What is your position on early dismissal? Is that dependent on the pediatrician?
- May we have total rooming in with unlimited sibling/family visitation?

If—so far—you are very encouraged with Dr. So Far So Good's attitude, and the Spirit bears witness to it, ask him about his philosophy on planned home birth with trained attendants. Your next question will depend on his answer. If he agrees that a planned home birth with skilled attendants is a viable alternative for the healthy woman, this is a good sign. (He will probably have to state a warning here, something to the effect that "sometimes things do not work out and problems can occur.") If he seems to be cautiously supportive, yet refuses to attend home birth, reassure him. Tell him that you understand his position with insurance and hospital privileges, etc., but that you were hoping that perhaps he would consider being your backup, should you decide to birth at home. You may have to educate him concerning the good care your midwife is giving you.

If his attitude changes, and he is less helpful than before, ask him, in a *gentle* way, why the change. Perhaps there has been a recent incident and he is playing it cool until he is sure of where you are coming from. The political climate is just as tough on doctors as it is on midwives in some parts of the country, so give him opportunity to get to know you, too. Some doctors are supporting midwives in a quiet way, and do not want their insurance companies to know, lest the insurance rates skyrocket, or their peers (and the hospitals they have privileges with) apply pressures or limit referrals.

If the physician agrees to discuss backing your home birth, providing your pregnancy is normal, you need to ask him more questions. "We realize the risks involved with birth, but feel they are the same no matter where we give birth. Will you meet us at the hospital should we need help? We will have someone at the birth who is skilled, and will advise us if we need to go to the hospital." If the doctor backs your midwife, now is the time to say that you are her client, providing you have her permission. Sometimes the agreement between mid-wife and doctor is very "silent." He doesn't fink on her, and she doesn't advertise his backup. A very precarious situation, but over a period of time, they can become a strong team. Once they recognize each others strengths, weaknesses, and skills.

You next need to determine who this doctor's partner is, or who takes his calls. Sometimes you have to interview another doctor, unless "Dr. Wonderful" can refer you to someone of like mind. Also determine his attitude about circumcision, and the hospital, will they routinely line up all boy babies, or are they careful about getting permission? Should your midwife not repair tears, will Dr. Wonderful repair in his office, the emer-gency room, or do you have to go to OB? The difference in fees for each area can be considerable, so it is important to ask. It may help motivate you to be diligent with prenatal perineal massage and practice your squatting.

If Dr. Wonderful is an Obstetrician-Gynecologist, you will have to get a pediatrician for the baby. The pediatrician can be a Family Practitioner or a specialist in children's health. In deciding which direction to go, inquire what status the family physician has in the pediatric ward. Some hospitals insist that only the pediatrician can be the primary care giver in pedi-atrics. Should your baby need to be transported, you would have to get a specialist at a time of stress, without the privilege of "shopping around," or take Dr. Potluck.

Some folks talk to a specialist, arrange for backup, and if not needed, continue with their family physician for well-baby care. Before going to the specialist, please check with your family doctor if he can be the primary physician should your baby need hospitalization. Ask him who his pediatric backup is. You may like this arrangement, or you may have to check around for someone with more amiable philosophy. Often your family doctor will have suggestions. He will have "inside" information that you do not have, and may be able to suggest someone close to your way of thinking.

This should be made clear with the backup that this is your intent, and be sure that it is agreeable with him or her. "We wish our family doctor could take care of the children in the pediatric ward, should they ever need hospitalization, but we understand that he does not have status above advisory level. That's why we came to talk to you. We want to get acquainted and understand each other before the situation arises." When all of you agree that you can work together, then be sure to say so; for example, "We like the family practice philosophy for health care, but if we ever would need a specialist for our children, we will certainly come to you." You don't want to make it difficult for the next couple by making this doctor feel like you have taken advantage of him ("Oh sure, you want me 'just in case,' but don't care about me otherwise.").

Questions you will want to ask the baby doctor are:

- May the baby go home as soon as he is stable and nursing well, or in 2–4 hours, which ever comes first?
- Will you do the PKU and T-4 test in the office, unless you plan to refuse it on religious grounds?
- Will you let me use unlimited breastfeeding and sun light to treat physiological jaundice instead of bili-lights, unless the jaundice is very high (over 18)? (Physiological jaundice occurs the third or fourth day, and it is not a blood incompatibility jaundice.)
- Who is your back up and will he or she honor our agreement?
- Will you meet us in the emergency room at the hospital of our choice?

- Would you rather meet us in the pediatric department, and would that require admitting the baby first?
- How do you determine the need for admittance without seeing the baby first?
- Are most of your clients breastfed, and for how long?
- When do you suggest starting solids?
- You may also want to discuss with him/her about immunization and circumcision. More and more parents are saying "no" to these formerly routine procedures.
- How does the doctor stand? Is doctor a traditionalist, or liberal in thinking?
- Will he honor your decision should you decide to go against the stream of what is routine and usual?
- Will he do what he deems is best and you just have to like it or lump it?
- Will he let you make decisions on all procedures after telling you what the consequences are for or against the procedure and not fuss about it?

Hospital Backup

Most hospitals offer guided tours through the maternal-child (obstetrical) units. This is your chance to pull out the list of questions and get the staff's reactions. This is the best way to discern the philosophy of the hospital. But keep in mind that what they *say* is not necessarily what they *do*. If the person giving you the guided tour is amazed, surprised, shocked, negative, evasive, or tries to put you off when you ask your questions, that is the area you need to zero in on. Find out why the reaction was anything but warm and enthusiastic, by asking related questions. If that fails to bring out the "skeletons in the closet," then ask the direct question. Maybe this nurse needs to be educated.

Another way to evaluate the hospital is to talk to people who recently birthed there. Call people whose births are reported in the paper (if you do not know anyone in town). Explain why you are calling them, and find out if their birth plan was followed, if their birth was what they hoped it would be, what was their experience like: good, bad or ugly. You don't need to pry into the details of their birth. You are looking for impressions of the nursing care, and the philosophy of birth in action.

Some towns and cities have more than one hospital. Unless you are in a large urban area, these hospitals are in great competition. Use this to your advantage. Let the guide know that you are hospital shopping about half way through the tour. Watch for changes of attitude. Is the guide suddenly buttering you up? Why? What is the division of all local births? Is this hospital getting their fair share, or is it more at the other place. . . or less?

If Hospital One has fewer births than Hospital Two, visit Hospital Two. See them in action. Has their popularity turned them into a baby factory? Is the staff just as happy to see you as they were at Hospital One? Ask the same questions as before. Be alert to attitude changes when you say you are hospital shopping. If they have to knock the other place, find out why. Maybe the census shift has started towards Hospital One.

Talk with your doctor/midwife and see if they have a preference. I have found that the hospital that is "trying harder" to get a higher census, will most often be the most generous with the birthing plan. They have the time to spend to do test strips, and things that are out of routine. Because of our local competition between hospitals, I have found that the staff at one is very friendly to my clients and to me, so I am more apt to transport there. I also know that we can get more options there. They are courteous, explain why some things are written in stone, and will follow the birth plan that the doctor agreed to without complaint. When we arrive, they are friendly to my clients and to me, and act as if we are the VIP of the week with complete entourage. But, they also act that way when anyone from CAPIE comes to labor support. That puts the hospital on the Rose List, and keeps them off the Radish List.

CHAPTER 7

LABOR AND BIRTH. . . IN THE FULLNESS OF TIME

"What was that? That pressure again—is this how labor starts? What did the instructor/midwife say in class? Oh, it's just the baby moving. Is this baby ever going to get here? Will it ever come? I'm so tired of being pregnant, and it is so hard to move around. Once I sit, I don't care if I ever stand up again, but it is so hard to sit still. Maybe if I just stand up the rest of my life, I'll feel half-human again. If only I could put this belly in a sling, or on a cart. If only these contractions would get regular and harder. If only I could sleep all night long. Just one night, Lord, before this baby is born." These are just some of the "complaints" you have, and I hear, the last month before birth day.

Now, don't be discouraged. Look at the bright side. When you start feeling like this and your fundal height has reached 38 cm or more, birth day is right around the corner. Just when you decide that "This is not the ordinary child. This one will take at least a year or more to 'make'." That is when you get that famous spurt of energy called "nesting." You feel wonderful! You get a long list of things done. You go to bed ready for a good night's sleep and you sleep like a rock. . . for five minutes. Then—*wham!*—you wake up with a start, wondering why you are awake. So, you get up and go to the bathroom thinking that must be it. Just as you get all settled back in bed and start to doze off, you have a strong contraction. Now you know why you woke up! That really got your attention.

Your first temptation is to complain about losing this good night's sleep that you were looking forward to. Resist that! Thank God! Your prayers are answered. The children are sleeping, your husband is home and you won't have to "find him" or call him home from work. All the things you wanted to get done are done. Everything is ready. Everything except. . . the cookies you were going to bake tomorrow! That's okay, you can bake them while you are waiting for the midwife. . . Oh yes! You *do* have to call the midwife when. . . oh, my, here's another one, and it is stronger. . . than the last. . . and only five minutes apart, too. Now, you wake up John and have him call the midwife, while you gather your birth supplies from their various "hiding" places. Once John hears that you are in labor, you won't have any trouble getting him up. It just may take some doing to get him to hear what you are saying at first.

It would be nice if that was all there is to knowing when you are in labor. Believe it or not, there are some women who are so blessed that it is that simple. Most of us, however have some uncertainty. Why? Because of those dear Braxton-Hicks contractions that the midwife and childbirth class instructor all think are so "wonderful."

Braxton-Hicks are intermittent contractions that are present all through pregnancy. They usually are not noticeable, other than an occasional tightening of your tummy, until your eighth or ninth month. They get stronger and more frequent as the pregnancy progresses and can become timeable in your last month. This is when it becomes confusing. We have been told that when the contractions are so many minutes apart, call the midwife. She has a long way to drive and you don't want to wait too long, etc. You don't want to have the baby on the way to the hospital, either.

Braxton-Hicks can be strong. They can be as close as two minutes apart and last a full minute. They can be strong enough to make you concentrate on relaxing and stop talking. . . so how do you know if you're in labor? What I've just described is just like labor, isn't it? Not quite. Braxton-Hicks, or "pre-labor" contractions concentrate in front, usually down low around the cervix. Their purpose in the last few weeks, is to soften the cervix up, get it thinned out (effaced), and help the baby to drop (lightening). They are getting the uterus ready.

Just like an athlete training for a marathon, these mild, irregular contractions put the uterus through a training program. Some researchers feel that they also massage the baby into proper position.

We are all familiar with Genesis 3:16. . ."I will greatly multiply thy sorrow and thy conception; in sorrow thou shalt bring forth children; and thy desire shall be to thy husband, and he shall rule over thee." Did you know that the word translated as "sorrow" in verse 16 is also translated as "sorrow" in verse 17, ". . .in *sorrow* shalt thou eat of it. . ."

The root word in Hebrew is *atsab*—meaning "to carve, fabricate, or fashion, and in a bad sense; to worry, pain, anger, displease, grieve, hurt, make be sorry, vex, worship (other than God), wrest." This verse is often used as the proof that women are to have great pain in labor. We are supposed to be "paying for enticing Adam to eat that apple, and deserve to be in pain when (we) bear children." Nobody has ever been able to answer why Adam didn't remind Eve not to eat from that tree, or why he didn't send the serpent on his way. After all, he was standing right there. Eve did not have to yell for Adam to come, nor did she have to find him. (Scripture says that Adam was with her; see v. 6.) As a consequence, women are told that they have to have horrible pain in childbirth, "because it was your fault."

I am not going to pass the blame to Adam. Adam and Eve must share the blame equally because, "*all* have sinned and fallen short of the glory of God" (Romans 3:23). God did tell both of them not to eat of the tree of knowledge of good and evil. However, in Romans 5:12, Adam receives the blame "for by one man sin entered the world and death by sin; and so death passed upon all men, for that all have sinned." God made a promise of mercy and grace to Eve and Adam in Genesis 3:15, or there would have been no hope. God fulfilled that promise of mercy and grace in the person of Jesus Christ. Galatians 3:13 tells us that Jesus fulfilled the curse of the law, and with His mercy and grace, gave us His righteousness. It is a gift of grace that we receive by faith, not by works (Ephesians 2:8–9). We are the blessed of the Lord, and we are to receive the blessing [of Abraham] (Isaiah 61:9).

I have a pin that says, "A baby is God's assurance that the world must go on." In other words, God planned for women to have babies. Men don't have babies. We need to get our attitudes in line with what God is doing in our lives. If we look to labor as a necessary process, accept it, and work with it, not against it, we will be surprised at the smoothness of it all. I refuse to say that pain reveals sin in your life. Pain does reveal several things about mother and baby. Such as: the baby needs to make some adjustments in the way he is presenting himself; mother should change her position to a more helpful one; or she needs to eat, drink, rest/relax and submit to her labor.

Pain is also present if you are exhausted, tired, thirsty, and undernourished. We can and want to prevent all of this. Scriptures tell us that severe pain is for the unredeemed, because they are not under the cleansing Blood of Jesus. Once you are under the Blood of Calvary, sin does not have dominion over you. You have dominion over sin. Are you exercising that dominion, or are you practicing sin? (Romans 6:1–23). If your labor and birth hurts, thank God you are redeemed by the Blood of the Lamb. What would it be like if you were *not* redeemed?!

Labor contractions usually begin in the lower back and spread around to the front. In the beginning, the contraction comes around to the lower front and then spreads up to include all of the uterus. Most of the concentration is in the lower area, deep behind the pubic bone. This is because the cervix is stretching and opening up. You can feel the cervix wanting to open with active labor contractions. That feeling is not there with Braxton-Hicks, or pre-labor, contractions.

Sometimes you can encourage Braxton-Hicks (pre-labor) and make them feel pretty strong by walking. If it is night time, go to bed! Sleep between your contractions. Have a cup of chamomile tea to help you sleep, or a nice hot soaking bubble bath. Often the hot bath will stop the contractions so you can sleep. If the Braxton-Hicks have been strong enough to time, and then stop after the bath, expect to go into labor in about 24 to 48 hours. Occasionally, we have to give Caulophyllum 6x, four to six tablets sublingually (under the tongue), every 20 minutes for two to three hours. This will either stop the Braxton-Hicks or bring Pat into active labor.

At about 4–5 cm, you can't ignore the contractions anymore. You may feel some pressure across your back, if the baby is posterior. This is not the time to go to bed, unless you are very tired. If you are *very* tired and it has been a big day, go to bed and lie on your left side. This should slow your contractions down sufficiently to allow you some rest. Lying on your left side in active labor can improve the position of the baby without slowing your labor appreciably.

If you are not really tired, and your contractions are getting stronger, stay up. Walk or finish up those cookies, sweep the floor (but not in the birth room please; we want to keep the dust settled there), and straighten up the house. In other words, keep busy, but don't get too tired. Your contractions are usually about five minutes apart now, and lasting about 30–40 seconds. If you haven't made the bed up with your birthing sheets, now is a good time to do it. One lady asked me after the birth was over, why did she "have to put those birthing sheets on the bed when she used the birth stool, and was never on the bed?" I replied, "Now we don't have to do it after the baby was born, and it is ready for you to hop into after the herbal bath." That brought a smile to her face. It always feels so nice to slip between fresh sheets after birth and a bath.

When you put your clean or sterilized sheets on your bed, you want to start with a clean plastic sheet or mattress cover. Next, comes a fresh mattress cover, topped with the bottom and top sheet (if you use a top sheet). Tuck the sides in well. Cover with a second plastic sheet, and a bottom sheet. Tuck in the sides well. Place a blue underpad about where it will be needed for mom. Now, lay a top sheet over, without tucking the sides in. If it is cool, you may want to put a clean, lightweight blanket on top. Put clean pillow cases on the pillows and you are ready.

Set out the supplies from the birth kit you ordered. You may want to set out the baby clothes, wash cloths, and towels you have readied for this event. The bassinet or crib makes a very handy place. You may want to clear off the top of the dresser for the midwife to put the birth supplies on if the crib is already "full," or in another room.

There is no rule of thumb as to when to call the midwife, doctor, etc. It really depends on how fast your labor is going, how far these people have to travel to get to your house, how much traffic there is on the way, and above all, how early you want them there.

If your contractions started out at two minutes apart, and you only have 15–30 seconds between them, you had better call immediately, and tell them to hurry. I wouldn't wait more than three contractions to call. If your waters break before the contractions begin, and 14% of all labors begin that way, it is nice to let them know about it. Your attendants would also want to know if the water is clear, and if the baby's head is tight against the cervix. You will learn how to check for this in Chapter 12. This helps them plan their day; for example, getting the afternoon appointments done in the morning, because they will be at your house in the afternoon.

Usually, when your contractions are about five minutes apart, and you have to concentrate on relaxing and breathing nice, normally paced, deep breaths, is a good time to call. That should give the midwife time to arrive and get settled without dashing in, "working" out of her bag and no time to wash her hands. (I always feel like I have "missed something very important" when I arrive just as the head is crowning.) Allowing the midwife enough travel time is less worrisome for you. You won't have those panicky moments of, "Where is Betty?" "Can you see her lights yet?" "Please hurry, Betty!" "Please, God, help her get here, *now!*"

The midwife is hurrying as fast as she dares and is praying to make it in time without any "personal attention" from the folks with the "pretty lights" on their cars. She is also praying for all green lights and no other traffic at the stop signs. If you are alone, the midwife has not arrived but the baby wants to birth, lie on your left side, and breathe your baby out. *Try not to push.* Say "ha-ha-hallelujah!" through the contraction. The baby will be born very gently with very little, if any tearing.

Labor has traditionally been divided up into three stages. The first stage consists of the cervix dilating from 1 cm to 10 cm. These contractions begin by being spaced far apart and mild in strength. Gradually they become closer together, until they are about 3–5 minutes apart and very strong. The second stage is is the "pushing stage." The contractions are very strong and are from two minutes to five minutes apart. As baby passes through the cervix, he presses on a spot that gives Pat the urge to push. As she pushes with her contractions, she can feel the baby move slowly but steadily down the vagina, crown, and be born. The third stage is when the placenta is born. Recently a fourth stage has been considered. This is the immediate postpartum period of 4–6 hours. Some folks say the fourth stage begins after the placenta is expelled and lasts until the uterus is completely involuted—sometime between the fourth and sixth weeks.

The First Stage of Labor

The first stage of labor has also been divided into three stages. The first is called many things: latent, prodromal, inactive, or pre-labor. I personally prefer the term pre-labor, because it *pre*pares your body for *labor*. The contractions are not very regular, and have a more aggravating and nagging nature. They feel like something could come of them, but nothing has as yet. It is this feeling of uncertainty that becomes so aggravating. The excitement and anticipation of active labor soon to begin is a contributing factor here. The contractions are strong enough to keep you awake when you try to sleep, but not hard enough to require concentration to relax and breathe through.

Thinking that walking will help your contractions along, you get your husband home from work and you walk, and walk, and walk. Sometimes you have a strong contraction but most of them are mild little hugs. The baby is usually quite active and wiggles around, first one way and then the other, as though he is trying to find the "open door." Some ladies even describe a nodding movement from the head, once the baby wiggles into the pelvis.

The only real danger in this phase is that you work so hard trying to go into active labor, that you wear yourself out. You have used up the energy you need for active labor. The cure is simple. Continue with normal living activities during this phase. If you are tired, rest. If it is night time, go to bed. If it is daytime, sit back in a recliner and relax. If you don't have a recliner, make one with a footstool and a comfy chair, or take one or two cushions from the couch for a back rest, add a few bed pillows for comfort and your bed becomes a recliner. Give the children quiet but interesting projects that will keep them busy for 30 to 45 minutes, or let them watch "Mr. Rogers" or "McGee and Me" so you can rest.

If they take naps, praise the Lord! You take one, too. If you are not tired, this is the day to do those short-term things that you have put aside for some other time. If you keep your mind busy, pre-labor is not as noticeable nor is it as aggravating as it can be. Catching up on the mending, crocheting, knitting, etc., or taking the children to the park, helps.

Maybe a picnic lunch in the park would be fun. Besides, cleanup is very easy. A park trip is more fun if your neighbor can go with you, just in case you need help with the children or getting home. When you tire of pushing swings, you can watch them burn up energy from the park bench. Have you ever noticed that children can squeal and shout at the park, but it does not grate on your ears like it does in your own yard? One benefit of a trip to the park is when the children go to bed, they will be so tired that they will go to sleep right away and sleep through labor. They may even sleep long enough to let you get a nap after baby is born.

The best coaching during pre-labor is emotional support. Keeping the children happy and occupied in quiet activities and including Pat as much as she wishes is very helpful. Pat needs to eat and drink just like any normal day. No fasting, please. Your body is using up a lot of calories, so you need to keep the normal supply of foods coming.

The good news is that birth day is coming within a week. Often, a lady will have one or two episodes of pre-labor and 48 hours later will go into active labor and have her baby very quickly.

I had a client who had three days of pre-labor with all of her children. Some time during the third day, her contractions would suddenly get very strong at two minutes apart and 60–90 seconds long. When that happened, the birth team had to get there pronto, because her baby would birth in less than two hours of the change. Up until that change in tempo, she would not dilate past 4 cm. She did the rest in about 45 to 60 minutes and would push her baby out in about four contractions. Expulsion of the placenta would take 15 to 30 minutes. Her babies all weighed from 8 to 9 pounds.

The second part of the first stage is active labor. This begins at 4 cm dilation. Pat is actively working during the contractions to continue deep breathing and staying relaxed, so each contraction can do its optimal work. Before and after each contraction she should take a deep cleansing breath. The contractions are about five minutes apart and last from 30 to 60 seconds. The closer you are to 10 cm dilation, the longer the contraction will last. At about 7 cm dilation, the contractions will be about 60 seconds long and vary between 4 and 5 minutes or less apart.

Pat has reached the "infamous" transition! This is the phase most often shown as the Hollywood version of birth. The actress is pulling on her "husband's" shirt, saying all sorts of nasty things, hollering, scratching and in general not being herself, due to the medication that used to be routinely given.

What is real life in transition? Real life Pat often will voice doubts of her ability "to do this." She may talk about fearing the increase of pain. She may even complain about not finding a "comfortable place." She is trying to find her nest. Give her encouragement! Praise her for doing such a good job. She does not perceive herself as being as calm and quiet, nor does she think that she is working well. She needs honest praise and reassurance from her husband, John, that he "loves her and is so very proud of her." Make some suggestions between contractions, for position changes. Keep her hydrated, give her a back rub or leg massage. Do what ever it takes to keep her relaxed during and between contractions. This is not the time for heavy, deep, conversations to solve the world's problems like: international famines, establishing peace by evangelizing the entire world and what is the best way to do it, revamping the education and medical systems of the United States, cleaning up government, etc. If Pat wants conversation to help her relax, keep it light. Save the laughs for between contractions. It's hard to laugh with a contraction.

Active labor requires varying amounts of coaching; from occasional gentle reminders to stay relaxed and breathe with your tummy (lifting it up so your uterus can work unencumbered by the weight of the abdomen pressing on it), to very intense eye-to-eye contact coupled with massage to keep hands and feet relaxed. Massage needs to be gentle enough to be soothing, yet firm enough to help those muscles to relax. This is not the time for trailing your fingertips up and down the arms and legs. Pat will not like that at all! She will experience sensation overload, and instead of relaxing her, it will make her very tense. If Pat gets a cramp, knead it and work it out as firmly and quickly as you can. Just as the cramp has no mercy on the laboring woman, have no mercy on that cramp!

Pat needs to change her position every two hours. This helps the baby to keep moving through the pelvis. If she doesn't change position on her own, a positive suggestion such as, "You have been rocking in your chair for some time, how about a trip to the bathroom or a walk around the house" will gently remind her that a change of scenery will do her good.

Women who have learned to yield to their labor have an easier time than those who are fighting it all the way. You cannot fight labor and win. It will beat you into submission. The best preparation you can do is to practice relaxation at home just before going to sleep. It is that same principle of going "limp as a wet noodle" that will help you most during labor. When you relax completely, your uterine muscles are able to do the most work in the least amount of time. That way, they do not have to repeat themselves, and each contraction accomplishes what it needs to do.

Rubbing the lower back, or giving steady counterpressure across the sacrum helps Pat relax. The baby is exerting a lot of pressure as he starts down into the mid-pelvis. The head pushes against the sacral promontory (that spot where your spine makes a quick dip in at the top of your "cheeks"). Often, the labor coach can feel the bulge of the head with the palm of her/his hand. Steady pressure on that spot gives the support to Pat's back and encourages the baby to tuck her chin, easing the pain/pressure.

Place your hand with the fingers lying loosely in the direction of her feet and the palm of your hand over "the spot." With firm and steady pressure, increase the pressure (with the palm) until Pat says "that feels good." Now you get to maintain that pressure. Don't change hands until the contraction is over, and then release the pressure slowly. If you release the counter pressure too fast, it will feel like a rubber band snapping her. She won't like that!

If the baby is in a posterior position, doing a "hula hoop" movement, or drawing a circle with her hips (sometimes called a circular pelvic rock) will help turn the baby. Hands and knees, coupled with pelvic rocks also are very good. If she has been up for a long time, she may be tired, so a left side-lying (dorsal) position helps turn the baby too. If all the above does not work, a few "flip-flops" (see Chapter 12) will do it, for sure. Most posterior babies will turn during the pushing in second stage, if not before. If Pat is experiencing a lot of pain and the baby is very slow in his descent, it is worth trying to change things around to an anterior position. The homeopathic remedy of Pulsatilla is also reputed to be of help with malpresentations. Four tablets Pulsatilla 21 X sublingual.

Maintaining good nutrition by eating at meal times, snacking between, and staying hydrated by drinking about one quart of fluids every three hours during long labors will not only keep Pat's energy level high, it will also keep her pain threshold up.

If your water has broken, you need to increase your liquids to one quart every two hours and take 500 mg of Vitamin C every eight hours until baby is born. This will keep the waters fluid and prevent infection in mother and baby. After the waters have broken, you want to limit vaginal exams to as few as are absolutely necessary. Each exam increases the possibility of introducing bacteria from the perineum into the uterus. Bacteria love it when it is dark and warm with easy access to a good blood supply as in the uterus.

If you absolutely need to do an exam after the waters have ruptured, use a povidone iodine solution (for example, Betadine®). Place an underpad under Pat. Pour the povidone iodine solution so it runs across the perineal hair and vagina onto your sterile glove. povidone iodine is antibacterial, but it also irritates vaginal tissue. If Pat is allergic to povidone iodine, you need to use hydrogen peroxide or an iodine substitute. Peroxide will foam, and will act as a mild anti-bacterial. It is best against aerobic (oxygen-loving) bacteria, because it takes the oxygen away from them. Peroxide does not irritate mucus membranes. Be ready to wipe with tissue after the exam because peroxide foams, and povidone iodine runs all over so it can be a bit messy.

Fetal heart tones should be taken every hour for at least one minute in early labor. Then, every 30 minutes as labor picks up, to assess the baby's health and well-being. It is a good idea to listen every hour to the heart tones through a complete contraction as a means of monitoring the baby a little closer, until the bag of waters (BOW) breaks. After the water breaks, you will want to take the FHT every five to ten minutes and listen through a contraction every 15 to 20 minutes. Listening during the contraction is the only accurate way to find baby's abnormal reactions to labor. The average normal base line range of heart tones is from 120 at the low end to 160 at the high end. You need to understand that if this child's normal base line prenatally was 156, that during labor it very likely will be spiking at 168 or even up to 170.

Normally, you do want to see a variance in the FHTs. Usually it speeds up six to ten beats per minute with the contraction as it peaks, then back to base line as the contraction recedes. This indicates that the central nervous system controlling the circulatory system is mature and healthy. This is a normal pattern seen in cephalic and breech presentations. Always be alert to abnormal decelerations and tachycardia as described in Chapter 11. Do not confuse the normal deceleration during the peak of the contraction in second stage with a problem. The difference is that the baby's heart beat returns to the normal base line shortly after the peak and before the contraction is over. If the return to base is slow and tends to wander into the rest period after the contraction, then you do have trouble. Change position immediately, and read chapter 11.

If Pat is following the Brewer Diet, her waters will probably not break until the cervix is completely dilated or during second stage. That is the way God planned it. The bag of waters acts as a wedge on the cervix. As the cervix opens up, responding to the pressure of the wedge, the forewaters (a "balloon" of waters preceding the presenting part), slips into the space left by the dilating cervix. This puts continuous pressure on the cervix, but because it is soft like a water balloon, it is gentler than the head. The forewaters also give protection to little Johnny's head from severe molding and cephalohematoma.

Cephalohematoma is a subperiosteal hemorrhage on the baby's head, caused by injury to the periosteum (the brain side of the skull bone) during labor or birth. It is usually noticed within 24 hours after delivery by forceps or vacuum extractor. If the labor was particularly difficult, cephalohematoma can occur at home, especially if the head had to mold a lot. The swelling does not cross the suture lines, and the scalp does not move easily across the swelling. It usually takes two to three months for the swelling to go down. In the meantime, the baby may act as though he has a headache. You need to monitor the swelling and make sure that it is not increasing or very large. If it is, the baby needs to see the doctor quickly. This may indicate new bleeding that could be causing pressure on the baby's brain. *Arnica montana* will limit the bleeding and aid in dissolving the hematoma.

A common swelling on a baby's head is called a **caput suc-cedaneum**. This is swelling on the bones of the head and does cross suture line. It is caused by uneven pressure on the baby's head during labor and birth. The scalp moves when you "wiggle" it. It will decrease in size in a day or two. Johnny may act like it is a tender place, but it is usually softer than a cephalohematoma. It is similar to a bruise and responds quickly to *Arnica montana.* Ice should not be placed on a new-born's head, because you could cause hypothermia.

One of my ladies who had planned a hospital birth arrived in the Labor and Delivery Unit dilated to 8 cm. As soon as the admission "ritual" was completed, she got up and started walking. When she had a contraction, she walked faster. . . much to the surprise and amazement of the staff. An anesthesiologist was overheard to say, "I have never seen a woman walk in labor, let alone at 8 cm, and during a contraction." Within the hour, her water broke. She went to bed to get checked. The nurse confirmed the baby was at +2 station and the cervix was completely dilated. The monitor said baby was fine, and "they gave Pat permission to push."

Pat didn't feel right in the semi-sitting position, so Pat turned over into a kneeling position. She kneeled facing the elevated back rest, supporting herself with her hands holding on to the top of the mattress. In 10 minutes Pat had a beautiful baby girl. The doctor had never seen a baby born "upside down and backwards," so it was a real challenge for him. All was well with only the tiniest of skid marks on the inside of her left labia, so no stitches were needed.

Even though Pat walked through all of her contractions, except while in the car en route to the hospital, she remained relaxed. Walking kept her breathing regular and deep. As she took each step, she thought of the baby moving down little by little, and the cervix opening up more and more. Walking helped keep her Kegel muscles open too.

Walking, rocking in the rocking chair, standing and doing the circular pelvic rocks, hands and knees, side lying ("dorsal recumbent"), and squatting are all wonderful labor positions. Whatever helps put pressure on the cervix so it dilates and helps gravity bring the head down is worth trying. If Pat needs a little extra room in her pelvis, have her kneel on one knee and put her other foot flat on the floor, with her leg bent at the hip (modified Parker position). Standing with one foot on a chair, is a little easier on the knees, and is called the Parker position. This will really give her extra space if she has a marginal pelvis for the size of this baby. She can switch raised legs as needed. The rocking needed to switch knees/legs may encourage the baby to move down the passage.

Transition is the last third of first stage. This is the stage that is the hardest to relax for many ladies and they require intense labor coaching. This is when a woman will say, "I've changed my mind, I'm not going to do this. I'm going to take a nap/go shopping, etc." Or, at one decibel level or another, "Get this baby out!" This is when the coach needs to get Pat relaxed and back on track with the job at hand.

Reassurance that the baby will be born sooner now than when she first began, helps. Knowing that it won't be long helps a lot. She needs to know that she is doing a very good job. What women are really saying with the above comments is: "This is not working in this position," or "I need something fresh to drink," or "give me a good massage and help me relax." Changing the "scenery" and a drink is a big booster. This is a good time to listen to heart tones or do an exam. It gives a slight change in the present rhythm and that change is refreshing because of the change of activity. It also allows everyone to stretch, move and get the kinks out.

It has been proven in a scientific laboratory that it is impossible to be tense and praise the Lord at the same time. No matter what the circumstance and severity of pain, if the "subject" would praise the Lord, the perception of pain would drop and the "subject" would have a sense of well-being. If saying, "Thank you, Jesus," or "Ha-ha-hallelujah!" feels artificial, pray in your prayer language. Say "Praise the Lord," or whatever. Remembering that this baby is going to be born sooner now, than if it were still yesterday should help you praise the Lord. It isn't *how* you praise God as much as just *doing it from the heart* that is important.

As the baby's presenting part begins to crown at the cervix, you sometimes feel a need to push. This is especially true if the presenting part is at a low station of +1 or +2. Do not push until you are completely dilated. Pushing too early will cause the cervix to swell, tire you out, and prolong the labor. Some midwives use an ice cube to move the cervix out of the way, if you only have an anterior lip left, or to decrease the swelling. If the cervix has followed the head down and has become a persistent anterior lip, you can brace the cervix by pushing it back over the head with your sterile gloved fingertips during the next couple of contractions. Persistent anterior cervical lips are caused by encouraging Pat to push too soon! Every subsequent pregnancy she will have that anterior lip, until it is braced and pushed back and taught to dilate completely before Pat pushes.

Another very effective remedy is the hands-and-knees position. This puts steady pressure on the cervix, encouraging it to slip back naturally. Obviously this is less interventive, and I would try it before manually pushing it back. Sometimes for Pat's ninth or tenth baby a 9 cm, dilation feels like an anterior lip, because she may not be or need to dilate evenly. A hands-off policy works much quicker than treating it like an anterior lip.

Always talk in a quiet and reassuring manner. If she isn't responding well, be firm but calm, as you would with a child in front of company. If the coach is upset, Pat will get even more upset. "Pat, pay attention to me, please. . . Relax this foot. Thank you, that is so much better."

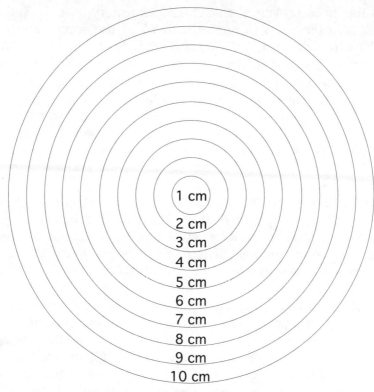

Figure 7-1: Diagrammatic representation of dilation of the cervix (to scale).

Inside the circles, from innermost to outermost: 1 cm, 2 cm, 3 cm, 4 cm, 5 cm, 6 cm, 7 cm, 8 cm, 9 cm, 10 cm.

Second Stage of Labor

Once you dilate to 10 cm (centimeters), you are on the home stretch. Frequently, there is a slight pause at 10 cm. The contractions may spread out from two or three minutes to five minutes or more apart. That's fine. Enjoy your break, and rest. It is very tempting to encourage women to push at this point. Actually there is nothing to prevent it. But for the most effective birthing of the baby, wait until the presenting part has slipped through the cervix and is pressing on that nerve that says "Push!" to your body. I personally believe that sometimes baby needs a little extra room, or mom needs the rest before she starts pushing. That is why she gets a short rest.

Pushing when the pushing reflex is operating is not only effective, it is the easiest. I have never seen a woman "push" the "wrong way" when she waited for the reflex to start her. If you encourage her to push before the reflex kicks in, you have to keep telling her how to push, and she never quite catches on. This can lead to a great deal of frustration and the danger of exhaustion physically for the laboring woman, and a loss of her attendants' patience. Another example of "improving on God's natural order."

The pushing reflex is caused by pressure on the posterior vaginal wall. This, in turn, stimulates the same nerve that makes one want to evacuate the lower bowel. If Pat is having a hard time pushing effectively, then coach her through the contractions, helping her breathe with them. When it is time to push, she will push naturally and correctly. Occasionally the desire to push comes before the natural urge.

If she needs instruction, teach her the "gentle pushing" method. Gentle pushing uses the same muscles and breathing that you use for singing loudly, or yelling "Johnny, *no!*" at the toddler that is heading for the street. Take good breaths for each push. Most ladies need to take three or four breaths per contraction, and give good "grunts" when they push. Just as if you were lifting the piano onto a platform, or a cow to her feet. . . all by yourself. One of my clients sang the most beautiful birth song while she pushed her baby out. Another spoke her children's names. Some ladies are very quiet. It does not matter, as long as your efforts are effective.

Some of the pitfalls of pushing without the reflex to help you are:

- The tendency of holding your breath for the length of the contraction can cause infant hypoxia.
- **Hypoxia** is a medical term meaning the lack of oxygen which can lead to acidosis. Acidosis is a serious imbalance of blood gases in the baby and can be very dangerous and lead to death.
- Interfere with maternal and placental blood circulation.
- Pushing while keeping all the energy in your shoulders and face. This causes capillaries to burst in your face and you will look like a battered woman the next day. It also holds the baby up in the pelvis and does not let the baby come down the birth canal.

All of the above reasons are why you should ignore the common labor room chant of "*Push, push, push, push, push!*" except in extreme emergency and if you are receiving oxygen, for the baby's sake.

It seems that Labor & Delivery (L&D) nurses think that Pat has suddenly lost her hearing, because the chant will get louder and louder until she convinces them that she can hear by doing it "their way." Coach, now is the time for you to be assertive. Whip out a copy of the Gentle Pushing Directions and tell them, "Pat will not endanger her baby and is going to use the gentle pushing method." Be firm and tell them to "Please stop shouting. The quiet rule is still in effect." Do not be swayed by any arguments that it doesn't work. It works all the time for midwife-attended births.

Occasionally, Pat will have invited a nurse with the Labor & Delivery department experience to her birth at home. You will need to educate her about gentle pushing before birth day.

Second-stage contractions are just as hard as they were at eight or nine cm, but because Pat can push, she perceives them to be easier. This is the time for those wonderful, hot, comfrey-leaf compresses. See "Midwifery Skills" in Chapter 12. Plain water works, too. Gently hold the hot cloth to the perineum, especially during the contractions. This helps Pat relax her perineum because she feels your touch and "knows" you are helping her. Some women have a feeling of panic if the hot cloths are not there, because of their fear of perineal lacerations (tears).

If Pat is having difficulty directing her pushing, try some of these remedies:

- Sitting on the toilet. Sometimes she has to go potty, and the emptying of her bladder or bowels, in the "right place" will relax her. You can't push effectively if you are keeping your Kegel muscles tight.
- Hot compresses to the labia help focus the direction of force. Placing them on the perineum may confuse her.
- Have Pat think of a tunnel that goes through the middle of her body from the uterus through her vagina, and the baby must travel down that tunnel. This directs the pushing effort in a more anterior direction. It is also more aesthetic than "push like you are having a bowel movement." Not many women want to have a bowel movement in such close proximity to others. Pushing "towards the end of the tunnel" also encourages maximum effort of the abdominal muscles.

- Changing her position to hand and knees, squatting, using a birthing stool, supported standing, or semi-reclining all might help with pushing.

In the semi-reclining position, she is to keep her back straight but relaxed, soles of her feet flat, knees bent, and holding on to the backs of her knees as she pushes. She definitely needs some back support with a pillow wedge, or she will waste too much energy curling up.

Pushing can be done in any position, and is more effective in one position than another for the individual woman. She needs to have the liberty to find her best "spot" or "nest." If Pat is throwing her head back while pushing, you need to give her head support, flexing it as much as you can toward her chest. After the contraction is over, put an extra pillow behind her head or find something to give her support. When she throws her head back, she is draining the energy out of the push and into her neck, and her effort in expelling the baby is made ineffectual. Sometimes it helps Pat to bring her knees closer to the sides of her body so her feet dangle loosely "in the air." She must remain relaxed or this position is counterproductive.

Occasionally Pat needs some help getting the rhythm of pushing established. A very effective trick is for the midwife to insert 2–3 sterile, gloved fingers deep into the vagina and apply pressure to the posterior wall (towards the rectum). This should give Pat the desire to push. Pressure on the right spot will be confirmed by definite progress of the fetal head, and a more natural push from Pat. It is very effective when Pat has been completely dilated for some time, but the baby is not descending well due to lack of force. The pressure from the fingers activates the expulsion reflex.

Okay. Now Pat is pushing and her baby is progressing down the birth canal. Each contraction causes the baby to go two steps forward and at the end of the contraction it will slip back one step. Ladies can feel this "slippage", and can get discouraged. The baby slips back to take some of the pressure off his head and also off of mother. This helps her body to stretch in a more gentle manner, and reduces the likelihood of lacerations (tears). If the baby did not go back one step, the pressure on his head could cause damage to very sensitive areas in the brain. God has everything well planned and thought out. Hallelujah!

As the baby begins to crown, sometimes there is a burning or stinging sensation, especially during the contraction. That is the signal that Pat needs to breathe through that contraction and *not push*. The burning comes from the tissues stretching as far as they wish for that contraction. Breathing, or saying "Ha-ha-ha-hallelujah!" through that one will help the tissues/muscles to relax and open up. The next contraction, you can push again. Sometimes you can push at the beginning of the contraction, but have to praise the Lord during the peak. That's okay. Just be sensitive to how your body is working and work with it.

Prenatal perineal massage usually eliminates this burning sensation because Pat will have learned how to relax against the pressure of the head. If the midwife applies warm olive oil with her gloved fingers (from a fresh, clean bottle) to the vagina and does gentle massage, it often will help the baby descend and relieve the tension that can build up. Keep changing the hot compresses, so Pat feels them on her perineum during the contraction to help her relax. Cool cloths have a tendency to tighten the perineal muscles. If a fan is blowing towards Pat, aim it so it is blowing toward her from the side and not at her perineum, or your compresses will cool too quickly. (Cool air blowing on the baby's head may not be in the baby's best interest, either.)

The baby's head often will push some feces (stool) out of the rectum, as it comes down the birth canal, because it needs the room. Remove it gently with tissue during the contraction or immediately after. If no mention of it and no faces are made on the part of the attendant, Pat will not be embarrassed. If Pat mentions the feces, pass it off as such a little bit and of no consequence. Being casual and reassuring her that it is normal and very common will relieve her embarrassment, too.

As the baby crowns, the attendant needs to be alert to many things. She needs to keep the baby's head flexed by applying gentle, firm, downward, and yet outward pressure on the occiput with the fingers of the dominant hand, while still supporting the perineum with the other hand. Between contractions, use the dominant hand either to apply more warm oil where the labia and the head meet, or to change the hot compresses. When the occiput is fully birthed, let the face sweep over the perineum. Should the head want to come too fast, have Pat breathe or "Ha-ha-hallelujah" through that contraction, while you control the speed of expulsion with the palm of your hand without putting too much pressure on the head. You don't want to cause compression of the cervical vertebrae.

The next thing you need to look for is a nuchal cord or hand. As the head is being born, look for that nuchal cord. If a nuchal cord is present you need to:

1. Give a gentle tug on the cord and take up whatever slack you have. If the cord responds easily, it is not pinched, and you can let the baby birth normally. Do keep a finger near to take cord pulse
2. If you don't have any slack, make sure the cord is not wrapped around the baby's neck.
3. Get the baby's head out very quickly, because her oxygen supply is compromised.

The cord may be compressed between the pelvic bones and the baby's head. Compression at this point is allowing little, if any, oxygen to get to the baby. Encourage to push very hard with and between contractions. Once the head is born, the compression should be gone. Check for pulse in the cord, and baby's condition. If there is any doubt, get the baby out fast!

If there is any doubt as to how fast mom can birth her baby, the midwife needs to bring one arm out to help the shoulders, with the same technique as for shoulder dystocia. Time is of the essence, so work fast. Once the shoulders are born, the pressure should be off the cord, and things can return to normal pace. If the baby looks like she needs some help, begin start-up measures. Check the cord to make sure it is functioning, first. If it is still working (you can feel the pulse), you have a small window of grace left. Clear the baby's airway, and stimulate the baby for a good cry. That should take care of it, but make sure the heart rate is over 100 at one minute. Crying will bring that up as well as filling the lungs with air, normally. If not, begin standard cardio-pulmonary resuscitation (CPR).

If you feel fingers by the chin, ear, or sometimes at the back of the neck, you need to bring that hand out. This is because the elbow will act like a brake and slow the descent, or as a knife on the perineum and cause a nasty tear. Tell Pat that you need to get a hand/arm out of the way and for her to breathe through this contraction. "Reduce" the hand by freeing it from the neck and pointing it towards the opposite shoulder. Then, grasping the arm near the elbow (bracing it so it bends in the right direction), sweep it across the chest to the opposite shoulder, above the head, and then out the vagina into a "Praise the Lord" position. Once the arm has been reduced, the elbow and the first shoulder are out of the way. The second shoulder then comes very quickly.

Once the head is born, the baby usually turns either to the left or the right on the next contraction. Now it is time for the shoulders to be born. Usually the shoulder towards Pat's front, or anterior, is the first to be born. Let the weight of the baby's head cause it to sag to the wrist of your hand supporting the perineum with the hot compress. This should allow the anterior shoulder to birth. Occasionally the posterior shoulder wants to come first, and you have to raise the head up slightly. You will feel the pressure on the hand supporting the perineum if the posterior shoulder wants to come first. Do not bend the neck more than is normal (five degrees).

Sometimes the baby will have broad shoulders, and they may not want to come without help. In a true shoulder dystocia, the baby will not rotate after the head is born, the chin will suck back against the perineum, and the head will start turning color from white-pink to black. (Usually the baby will give you warning earlier—during pushing—that he has wide shoulders. His progress will be slower, and sometimes it seems that it takes 2–3 contractions with good strong pushing to do what usually only takes one good push to do.)

Techniques with increasing interference corresponding to the severity of the dystocia are:

1. Changing Pat's position to hands and knees.
2. Reducing and delivering one or both arms, will free the anterior and/or posterior shoulder enough and the baby will slide out by the next contraction.
3. Supra-pubic pressure on the anterior shoulder will help it slide under that pubic bone and the baby will be born right away.
4. The corkscrew technique is the last trick. Sandwich baby's body between both hands inside the vagina. With both hands working together, move baby from 10 o'clock

to 2 o'clock while applying gentle downward and outward movement, "corkscrewing" the baby out.

You may have to use a combination of all of the above. When progress stops with one technique, you go on to the other. In a severe dystocia, you have five minutes to get a live healthy baby out and eight minutes to get the baby out for a live, but potentially severely brain-damaged baby. The less time it takes you to get that baby out, the better the outcome for the baby and everyone else. The important thing is to work fast and use your muscles! *Never, never, never pull on the baby's head—you will decapitate him before you will reduce the shoulders that are stuck.* Perineums can be repaired, only God can resurrect babies.

Third Stage of Labor

As soon as the baby is born, lift him up onto Mom's lap. If the baby needs resuscitation, do it there. He needs mom's touch and voice to stimulate him. If all is well and the cord is long enough, put him to the breast. Skin-to-skin is best, especially if the room is about 70° F. Cover him up with mom's gown and a blanket to keep him warm. If he shows interest in nursing, help him get a good latch. If he just wants to lick the nipple, that will also stimulate the uterus to expel the placenta.

Sometimes the baby is so interested in memorizing mom's face and matching dad's face with his voice, that suckling at the breast is not his first priority. Once he finds out that he can do both, he is usually interested in the breast. Some babies are born hungry, others are content to wait until the milk comes in, and just tolerate the colostrum. What they don't understand is that they have to have the colostrum to get the milk flowing. A little encouragement is all that this type of baby needs.

The **Apgar scoring** should be taken at one minute and again at five minutes after the baby is born. If you suspect the baby is a premie (under seven pounds or less than 38 weeks), then you need to evaluate his development using the Dubowitz scale. Occasionally you will find a full-term baby with a low Dubowitz score, that will date him at 36 weeks. In about 12–24 hours he will score full term (40 weeks). Just keep an eye on him and make sure he eats, sleeps, and maintains his body temperature like a newborn should. This baby was a bit slow in "waking up" at birth. As long as the rest of his development is in normal limits, I would not be overly concerned, just attentive. You would not be out of line to suggest that this baby see a physician within a couple of weeks to make sure everything is all right.

Well, the baby is born! Congratulations! That means everything is over, right? Wrong! We still have the cord to cut, the placenta to birth, and the herbal bath to do! Everybody is ready for the herbal bath, but getting that cord cut and the placenta birthed can be an exercise in patience.

Wait to cut the cord until after it has stopped pulsating. This can be within five minutes, or up to 45 minutes. I have heard of it pulsing for two hours, but that is very unusual. When the pulsing stops, put the cord clamp from the birth kit, around the cord about one inch from the baby's tummy. You may apply a hemostat about one inch from the baby's clamp toward the placenta side and cut between them with a sterile scissors. Or, instead of the hemostat, you may also lay a 4×4 gauze square under the cord where you are cutting it, to catch the few drops of blood that may be present. Now lay the long end of the cord in the pan.

I used to move the hemostat on the cord from where it was cut to just clear of the labia hair, and waited to see a lengthening of the cord. Now I rarely clamp the cord (on the placenta side), even when cutting the cord, because I don't notice any bleeding from the cord beyond one or two tablespoons. This is the pooled blood in the cord from the cut site to the placenta. It is not from the baby. If you wait to cut the cord until after the cord pulse has stopped, the placenta is no longer functioning, and mother is not going to bleed through the placenta in a normal implantation. I still have a sterile clamp (hemostat) handy should I need it.

I let daddy cut the cord for two reasons. The first is that it is a special honor to let daddy officially "separate" the baby from mother and "put him on his own." The other reason is legal. If daddy, mommy or sibling cuts the umbilical cord, it is not considered a surgical procedure. If the midwife does it, it is a surgical procedure, and may be grounds for legal prosecution. Don't try to understand it. . . that's the way the world is. After the cord is cut, Pat and John have more freedom to wrap the baby and hold him.

I lay the cut end of the cord in or let it hang over the sterile fracture pan that I use to receive the placenta. Now patience will have her work. Mark the end of the cord on the underpad if Pat is sitting on the birth stool, so you will know when lengthening has occurred. If the end of the cord is in the pan, then watch for a sag. That sag tells me that the cord is lengthening, which is the classic sign of placental detachment. Usually, as the placenta separates, there is a slight gush of blood, about $\frac{1}{4}$ cup, accompanied by a uterine cramp.

Usually the placenta is birthed within 15 to 20 minutes after the baby, especially if the baby is an eager nurser. It is all right to wait two hours or more if there is no unusual bleeding. What is your patience level? If you think the cord has lengthened, or Pat has had a gush of about $\frac{1}{4}$ cup of blood, ask her if she has had a cramp. Sometimes she won't even notice, because the baby has her full attention.

Brandt-Andrew Maneuver

After about 20 minutes and you're not sure if she has had her cramp, you might ask Pat to give you a push while you give a gentle tug on the cord. At the same time, you want to brace the uterus by placing your other hand just above the pubic bone to prevent it from prolapsing or inverting, should you tug a little hard. Sometimes you have to give a little extra tug, but don't pull so hard that you pull the cord off the placenta or tear the placenta. Either one can cause serious bleeding or hemorrhage. Sometimes the cord is not attached very well, or the placenta is not very healthy, and the cord will tear off very easily. Caution is the best policy.

If the cord "gives," ask Pat to give a nice strong push. If it still does not come, you can either wait as is, or change her position. A change to any upright position usually does the trick. Position changes from sitting to kneeling, lying down to sitting up, to hands and knees, or to standing often causes the placenta to slip right through the os and into your hands. If that didn't do it, but you can feel the contractions with your hand, slip a disposable diaper on her and walk with her to the bathroom. The walk and sitting on the prepared commode (where you've been trained to "get rid of stuff") often causes that placenta to come right out. Sometimes it falls into the diaper on the way to the bathroom.

A slight tug as Pat pushes, and the placenta will slip out. Be sure to support the placenta and twist it to get all the membranes out as you move the placenta away from her body. Rapidly twist the membranes by rolling the placenta 360° either to the left or right as it is expelled. This causes the membranes to stick to each other like plastic wrap, making them stronger and less likely to tear and remain inside Pat. If pieces of membranes remain inside, the possibility of hemorrhage and/or infection increase.

It is always a good idea to measure the amount of "blood" loss, and catch every thing that is expelled with the placenta. That is easy to do at the birthing place, but how do you catch it in the commode? You carry small, (17"×18") garbage bags in your birth bag. Take one out, open it up, drape it over the bowl, using the seat to hold it in place. When Pat sits on the commode, the placenta and anything else that she expels will go into the bag. This makes it easy to examine and to measure blood loss, if any.

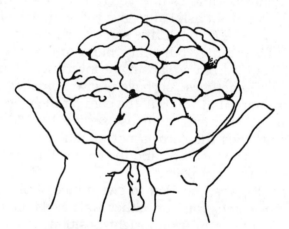

Figure 7-2: Placenta, maternal side, open

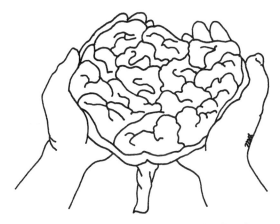

Figure 7-3: Placenta, maternal side, closed

Examine the placenta as soon as it is expelled. You want to make sure all the cotyledons (the bumps on the maternal side) are not torn. If you see a torn place, lay the placenta flat and see if the ragged edges meet and fit together like a puzzle. If not, check out the blood clots for that piece. If you do not find it "outside", you have to look for it "inside" Pat. If it is a large piece, go after it, or transport to your backup to get it. If it is a small piece, watch for it to come out by itself in the next 24 hours. Describe to Pat and John the size of the piece you are looking for, so they can save any clots for you.

I have found goldenseal or Hydrastis 30X will expel membranes and retained placenta pieces very neatly. It also prevents infection as it has antibacterial and hemostatic properties. Gossypium Homeopathic Remedy is excellent for expelling placentas, too. See Chapter 11, page 280, Other Herbals.

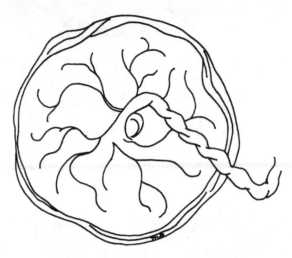

Figure 7-4: Placenta, fetal side

Now that the maternal side has been examined, check out the fetal side. This is the side that is smooth and has a very iridescent color to it. You want to make sure that all of the blood vessels are complete and do not continue past the edge. If they do, it is not good; they should have a closed end, not open and torn looking. They are supposed to turn when they get to the edge of the placenta. If they continue on, they may have been connected to a smaller placenta in the membranes. This is called a "succenturate" type placenta. (I remember it by thinking of "satellite.")

If the small placenta is not complete with the large (main) placenta, you have the option of removing it yourself, waiting until Pat expels it, or transport. After two hours, the possibility of unusual attachment of the placenta to the uterine wall increases. Manual removal is described in detail in Chapter 12. It is an advanced procedure and not to be considered unless the condition of your client and the time it takes to get to backup or other emergency care are in conflict. If Pat is suddenly losing a lot of blood and doing so very fast and the nearest emergency care is 45 minutes to an hour away, you had better pray hard and quick, be skilled and take care of it.

Placentas come in a variety of shapes. The majority are round, but they can be bipartita (two-lobed or heart-shaped), rectangular, square, oval, V-shaped, triangular, or triplex (three-lobed). They can be thin and cover a lot of area, or very thick but small in the area of contact with the uterus. Just as God has made people of different sizes and shapes, so He has made placentas. God puts the blueprint for the placenta in the baby's DNA, and the placenta then is formed after the fertilized egg (eight-day-old baby) implants in the uterine wall. The baby lives off the egg sac until about eight to ten weeks of age, then the placenta takes over.

Cords come in a variety of sizes and insertions into the placenta. The length can be as short as zero inches—the baby has no cord and is attached directly to the placenta. Or it can be as long as 5 feet long. Those are the extremes. The average is from 12 to 24 inches long. The longer the cord, the easier it is for the baby to get tangled. Anything shorter than 12 inches will make it hard for the baby to birth vaginally, depending again on where the placenta is attached. If attached in the lower segment of the uterus, a shorter cord is not the problem an attachment high in the fundus would be with the same short cord.

The baby with a short cord will not descend during labor and second stage. This, thankfully, is a rare occurrence, and is mentioned only because it may be a reason for an inverted uterus, abruptio placenta and cause for umbilical hernias. A very short cord would necessitate a caesarean birth. As long as the cord reaches from the placenta to the labia it is long enough. Praise the Lord, the majority are long enough!

Figure 7-2: Postpartum herbal bath

Postpartum Stage

What a relief: the placenta is out and has been checked thoroughly for completeness, the cramping is gone, and you are contentedly nursing your baby. Some midwives want to check for any tears or clots in the cervix before you have your herbal bath. Others wish to wait until after the herbal bath. If you wait until after the bath, Pat and little Patty are able to enjoy the bath longer, than after any needed suturing has been done. I think it is easier to do visual exams after Pat has been cleaned up. Always explain to Pat what you want to do and why, before you do it, so she can give or refuse informed consent.

Always put a fresh sterile glove on when checking for tears with your fingers (digital). You want to maintain sterile technique, so you do not introduce any unnecessary and unfriendly organisms to this freshly parturient uterus. While visually checking for vaginal tears, check the cervical os also. Usually, you do not have to do a digital check of the cervix and upper vaginal vault after a normal spontaneous birth. Indications for inspecting the cervical os and upper vaginal vault are:

- A steady trickle or flow of blood from the vagina, even though the baby is nursing well, and the uterus is well-contracted.
- Mother was pushing before her cervix was completely dilated.
- Labor and birth were very quick and precipitous.
- Needed to manipulate the cervix during labor, e.g., bracing an anterior cervical lip.
- Baby was large, or had shoulder dystocia.

Bringing clots out from the os is an uncomfortable and sometimes painful procedure for Pat, so you need to warn her, and remind her to do some deep breathing (as she did during transition), or the "Ha-ha-ha-hallelujah." Pat needs to stay as relaxed as possible, and the midwife needs to do the procedure as gently and as quickly as possible.

Leaving a large clot inside the os may keep Pat's uterus from clamping down and her bleeding the first 24 hours will be heavier than necessary. Plus, when that clot does come out, it can be very startling to Pat. Especially at 3:00 o'clock in the morning, and the midwife has gone home. Those large clots are usually accompanied by a small to medium gush of blood and other small clots. The gush is from the pool of blood behind the clot that is holding the uterus from clamping down and involuting. Most of the time, there are only a few small clots in the os or in the vagina, which are of no real consequence, and are usually expelled in the bath, or before the midwife goes home.

After birthing a baby, there is a "discharge" that resembles a menstrual period. It is called lochia. The first few postpartum hours it is like a very heavy day of your period and is called **lochia rubra** because it is made up of blood and deciduous cells. Lochia rubra becomes moderate in flow within 12 hours. The next stage is called **lochia serosa**. It begins about the second or third postpartum day. Lochia serosa is composed of serous fluid, decidual tissue, leukocytes (white blood cells) and erythrocytes (red blood cells). Lochia serosa begins as a light red and fades to pink, then yellow and finally white after about seven or eight days. The final lochia is **lochia alba**, and is mostly leukocytes and decidual cells. It is creamy white and begins about the tenth postpartum day.

These stages vary from woman to woman. Some are finished by the tenth day, others have lochia serosa for five weeks. Some go from red to pink to brown to tan to white, and the white remains for several months. As long as there is no bleeding (pink or red), and everything else is normal, intercourse may be resumed when Pat and John are ready to resume "normal living" again.

The total amount of lochia is about eight or nine ounces, and has a characteristic odor similar to menstruation. If the odor becomes foul-smelling, infection must be suspected and proper measures taken. Pat should expect a sudden gush with change of position, e.g., from lying down to sitting up, the first few days postpartum. This gush is from the lochia pooling in the vagina, and then answering the call of gravity when she becomes upright, or rolling over in bed. This gush should stop right away, and be no more than a teaspoon or so. If she feels a trickle following, she needs to massage her fundus (the top of uterus), and make sure that it is hard. After the first 12 to 24 hours, the uterus normally remains firm on its own.

I recommend using the super "overnight" size napkins for the rubra stage. The kind that have the tabs that wrap around the sides of your panties save a lot of laundry. Some ladies use the adult diapers/shields with the gathered legs and elastic belts for the first few days. The diapers are very nice, but you need to change your pads every three to four hours when you go to the bathroom. That can get very expensive. One lady used the regular napkins and slipped a baby disposable diaper inside her panties as her "insurance" against leaks. She didn't have to change the diaper as often as her napkin, and only used a couple of diapers the first 24 hours.

Another alternative is to make your own out of old flannel and old diapers. You use a commercial one for a pattern for length, but make them a little wider (about three inches), with light elastic to hold it close to the body. She used buttons and button holes on a one inch wide elastic "belt." Velcro will do the job too, and easier if you and the sewing machine are not real friendly yet. All you need is about a dozen for the first 24 hours. They are recyclable and environmentally safe, plus available for your next bundle of blessing.

Tampons should not be used for lochia. There is a higher incidence of toxic shock at that time. Another, and I think a more compelling argument, is that the vaginal walls do not return to their pre-birth tone until about the third week. It is the vaginal walls and perineal muscle tone that hold the tampon in. The perineum does not regain its pre-birth tone until about six weeks postpartum, providing you are diligent in practicing your Kegels every day. By that time you don't need the tampon.

To encourage your first bowel movement after baby's birth, you will want to drink something warm, like tap water, or hot tea, first thing in the morning. Avoid drinking something cold first thing in the morning. Cold drinks cause the bowel to contract or have mild spasms, causing constipation. Fresh fruit and vegetables, fruit juices and whole grains will provide the roughage to stimulate your bowels. Enemas are usually not needed, and a laxative will work on baby as well as Pat. (Remember, it isn't baby with the anticipated problem.) When you have the urge to go, do not hold it back. Relax, and the normal process will take place. It really is not as bad as you anticipate it to be. I guarantee that it will not be as difficult as having the baby. The first bowel movement usually occurs in the first 24 hours post-birth, depending on how many stools you had at the start of and during labor.

The peri bottle should be used after going to the bathroom for the first week. Pour about a thumb's width of povidone iodine into the bottle, and fill it up with warm water. After answering nature's call, and changing your pad, squirt the iodine solution over your labia and perineum, "rinsing" well. Blot dry from front to back with tissue. *Never, never* wipe from back to front. The bowel has lots of organisms that are needed in the bowel to digest foods and process the contents of the bowel until it is time to expel the stool. Not all of these organisms are helpful when they get to the vagina, or the urethra. Wiping from back to front gives these little "hitchhikers" a taxi ride to areas they do not belong in. This is the leading cause of bladder and vaginal infections in women at any time of their life, but especially postpartum. So remember, wipe from front to back for the rest of your life, and teach your daughters the same, starting when they first use the potty.

Pat should continue with her prenatal diet for at least six weeks postpartum. This will give her the energy to be awake at all hours of the night and day, taking care of her baby, and to make the amount of milk her baby needs. A good habit is to drink a glass (12–16 oz.) of something every time you nurse your baby during the daylight hours. This will keep your "plumbing" in good order, and helps with the milk supply. Caffeine will stimulate and give the baby lots of "zing," so the decaffeinated stuff is better if you need that coffee in the morning. If you are trying to get him to sleep at night and not in the day, try the regular caffeinated stuff. Sometimes it backfires on you with a crying baby for 24 hours, because caffeine accumulates in the baby.

Christian Childbirth Education usually does seven postpartum checkups. On day one (first 24 hours), we check for time of the first meconium and urine of the baby, if first voiding (urine) and meconium was done after the midwives left (4–6 hours after birth), and before they returned the next day. A very important part of the postpartum visits the first week is evaluating the baby.

Most babies have indicated a desire to nurse and do well before the midwives leave on birth day. Occasionally, the baby indicates that sleep is the number one priority on the agenda. If we are coming back within 12 hours we encourage Pat to let the baby sleep in bed with her, hoping the baby will be more interested after a nap. This is the usual pattern. The closeness of Pat to little Johnny encourages her to offer the breast when he stirs. Most of the time Johnny latches on, and breastfeeding is well established by the time the midwives return on the first postpartum visit. If Pat is a first-time mom, then one of the midwives will stay (napping on the couch) to help Pat get a good start.

We usually ask Pat and John about their perceptions of the birth on the first or third day. We want to know if they felt we allowed them to flow as the rhythm of the labor directed them, or did we impose our wishes on them. We have found that the fine details start to blur if we wait past the third day, and sometimes clients will give us a new insight that will help others. Even reassuring us that all went as beautifully as they had dreamed, helps us reach for that goal of the invisible midwife (see Chapter 12).

Each visit, the color, amount and odor of the lochia is recorded as is Pat's temperature, if any. The blood pressure (B/P) is taken, with pulse and respiration, fundal height and if the uterus is hard or soft. Pat's hemoglobin is taken on the fifth day postpartum and at the six-week checkup. Note is made when the milk comes in (second or third day, usually), and how well the cord is drying, when the clamp comes off and when the cord falls off. If circumcision is done, by whom and how the healing process is doing is recorded. Baby is checked for jaundice using an icterometer at each visit the first week and when indicated throughout the first six weeks of life. PKU and other state-mandated tests are done with parent permission on the fifth or seventh day. These tests cannot be done before the baby has had milk for 48 hours or they will not be accurate and will have to be repeated. Baby's weight is usually done on the third week (21st day) as a reassurance to Pat that all is well and baby is gaining. Watching for signs of dehydration, e.g., sunken fontanelles (soft spots) and "old man" appearance are routine evaluations at each visit. Since birth day, baby should be nursing every $1\frac{1}{2}$ to 2 hours during daytime, and every 2 to 3 hours at night. We encourage discussion of baby care at each visit, and how the family is adjusting to this new person.

Natural family spacing concerns are discussed as the clients wish. Generally, frequent nursing during night and day postpones the return of fertility. Nursing your baby at night with very little, if any, light (by moonlight, for example) also helps postpone ovulation, according to some researchers.

At the six-week checkup, pap smears are done if Pat requests it, if none had been done at the initial prenatal visit, if there was a reason for a repeat smear, or it has been three to five years since her last. Involution is checked with a bimanual internal exam, and the usual B/P, weight, "dip stick" and breasts are examined. If I know that Pat's family has had a siege of upper respiratory infections (URI), or she will not have a physical until the next pregnancy, I will listen to her heart and lungs and check for enlarged lymph glands. If Pat has varicose veins, they will be checked too. Usually they will be almost "normal" looking at the sixth week postpartum. She should be encouraged to continue with her homeopathic medication or herbs for six months, and then start tapering off slowly for lasting benefits. Pat is reminded to call if she has any questions concerning breastfeeding, or *whatever*, whenever she wishes or has the need. Class reunion reminder and preference is asked concerning where they would like it; e.g., in the country or in town at the park. We try to have the reunions in places where children of all ages can have fun, like playgrounds near softball diamonds. We also like to have kitchen facilities to warm up the hot foods and keep cool things cool, and handy bathrooms. All of the clients from previous years are invited as well as the current year. Many friendships have developed over the years among clients that would never have met otherwise, because of distance or lifestyle differences.

CHAPTER 8

ꟈATURAL ꟈIRTH ꟈFTER CꟈESAREAꟈ... ꟈEW ꟈEGIꟈꟈIꟈGS

The woman that has experienced birth by caesarean has a legion of questions about herself. Most of these questions deal with the function—or perceived *lack* of function—of her body during labor, and whose fault was it, really. Most of the time it was no one person's fault, unless your doctor was one of the few that are "caesarean happy" and has the middle name of "MacKnife." Caesareans are usually the result of events that have snowballed and you find yourself on the low side of an avalanche of circumstances.

The first thing you must do as a couple is forgive each other. Next, you must each forgive yourselves. "For what?" you say.

- For not fulfilling your dream birth.
- For not being the labor coach you think your wife needed.
- For not being the advocate she needed.
- For hitting the panic button when the doctor and nurses started listing all the "dire consequences" of not doing whatever they were pushing at the moment.
- For not pushing "hard enough."

- For not being active enough (position changes/choices) in the labor.
- For not being able to handle the pain.
- For not resisting the epidural, medication, IVs, etc.
- For going into labor on a holiday or the evening before doctor's weekend off or start of his vacation.
- For not dilating fast enough.
- For going to the hospital too soon.
- For "allowing" your water to break hours before active labor began.
- For submitting to an "unnecessary" caesarean.
- For not being the "real woman" you needed to be to birth a baby.
- For failing again, and again. . . and again.
- For being "distant" and reluctant to resume sexual activity with your husband after the caesarean.
- For being afraid of another pregnancy.

And the list goes on. . . .

If forgiveness of each other and of the attendants is not given, bitterness and resentment will grow, and the enemy will have won another battle against the family. Love does not flourish where bitterness and resentment live. So, forgive each other! Tell each other how much you really do love one another. Renew your marriage vows and hold one another close. Cry together. There is a lot of healing and cleansing when you cry together. When the tears stop, pray together. Ask God for wisdom and grace, guidance, and forgiveness for having sinned against each other for "letting each other down," for having bitterness, resentment, unforgiveness, etc. Put the enemy (Satan) on notice and tell him (don't *ask* him) to pack up and get out with all his little friends. He has no part in your lives, in the Name and by the shed Blood of Jesus.

Purpose in your hearts to go to an independent childbirth educator that teaches consumerism as well as the processes of birth, pregnancy and postpartum, such as Apple Tree Family Ministries, or a Christian midwife's class. If you cannot find a Christian Childbirth Educator, look for a neutral type like an American Academy of Husband Coached Childbirth (the Bradley Method) or International Childbirth Education Association teacher.

Most hospital-based classes are little more than "obedience classes." They tell you what to expect them to do to/for you in labor, not what you could do to help yourself or will experience in your childbearing year. Read every book you can get your hands on. What you read will help you sift out what is consumerism and what is obedience class. Authors such as Penny Simkin, Helen Wessell, Sheila Kitzinger, Nancy Cohen, Gail Brewer, Roberta Scaer, Diana Korte, Michel Odent, Barbara Katz Rothman, Lee and David Stewart to name a few, have written prolifically on alternatives and consumerism in birth and can give you perspective on what you hear in class.

Please be as wise as a cow and spit out the sticks. Cows eat a lot of hay and sometimes there are sticks in it. . .they don't just swallow the sticks and get a bellyache. They spit out what they can't chew (what does not agree with Scripture) and swallow the rest. Cows also bring up their cud (what they have already swallowed) and chew it over again, until it is in a form that can become a part of them. If you can't find independent classes, contact International Caesarean Awareness Network, 870 Bowers St., Birmingham MI 48009 (877) ASKICAN. ICAN can give you contacts near you for childbirth classes, support groups and attendants that will help you have your Natural Birth After Caesarean. NAPSAC (interNational Association of Parents and Professionals for Safe Alternatives Childbirth), Rt. 4, Box 646, Marble Hill, MO, 63764 also has a listing of parents, practitioners, educators and support groups that promote NBAC. Please send a self-addressed envelope with your request.

I personally feel that 86–90% of all caesareans done today in the United States are not necessary. We are the only country in the world with such a seriously high caesarean rate. Our infant mortality rate is also one of the highest in the world. We rank a sad #22 among the industrialized nations, and worldwide, there are *third-world* countries with better infant mortality rates than the United States! According to the World Health Organization (WHO), of which the U.S. is a charter member, we should not have more than a 10% caesarean rate. In fact, the U.S. is over 25%. In some United States hospitals, it is a shocking 90%! One has to wonder about the skills and training of the physicians and obstetricians with such high caesarean rates. It is obvious that they are highly trained surgeons, but obstetrics is more than surgery. The greatest difference between the United States and the rest of the world is the basis of care. Canada and the United States are the only countries of the world that do not consider midwifery as the standard of care. In all the other countries, midwives are respected and considered the experts in the care of women. Obstetricians are called in for consultation by the midwife at the midwife's discretion, and midwives *must* approve of the need for any caesarean or other intervention to the natural process.

Physicians need to trust the human body more, instead of fighting it so desperately. Until obstetricians begin to think more like midwives, the caesarean rates will increase until vaginal birth will not be available with a physician. I heard a physician who is prominent in the AMA state that he expected 100% caesarean births by 1995. That is outrageous! It is also a terrible indictment on the failure of medical schools and teaching hospitals to teach physicians and nurses what normal functions of the human body are and how to work with those functions.

Vaginal and natural birth are not necessarily the same. Just because a baby enters the world through the vagina or without an episiotomy, does not make it natural. Forceps and vacuum extraction assist the baby to be born through the vagina, but they are not natural births! Just ask a mother that has had a forceps or vacuum extraction delivery. Natural birth occurs without the interference of intravenous (IV) fluids, medication, or electronic monitoring and the laboring woman is allowed to change positions and move about freely. She is encouraged to eat and drink frequently whatever and whenever she desires, and fetal heart tones are monitored with a fetoscope.

I encourage NBAC women to get out and walk, as briskly as possible, every day for one mile. This can be done in the park, around the block, at the mall, or wherever it is convenient. Just do it. This exercise will help you feel better about yourself and is aerobic enough to be of benefit to your body, without undue strain. Between exercise, good nutrition, you and your spouse educating yourselves, getting the inner healing you need, and with good prenatal care from a supportive attendant, you *will* have your NBAC.

Myths

Let's address some of the myths you will hear. The oldest one around is: "Once a caesarean, always a caesarean." This was first stated at the early part of this century, and was lifted, out of context, from the middle of a sentence in a speech. This line of thinking is now considered very old-fashioned and out of step of current knowledge and skills.

Caesareans were not done on living women before the late 19th century. Until the advent of general anesthesia (chloroform and ether), the mother rarely lived through caesarean surgery. So, they were usually not performed until the mother died and then only to save the living baby. The other option, was to kill the baby, as in present-day third-trimester abortions, in order to save the mother's life. This was a horrendous decision to make, but very necessary for the times. The mother was saved because she was needed to care for the rest of the family. A live baby and a dead mother would be an added burden, with no guarantee the baby would live. Baby would have to be boarded out or given up for adoption. Families were large, and it was generally understood that more children would be coming along, so a live mother was definitely a priority. Birth control was not practiced as religiously as it is now, because children were the delight of the home.

Taking care of a motherless infant was a monumental task until this century. Unpasteurized milk and disease claimed the lives of many infants and young children. Pre-packaged formula was not available and often the lead bottles and nipples claimed the baby through lead poisoning. Glass baby bottles and rubber nipples are a modern convenience. Prior to the late 1920s, the demand for glass baby bottles was not great enough to mass produce them because *all* women breastfed their babies. It was considered unwomanly and the greatest denial of motherhood to choose to bottle feed your baby. Even the wealthy breastfed their babies. If mother was a public figure such as a queen, or movie star, she had someone else wet nurse the baby for her during public hours. Wet nurses were not that easy to find, to live in and take care of the house and children of a widower.

Chloroform and ether were the only anesthetics until the 1930s. Both had severe effects on the baby if mother got enough to render the procedure painless. (Drugs to counteract the effects of mother's medication on the baby were not discovered until the 1970s.) The suture materials were not really reliable, and often would dissolve too soon, cause severe allergic reactions in the patients or, because antibiotics were not discovered yet, wound infections would cause imperfect healing of the incision. These factors all compromised the muscle integrity of the uterus. Also the placement of the incision in the fundus was a major contributor. Uterine rupture at the site of the scar was a real factor to be dealt with, and the risk factor for a live mother and baby were very high (about 50%). All of the above was true at the turn of the century. *Any* surgery was a major risk 70 years ago. Tonsillectomy or appendectomy were considered as major a procedure as brain surgery is today, and with equal outcomes.

It is true that having a caesarean is having major surgery and having a baby at the same time. But the risks are not as bad as they were then, at 50%. Caesarean birth is 10 times more risky for the mother than vaginal birth, and each succeeding caesarean multiplies the risk factor by 10. But, recent research has proven that the uterine muscle heals very well, and in six months will show little, if any, scarring, providing there was no infection and the suturing was done well. If circumstances dictated that you had to have a classical incision, you can still have a NBAC. You will just have to look harder for an attendant.

The classical incision was the only incision done until after World War II. It is made in the fundus, the area of the uterus that does the most work during labor. It is also the area that must stretch and thin out the most during pregnancy. The advantage is that it is the easiest incision to do. The biggest disadvantage is it is the most vascular (has the most blood vessels) and must work the most during pregnancy and labor.

Today, the low cervical or "bikini" incision is made right at the pubic hairline. The bladder is gently eased out of the way, and the uterine incision made just above the cervix, in the lowest segment of the uterus. The resultant scar is like a "smile." Sometimes this is called the "low transverse." Women who have low cervical or low transverse uterine incisions *can have* NBACs, even after several caesareans.

The low vertical incision is made in the lower segment of the uterus also; however, it is vertical like the classical. Because it is in the lower segment, the scar will not "interfere" with the uterus stretching in a subsequent pregnancy or during labor.

The next myth is that the uterus will rupture when you go into labor. My first thought when a physician says this, is: "Don't you have faith in your suturing skills?." If he/she has stitched the muscle together properly, the body will heal correctly. I heard a testimony of a lady who planned a home NBAC, with her doctor attending. Certain events occurred during labor and it was agreed that they should go to the hospital and have a repeat caesarean. When the physician made the low transverse (bikini) incision, he looked for the uterine scar. He found none. He was the physician that had done the previous caesarean, and he knew where he had cut. Not a sign, not a scar! This has precipitated the research on the healing and integrity of the uterus. God does all things well, and He made sure that the uterus would be strong and healthy!

Another cause of poor healing is due to infection at the site of the incision, either inside or outside. The best prevention is to have a good diet, so you are healthy and well nourished. The healthy body will fight off any invading bacteria, if it is not overwhelmed by same. Taking some extra Vitamin C and immune-booster herbal teas prior to your caesarean will help prevent infection. The best prevention of infection is for the surgical team to maintain sterile techniques in surgery and clean techniques by the staff in postpartum. Don't allow anything that has fallen on the floor to be used anywhere near your IV or your dressing.

It does not matter that it is still in the unopened package. Sterility is not guaranteed if it has bounced on that (bacterially speaking) dirty floor. Paper is porous, that is why it is such a good wrap. . . it allows the steam or gas to penetrate the enclosed item, yet protects from airborne contamination. When the item falls on the floor, it stirs up all kinds of bacterial and viral creepies, some large and some very small. . . none of them visible to the naked eye. The impact forces some of them into the package. Any one of them could take up residence on the enclosed item and have a party harassing you in your body. There is no better medium for viruses and bacteria than a warm, dark, bloody place, such as a newly parturient uterus or a surgical wound.

There is also no better place to get an infection than in a hospital. Where else do you find a greater concentration of sick people with the corresponding concentration of unfamiliar germs? You can find a greater concentration of "super germs" in the hospital than at your local sewage reclamation facility. Nosocomial (hospital-caused) infections and injuries are at an all-time high. Medical professional media is full of warnings about this issue, and we need to do our part by being alert and giving reminders when clean or sterile technique is broken. (Please be gentle and tactful when doing so.) Staff members often are overworked and have picked up shortcuts that are not always to our advantage.

Today the incidence of uterine rupture is 0.01%. Most uterine ruptures occur in the first trimester of the pregnancy, and rarely during labor. One hundredth of a percent is not nearly as often as the possibility of being in an auto accident, or slipping in the bathtub. The leading cause of uterine rupture today is poor nutrition. You can be poorly nourished and still lack clinical symptoms of malnutrition. If you live on fast foods or poor protein sources, white flour and sugar, rarely have fresh vegetables or fruit, and few dairy products, you will qualify for a poor diet. You also become a high risk for a uterine rupture with or without a previous caesarean or other uterine surgery. Another cause of rupture is a severe blow to the abdomen.

Improved suture materials and antibiotics have increased the safety factors from the 1940s. Caesarean birth is still not as safe as having the gall bladder out, however. There is still a 10% mortality rate for mothers, and every time you have a repeat caesarean, the mortality rate risk factor increases 10 times. ACOG, the American College of Obstetricians and Gynecologists, has published a paper encouraging planned NBAC, and discouraged planned caesarean. Unfortunately, it rarely happens in many areas. Those doctors that do planned NBAC have a 80–95% vaginal birth after caesarean rate.

Women that do have labor, but end up having a caesarean anyway, recover much quicker than those women who have caesareans without labor. It is because the hormones responsible for healing the body after birth are present as a sequence to labor. The mental attitude and emotional response of having done all that could be done and "tried my very best, therefore, the caesarean was necessary" also aides in the healing process of the body. Mentally, she is cooperating with her body, and not at war with it. She also knows that at another time, with another baby, she will probably have her NBAC.

Another major factor in her recovery is that she has experienced labor. Now, she can enter into the conversations with women when they discuss their births. She no longer has to sit quietly, or leave the room when women talk about such an important time of their lives. She no longer suffers the reproach of the implications of "wimp" or "failure." She is finally part of the Sisterhood of Mothers.

My approach to women preparing for NBAC is very much the same as helping a first-time mother prepare for labor and birth. The only exception is helping her work through her emotions and fears. (Some first-time mothers have the same hurdles.) Doing a Bible word study on fear, sound mind, strength, trusting God, having faith in God, and the scriptures on how He is forming your child is of great benefit. As you study how God forms your child within you, realize that He made you the same way. If God formed all of creation and said it was good, then you are also made good. God does not make junk!

Then, when your confidence in the Lord is strengthened, read a good book on birthing normally, such as Chapter 7 of the book *Childbirth Without Fear* by Grantly Dick-Read (second edition, edited by Helen Wessell) and *Husband-Coached Childbirth* by Dr. Robert Bradley. Notice how your body works together with the baby. Notice how the hormones and the muscles and the bones all work together to gently move your baby out into his new address. He doesn't just fly out like ketchup suddenly shooting out of the bottle. Everything works together, so baby is gently squeezed, hugged and eased out into this new environment.

Baby is also working with your body. He wiggles and turns his head so the smallest diameter is coming first. As his head finds the best way, the body follows. Just like an otter swimming in very slow motion. Sometimes baby kicks or pushes off his mother's ribs to help himself get into the right position and place. As startling as that is, it is good for your baby to be so helpful.

Now your preparation is complete, and birth day is here. Labor is established, your birth team is assembled, and suddenly you notice that your body seems to be at a plateau. Your contractions seem to be on hold as if your body is expecting something to happen, but it isn't happening. Don't panic. This is not uterine arrest. This is a normal but not frequent situation, especially with ladies having NBAC. Your body is waiting for something. If you stop and think back, this is exactly when you had your caesarean! So, does this mean that you have to have another caesarean? *No!* What it does mean is you must tell your body, "I am not going to interfere with my body this time. You must continue to work and bring the baby forth as

God intended you to. Body! You will function according to God's plan."

If you have been laboring for a while and you are tired, take a nap. If your contractions are keeping you awake, then get up and walk. To help you relax, take a ride if you have some pretty scenery to look at or if you have "cabin fever." Driving slowly on a bumpy road can help baby move lower in the pelvis. Maybe a light meal and something to drink is what you need. Your contractions will kick back in as soon as your body realizes that it will not be stopped from its appointed task. When the body returns to its work of labor, you will notice a renewed strength and energy to your contractions. One of my clients described it as her "body was working with joy that it could finally do the task it was made for." (She had had three caesareans.) I thought that to be very descriptive of what was happening. We all rejoiced and praised the Lord for His faithfulness, love and grace. Thirty minutes later, she had her baby.

This temporary rest can occur in early first stage, as well as well into labor. If your caesarean was done because you went to the hospital during pre-labor, your body may try to start labor several times but never quite kicks in. For the same reason, women who have had oxytocic augmentation have a similar problem getting started in labor. Keep up your exercise walking as much as you can. Be sure to not get overly tired, and keep up your nutrition. If you have a difficult time sleeping at night and don't get any make-up naps during the day, or just feel worn out, you probably need to do something to get the labor established. Don't do this unless you are sure the baby is ready. Usually the baby is ready when the cervix is ripe (soft) and the surrounding tissues is very soft and mushy.

Sometimes making love will get things going. If you are too uncomfortable for intercourse, try a body massage from your husband to help you relax those tense muscles and feel "spoiled." A cup of chamomile tea before bedtime will relax you and help you sleep through the minor, but aggravating, contractions. Husbands, pray for your wives. Take authority over that enemy of her sleep, pray blessings on her, read Scriptures about sleep; for example, Psalm 127:2, Proverbs 3:24, etc., and incorporate them in your prayer. God honors His Word. . . it is the one law that covers everyone, in or out of grace. If God said it, it is for all time, so don't hesitate to repeat His Word in prayer. Hebrews 4:12 says God's Word is active. That means it is alive. As we pray, angels receive their orders and go forth doing the Lord's bidding (Hebrews 1:14). Therefore, when you pray for your wife to get a good night's rest, the angels station themselves so nothing will disturb her from the outside. Singing worship songs and reading Scripture keeps her mind on God, giving her peace and undisturbed composure thus speeding her off to sleepy land.

Sometimes making a backrest with the sofa cushions and bed pillows or one of those wedge cushions for reading in bed will help you get comfortable enough to sleep. If you have pre-labor at night and that keeps you awake, try some chamomile tea before bedtime. If you need more than that, perhaps some blue cohosh tea will quiet your uterus enough for a good night's sleep. If you try the blue cohosh, brew two cups of hot water with one teaspoon of blue cohosh and drink it within a couple of hours. You may sweeten with honey or lemon.

If the contractions are getting stronger, time them for a while. They may quit later, to begin "for real" in about 12–24 hours. However, when they get stronger, they really want to keep going, and may need some encouragement with some walking. Many ladies have found that walking through the contractions actually helps the baby come into the pelvis. I was labor coaching in the hospital and my client was admitted at 8 cm. As soon as the test strip was taken on the monitor, and all the admission things were done, she got up and started walking. The harder the contraction, the faster she walked. Soon she had the entire OB staff on their feet watching her. They had never seen a woman walking during labor, let alone at 8 cm. I had to jog to keep up with her.

When her water broke, she was completely dilated, and at +2 station. My client was ready to start pushing then. Push-ing did not seem to work well in the semi-sitting position, so she turned around and kneeled on the bed, facing and sup-ported by the raised back rest. Pushing worked very well then and the doctor learned how to catch a baby "upside down and backwards," as he put it. My client had a tiny "skid mark," and the doctor graciously declined to repair it, "because the cure would be worse than the problem." How refreshing to hear that from an allopath! As soon as the baby was born, she turned around and sat down on clean underpads, received her baby and nursed him. When it was time for the placenta, she decided to go back to the supported kneeling position, and it slid right out. Daddy was able to hold his new baby while Momma was busy changing positions and expelling the placenta.

So, the lesson to be learned is to do whatever works for you. Don't limit yourself in labor or birth to what has become traditional. You are an individual. You are the only one of your kind. God made you that way. You are special. Make your birth special by listening to the message your body is giving you, and doing what it says. Sometimes you just have to try every position over and over again. Do not be discouraged, because the position that you rejected early on, is usually the one that works at birth time!

Start searching for a caregiver you can talk with and agrees with you early in your pregnancy. Even before you get pregnant is not too early in an area that has 25% or higher caesarean rate and you don't know a midwife. Ask the local Chiropractor's Association for recommendations of MDs that are non-interventive or for midwife referrals. La Leche League is a good resource too. Have interviews with the doctors. Even if it costs you for an office visit, do not have an exam without talking first.

At the interview, mention to him that you read an interesting article in the "Such-and-such Journal" concerning whatever "pushes the buttons" on the local medical establishment, and has he had a chance to read it? That may be a trigger for him, because he knows you will put that in your birth plan, and he had better find out for himself what you are basing this on. After all, he doesn't want to look ignorant in front of a mere patient. This kind of strategy will serve you well and will set up a positive relationship with him, most of the time. If he gets all bent out of shape, shake the dust of that office off your feet and find someone else. Fast. This doctor will give you lip service until he gets you where you can't run, and then it is knife time, whether you want it or not.

Immediately, you want to develop a birth plan. Talk with your caregiver about it as you go along. Have it ready for your final discussion and agreement about 4–6 weeks before your due date. Have the documentation, preferably from the doctors' own publications like the *New England Journal of Medicine*, *Journal of American Medicine* or the OB-GYN journals on every point he may balk on. Things like moving about on your feet during labor, monitor test strips only, no IV, position choice is yours, not his (in the normal situation), etc. Please do not quote *Reader's Digest* or other "non-trade" magazines as your documentation for your birth plan. The doctor will laugh you out of his office. They do not respect those articles, even though they may be word for word what is in their own journals. (Probably because they hardly have time to read the medical magazines, let alone the common folks' stuff, and don't want to appear out of step).

Caesarean prevention boils down to:

- Study and show thyself approved (I Timothy 2:15). Especially the husband, because he is your protective covering in that hospital.
- Good prenatal care. Be active, don't let someone else take all the responsibility—that is the same as saying "Take me, I'm yours to do with as you will." A fine attitude of submission to God, but not to the doctors, without discussion first.
- Do your part. Eat right. Exercise, both physically and spiritually.
- Agree on your birth plan and stick with it. Know what you will negotiate and what you won't, unless truly medically indicated.
- Be healed of the pain from your caesarean birth, in your spirit, soul and body, or at least be started on it. Go to the Master Healer, Jesus Christ, and accept His healing.
- Find a midwife and plan to birth with her/him.
- Hire a monitrice or professional birth coach.

The key to having a Natural Birth After Caesarean is be prepared. Study! Both of you must study. If only one of you are committed to having a natural birth, it isn't going to happen. You have to be together on this. Pat, you have to pour out your heart to your man and let him know how this caesarean has affected you. If Pat is still in the grieving process and it is John that is pushing for the natural birth, John will have to tell Pat how devastated he feels that they did this to his wife. So, communicate your feelings, thoughts, dreams, goals to each other.

I know that midwives are not easy to find in most parts of this country. . . I hear that everyday. But be persistent. You may have to convince her of the safety of NBAC. International Caesarean Awareness Network and NAPSAC can help her with information on that. The sad truth is that if you want NBAC, you have to do it at home in most areas of this country. The restrictions put on by most hospitals and birthing centers are a greater hindrance than a help, and will almost surely cause a repeat caesarean. The leading causes of Caesarean today are the internal fetal monitors and IVs because they restrict your position choices and nutritional needs during labor. The few (hopefully increasing in number) doctors that specialize in NBAC have a 90–95% success rate. None of them insist on constant monitoring and IVs.

Time for a few birth stories. One of my first NBAC ladies had her first caesarean for CPD (cephalopelvic disproportion). Her son's head was a normal 14 inches plus at birth. Large heads ran in the family. . . on both sides. Pat and John decided not to have a caesarean again and looked for a midwife. I was the only one around within a two-hour drive, and very enthusiastic about NBAC after having heard Nancy Cohen (author of *Silent Knife* and *Open Season*) recently. The pregnancy was very normal. They attended classes and anticipation for birth day was running high. Finally the day came. Pat called me and reported that her contractions were five minutes apart and she was feeling a lot of pressure. I said that I would pick up my partner and we would be there as soon as we could. It was approximately a one-hour drive to Pat's.

I called my partner, who said her husband was on his way home from work, but should arrive about the same time I would. He would be watching the kids because her baby sitter was out of town. My partner lived about 18 minutes from my house, and was also on the way to Pat's. I packed up the car with the bean bag chair and my birth bag, cleaned up, changed my clothes and was on my way. I get to my partner's and her husband is not there. We wait and wait. Every minute seemed like hours. Finally, after 10 minutes, he arrives; he had stopped to get groceries. Just then, the phone rang. It was John: "Please hurry!" Off we flew. We arrive just as Pat is starting to push. A beautiful baby, one and one-half pounds heavier and with a head measurement of $15\frac{1}{2}$ inches, slid out into our waiting hands. Her labor was $3\frac{1}{2}$ hours long. She had four hours of labor until interrupted by caesarean with the first baby.

Another favorite story about Pat and John. After recently attending one of Bill Gothard's "Advanced Seminars"/"Life Purpose Seminars," they came to me for an interview. (You all need to attend an Institute for Basic Youth Conflicts seminar.) They were very intent on NBAC and wanted very much the support and education needed for one. When I listened to her story, I wanted to cry. Her first baby decided to come on Thanksgiving, the absolute worst time for a first baby. They were visiting family and just ready to sit down for the turkey dinner when her water broke! Following doctor's orders, they immediately left to go to the hospital on the other side of the state where they lived and where they planned to birth (a 90-mile drive on the Interstate). On admission, the contractions had not yet become regular.

After the contractions were about 10 minutes apart, the IV with oxytocin, and internal monitor were in place, Pat was informed that she had to have her baby within a certain time frame, or wait until 9:00 p.m., because doctor was going to have his turkey dinner! Pat and John were young, college students, having their first baby, they thought these instructions were written in stone and had to be obeyed. They were so worried the baby would come at the "wrong time." Well, baby did not come before 9:00 p.m. . . but the doctor wanted to have the baby so he could get a good night's sleep. So they did. . . caesarean. The wildest part of this whole story, is that all of the above commentaries by the doctor are in his notes on her record! Ladies, your hospital and doctor's records of your care are very informative!

Pat's next baby was caesarean because she "couldn't have the first one vaginally" said Doctor Number Two. Doctor with Pat's third pregnancy said, "Sure, you can have a VBAC." But on birth day, it was his substitute who said, "No, no, you already had two caesareans." This time, he had planned on attending a doctors' conference, but it would be over by the due date, and he agreed to let her have her long awaited VBAC (vaginal birth after caesarean). Labor proceeded well, and they wheeled her into the delivery room (ready to convert into operating room in five minutes) because she had had three caesareans already. As Pat was pushing, a very observant nurse stated, "Oh look! It's a girl!" The doctor spun around as he was putting his gloves on, took a quick look and said, "Caesarean! we can't deliver a breech VBAC! So he pushed the baby back inside. Pat had painfully huge bruising on her thighs and in her vagina plus another caesarean to heal from. Doctor Number Four was not a novice. He had 15 years experience and taught in a teaching hospital. He was considered a skilled physician, but he had never done a breech birth vaginally in all of his years as a physician. Not even in medical school. What a shame that his instructors had never completed his education!

Now Pat and John are in my office and I agree to help them. Pregnancy was fine, they attended classes, and birth day came. Pat had a favorite, special place in her living room that was to be her birthing place. The children were sent to Grandma's immediately after participating in a special program at church. Pat and John went home, called the birth team, and settled into Pat's little nest. In the fullness of time, God called him forth, and a new baby boy came into his mother's arms. Such joy! Such a blessing! Her labor was one hour longer than the doctor allows for NBAC births.

My first twins were NBACs. The first caesarean was for prematurity. The doctor felt the eight-week premie would not tolerate labor well. She was home in five weeks gaining weight and maturing very speedily. When baby number two came along, Pat found a midwife, and planned a NBAC at a motel near the backup doctor's hospital. However, the day before Pat was to deliver, the midwife was arrested (practicing midwifery when the state refused to give licensure in violation of its own law to provide one). She was out on bail by labor day. Pat and the birth team gathered as planned, but when the midwife checked for dilation and heart tones, she discovered that the baby was breech and was a big baby (confirmed by sonogram). Given the political climate, Pat, went to the hospital and had a caesarean. They did have family rooming in for two days when Pat went home with her 10-pound, 16-inch-head baby!

After that history, Pat and John came to me ready to beg for a chance to have a NBAC. The previous midwife was no longer practicing. Everything went well, until we discovered twins! Then the other midwives who lived closest to Pat and John, resigned so we were down to me and an apprentice. Fortunately the apprentice was ready to go on her own as a full fledged midwife, but had not seen twins or breech born yet. We determined that Baby A was head first, and Baby B was in a transverse lie. Labor day came and Pat and John drove two hours to be close to us. They had made arrangements to birth near me. Pat's water broke about 9:00 a.m., and by 2:30 were settled in at their birthing place. Labor moved right along.

Baby A was born at 4:00, all 5 pounds 6 ounces and Apgars of 9 and 10. We wrapped him in warm dry towels and gave him to Mom to enjoy. He nursed until contented, and looked around at Dad. We waited patiently, but no contractions, after two hours, we called the backup. His suggestion was to come in for Pit induction or a caesarean, or we could wait. Pat decided to wait, so we waited. At two hours and 10 minutes, we thought we had a contraction, but Baby B was still transverse. We prayed! The Holy Spirit brought to my remembrance a procedure a doctor did and discussed with me at great length (teaching me and I didn't know why then). It is called Podalic Version. We will go into detail in Chapter 12. We did the podalic version. Baby B was born two hours 19 minutes after his brother, weighing four pounds 12 ounces and had Apgars of 9 and 10. We called the backup and told him what we did. He congratulated us and went out for the evening with his family. Pat and John were ecstatic! Needless to say, we praised the Lord for His goodness. In the hospital, Pat would have had a routine caesarean for two reasons. One, twins and the other for the transverse lie of Baby B. By the way, here is a picture of the twins with proud and happy daddy!

Figure 8-1: NBAC twins born at home after two previous caesarean births. Babies are 20 minutes old and 2 hours, 20 minutes old, with proud daddy.

And how about the daddy who delivered his own baby by himself? Pat had a 30-minute labor, and the baby was a 10-pound, 8-ounce double footling breech. Apgar scores by daddy was a "10 and a 10 because the baby was a squalling the minute the nose was born!." The midwife arrived one hour after birth. Everybody was doing well. Mom was dressed for company and baby was too. And Dad? His buttons were popping all over the place. Yet, in the joy and pride of doing the impossible, Pat, John and I all thanked the Lord for making the impossible possible!

In my area of the world, caesareans are done for many reasons. The only time they are not done is if the baby is born within 14 hours for a primipara (first-time mom) and 10 hours for a multipara (second or third time mom), providing the baby is head first and second stage does not take more than two hours for the primipara and no more than 45 minutes with the multipara. Breech and multiple pregnancy are mandatory caesareans, with no labor, unless baby happens to fall out before the doctor gets there.

Midwives have many birth stories that tell about saving a mother from a caesarean. It is fine and wonderful to prevent or rescue women from caesareans, but the midwives also can say the mother and baby are healthy! We constantly disprove the theory that intervention is safe. We know that non-intervention is safest. Midwives know the normal, natural way to birth. Every woman has her own variation of normal. As long as mother and baby are doing well, be patient. If you are not patient, you will be sorry. The old, old margarine commercial said, "It's not nice to fool Mother Nature!" It is well to remember that with birth. Never forget that the living God is sovereign. He alone is Lord! We may have wonderful skills, but it is the Father in heaven that gives the skill, knowledge and wisdom and above all the grace to every birth. It is the Lord that gives and the Lord that takes away. To Him we give honor, glory, blessing and praise. Keep your heart humble, because without Jesus, we would not have birth miracles.

"And God saw everything that He had made, and behold, it was very good—suitable, pleasant—and He approved it completely. And there was evening and there was morning, a sixth day." (Genesis 1:31, Amplified)

CHAPTER  9

MIDWIFERY AND THE LAW...
JUDGMENT

When I first began writing this book, I tried to keep up with the day-by-day changes in midwifery law, state by state. I soon gave up. Those states that appeared to be "safest" often had proposals before the state legislatures to restrict midwifery; and it soon became impossible to keep up without having a contact in each state capitol. State midwifery associations even had a difficult time keeping up because amendments to the midwifery law were "stapled" onto the backs of popular new laws and they suddenly found themselves knee-deep trying to preserve what they had.

If you think you are safe because you are in a "legal" state or your state tolerates midwives without harassment, wake up! Get your head out of the sand! No one is safe until every midwife is as recognized and "honored" as allopathy is today. We are at war and the prize is the turf of who gets to catch the babies. Allopathy wants to be the only health provider and the only baby catcher in the United States. Yes, I know, there is room for everybody. Have you ever noticed the bully in the sand box that has to have *all* the buckets, *all* the shovels and *all* of the sand? He only has two hands to use one shovel and one bucket, but he will hoard them all, keeping his hands so full that he can't play in the sand. That is where we are now. Doctors are so busy they can't truly care for the people that go to them. They end up with this assembly-line practice, putting themselves at risk for litigation because they don't know their patients and the patients don't know them.

Only when all midwives have attained public recognition with full rights to care for our clients in or out of the hospital and allopathy has been forbidden to harass us, will we be able to take a deep breath. But, before we let that deep breath out, we had better watch how much breath to let out. Allopathy will not give up its harassment of non-allopathic health care givers until that harassment no longer serves its purpose. In other words, when the public understands that the current mindset of allopathy, which attacks non-allopathic health care, serves only allopathy and not the public at large, then, and *only* then, will we be free to be what we have been called to be. Midwifery already has the statistics that prove "we do it better." The public and the medical schools also must recognize midwifery care is best for normal *and* poor women. In many areas, the public does not know that midwives are a positive alternative.

The quickest way to educate the public is to do public events, like health fairs, booths at county and state fairs or rodeos. Any place the public gathers is a possibility for education. Local TV channels have public access times; use them. Every bit of positive public relations work you can do, do. If a negative letter is in the public opinion section of the newspaper, respond with a positive letter. You say the writer is a known nutso? Respond anyway with a very up and positive attitude. The more ignorant the original letter was, the more positive and non-accusatory you must be. Just educate, don't sling mud. You are called to a higher calling than accusation and mud throwing. Speak at women's groups, service clubs, church groups, college and university "women's studies," high school "adult living" classes, etc. Every person that hears you speak will share those words with at least five friends. Do you see how that multiplies? Moses wasn't fluent either, but God used him. Do you remember Jonah? He couldn't run away from God. God said he had to speak.

When a story runs about a baby born en route to the hospital, get in there with your letters to the editor, call the local TV or radio stations. Write a congratulatory note to the parents (they've been getting lots of flak about not getting to the hospital on time.) Tell them the statistics of home birth—attended and unattended—vs. attended hospital births. You don't have to identify yourself as a midwife. Be a concerned and well-read parent or childbirth educator. If you have had a home birth, say so (without giving all the details), and why you would do it again. Do this often enough and the media will start thinking of you as a local resource. It may get you an interview. This interview will be a source of information to the public concerning NBAC, what real natural birth is, how to avoid that episiotomy, caesarean or forceps/vacuum-extraction birth, or whatever the local debate is about. It may even get local doctors that want to do more natural births thinking. NAPSAC's *Childbirth Activist Handbook* is full of excellent information on how to feed the media information and have successful public events.

There have been lots of books written on the history of midwifery in these United States in recent years. I'm not going to reinvent the wheel, but I do want to look at history from a slightly different point of view. Post-World-War-II people were so busy getting their lives together after being completely disrupted for five years that no one wanted to make waves. Military discipline filtered into society, and if the experts said something different than what people were used to, they accepted it. It was a "Don't bother me now, I'm busy, I'm too busy to think about that, go talk to the expert" mentality. After sacrificing and doing without many of the "basic necessities," people became materialistic to make up for those years of want.

Midwives were overconfident about their place in society. After all, midwives were the primary baby-catchers since Adam and Eve, and thought they would always be considered a vital part of society. Midwives were busy catching babies and didn't understand the political need to talk, but the doctors were only too ready to give their viewpoint. Doctors also needed to let everybody know they were home from military service and ready to open the office (it was "unprofessional" to put an ad in the paper stating your office was open). Doctors had learned in the military that they could see a lot more people if those people came to the doctor, rather than the other way around, so house calls disappeared. If he wasn't doing any house calls, he didn't have time to sit for a labor and birth at home. After all, the nurse at the hospital could call him "when he was needed," and he could see his hospital patients or be at the office getting something done instead of "wasting time." The post-war baby boom gave everybody plenty to do and no one was looking ahead to the natural cycle to slow down, igniting the current "turf war."

In keeping with the self-gratification and materialistic society we had become, we began to look at the traditions around us. The Civil Rights Movement addressed and corrected serious abuses of not only racial but of the handicapped and those that women traditionally suffered. In the process of setting those abuses aright, we "threw the baby out with the bathwater" and lost more than we gained in some areas. This was the beginning of the all-out attack on the home. People stopped taking responsibility for their own actions, blaming socio-economic factors for their problems.

While women were battling for recognition and equal opportunity in the marketplace, a curious thing occurred. Men became emasculated, which essentially killed their drive to protect and provide. Men have a tendency to allow women to take the ball and run while they are content to be sure and steady. . . sort of the hare-and-tortoise syndrome. It began with Adam and Eve, and short of Divine Intervention, it seems to be destined to continue until the Lord returns. Adam knew they were not to eat of the tree in the midst of the garden. But, for whatever reason, only God, Adam and Eve know, he did not stop her, but he ate of the tree, too. He allowed Eve to usurp his headship and women are still doing it today.

Godly submission, where the husband loves the wife as Christ loves the church and the wife submits to the husband as the church submits to Christ (Ephesians 5:22–25), is the only answer. When the church assumes headship, denying the headship of Jesus Christ, it is out of order and begins to disintegrate. The same thing happens in the home. When Jesus is no longer the head of the house and there is no male head of the home, the devil can easily come in and cause destruction. If the husband is no longer the head of the house, the children are soon out of order. When the children are out of order, nobody wants them around.

We have developed a whole system of how to keep the children so occupied with "supervised activities" that Mommy and Daddy don't need to worry about them. The "experts" will take care of them. Our children are being raised by babysitters at night and daycare by day. We see our children long enough to say "brush your teeth, be good today at day care/school, and

I'll see you after work." After work, we grab a hamburger or pizza which everyone eats on the way to soccer practice. After all, that's why you pay for hot lunch. After soccer practice, Mom and Dad have a meeting, so the baby sitter comes over. By the time Mom and Dad are home from their meetings (separate, of course), the children have been in bed for hours. Both parents are working to pay for daycare, music lessons, sports camp/clinics, and all the "necessities" of modern life. . . because someone has convinced us we need all these things.

What our children need is loving guidance and Godly instruction from their parents on a continuing basis, hour by hour, day by day. No child remembers from Monday to Saturday that situation they wanted to talk to her parents about. If Saturday is the day set aside to discuss the week, you will probably be a week late. Whom does she see the most? Her classmates and her teacher. And those are the ones to whom she will go if she needs a quick answer. Neither of them will necessarily give your child the point of view you would. Will your child find Godly counsel? Or will your child instead learn that parents truly are too busy, and only the teacher/peer group "understands." The next step is acceptance of secular humanism, New-Age "situation ethics," and self-gratification by any means.

This parallels what has happened to midwifery. Typically, midwives are not political or assertive folks. They have assumed that people know the worth of the midwife. They have assumed that people understand that certain interventions are kept down when midwifery is active in an area. They have assumed that people know that midwifery raises the standard of maternal/child care in an area by lowering the infant mortality rate. What is not properly addressed is the media attention to encourage such progress. Midwives do not run about, waving the *Five Standards for Safe Childbearing* and shouting from the housetops: "This is what I do and the doctors must do it too, or they will be out of business because this is the kind of care the public wants." She may not want to draw attention to herself because it would be political suicide and she would be the one out of business. Another major reason she has backed down politically is because her local/state organization is not active politically and midwives are not in a numerical majority. She also knows that she can only serve a very small portion of the community. If she makes too much noise she won't be able to handle it by herself, and there is no one else to help her.

All of these entities—both parents working, children farmed out to school and baby sitters of one brand or the other, and the persecution of midwives—have the same root cause. Midwives bring the family together. The bonding that takes place at the family-centered birth is immeasurable. When God is the head of that home, the bonding is a cement that will hold that family together, no matter what comes their way. That family will know that God has the answer for *all* circumstances and will not be easily swayed or discouraged. It does not serve the purposes of Satan to allow strong, Christ-centered families.

Most of us have already heard of the various social studies of inmates on death row. The common bond they virtually all had, other than violent crime, is prolonged separation from their family/mother from birth until they were several months old. These people were usually premature or sick babies at birth and had to spend prolonged separation from their families in the intensive-care nurseries. When they were finally able to go home, they were "strangers." Mother and Daddy were uncertain of their ability to care for and were frightened by this child that needed so much attention and special care. The baby was frightened by their uncertainty and unfamiliarity, so he cried. This alienated him even more from his family. The mothering instincts were stifled at birth and denied because of distance and lack of transportation or economics (Mother and Daddy both needed to work to care for rest of family, or Mother is a single parent). It is hard to fall in love and stay in love with a baby if you only see him once through a window, hooked up to every imaginable kind of machine, and your strongest memory of the birth was how horribly difficult and painful it was. All of this snowballs, until the family is defeated and destroyed.

That is the modern version of the enslavement of Israel to Pharaoh. He was frightened because there were more Hebrew slaves than Egyptians. Then there was the belief among the Hebrews that God would raise up the deliverer to free them. So, Pharaoh decided to kill all the boy babies. He had some very good reasons for that action:

- If all the boys were killed, the chance of a leader to lead the "rebellion" and free the slaves was very slim.

- Killing the boys would remove the protectors from the girl slaves. This meant that the family unit was no longer possible in the next generation. If there was no family unit, national identity and personal dignity would quickly be erased.
- With no brothers, husbands or fathers, the girls would lose their resistance to be used for and at the pleasure of their "owners." This perpetuates the slave mentality and erodes all self-worth, will and dignity from the girls.
- This would also guarantee a continuous supply of very submissive slaves who would be unable to overpower their owners.

The only problem with Pharaoh's order was that the midwives decided to trust and obey God, not Pharaoh. I find it very interesting that in spite of the midwives being slaves, Pharaoh had enough respect for midwives that he spoke with them face to face. He could have given the order to a messenger or taskmaster to tell the midwives to kill the baby boys. But he didn't, because even the enslaved midwives were respected.

In Exodus 1:17, we see this first recorded incidence of civil disobedience. "But the midwives feared God, and did not do as the King of Egypt commanded, but saved the male children alive." Disobedience to a direct order from Pharaoh was death because that was considered an attack on his authority and person. No fine and/or prison term here. It was a matter of *how* you were going to die, fast or slow, depending on how deeply Pharaoh was offended by your disobedience. We have to remember that even though Shiphrah and Puah had Pharaoh's respect because they were midwives, they were still slaves and did not legally have any rights to make decisions. They were expected to do what they were told and had no choice to alter that order in any way.

But Shiphrah and Puah believed God! To them, that was more important than any Pharaoh or Pharaoh's orders. Do we have the courage of our convictions? Do we believe that God anointed us to do the office of the midwife? Is God's anointing less than Pharaoh's orders? We need to pray and seek God and know without a shadow of a doubt whence our anointing is. If it is of man, then we must throw it away, repent before God, and stop being presumptuous.

If the anointing is of God, we need to stand up and declare, "If God be for us, who can be against us?" (Romans 8:31); "When you pass through the waters, I will be with you; and through the rivers, they shall not overflow you. When you walk through the fire, you shall not be burned, nor shall the flame scorch you." (Isaiah 43:2); "For the Lord will be your confidence, and will keep your foot from being caught (tripped up)" (Proverbs 3:26); "The Lord is my light and my salvation; whom shall I fear? The Lord is the strength of my life; of whom shall I be afraid: When the wicked came against me to eat up my flesh, my enemies and foes, they stumbled and fell. Though an army should encamp against me, in this I will be confident." (Psalm 27:1–3). These are just a few that I either sing or repeat to myself when the knees start to knock. Memorize Scripture and sing or say it back to yourself until fear is gone and the confidence and peace of the Lord floods over you.

If you have not come to the place where God's peace and confidence reign, but you are sure that you are doing God's will, if your family and local expression of the Body of Christ are in agreement with you, and giving you their full support, then it is time to "put on the full armor of God. . . and having done all, *stand*" (Ephesians 6:13, emphasis mine). This means:

- **Gird your loins with the truth.** Avoid the New Age and Feminism so prevalent in midwifery and seek Godly knowledge and wisdom. Jesus is Truth, and He freely shares it in His Word.
- **Put on the breastplate of righteousness.** Walk in rightstanding and holiness before God, avoiding the appearance of sin. Accept the righteousness that Jesus imputes to His believers.
- **Shod your feet with the preparation of the gospel of peace.** Walk in the peace of Jesus; be a peacemaker, not a peacetaker. Be instant, in season and out of season, to speak the gospel. Share the word of God freely, especially how it applies to the family and birth.
- **Take the shield of faith** so you can ward off the darts of the enemy. Trust God. Put that hedge of thorns around you daily and wash yourself in the Blood of Jesus daily. Do not look to man for your deliverance, but look to Jesus!

- **Use the sword of the Spirit,** which is the Word of God, as an offensive weapon against the lies of the enemy. Jesus in the wilderness quoted scriptures, even correcting the misquotes of the enemy, and overcame the temptations. Pray the Word! There are many prayers in the Bible: use them, quote Jesus and what God says. Use the stories of the midwives when in doubt of what to do and ask Jesus to help you as He helped them (the birth of Esau and Jacob, etc.).

Now, let God do the fighting. You have done all you know to do and now you are going to rest in the confidence that He and He alone is able to bring the victory. During this time of resting, we have a hard time understanding because we look at *circumstances* instead of what God says. What God says is that Jesus already won the war against Satan 2000 years ago. We are just doing mop-up duty. It is our responsibility to capture, disarm and imprison the snipers.

Did you ever have to babysit a spoiled brat? Remember how this child would scream and kick every time he would lose a game or not get his way? Such a commotion, and rolling around on the floor, holding his breath, etc. Then he would want to play the game over and over, always accusing the winner of cheating and complaining how he never wins. The more he lost, the more he complained and accused everyone of such outrageous behavior. . . and his, of course, was the worst, but he would never admit it. Well, I think of the devil as a sore loser. Jesus won everything. He has complete victory and has imputed that victory to us by His blood and the word of our testimony. The devil has no hold on us except what we give him. He hollers and shouts and kicks at us and makes us think that he has rights that Jesus took from him. The liar! He has no rights. We have the victory through Jesus, and we just have to kick that sore loser off God's property. He is trespassing on posted land.

The devil is trying to steal our inheritance of birth from us. We have allowed him far too much "land" already, so it will not be easy to get birth in the family back from him. But we must press on and take the land. Another reason the devil is opposing us in birth is because he does not want Godly seed to be born. When our children are taught the precepts of the Lord from conception on, the devil will have to face up to his limited time. He does not want that. He knows Jesus is coming soon, and that the overcomers are on the move. He does not want us to know that, so he screams and shouts and acts like he has lots of authority. This is just a smoke screen. His authority ends where the blood of Jesus begins. If you stay under the blood, humbly walking in righteousness and holiness before God, the devil cannot permanently harm you. He can toss the bombs and arrows at you, and you may become concerned and even wounded, but lift up your head. . . your redemption draws nigh. Jesus was with the three children in the furnace. They were thrown into the furnace and they saw the ropes get burned off their hands, but they kept their eyes on Jesus and worshipped and praised Him with their whole hearts. Then God gave them grace. They were not burnt, and did not even smell like smoke. You don't have to be in a fiery furnace to understand that miracle. Ever try to be within ten feet of a campfire or a cigarette smoker and not get any smoke smell on you? With God, all things are possible. The trick is to stay with God, and not run ahead of or behind Him.

We need to keep our conscience clear by avoiding the appearance of evil. Study and drill yourself, using dolls, or mentally going through each step of every procedure until you can deliver a breech baby in your sleep, for example. Continuously go over emergency procedures so when that rare event comes along, you won't have to dig out a book or "crib" cards to refresh your memory. (If you need a reminder, you are too late and tragedy can strike before you are ready.)

Colossians 4:5 reminds us to walk in wisdom, especially with those that are not believers and to redeem the time. Matthew 5:13 also reminds us to be good influences, just as salt enhances food. As you interview potential clients, be open to what God wants. In the beginning of my ministry as a midwife, I would turn people down if they were not my "brand" of Christians. I thought I would "cast pearls before swine" if I accepted "unbelievers." Then one day the Lord spoke very loud and clear. . . in fact, He literally shouted at me. He said, "You will serve this couple!" and I said, "But, God. . .!" "Silence! You will serve them." Now, what choice did I have? So I did, and God worked in their lives so gently, yet very strongly. Some time after their birth, she called and told me that they had made a strong commitment to the Lord, were now filled with the Holy Spirit, and how did I put up with all of their "new age garbage?" She apologized, but admitted they hadn't known better, because it was being taught from the pulpit at their former church. Seeds were planted during that pregnancy and birth. Praise God, someone else watered and another harvested! We do not know what role we will play in their lives. God does, and sometimes He asks us to do what may seem totally "wrong" in our eyes. Then, we can be vessels and God will reap the benefit. And isn't that what we are about? Glorifying God, not ourselves.

Guidelines for Screening Clients

Below are some general guidelines for selecting clients. Some may be appropriate for you; some may not. Prayerfully consider which ones you feel God wants you to use.

- Don't allow the devil to tempt you to take on clients that are beyond your skills without making arrangements for someone with appropriate skills to be with you. Always pray before committing yourself to a client and ask God what His will is for you in this situation.
- Don't answer questions on the phone that could compromise you; for example, "How much do you charge?" "How many babies have you delivered?" "What kind of equipment do you carry?" etc.
- If things are politically hot, or could be at any time, always find out how they heard about you and why they called you. If you do not know the person that referred them to you, ask for that person's name, address, and phone number. Then call people you know in that area and do your own inquiry. In the meantime, just say that you will contact the local midwife and if she has an opening, she will contact them.
- If all checks out and the referred is a reliable sort, you can set up an interview appointment. This is when you get real specific about their motives. If you are the least bit suspicious, refuse them on the grounds that you are too busy at that time, or you are not taking any new clients. If you are suspicious of a potential client, it is wise to not let them realize/suspect your suspicions. You must have a reasonable cause for refusal. The best one is that you are booked up. Explain that because of

family obligations, you limit yourself to. . . however many births you have already booked for that month, and how sorry you are because they seem like such nice people to work with. Suggest that you will inquire of the other midwives in the area and if they are not booked up, will give the applicant's name, address, and phone number to one of them.

- If questioned why she can't contact the other midwives, tell her the other midwives do not know the contact person that gave the applicant your name, and they probably would not accept her on that basis. Or, you could say this is the way we refer new clients between midwives. Or, sometimes if the midwife is going to be in your area sometime in the near future, she could stop by and meet you at your house. This gives you the opportunity to check the address out at the local library in the city directory. The directory is updated yearly giving the name, address, phone number and occupation of everyone at that address. This will tell you all the basics you need to check of that person. People have been hired to pose as prospective clients, so if you do not know them, double-check their references.

- Have your clients that are referring someone to you call you first (before the applicant calls) and say; "John Doe will be calling you. He's a real neat guy. We have known John and his wife Pat for n years through church or work," etc. They should give you any other information that is pertinent and helpful. Then you can ask your client concerning any reservations or evaluations you may have about the potential client.

- Network with other midwives. Find a more experienced midwife, or someone you admire for her experience or quickness of mind and ask if she would be available should you need consultation sometime. Ask if you can call during the night should something serious come up, or something you do not understand. She may even know of a good doctor that will support midwives. Make an appointment with him, so he can get to know you and you him. If he is too far away from you to help with transports, maybe he would help you by phone, and tell you if "this situation will usually work itself out, but be alert for . . ., and if that occurs, then transport unless birth is imminent." Sometimes, it just helps to bounce ideas off someone else. This doctor may even teach you some skills like suturing, or starting an IV, so your client can be stabilized en route to his hospital. Having a prescription to do certain procedures or give certain medications will save your neck and his. A prescription would give you proof that you have "doctor's orders." He can teach his staff/clients/patients procedures that he deems "safe and prudent," and usually gives protection from open interference from a third party. If you use it rarely and only in dire circumstances with hospital transports, no one will pay attention to it.

- There are many women out there that want home birth to avoid the pain, agony, medical "rape" and "assault" their hospital birth experience was. These women are just as emotionally fragile as NBAC ladies. With women who have had traumatic births, the midwife needs to be very careful to help the woman heal and recover from that birth in time to prepare for the present birth, or you will have history repeating itself. If her hopes are dashed with this wonderful home birth she planned, the midwife could find herself dealing with a very bitter lady. Love her and pray for her—in your prayer closet, if she doesn't want to pray with you. Visit her in the hospital, take a bouquet of flowers and let her know that you grieve the loss of the home birth with her. If her grief is not ministered to, it may grow a root of bitterness, and that may produce anything from vindictive gossip to court dates. Both are very difficult to deal with. The first will spoil your reputation as a midwife, and the other will lead to financial drain or ruin, emotional trauma for you and the family, and lots of publicity. Not all of the publicity will be positive, supportive or correct. Use any publicity as a way of educating the public, and the reporters.

Preparing Against the Unthinkable—
Legal Hassles

Everybody thinks he or she won't have a legal hassle. "After all, midwives do not get sued, and I screen my clients well." That is true. But third-party involvement is what causes the hassles. Our hassle began because a third party asked the District Attorney to get "rid of the midwife problem." Hopefully, the rest of this chapter will be an exercise in the legal history of midwifery by the time you read this, but as of this printing, 1992, the reality is that we are in the midst of a landmark case to determine the legal status of midwifery in Illinois and possibly in the entire United States.

We believe that:

- Midwifery should be available as an option to all pregnant women.
- Women should be able to chose the kind of care they want, be it from a physician or a midwife, and choose the place for birthing their babies, be that at home, in a birthing center, or in the hospital.
- Students and apprentices should be able to receive skills training, and academic education in traditional midwifery from traditional midwives.

We believe that the U.S. Constitution protects our right to pursue these three points, and to prohibit our pursuit of midwifery and choice of caregiver is a violation of those rights. That is our proposal in a nutshell. We wish to establish midwifery as a profession on a par with chiropractic, osteopathy and allopathy. Because we are in court as of this writing, we cannot go into details of our case.

We were prepared, because I had found lawyers that were educated in alternative health care, and had talked to them about a different matter about a year before we really needed them. That was the first thing we did right. Every midwife should have a lawyer, not on staff, but someone that you can educate before you need him. Educating a lawyer while dealing with the stress of the arrest, getting booked, the media, court appearances, birthing babies, and trying to keep your family and clients cool and calm and remain "sane" yourself is not possible. Your head cannot handle all of that. If you can keep your family from leaving you and your clients from freaking out, and your head about you long enough to get through each birth without doing something stupid, count your blessings! Your lawyer needs to be educated before he/she has to start defending you.

The first step in their education is the *Ballard v. Andrews* case on acupuncture heard in the United States District Court for the Southern District of Texas, Houston Division, Civil Action No. H-77-999. Next, give your lawyer a copy of *Divided Legacy*, by Harris L. Coulter (North Atlantic Books), *The Five Standards for Safe Childbearing*, from NAPSAC, and the two volumes of *21st Century Obstetrics Now!*, also from NAPSAC, to read for background and his/her general education. After reading the NAPSAC books, tell him/her to re-read *Ballard*, and substitute midwifery for acupuncture. The case becomes very interesting.

You need to read *The Childbirth Activist's Handbook, The Five Standards for Safe Childbearing, 21st Century Obstetrics Now!, Compulsory Hospitalization or Freedom of Choice* (three volumes), and *Safe Alternatives in Childbirth*, all by NAPSAC. These books will give you many published studies and statistics on home birth, and the safety of home birth. Now, to beef up those stats, you may want to keep a running total of your own stats, to "prove your worth." Check with your state organization, they should also have stats. No matter how incomplete your state and local midwifery stats are, they will be incredibly better than the allopath's stats!

The reality of the real world, is that when a tragedy occurs in the hospital, with a physician present or in charge, it is an "act of God, so sorry." If that same "act of God" occurs and a midwife had anything to do with that birth (like a transport, or planned hospital with labor at home as long as possible, or a planned home birth), it is no longer an act of God, but manslaughter or murder "caused by the midwife." Even if there was nothing anyone could do—say, because of tremendous congenital (developmental) anomalies—the charges would be the same against the midwife. There is no justice, logic, or rationality in those kinds of mental gymnastics. The only explanation I can give is that we are held to a higher standard because our stats are so much better than the allopaths, even though they have many more years of formal training. And that is why they get so bent out of shape when we have a rare stillborn. Did you know that a baby dies with an allopath, in the hospital, every 20 minutes? Except for the parents and families, no one gets too upset over that, or even hears about it. But let any midwife in the state have "an unusual obstetrical event" as it is called, and it becomes headline news all over the state.

If the unthinkable happens and the investigation begins, *do not answer anybody's questions..* Give them your name and your lawyer's name: "Thank you for your interest, but because this is an inopportune moment to talk to anyone, and I have authorized my lawyer to answer all questions, please call him/her at. . ." This is a routine answer, and *everyone will think you are very smart!* Be prepared for very "understanding" reporters that are apparently very much on your side. If you do not know them, give them the same answer: "Talk to my lawyer." Sometimes they arc not reporters at all, but on a fishing expedition for the other side. Remember the super great reporter, "Rhonda," that gave you all that great publicity about that public event you participated in last year? Ask your lawyer about giving that reporter opportunity for positive publicity. Show the lawyer the article "Rhonda Reporter" did about the event. Maybe this will be a great story for "Rhonda Reporter" and her candid camera, plus you will be able to educate the public how smart and skilled midwives are, and the safety of home births.

This brings us to the courtroom. Dress as for church, but not "too well" (save your one "designer" dress for the celebration party). Pray without ceasing during the proceedings, keeping a pleasant smile/expression on your face, and have intercessors praying for you from day one until it is over. You want a nice balance that gives your supporters encouragement (praising the Lord as in I Thessalonians 5:16–22), and makes the other side think you know something they don't, without looking cocky.

As a Christian, you should not swear on the Bible, or by anything else (James 5:12). Matthew 5:33–37 reminds us that our word is to be good, so state that you will affirm (declare to be true) your testimony. Remember, the Holy Spirit will bring to your remembrance what you should say. Put a guard on your mouth before replying. You want to tell the truth, but you also do not want to say more than you need to say. Do answer in a reasonable length of time, but don't spit out what ever comes to your head. If you have to think a long time about every answer you give, some question may be raised about your integrity. The "prize" goes to the one with the most believable testimony, with the most true facts, not who can talk the fastest. Act like a professional, because you are one, and watch God work.

In a word or two: *be careful.* "I send you forth as sheep in the midst of wolves: be as wise as serpents and harmless as doves" (Matthew 10:16). Serpents know when to strike and when to flee. They don't go out of their way for trouble, but if trouble comes their way, they evaluate the situation to determine their chances of winning. Surely with the guidance of the Holy Spirit, we can be at least as wise, and not try to destroy the opposition if we can win them to our side. This leads us to the next thought:

Steps to Get Legislation Passed

Part of winning them to our side is to get legislation passed. If the midwife is legal, she can practice in a safer manner. She can openly get a local laboratory to run blood tests and thus give better care. Testing for Rh antibodies, if she is Rh negative and has never had RhoGam, can be life-saving for a woman's baby if she does not know that she is Rh negative. Certain precautions can be made in her care that will protect her babies both now and in the future. It can also, among other things, determine the type of anemia she has, so you can get to the root instead of guessing. Guessing and trial-and-error can lead to preventable distress and even tragedy in certain circumstances. Practicing legally takes a big burden off the midwife's family also. Imagine having an interview without suspecting the couple to be investigators trying to trap you. Or needing a consult with a specialist and actually speaking freely without fear of arrest, and when the need for transport arises you can admit what you are with pride and dignity instead of claiming to be a family member or friend. (I have more "daughters" than any woman could possible birth in one lifetime.)

If you are working on legislation, start educating your local representative and senator from day one. They are not going to blow the whistle on you. You represent about 11 votes to them. For every contact they receive from the public, they add ten others that do not take the time to say they agree with the one that contacted the representative. If you do your job right, you may have a sponsor for your bill, or a referral to someone interested in your type of legislation. You may even get suggestions on wording, tactics, or who to look out for. The one thing that should be pretty obvious, is that the AMA lobby will be out to get you. The nurse's lobby will not greet you with open arms either, so you need to educate them concerning your skills and education.

Your wording needs to be broad enough that you are not limited in what you do, and can modify your care of clients according to latest knowledge, but not so broad that it says nothing. Midwifery needs to be defined in such a way that allopathic physicians cannot be included in the definition. The NARM definition is:

> *A Certified Professional Midwife (CPM) is an independent practitioner who has met the standards for certification set by the North American Registry of Midwives (NARM) and is qualified to provide the Midwifery Model of Care. The NARM certification process recognizes multiple routes of entry into midwifery and includes verification of knowledge and skills and the successful completion of both a written examination and skills assessment. The CPM credential requires training in out-of-hospital settings.*

> *The Midwifery Model of Care is based on the fact that pregnancy and birth are normal life events. The Midwifery Model of Care includes: Monitoring the physical, psychological and social well-being of the mother throughout the childbearing cycle: providing the mother with individualized education, counseling and prenatal care, continuous hands-on assistance during labor and delivery and postpartum support; minimizing technological interventions; identifying and referring women who require obstetrical attention. The application of this woman-centered model has been proven to reduce the incidence of birth injury, trauma and cesarean section.*

The Christian midwife is also:

- A totally committed and maturing Christian
- A person of prayer and faith
- Obedient to the Lord, and filled with the Holy Spirit
- A listening and compassionate Christian
- Knowledgeable, yet teachable
- Secure in her identity in Christ

- Confident in her authority in Christ
- In Biblical submission to her husband and local Body of Christ

You also need to have midwives on the state midwifery board (allopathic doctors do not supervise chiropractors). Somehow, you need to get wording that allows emergency medication, like an IV line, oxygen, oxytocin or ergotrate to stabilize the client until medical care is available, especially if you have large rural areas without local hospitals. You may have to drop this to get legalized. Once you get established, and your reputation as a professional body is developed, that may be included at a future date, as an amendment.

Avoid requiring a physician (allopath only) to back and/or supervise you. Some areas have no physician, and that would put the midwife out of business before she started. You also do not want to limit yourself to herbs only. Many times homeopathic remedies work quicker and better than the herbal teas. Vitamins are not herbs either, so it will take time to make a good law. Start out by analyzing the good ones that are working well. You may be able to borrow from several laws, add what is especially necessary for your area (Alaska will have different needs than New Jersey), and come up with a great hybrid, custom-made and very workable.

Now, while your legislation committee is working on wording, etc., you need a group working on publicity and educating the public. This group could go by ones, twos and threes, giving public events, presentations to organizations, and developing coalitions. They may not have 100% agreement on everything, but agree that the midwifery law needs to be passed. You, in return, think that their project for helping crippled puppy dogs is worthy of support. That may be the only thing you agree on, but by having a coalition, it tells the legislature that there are lots of people of diverse culture and thinking that supports midwifery. This makes them think you have a worthwhile idea, long enough for you to talk to them. Get feedback from them. Find out why they will or will not support your bill. Write down all of their reasons, and go back to your committee and compare notes. Is it possible that you could compromise on the really big objections. . . or are those objections out of the AMA lobby? Your friendly legislator will tell you who is lined up with whom, and it does not always follow political party lines.

The following steps to get legislation passed were given to me by a friend who has worked with a U.S. Senator for many years. This is how it is done:

I. Getting a bill written:
   - What have other states done successfully? Get copies of their laws and see how they address the following questions:
     - What are our needs and does it meet them?
     - What does the law cover and does it help or hinder the traditional midwife?
     - How did they get it written and how clear is it?
   - Don't reinvent the wheel:
     - Don't repeat what positive legislation may already be on the books in your state.
     - Be specific about what you need, and what you want.
     - Agree what cannot be changed and what you will negotiate or compromise.

II. Coalitions are temporary alliances or combinations of groups that help each other get what they want. They are special interest groups or political parties.
   - Form coalitions with groups that have effective lobbies that will support you as promoting their basic program, i.e., maternity care as a public health issue:
     - What can this group do for us, and what can we do for them? (You may need them more than they need you, so "scratch their backs" if necessary).
   - Don't pity-party at meetings; start acting on convictions. Use meetings as report and assignment time.
   - There is strength in numbers. The more groups you can gather together, the larger your base and support appears to be. Strength brings votes!
   - Overlook minor differences for the common goal
     - Compromise without sacrificing principles. NOW is not a Christian organization, but midwives are not exclusively Christians. Will NOW support you (providing they are strong in your state) and you will support them in getting a bill passed that will promote a principle in keeping with your ideals, e.g., a woman's job is

protected while she stays home to care for a family member during a crisis situation/illness?

- Minorities and groups championing the poor make good coalitions especially if positive legislation has been passed by them, or need a few congressmen to get their bill passed. Sympathy to their cause may get more public attention and open ears for you.

III. Face political realities. . . be in the real world: *Altruism is noble, but does not get legislation passed.*

- The reality in most of the country is that a right-to-life emphasis polarizes abortion proponents that may otherwise sponsor midwives. Such group oppositions can kill your program. Let them work for you in the invisible background. Both groups have powerful lobbies and powerful sponsors. Choosing one side over the other will defeat you. Use both to your advantage. This does not cause you to endorse one or the other, because part of the midwives in your state are militantly pro-life and others are not. Each faction can deal with their favorites. You can "lick stamps" for your favorite group as your trade off, but stay away from bumper stickers that say "Midwives for One Group Or The Other." You will lose valuable votes from the other side. Remember, *the issue is getting midwives legal in your state.*
- Good choices/issues are minorities, pregnant teens, uninsured, poor, anti-domestic-violence groups, health-care-crisis activists, prominent service organizations, and in some states where churches are still respected, perhaps they will speak in your favor.
- Accentuate the lowered medical costs for both the private and the Medicaid consumer.
  - Use your state's midwives' association statistics and compare them with the doctors stats and the cost effectiveness of midwifery care (you win here).
  - Statistics concerning the needs of the state for obstetrical care for teens, poor, uninsured and high insurance rates and the cost of health care in your state, lack of doctors, hospitals, and birth centers.

IV. Legislative sponsors are legislators who will work for your bill.

- Get as many as you can that will work for the common good. Your coalitions help here. They can ask their lobbyists to convince other representatives to support, sponsor and vote for you.
- Start a letter-writing campaign to the entire Assembly/Legislature and Senate when the bill comes to committee. Your legislative committee and clients should walk the halls, knock on the doors of the State Capitol offices, shaking hands with your elected representatives, and lobbying for your bill while the official language is being applied. (There is a special official committee that puts legalese to your proposed bill in each state. . . they also check for duplication of bills/laws).
- As many supporters you can muster should be at the committee hearings (the more bodies, the more interest, or so the committee thinks) with appropriate name tags, t-shirts, colors of clothes (white blouses/shirts and dark skirts/slacks), so when your sponsor introduces the bill he/she can mention that "the white-shirt group" is very interested in this bill. Carrying signs out in the hall ways promoting your cause may be permitted, but usually is not in the hearing rooms. Find out what you are allowed to do before you try to do it.
V. Educate the public, your Representatives and your Senators.
  - Walk the hallways, knock on those doors and shake those hands at the State Capitol, over and over again.
  - Have people call their representatives at their district offices, and educate them about midwives: what they do, skills, education, etc.
  - Have media events: get on local talk shows (radio and TV), and do newspaper interviews or news conferences.
  - Speak at women's clubs, church groups and other community organizations.
  - Have booths at health fairs, rodeos, state and county fairs. Maybe one of your coalitions will share table space at the fairs or rodeo with you. The more wholesome, family-oriented publicity you can get, the better.
  - Organize a phone tree (like a prayer chain: each one calls five people) to call the Legislature members when your bill comes up for a vote, asking the assemblyman/repre-

sentative or senator to vote "yes" on your bill. Especially if he/she previously indicated opposition. Get that district to call and tell him/her to vote for midwives. You don't want to forget the faithful ones that said they would—assumptions never work in politics. You do not want to take the chance that the opposition is trying to put pressure on "your votes." ("Sam, if you vote against those midwives, I'll vote for that hospital you folks have been wanting for ten years.")

- Have informational "picket" lines and demonstrations at the capitol and in front of the opposition's headquarters.
- Use clients or sympathizers for the high visibility positions, if you are concerned about legal backfires. Usually you do not have to fear visibility in your representatives office, or at the state capitol; it is your local media that may cause the wrong folks to keep their eyes on you. Politicians look at people as voters, and what those votes mean to their career.

You also need a lobbyist. They do not come cheap, but you may be able to share one that works on other women's issues. This lobbyist can keep his/her eyes and ears open for a popular bill to piggy-back your bill on, for easy passage. Lobbyists make it their business to know what is going on in all the committees, and who is supporting what, who always backs rural health issues or the unusual, especially if it bucks the "establishment;" in general, the idiosyncrasies of each legislator and senator, as well as the corporate bodies of committees, and the assembly. They even know what the governor and the other department heads support, privately as well as publicly (they are not always the same).

Well, this is not complete, but it hopefully will give you something to think about and have big fundraisers for. Pray daily for guidance, wisdom, knowledge, and discernment from the Lord. Keep your armor on, and be armed with the Word of God. Then, no matter what comes your way, you will be ready and not overwhelmed, but able to do battle and conquer the enemy. "In all these things we are more than conquerors through Him that loved us." (Romans 8:37). Praise God!

The time has come to get radical about what you believe. We gave up our legality by not paying attention. Now we have to work hard to gain back the ground that belongs to us. I know that midwives are not political persons, especially Christian midwives. Somehow we have gotten the idea that politics is a dirty business. Well, how did it get that way? Christians didn't get involved. We let the "other guy" do it for us. Where is the leaven? Where is the salt? Where is the light? Without the leaven, salt and light of Jesus Christ in our capitols, we have very unsavory situations, and should not be surprised when scandals occur. Let's do it! Let's get involved and be legal!

Importance of Charting

Always document by a written record what you do at each visit with your client. This includes noting on her chart each phone call and what was advised/talked abut. Include on your chart all prenatal, antenatal postnatal care, birth plan, conversation and events.

We need to be diligent about our charting. If you don't have it in writing, you cannot prove it ever occurred. That includes your phone conversations, prenatal care, nutrition counseling, intrapartal and postpartal care—anything you did or did not do with, to, or for your client. Your defense could hinge not on what "you always do" but what was or was not written down on a form that is accepted as your chart. Scraps of paper get lost, and are not legally accepted.

The bright and positive side of this is an accurate, clear chart serves as a reminder of what you have done and what you plan to do. You may be able to remember if you only have one or two clients, but when you have more than three it becomes hard to remember every single detail in each of their pregnancies and births, plus what you have to keep track of for your own life. A permanent record also helps remind you of Pat's little idiosyncracies that made her birth unique five years (and thirty births) ago, when she comes back for her next baby or well-woman check-up.

Christian midwife, Kim Perry, has developed some beautiful charts with plenty of space to make your notes, and remind you of what you did and what you want/need to do, including a lovely souvenir Birth Certificate. Kim's address is in the Resources Appendix E.

CHAPTER 10

THE NEWBORN: THE HERITAGE OF THE LORD

My, what dreams, plans, hopes we all have for our babies! During our pregnancies, we daydream about the hair and eye color, if the nose is going to be long or short, fat or thin, will he have a strong chin or a weak one, large ears or small ears, and on and on it goes. Anticipation is 90% of the surprise! The nice thing about a baby is he is the most beautiful child ever, when we see him. Then, after birth day, we spend days and sometimes weeks looking for this or that virtue and attribute of our favorite relatives. There is nothing wrong with that, as long as we do not try to make little "Johnny" or "Patty" fit someone else's mold. That mold has been broken. Each of us are one of a kind, a very special someone for this particular point in time. Made with the special attention of our Heavenly Father, according to His good pleasure (Psalm 139:13–16, Ecclesiastes 11:5).

When the vagina begins to open up, the first thing you see with the contractions in the cephalic presentation, is hair on a bluish-white wrinkle. The scalp is very wrinkled, and does not appear like a a head at all, but more like a very large, white (or varying shades of blue) prune as it comes closer to the opening. This is from the molding of the head so it could pass through the pelvis. Some babies have more molding than others, and their heads do not round out until almost 24 hours old. If your baby is born with a decided point, it may take two to three days to round out, but it will round out. Molding is thought to be caused by the baby's head being in the mid- or low plane of the pelvis for the last few weeks. Others think it is only from labor, and the amount of molding baby needed to pass through the pelvis. It is interesting to note that some babies in a family may have a lot of molding, but others, even larger babies in the same family are not molded as much. I guess that is a question the Lord will have to answer (among the many others we have on the back burner to ask Him).

As the baby is born over an intact perineum, an interesting phenomenon takes place for the careful observer. The baby lets a big glop of fluid and mucus out of her mouth. This has been called the "newborn Heimlich maneuver." If you carefully observe this (and it happens very quickly), you will not need to suction the baby with the bulb syringe before giving baby to Mother. (Do keep the bulb syringe handy should you need it later.) This does not happen with episiotomy or lacerations, because it requires the pressure of the intact perineum to "milk" the chest and diaphragm. Another of Mighty God's mysterious plans and provisions.

The first thing we do after the baby is born is give him to his mother, and place him on her lap/tummy. I always like to let "Pat" and "John" discover if the little package is pink or blue— girl or boy. They are the ones that have the vested interest and have waited the longest, so they deserve to be the first to know. That is not always the easiest thing to learn as apprentices, to not shout out "It's a boy!" or "It's a girl!", but we catch on soon.

Next, we cover baby with warm blankets or towels from the oven (set at 140° with a pan of water between the heat source and the cloth). If the summer sun is quite warm, we lay them in the sun. Baby has just come out of an environment of 100° into a room that rarely is above 80° . Remember how you feel getting out of the hot shower into a cool bathroom, or out of the heated swimming pool into that cool breeze? Remember how nice that towel feels wrapped around your wet body? Your body has learned to adapt to the temperature of the air, but your baby has never had to do that before, and sometimes her internal "thermostat" is a little slow kicking in. Baby will lose 90% of her body heat through her head, so make sure the blankets or towels cover her head. You can make a "peep hole" for her to look at Mommy and Daddy, and for them to look at her. If it has been a long labor, a nice warmed flannel sheet or lightweight blanket from the oven will feel good to "Pat" too.

When you give the baby to mother, if the cord is long enough, try to get the baby started nursing. Some babies act as if they are related to a leech. They latch on tightly, and object loudly if the least suggestion of letting go is given. Other babies are very nonchalant about the whole thing, and act like they are nursing only because you are so persistent about it. This attitude usually changes to "I'm sure glad you thought of this, Mom" when the milk comes in. Most nipple problems are prevented by good positioning. Be sure the baby's tummy is flat against Pat's, so the baby does not have to turn his head to find the nipple. This position puts even pressure on the nipple, and is easier for the baby to suckle.

The one-minute Apgar should be taken about now. The baby is evaluated on five easily-observed signs: Appearance (color), Pulse (heart rate), Grip (muscle tone), Attitude (reflexes) and Respiration. The total score is on a scale of 0 to 10; each category is scored from 0 for "nothing" to 2 for "perfect." Please see the chart to understand how scoring is done. Most babies have a 7 or 8 at one minute and 9 or 10 for five minutes. Homebirth babies generally score higher than hospital-born babies.

Sign		0	1	2
A Appearance	Color	Blue, pale	Body pink, extremities blue	Completely pink
P Pulse	Heart Rate	Absent	Slow (below 100)	Over 200
G Grimace	Reflex Irritability	No response	Grimace	Cry
A Activity	Muscle Tone	Flaccid	Some flexion of extremities	Active motion
R Respiration	Respiratory Effort	Absent	Slow, irregular	Good crying

Figure 10-1: Apgar Scoring

The normal newborn has firm skin tone, has a wise, questioning look on her face, follows movement and light, and responds to sound. There are creases and folds at the joints, especially at the neck. The newborn has a very short neck, and almost appears as though her neck is missing. She may or may not be covered with vernix, a cheesy substance that is very good for baby's skin. This should be rubbed in as it does help prevent the dry, cracking skin that plagues some newborns. The vernix protects the skin from the amniotic fluid the first nine months of life. It is easier to massage the vernix into baby's skin in the warm herbal bath, as the warm water helps keep the vernix soft.

The head weighs $\frac{2}{3}$ the body weight, and has a "boneless" triangular area just behind the brow on the top of her head, called the anterior fontanel that closes in about 12 to 18 months. At the back (slightly pointed end) there is a smaller fontanel that will close at six to eight weeks. The suture lines between the fontanels and across the occiput make a "Y". The cranial bones appear to be overlapped across the suture lines immediately after birth, but within a couple of days will be end to end, with the suture lines palpable. Gradually they will lose their prominence, and in a couple of years you will not be able to palpate them at all.

All babies, regardless of race, are born with light skin. The melanin that gives the skin color becomes active after birth, and over a period of days or weeks the color darkens depending on what the baby's complexion will be. Babies of color (non-white), usually have a blue area called **Mongolian spots**, that sometimes looks like a little butterfly over the base of the spine and across the lower back. Mongolian spots can be very small or large. This is where the pigmentation of the skin begins, and gradually spreads until all of the skin is the color she is to be.

Sometime during the first four hours post-birth, you need to give the baby a good exam. This is to screen for any obvious problems requiring immediate referral to physician care. I usually give the exam after the herbal bath, unless more immediate checking is indicated by the Apgar score. The herbal bath is about 100° (the same as the inside of your upper arm). Baby and mother can take the bath together. Baby may be allowed to float, or be submerged up to his face. You may massage any vernix that is on the baby's skin, into the skin. It is easier when the baby is in the water, because the water softens the vernix. Air makes it sticky and dry. After the bath, the baby is nice and warm. You may want to give the exam in the warm bath room, or on the bed after "Pat" gets dressed. Try not to chill the baby while checking him over. Keep him covered as much as possible.

Estimation of Gestational Age by Maturity Rating
Symbols: X - 1st Exam   O - 2nd Exam

Scoring system: Ballard, J.L., et al, A Simplified Assessment of Gestational Age, Pediatr Res 11:374, 1977

NEUROMUSCULAR MATURITY

	0	1	2	3	4	5
Posture						
Square Window (Wrist)	90°	60°	45°	30°	0°	
Arm Recoil	180°		100°–180°	90°–100°	<90°	
Popliteal Angle	180°	160°	130°	110°	90°	<90°
Scarf Sign						
Heel to Ear						

MATURITY RATING

Score	Wks
5	25
10	28
15	30
20	32
25	34
30	36
35	38
40	40
45	42
50	44

Gestation by Dates _____ wks

Birth Date _____ Hour _____ am/pm

APGAR _____ 1 min _____ 5 min

PHYSICAL MATURITY

	0	1	2	3	4	5
Skin	gelatinous red, transparent	smooth pink, visible veins	superficial peeling/rash, few veins	cracking pale area, rare veins	parchment, deep cracking, no vessels	leathery, cracked, wrinkled
Lanugo	none	abundant	thinning	bald areas	mostly bald	
Plantar Creases	no crease	faint red marks	anterior transverse crease only	creases anterior two thirds	crease cover entire sole	
Breast	barely perceptible	flat areola, no bud	stippled areola, 1–2mm bud	raised areola, 3–4mm bud	full areola, 5–10mm bud	
Ear	pinna flat, stays folded	sl. curved pinna, soft, slow recoil	well curved pinna, soft, ready recoil	formed & firm, instant recoil	thick cartilage; ear stiff	
Genitals (male)	scrotum empty, no rugae		testes descending, few rugae	testes down, good rugae	testes pendulous, deep rugae	
Genitals (female)	prominent clitoris, labia minora		majora and minora equally prominent	majora large, minora small	clitoris and minora completely covered	

Scoring Section

	X - 1st Exam		O - 2nd Exam	
Estimating Gest. Age by Maturity Rating	_____Weeks		_____Weeks	
Time of Exam	Date_____ Hour____am/pm		Date_____ Hour____am/pm	
Age at Exam	_____Hours		_____Hours	
Signature of Examiner	_____ M.D.		_____ M.D.	

(Reprinted by permission of Mead Johnson and Company, Evansville, Indiana 47721J)

Figure 10-2: Estimation of Gestational Age

Name: _____   Parents: _____
Address: _____   Birth#:___ Sisters:___ Brothers: __
Apgar: ___@1min, ___@5min   Birth date: _____
Exam Time:_____ Date: _____   Head:_____ Chest: _____
Blood Type: _____   Weight:_____ Length: _____

1. General Appearance
   Cry:_____Activity: _____
   Tremor: _____
   Comment: _____

2. Skin
   Color: Pink___ Pale___ Cyanotic
   Jaundice_____ Mec. Stain _____
   Peripheral Cyanosis _____
   Circumoral Cyanosis _____
   Comment: _____

   Special Marks: Milia____ Cuts __
   Petichiae_____ Bruising _____
   Abrasions___Mongolian Spots __
   Peeling_____ Birthmarks _____
   Comment: _____

3. Fontanelles: Open____ Closed ___
   Widely spaced sutures _____
   Overriding sutures____ Caput ___
   Facial Asymmetry _____
   Cephalohematomas _____
   Scalp wound _____
   Comment: _____

4. Eyes
   Normal____ Drainage____ Edema __
   Follow Objects_____ Light _____
   Comment: _____

5: Mouth
   Normal_____ Epstein pearls ____
   Natal teeth _____
   Maxillofacial defects _____
   Comment: _____

6. Nose
   Patent_____ Flaring _____
   Noisy Grunting _____
   Comment _____

7. Ears
   Normal placement _____
   Canals open_____ Skin tags ____

8. Neck
   Clavicles intact____ Full ROM __
   Comment: _____

9. Cardiac
   Rhythm: Regular____ Irregular _
   Murmur _____
   Fem. pulse: Present___Absent _
   Comment: _____

10. Chest
    Respirations: Clear___Noisy __
    Retractions___ Grunt___ Apnea _
    Comment: _____

11. Abdomen
    Soft____ Hard____ Distended ___
    Masses _____
    Cord: Clamped_____ Oozing _____
    Number of vessels____ Intact __
    Comment: _____

12. Genitals
    Edema_____ Vaginal Tag _____
    Hydrospadius____ Hydrocele ____
    Testes descended _____
    Comment: _____

13. Extremities
    Normal_____ Webbing _____
    Extra digit_____ Edema _____
    Missing digit ____ Hip click __
    Comment: _____

14. Spine
    Straight___ Curved___ Masses __
    Sacral dimple_____ Sinus _____
    Comment: _____

15. Anus
    Patent_____ Imperforate _____
    Comment: _____

16. Neurological (1=normal, 2=abnor-
    mal; comment on abnormalities)
    Alert_____ Posture _____
    Muscle tone _____
    Muscle strength _____
    Moro reflex _____
    Comments: _____
    _____
    _____

Figure 10-3: Newborn Exam Form

Please look at Figure 10-3 to see what should be covered. I always write in the heart rate next to "**Cardiac**," and the respirations next to "**Chest**." If the baby has urinated or had a meconium *stool* (not meconium *staining*), I enter that at genitals and anus, respectively, and include age; for example, "Mec @ 4 hours" next to "**Anus**." In "**Comment**", I describe location of bruises, birth marks, or anything unusual or in variance from "normal" in that category. If nothing unusual is to be noted, I write in "normal newborn." This should be with the parents when the baby has her first physician checkup, so get it copied for your files as soon as possible. A good habit is to do it when you get home from that birth. Then, it is ready if something comes up and you need to have a doctor check this baby out sooner than one week. Most pediatricians want to see the baby in 48 hours, because that is when a heart defect, or anything major will show up. Having the newborn exam to compare with what he/she is seeing at 48 hours will be a great help.

If the baby scores less than the above average, closer evaluation must be made. Babies with one-minute Apgars of 5 or less need help from gentle stimulation to full cardiopulmonary resuscitation (CPR). It is strongly recommended that a baby with an Apgar of 5 at one minute, even though she is 8 or 9 at 5 minutes, should see a physician within 24 hours. This baby may just be a slow starter, or could have some serious heart, lung, or brain anomaly. It isn't worth the heartbreak to ignore such signals. It is always much better to get a clean bill of health than be awake at night worrying about possibilities. Some times a baby with a low glucose level will be slow to start. . . another reason for mom to eat and drink during labor.

I always make it a point to go with the parents for such checkups. The doctor usually asks questions that the parents may not understand, i.e., Apgar score, or if there were any "decels" during labor or other unusual fetal heartbeats. If the midwife goes, she can produce a copy of the labor and birth record, plus answer questions concerning the prenatal period. This may open doors for backup for you. Pediatricians, unless they had training or worked with midwives, are usually very strongly opposed to midwives. By being open, honestly concerned, humble yet intelligent, and polite, you may make a slight chink in their prejudice. Always keep in mind the political atmosphere in your area. . . you may have to preface your answers with "The midwife said. . ." If asked how you understand all of this, just reply that you are the childbirth educator, and were present at the birth as an extra support person.

You have to treat doctors with a certain deference, yet let them know by body language and how you are dressed, that you are a professional. "Bluff 'em 'til they believe it. Fake it 'til you make it. Act like you belong here." are my attitudes when I transport. . . and it usually works, especially with the nursing staff. Just don't forget you have no authority without staff privileges. If your bluff works too good, the nursing staff will think you have more clout than you really do, and that can lead to lots of explanations. Your official ranking at that hospital is below the level of the parents. Forgetting "your place" can lead to problems.

Once I diagnosed pyloric stenosis in a little girl at four weeks of age. When the doctor met us at the hospital, I mentioned that the symptoms "were so much like pyloric stenosis, but I didn't think girls ever had it, so it must be something else, right?" He looked rather startled, but centered his exam in that area. When the x-rays came back positive for pyloric stenosis, he thanked me for my observation. Pyloric stenosis is very common in little boys, especially if their fathers had one (follows family lines), but it is quite unusual in girls. He related that he probably would not see another pyloric stenosis in a girl the rest of his years as a doctor.

Some babies will "upchuck" most of the feeding if they have a big burp that didn't get out, so be sure to burp the baby after the feeding. If they have had to cry and get mad before the feeding, stop after the initial frantic nursing is over, and burp them before going on. This will help you know if you have a "spitter" or if you should look into something more involved. "Spitters" usually outgrow spitting up about three months of age, and seldom lose more than a tablespoon at a time. Most spitting up is accompanied by a quiet burp. The baby with pyloric stenosis will have projectile vomiting. They lose most of the feeding and it will arc and fly out of the baby's mouth. Baby will always be hungry, and will look like a little old man/woman from weight loss and early dehydration.

I do not feel that it serves any good purpose to let your baby squall until he gets red in the face and mad before you stop to nurse him. It could allow the demon of anger and rage to take up residency, which you will have to get rid of later on, when it has taken deep root. (Ever notice the difference in pulling a weed when it has just a few leaves to pulling it after you let it grow about two feet tall?) It also plants a seed of "If I make a big enough fuss, I will get what I want". Children have enough "weeds" in them (from Adam), we do not need to plant more.

Evaluating the Newborn

The most frequent screening test of physical/neurological development is for gestational age, and is done at the initial examination. Before 36 weeks gestation, baby has only one crease on the anterior surface of the sole, the breast nodule diameter is 2 mm, scalp hair is fine and fuzzy, the earlobe is pliable with no cartilage formed yet. The testes are still in the lower canal, the scrotum is small and has few rugae. The skin is usually covered with fine hair called lanugo.

From 37–38 weeks gestational age, there are occasional creases in the anterior two thirds of the sole of the foot, the breast nodule diameter is 4 mm, and the scalp hair is fine and fuzzy. The external ear (auricle) is developing some cartilage, but stays where you bend it, and the testes and scrotum are in the intermediate stage. Most of the lanugo (fine downy hair that covers baby's body until now) is gone.

After 39 weeks gestational age, the sole of baby's foot is covered with creases, the breast nodule has grown to 7 mm, and the scalp hair is coarse and silky. The auricle of the ear has stiffened with thick cartilage, the scrotum is pendulous with the testes completely descended and there is extensive rugae on the full scrotum. All of the lanugo is gone.

If there is any question about the neurological development to confirm gestational age, the Dubowitz scale is very helpful, as is the Ballard scoring system. The Dubowitz scale rates the posture of baby from arms and legs extended seen in a very preterm baby, to the usual flexed position of the full term baby; the angle/flexibility of the wrist (square window); the amount of recoil when the arms are pressed to the sides and then released (arm recoil); the angle of the knees to the legs when the knees are brought up to the abdomen (can be misleading if the baby was a complete or frank breech birth), the flexion and recoil when baby's arm is crossed over the chest with the hand towards the ear and then released (scarf sign); and finally, the angle of the legs when the toes are pointed to the ears (popliteal angle). Again, this can be misleading if baby was a frank breech birth. It is helpful to carry an "Estimation of Gestational Age by Maturity Rating" score sheet, available through Mead Johnson and Company, Evansville, Indiana 47721, in your birth bag (see the section "Newborn Screening," later in this chapter, for more information). If ever in doubt you can quickly do the scoring. There is a place to write in your scores taken from two different dates and times.

Occasionally a baby will take a few hours to "get born" mentally and emotionally after his physical birth. I have had two babies that at first I was going to classify them as premies or immature for gestational age, but later, one at two hours and the other at 12 hours, were acting as most babies do at birth. One baby needed stimulation and oxygen at two liters, because he did not want to inflate his lungs. We had a terrible time getting him to even mew at us. His breathing was very shallow and even had some retractions. We kept him warm and gave him oxygen at two liters by mask. We decided we would give him two hours to "shape up" or we would transport. Mom had her herbal bath, and "Pokey" decided to enjoy the bath too, but we couldn't keep him in as long as we would have liked. I decided to do a quick newborn exam, so the doctor would not think me lacking. As soon as I took that baby out of Daddy's arms and laid him on the table to exam him, "Pokey" let out the biggest yell I have ever heard from a newborn. He let me know his opinion of the whole thing, and I do not think he liked it. . . he bellowed at me all the way through the exam, but after worrying over him for two hours, I was glad to hear it. We didn't have to go after all. Thank you Jesus! We did have the doctor look him over within 24 hours to make sure everything was okay, because of the low Apgar score. Everything was fine, he just wasn't quite ready to be, yet.

The other baby had a good cry, and was alert, but his muscle tone was very poor. The muscles were soft, like angel food cake. The arms and legs would just stay wherever you put them, and he would stare at you with big dark eyes, as if to say "What am I supposed to do?" The Dubowitz scoring was a gestational age of 30–34 weeks. The nursing reflex was good, and the baby was maintaining good body temperature, so I decided to see what the next day would bring. In 12 hours, the muscle tone was normal and the arms and legs had normal recoil, etc. The Dubowitz score was normal for 39 weeks, which is what this baby was. Praise the Lord! We had the doctor look him over within the week. Our concern was possible retardation, but the baby checked out normal.

Needless to say, when I have a baby that even hints at being a special situation, I am in prayer. I start praying for every baby before the special situation is known, or when they start to show the proverbial 50 cents of scalp during birth, and don't stop until all is shown to be well. This is the time the enemy wants to interfere the most, so the battle in the spirit is at the greatest pitch. The greatest battle for the baby is from just before birth until breathing and heartbeat are steady, usually one minute after birth. Anyone that has ever been in intercession for a birth can attest to that. The battle for Mom's safety continues until six hours after birth in a high-risk situation. In a normal low-risk situation, the battle is usually over by three hours postpartum.

When I do the newborn exam, I put powdered goldenseal root stock on the the cord stump. Powdered goldenseal should be applied to the stump at each diaper change. Every day, the baby should take an herbal bath with Mom to cleanse the stump and baby. Put goldenseal on the stump again after each bath. This care dries the cord and it usually falls off in four to six days. Goldenseal has antibacterial action and is effective against pneumococcus, staphylococcus and streptococcus (all three can cause nasty postpartum infections). It is also an astringent, and antihemorrhagic. The major drawback is that it is extremely bitter and expensive. It is about $50.00 a pound, but it may also be purchased by the ounce in larger health food stores. It is also a yellow dye, so you may want to wait until after the stump is healed to put pretty, new undershirts or outfits on the baby.

It is a good idea to instruct the parents, especially if this is their first home birth, on the normal actions of a newborn baby before you leave, or your phone will be ringing when you walk in the door.

- Newborns make all kinds of gurgles, squeaks, grunts, snuffles, snorts, etc., the first 24 to 48 hours. Especially at night, when the house is quiet and you want to go to sleep. Just put the baby in bed with you, and go to sleep. You will be acutely aware of the baby, and can check him out easily without getting completely awake. Besides, the "noise" is over by the time you get to the crib on the other side of the room. When the baby cries, put him to breast, and Mom can doze off without worrying about dropping the baby.

- Always put plenty of surgical lubricant on the baby's bottom when you change his pants. The stool of the first 2–3 days is called **meconium**. Meconium is made up of bile, waste blood cells, waste or dead cells from growing in utero, digested amniotic fluid, etc. This substance resembles road tar.

Only mothers of half-grown boys or wives of men who work on road crews, know what a blight road tar can be to clothing; it doesn't come off whatever it sticks to. Meconium acts the same way on baby's tender skin. If he were to fill his pants when he went to sleep, and you didn't know it until 2–3 hours later, you would have to scrape and peel it off the baby, unless you used lots of lubricant. The lubricant is water soluble, so it is easy to wash off baby and the diaper. The meconium doesn't stick to baby, because the lubricant "greases" the skin. Fortunately meconium gives way to normal stools after the milk comes in or, after four major "blowouts." A major "blowout" calls for a complete change of clothing, head to toe. . . everything is soiled, and baby needs a bath. You experienced mothers know that such an occurrence (not necessarily limited to meconium) happens every time you are ready to leave for church, have pictures taken, or any time you have the baby dressed in his/her prettiest, nicest outfit, ready for company, and the second best is in the wash. Meconium will come out of clothes, if they are soaked in soapy water right away and get washed with the next load of clothes.

The cycle of stool color in the first week is:

- Meconium: black to dark green in color, gradually turns brown.
- Transitional: Green with yellow caused by a mixture of meconium and breast stool.
- Normal breast-fed baby stool: yellow with consistency of cottage cheese. (Breast-fed babies rarely get constipated).
- Formula-fed baby stool: yellow pasty to chunks (from constipation).

It is a good idea to check on the new family within 24 hours after birth, for: sore nipples. . . helping "Pat" teach the baby to latch on properly; checking Pat's recovery rate and if she is getting the rest she needs making sure "Pat" has help, so she can concentrate on taking care of and getting acquainted with this new member of the family; getting the birth certificate signed; reviewing the birth, and getting the family's point of view of the birth and did it follow their birth plan.

When you consider the almost miraculous changes in the baby's circulatory and respiratory systems at the time of birth, it is amazing that there are so few problems at birth. In all of the excitement of greeting this new person, it is hard to take a subjective look for variances from the normal. Most serious problems are very noticeable at birth. Certain internal difficulties like rare developmental anomalies in the heart, lungs or digestive system may not show up for a few hours or, more rarely, not for two or three days. I will try to give you screening tools to help you find the most obvious ones. Your intuition will be your best guide. If the baby does not seem to "act normal" or something is nagging you about how baby is doing, etc. it is best to get a second opinion. Better to be overly cautious than overlook something important.

Circulation of Blood and the Neonatal Heart

Before a baby is born, and still in his "private apartment" in the uterus, he does not breathe air, but he does occasionally practice breathing by "inhaling and exhaling" the waters that surround him. The purpose of the lungs is to oxygenate the blood, but because he gets his oxygen from Mom through the oxygenated blood in the placenta, his heart pumps only a small amount of his total blood volume to his lungs. In the unborn, mother's blood passes through the placenta and picks up the waste products from baby and eliminates them through her lungs, kidneys and bowels. At the same time, she gives baby fresh oxygen, antibodies and nutrients through her blood as it passes through the placenta. This is through a process known as **osmosis**.

Baby's oxygenated blood from the placenta goes to his liver and the ductus venosus, then to the inferior vena cava and on to the right atrium with enough pressure to cause it to go through the hole in the ventricle called the foramen ovale into the left atrium. It then goes to the left ventricle and on to the brain and upper extremities. Coming back from the brain and arms it travels through the superior vena cava and enters the right atrium with less pressure than before. Passing the tricuspid valve down to the right ventricle it then goes to the pulmonary artery and the ductus arteriosus in to the descending aorta for circulation in the lower parts of the body. A little bit of blood goes back to the lungs and is then returned to the heart with the rest of the blood in the above pattern. After making one complete pass through the baby the blood is passed to the placenta through the umbilical arteries.

Baby has been pumping his blood through the placenta and his own body since he was about 22 days old (22 days after conception). For eight months and ten days this has worked very well. Now, on birth day, it has to change! The hole in the septum between the right and left atria, called the **foramen ovale**, has to close so the blood goes from the right atrium to the right ventricle. From the right ventricle it goes to the lungs, then to the left atrium, then to the left ventricle. From the left ventricle it goes to the aorta and back to the body and brain. It goes without saying that there are valves in the atria and ventricles where the blood enters and where the blood exits. Looking at a beef heart will clarify how this works. The atria are the top two chambers and the ventricles are the two strong lower chambers.

If you hear any "whistles, squeaks, shushing" sounds or soft "rumbles" during the heartbeat (before, after or between beats) there is a developmental problem and the doctor needs to see the baby within six hours. Especially if baby does not stay pink. Any bluish coloration in the face or extremities combined with any of the above sounds could indicate a potentially serious problem, especially in response to the baby crying or spontaneous moving of his arms or legs.

Breathing

When baby takes his first breath, the foramen ovale closes and the air sacks (**alveoli**) in his lungs inflate with the inhaled air. This is a startling sensation, and sometimes that is when the baby begins to cry. Others have a momentary startled look on their faces, before getting distracted by all the other sensations of touch and loud voices. Many home-birth babies do not cry, unless caused by stimulation, and look about their new world with wonder and concentration. This is the quiet, alert stage, and is very normal. I count it the same as crying on the Apgar score.

Breathing, of course, is most important once baby is out in his new world. If there is any doubt about how efficient baby is breathing, don't cut the cord unless it is no longer functioning. Baby needs the oxygenated blood coming from the placenta to help him adapt to this new stage of his life.

Babies have a very irregular breathing pattern, especially in the first 24 hours. As long as he is pink and is taking deep breaths, all is well. The normal pattern for a just-born baby can be several shallow breaths with deep breaths mixed in, and short periods of **apnea** (he stops breathing for a short time and then "makes up for it" with several quick short breaths ending with a deep breath). It is all right if it is irregular in the first 24 hours. About 30 to 60 breaths per minute is within normal limits.

Mucus Trap Suction

In this text, I refer to mucus trap suction devices as "DeLees" as a generic term for mucus trap suction device, because I personally preferred and used that brand. In all, there are probably five different brands. Each one has its own peculiarity that one person may like over another. I encourage you to try them all, and then concentrate on the one you like the best. At present, each brand has two types of mucus traps. One has a valve that prevents a backflow from the trap into your mouth, and the other does not. The former can also be hooked up to a wall suction. The safer one is from $5.00 to $7.00 and the other about $2.50 to $4.00. Both are disposable and restricted, so you need a license to get them.

In the event of meconium in the waters, suction the baby's mouth and throat (pharynx) and then the nose on the perineum. Immediately after baby is born, place him on Pat's tummy or chest, with his head slightly extended, cover with warm towels and suction again, this time get the lower throat and the trachea.

Slip your clean gloved index finger into baby's mouth to the back of the throat. *Do not touch the back of the baby's throat with your finger!* Gently slip your finger down to the base of the tongue, and palpate for two little holes. One has "strings" across it. That is the trachea and the strings are the vocal cords. Carefully thread the DeLee tube between the cords. Remove your finger once the tube is in place and suction as you rotate the tube about between your first finger and thumb. An easier way to do this is by intubation, but this requires specialized training, so I won't go into it here.

Don't be afraid to suck hard, it takes a lot of suction to get meconium up that little plastic tube. If the fluid you get is clear, praise the Lord! You are done with the suctioning. If not, continue as thoroughly and as quickly as you can. If the meconium is very thick, and you have sterile water, draw some up in a syringe and put $\frac{1}{2}$ cc down the tube to thin the meconium out a little. Make sure you suck that out before you withdraw the DeLee. Later, when baby is a few hours old, you can suction out the stomach. Right now, you want to get this baby breathing and on with life.

Any baby that requires tracheal suction because of meconium should be transported to make sure the lungs are clear and there is no chance of Respiratory Distress Syndrome. That is the conservative and standard of practice. No one would fault you if you transported needlessly, because it is "always better to be safe than sorry." Because of the penalty of unnecessary tests and the rude treatment my families received from doctors just because the baby was born at home, I only transported if I was not sure about the cleanness of the lungs. Since I discovered Laurocerasus, that is no longer a problem.

Laurocerasus dries up wet lungs and gives babies open alveoli to breathe with. I did use it with a baby that had foul-smelling, meconium-stained waters. It was the one time I did not have a DeLee or a bulb syringe and I desperately needed both. The homeopathic birthing manual said Laurocerasus, and this cyanotic, apneic baby was pink and squalling for mom ten seconds after getting one pellet between his cheek and gum. I had given him oxygen, but it was not good enough. He needed resuscitation and my bag had not arrived from the local supplier that I had ordered it from three months before! (I lost my original when the hospital thought my autoclavable Laerdale bag was disposable.) This was a real setup for a miracle, and we got it! Thank God for His mercies!

Apgar scores are not indicative of the baby needing or not needing resuscitation. That only indicates how quickly baby returned to normal if resuscitation was needed at birth. Praise God, 95% or more babies never need any help to get them started! The ones that do, cannot wait for the one-minute Apgar score. It may be 45 seconds too late and irreversible apnea may have set in from lack of action on the part of the midwives. Evaluation of the baby should take place as he is being born. This evaluation consists of:

- Is baby breathing? What is the rate and quality of respirations?
- Is baby's heart beating? What is the rate and quality?
- What is baby's color? Pink? White? Grey? Blue head? Blue body? Blue hands and feet but pink body?

Is Apnea present? Always make sure the airway is open and unobstructed before diagnosing apnea in a gasping baby.

Take the Apgar scores at one minute and again at five minutes. Wait for the cord to stop pulsating before you or John cut the cord. This can take from one minute to 15 minutes. While waiting, you can get baby started on the breast. See chapter 7.

Apnea and Resuscitation

If the baby needs resuscitation, follow the steps you learned in resuscitation class or for Cardiac Pulmonary Resuscitation at the American Heart Association or Red Cross classes. Resuscitation must be initiated immediately to prevent irreversible apnea. Remember, that baby has had some apnea in utero, or he would not be in trouble at birth. Practice! Practice! Practice! until the steps are automatic. If you have to get your cue cards out, or have someone read the steps to you during a real emergency, the baby, parents and midwife are in serious trouble!

Now to review what you already have learned in class and apply it to the birth at home situation. This is only a summary. A CPR class is a minimal necessity. Taking the Infant

Resuscitation workshop is necessary if you plan to catch babies as a regular thing. Sooner or later the law of averages will catch up, and you will wish you had oxygen and knew what to do with your equipment.

Ninety-five percent of all babies will start breathing right away and you will wonder why you invested in something you "never" use. Then, out of the blue, you will have a baby that needs just a little extra help, and you will be so thankful you have the equipment and the skills to help the baby get a good start on life. Besides the physical skills, you need to be armed with your "Sword of the Word." Genesis 2:7, Ezekiel 37:5–10, II Samuel 22:16, and Job 33:4 all speak of the Breath of God bringing life into the body. Memorize these scriptures, and use them appropriately. Ezekiel 37:5–10 is the story of the dead bones having muscle, sinews and flesh grow back and the breath of God causing "dead bones to come back to life!" That's needful when you've had heart tones that seemed fine and then the baby just doesn't want to breathe when he should. God is the giver of life. He gave life to the child at conception, and just because the devil wants to interfere, he doesn't have the power over life and death. God does. The Bible says so. So use the authority of the Word of God and the devil must flee (Ephesians 6:10–12). James 4:7 tells us to submit ourselves to God, and resist the devil and the devil must flee from us.

There are two types of apnea:

- Type I (**primary apnea**)
  - Initial period of rapid breathing
  - Breathing stops
  - Heart rate begins to fall below 100
  At this point, 100% oxygen and flicking the feet or rubbing baby's back may start him breathing.
  - Deep gasping respirations (ribs show, see-saw abdominal motions, grimace may or may not be on face)
  - Heart rate continues to decrease
  - Blood pressure begins to fall
  - Respirations become weaker and weaker until baby takes last gasp
  - One-minute Apgar will be 1 or 2

- Type II (**secondary apnea**; it is a continuation of the deterioration of Primary, Type I)
  - No breathing
  - Blood pressure falls
  - Oxygen level in blood continues to fall without ventilation and oxygen
  - Baby not responsive to stimulation
  - Homeopathics may be given immediately while stimulating baby and evaluating heart rate before positive-pressure ventilation and 100% oxygen and chest compressions or CPR
  - Heart rate falls; initiate chest compressions if below 80 beats per minute and ventilate once every five chest compressions

If baby has not responded to homeopathics, or they were not available and artificial ventilation and oxygen is not started at once, brain damage or death will occur.

Some authorities feel that any baby that is born without spontaneous breathing should be treated as though in secondary apnea, and CPR should be immediately initiated. This is because you do not know how anoxic the baby was in utero, and if the baby tried to breathe before birth. Usually a whiff of oxygen and stimulation will start a baby right off.

Homeopathics for resuscitation are:

- *Aconite:* asphyxia, hot purplish color, breathless, little or no perceptible pulse, retained urine, traumatic birth.
- *Antimonium Tart:* pale face, rattling in throat or lungs
- *Arnica:* asphyxia, face hot, body cold, face hot, nose cold, jerky breath, tremor in limbs
- *Arsenicum Album:* pale, warm, lifeless, breathless, distorted features, stiff knees and feet with tetanic spasms
- *Belladonna:* Red face, asphyxia, dilated pupils, eyes staring, inability to swallow, spasmodic respiration
- *China (Cinchona officianalis):* Cold sweat, faint pulse, lifeless as result of great blood loss by mother in labor
- *Cicuta:* spasmodic rigidity, with frequent jerking
- *Ipecac:* suffocative breathing, chilly or warm
- *Laurocerasus:* asphyxia, blue face, gasping for breath or imperceptible breathing, twitching in face chilly
- *Lachesis:* cyanotic (blue) in face, nails, extremities

All homeopathic dosages are one tablet between the cheek and gum (at baby's molar area). Dosage is one tablet 200C or 1M. If there is no response in 30 to 40 seconds, depending on the urgency of the situation, go to the next possible remedy. Resuscitation procedures should be initiated while you wait. My experience is you will see results immediately if it is the right remedy. As in all remedy pictures, the baby does not need to show all the symptoms listed. If most of them are present, try the remedy. You will not make it worse. If it is the wrong one, there will be no change, and you can try the next one.

You need to do what you are most comfortable with and what the possibilities are for you. If the baby is in trouble, calling the ambulance may or may not be the best. If they do not have newborn-sized equipment, you are better equipped than they. To compound the error, they are often too arrogant to admit they don't know how to resuscitate the newborn, so offering them "use of your stuff" will not help. You need to know the "First Responder's" skills and what they have on the ambulance. If you are better trained than the ambulance crew keep your current certification card at the ready, to prove to them you know what you are doing, so your efforts can continue en route to the hospital.

Side note: Some ambulance services will appreciate you speaking to them concerning what midwives know and do, what your skill level is, what emergency supplies you carry, and why or when you would be apt to call them. If your local ambulance service is "friendly" and open to an in-service with you, use it as a public relations tool. Most ambulance people are terrified of birth. They would rather answer massive freeway pileup calls than get a maternity call, because they have been warned by doctors that birthing babies is "so very dangerous and only doctors know how!"

To properly resuscitate a baby, you must take an infant resuscitation course. MANA usually has a workshop at their conferences. As a reminder, we will go through the steps of evaluation and resuscitation.

As soon as baby is born, do the following assessment. Is baby:

- Breathing? Rate? Quality? Decreasing? Increasing?
- Heart rate? Over 100? Increasing or decreasing? Regular?

- Color? All over? Extremities? Body different from extremities?

This is done while you dry the baby off, and place him on Pat's lap in the first 20 seconds. Usually drying the baby is enough to make him cry. This causes him to take deep breaths, opening up the alveoli (air sacs) in the lungs. Good oxygen exchange will force any fluids in the lungs out of the lungs. You need deep "hard" breaths for that. Crying does the job. Some babies can open up their lungs without crying. Auscultation, (listening with the stethoscope) will confirm that. Listen for breath sounds in the lower lobes (at the bottom of the rib cage).

When you suction the baby, avoid touching the back of the throat with the bulb syringe. The danger in irritating the pharynx (the back of the throat) is activating the **vagal reflex** because the vagus nerve was stimulated. This causes a severe slowing of the pulse rate. If the baby already is in bradycardia heart pattern (pulse below 60), you do not want it to get slower! The vagus nerve is the longest pair of cranial nerves and is responsible for swallowing, speech (crying), and the sensibilities and functions of many parts of the body. When you suction, aim your syringe at the sides of the mouth in the molar area, then sweep across the tongue to the other side. It is not safe to suction into the trachea with the bulb syringe. Besides activating the vagal reflex, you could do serious harm to the vocal cords. The damage may not be repairable.

Evaluation steps are:

- Dried baby placed on warmer (Pat)
- Wet towels discarded, Dry, warm towels around baby
- Head slightly extended, aligned with body
- Mouth, pharynx and nose suctioned with bulb syringe

Respirations evaluated:

- Rate of 30–60?
- Quality: deep? Regular? Apneic? Gasping?
  - Initiate Positive Pressure Ventilation (PPV) if respirations are below 20, or baby is apneic or gasping with breaths
  - PPV is at 100% oxygen, initial ventilation is 30–40 cm H_2O pressure, succeeding ventilations are 15–20 cm

pressure or 20–40 cm pressure if meconium was aspirated.
- Check HR after 20–30 seconds of ventilation or after determining the respirations are normal. Is the:
- Heart rate between 60 and 100 but increasing? Continue PPV
- HR between 60 and 80 but remaining the same? Continue PPV
- HR below 80/minute? begin Chest Compressions (CC) at rate of 120 per minute and PPV (ventilate 1 time per 5 CC)
- HR below 60/minute? evaluate PPV and begin CC
- HR above 100/min. with no spontaneous respirations? Stop CC and continue PPV
- HR above 100/min. with spontaneous respirations? stop PPV and CC
- Color
  - Pink all over? Keep warm.
  - Body pink, extremities blue? Keep warm if all else is normal.
  - Body blue (cyanotic), Respirations and heart rate normal? Give free flow oxygen, keep baby warm

To give free-flow oxygen properly, hold the oxygen tube $\frac{1}{2}$ inch from, and pointing across the upper lip of the baby at the rate of 5 liters per minute. Avoid pointing the oxygen tube toward the nose from the chin up. This causes oxygen to blow into the eyes and cause eye damage. Always point the tube across the lips "from" ear to ear so the oxygen flows across the nares.

All of the above evaluation must be done in 20 to 30 seconds at the most, or resuscitation will be increasingly difficult to impossible. Because we do not know exactly when the apnea occurred in utero, we must act as though we are at the outer limits of time. You have three minutes from the onset of apnea to successful resuscitation for a healthy baby. From three minutes to the five-minute mark, you have varying amounts of brain damage to death of the baby. Time is of the essence, so please practice on a doll the procedures you need for full resuscitation, until it is as automatic as your own breathing.

All babies are born with a high concentration of carbon dioxide and a low level of oxygen. This is to help stimulate the baby to breathe. Only the stressed baby will have trouble compensating for this by breathing faster the first hour after birth. A little oxygen (one to two liters per minute) given by mask or holding the open tube by baby's nose (pointed across upper lip) will help the stressed baby with the oxygen balance. When using oxygen therapy, you want to be sure the oxygen flow is not aimed toward baby's eyes. Serious complications to the eyes can occur (even blindness) if certain oxygen concentrations occur over a period of time. Keeping the flow of oxygen away from the baby's eyes or protecting the eyes with a mask in an high oxygen environment (like an incubator) and keeping the rate below 4 liters will prevent eye problems. Higher concentration requires medical supervision (hospital), not a birthing center. *Baby needs to see a doctor as soon as possible*, less than six hours after birth if he:

- Had an Apgar score of 5 or less after 5 minutes;
- Required oxygen to stay pink after 5 minutes of oxygen;
- You had to do full CPR or work on the baby to get him started;
- Had "weird" heart sounds;
- Aspirated meconium and you didn't/couldn't use a DeLee mucus trap;
- Has an obvious serious deformity (spinal bifida, cleft palate, etc.);
- Has an obvious genetic problem requiring constant help/stimulation;
- Has an imperforate anus (closed rectum);
- Can't swallow (comes back up) or pooling of saliva, requires immediate transport (first signs of tracheoesophageal fistula);
- Has a blockage in the trachea or esophagus (couldn't get DeLee tube down).

Sometimes if there was a tight nuchal cord, face presentation, or shoulder dystocia baby's face and/or head may be blue or purple for up to forty-eight hours. As long as the rest of the body is pink, baby is fine! The color is from surface blood pooling and causing temporary bruising.

If the acid base (blood pH) is less than 7.20–7.40, make sure the baby nurses well. This baby will need encouragement to nurse. He may be too tired to care much from his long labor and mother's fasting in labor. Your alternative is hospitalization, because low blood sugar is not good for baby. As a last resort, give him one bottle containing 1–2 oz. of warm water with a couple drops of Karo syrup dissolved in it, or a couple of ounces of Pedialyte (Pedialyte is a balanced electrolyte solution). A low blood sugar is usually the culprit. Nursing will bring it up, but you can "pour" (force feed a couple of ounces) a bottle into a baby easier than colostrum from the breast if baby will not suckle at the breast.

You can check the baby's acid-base by sticking the heel and using a blood pH strip. Of course, this is not a routine thing, but handy to know why baby is lethargic (hard to arouse), and can turn a baby around very quickly. Baby often cries quite loudly when stuck and is very happy to nurse when he finds the nipple in his mouth, so Mom has to be ready. Homeopathics are very handy, too. Check your manual for proper medication by symptoms.

If all of this sounds too "high tech" for the ordinary midwife, it probably is when she has great back up and practices in a legal area. But if it saves transporting a baby in a politically unsafe area, it is worth it.

The bottom line is to evaluate, stabilize at home, and if the baby or mother needs further evaluation or care, then get it from the appropriate medical source. A heel stick is less invasive than the risk of legal difficulties in a politically risky environment. The Dextro-stix checks for low blood sugar and the pH strip will check for the acid base or low oxygen level in the baby's blood. You do not need to check this in the normal baby, but if the baby is having difficulty, then one heel stick will save some headaches.

Any deviation from normal of the shape or placement of eye or ear should be referred to a doctor, but it is not an urgent situation. Purulent discharge from the eyes should be treated either with antibiotics or goldenseal eye wash. The top of the ears should be in line with the pupils of the eyes. If they are lower, look for other variations. Baby may have Down's syndrome, Potter's syndrome, kidney malformations, autosomal chromosome abnormalities (trisomy 15 and 18).

Neck webbing may indicate Turner's Syndrome or Down's Syndrome. Brachial palsy or fractured clavicle causes reflexes to be absent on the side of the fracture, and baby does not use that arm. A single, deep, sharp, transverse crease across the palm with stubby flat thumbs, and short little fingers usually curved towards the next finger are characteristic of Down's Syndrome. Basically, the baby should be symmetrical. . . what is on one side should be equal to the other in number (fingers, eyes, etc.) and size (length, thickness, etc.).

Birthmarks

Port wine stain is the red- to purple-colored areas on the skin that occur very infrequently. Port wine stain is caused by an "overpopulation" of blood vessels close to the surface of the skin. It does not interfere or cause any problems with circulation in that area. The problem with them is that they are so very noticeable. Laser surgery can usually remove large ones with little scarring. There is a much less invasive cure. If you are very concerned about others thinking you are weird, you may hesitate to do it. That aside, it does work, and it is very inexpensive. After baby has her bath, mother should lick the stain. Now when you finish laughing, let me tell you about Pat and Patty.

Patty was born with port wine stains from her big toe to her hip. It looked like red ink had spilled and splashed on her. Her mother, Pat, was torn between the cost of the laser surgery and the emotional trauma for a little girl growing up with such noticeable large birth marks. Knowing that the doctor would not do anything about it until Patty was older, she decided to try licking. Aside from feeling silly the first few times Pat felt she couldn't lose. The nice thing about it is that in a week, we could see a definite difference. The stain was fading, and the small spots were smaller. In six months' time, the stain was almost gone! Praise the Lord! Patty is now four years old, and the former stain areas are the first to tan, but that is the only noticeable effects. You cannot see the places that were stained!

"Stork bites" are red spots, usually found at the base of the occiput, on the bridge of the nose, eyelids, forehead, or around the nose. They are caused by dilation of capillary vessels and minute arteries. They usually fade in the first year, unless baby is crying when they show up. By the end of the second year the facial areas are gone completely. Occasionally stork bites remain in the hairline at the base of the occiput for life.

Strawberry mark is a bright red, raised area that shows up sometime in the first six weeks and may increase in size until about 12 months of age. Most get smaller and disappear by 10 years of age. No treatment is necessary. Licking may fade them to pink, but it is not as effective with the strawberry mark as it is with port wine stains.

Hernias

Hernias are a loop of intestine through a muscle. They are named by the area they affect. The only hernias that are troublesome are the **inguinal** and the **diaphragmatic**. Umbilical hernias usually close by themselves by three years of age. Sometimes putting a clean coin over the healed umbilicus and holding it in place with a strip of adhesive helps them heal quicker. Change the coin and clean the umbilicus regularly during the tub bath.

A diaphragmatic hernia can be very dangerous and sometimes fatal because it may interfere with the breathing process. This needs medical evaluation and probably surgical repair. The inguinal is a loop of intestine through the inguinal ring and 90 % occur in males. The intestine follows the testes down into the scrotum, and needs surgical repair as a rule, before it twists, or becomes gangrenous when the inguinal ring begins to close. The inguinal ring usually closes in the first month of extra-uterine life so the testicle will stay in the scrotal sac. If only one testicle has descended, be patient. It has until the boy is 6 to 10 years of age to come down. Actually, no problem is expected until he becomes prepubescent; the body temperature can be too high when the undescended testicle is to start functioning with proper male growth hormones.

Genitals are normally swollen at birth because they respond to mother's hormones. The breech baby not only has swollen genitalia, but his bottom is often bruised, and keeps his thighs drawn up as though in the lithotomy position. Forcing the breech baby to keep his legs in the "normal" position of the cephalic baby can be painful. Be patient, they will come down on their own within two or three days.

Newborn Screening

There are some state mandated screening tests to be done after the baby has had breast milk or formula for 48 hours.

We are required to test by heel stick for: biotinidase deficiency, congenital adrenal hyperplasia, galactosemia, congenital hypothyroidism, phenylketonuria (PKU) and sickle cell disease. The state agency requiring these screening tests (usually the health department) will supply the forms. There is a blotter-like pad attached to the form with five circles on one end. The attendant sticks the baby's heel with a lancet and soaks each of the five circles with baby's blood. The blood must soak through, without layering. If there is too little blood or layering, the test will have to be redone. You may want to practice on yourself, to get the knack of how much/little is enough. After filling in the correct information, drop the form into an envelope and mail it to the address on the form. You will get two copies of the form back, one for you and one for your client, in about four to six weeks. If the test needs to be redone, the two form copies will be back in two to three weeks with a letter stating what or why it needs to be redone. The state then bills you for all of the tests done at the end of the month. If you have sent in one or ten tests, the bill will come itemizing who had the tests done. Retests are free, and there is a square to check. See the illustration on the next page:

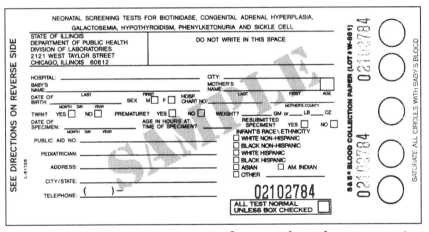

Each state has their own set of required newborn screening tests. If you do this service for your clients, get the proper forms from the local health department or agency responsible for these tests.

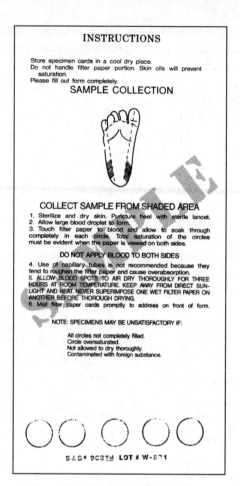

INSTRUCTIONS

Store specimen cards in a cool dry place.
Do not handle filter paper portion. Skin oils will prevent
   saturation.
Please fill out form completely.

SAMPLE COLLECTION

COLLECT SAMPLE FROM SHADED AREA

1. Sterilize and dry skin. Puncture heel with sterile lancet.
2. Allow large blood droplet to form.
3. Touch filter paper to blood and allow to soak through
completely in each circle. Total saturation of the circles
must be evident when the paper is viewed on both sides.

DO NOT APPLY BLOOD TO BOTH SIDES

4. Use of capillary tubes is not recommended because they
tend to roughen the filter paper and cause overabsorption.
5. ALLOW BLOOD SPOTS TO AIR DRY THOROUGHLY FOR THREE
HOURS AT ROOM TEMPERATURE. KEEP AWAY FROM DIRECT SUN-
LIGHT AND HEAT. NEVER SUPERIMPOSE ONE WET FILTER PAPER ON
ANOTHER BEFORE THOROUGH DRYING.
6. Mail filter paper cards promptly to address on front of form.

NOTE: SPECIMENS MAY BE UNSATISFACTORY IF:

All circles not completely filled.
Circle oversaturated.
Not allowed to dry thoroughly.
Contaminated with foreign substance.

S&S* 903™ LOT # W-071

Figure 10-4: Newborn Screening Form

Sickle Cell Disease

The sickle cell disease trait is carried by 7% of African-American women. Only about 0.2% of the black population actually has the sickle cell anemia. One can carry the trait without having the disease. It is so named because the red blood cells become sickle-shaped. As of this printing, no cure has been found. It is chronic, and few with the disease live beyond 40 years of age. It is race specific.

Phenylketonuria

Phenylketonuria (PKU) occurs in 1 out of 12,000 births, except in certain Amish communities, where it occurs in 1 out of 200 births. The baby appears normal at birth, but due to inability to digest certain amino acids in the protein molecule, does not assimilate protein well. This can lead to poor development and cause mental retardation. A special diet will prevent these problems, if started early. It is thought that the child will outgrow the problem and will be able to digest the entire protein molecule at about school age. There are some exceptions, so please continue getting the urine and or blood tests until normal values are consistent. Once the brain has stopped growing, it is assumed by some that the danger is over, as many adults have PKU characteristics in laboratory tests, but have normal mental capacities. Please read *The People's Doctor* newsletter by Robert Mendelsohn, MD, Vol. 9, No. 1. Breastfeeding can be successful, and if the PKU is severe, mother drinks the Lofenalac formula instead of baby.

There are three types of PKU syndrome:

- The true type shows a rapid rise in blood serum phenylalanine. This is usually found in 25% of all low-weight infants.
- Some normal-weight infants have delayed maturing of enzyme systems involved with metabolism of phenylalanine and the amino acid tyrosine. Increased levels of phenylalanine and tyrosine can become normal with taking vitamin C.
- "False PKU" has a rise of serum phenylalinine that is slow but is elevated above true phenylketonuria.

Treatment: Mother should take vitamin C for three days before the screening test. If test needs to be redone, take it at about three or four weeks of age, after mother has taken vitamin C for at least three days, to eliminate a false reading. If it repeats as positive, continue to breastfeed and mother will make the diet adjustments for herself. The company that makes the Lofenalac advises putting the child on a normal diet sooner than the medical standard of practice. (It is not often that a company puts the interest and health of their customers first.) Please read their information, too. They have a hotline and lots of help for you in getting you started with the special diet, and any consultation you may need.

Congenital Hypothyroidism

Congenital hypothyroidism may occur in one out of 4,500 newborns. The thyroid hormone is low or absent because part or all of the thyroid gland has failed to develop. This is more likely to occur if the mother is on thyroid therapy. Early discovery aids the baby to develop normally by giving her proper replacement therapy. Animal fetal cell therapy (from specially developed breeds of animals) has been successful in stimulating normal growth of thyroid glands in babies. You may want to investigate this. Europe has great success with animal cell therapy.

Galactosemia

Galactosemia occurs in 1 out of 25,000 newborns. This prevents the baby from digesting a milk sugar called galactose, leading to problems with the liver and brain damage. This is also treated with a special diet. Recent studies have shown that mothers can successfully breastfeed the galactosemic baby, because there is less galactose in breast milk than in cow's milk. La Leche League has a very informative and recent reprint of a study that is of great help to the parents of a galactosemic child.

Congenital Adrenal Hyperplasia

Congenital adrenal hyperplasia occurs in 1 out of 15,000 births. It is a genetic disorder that causes a lack of a sugar-producing hormone called **cortisol**, and may cause a lack of salt-retaining hormone, from the adrenal gland. This results in severe dehydration and failure to gain weight.

Biotinidase Deficiency

Biotinidase deficiency may occur in 1 out of 40,000 births. It is an enzyme deficiency causing the inefficient use of vitamin B. If left untreated, the child will experience hair loss, skin lesions, hearing loss, poor muscle tone and developmental delay. Treatment consists of biotin replacement orally.

At a workshop I attended, a pediatrician stated very emphatically that these screens can be done at any time before nine months of age. Should a problem be found, damage would be minimized by instituting treatment immediately. It would not repair damage done, but, breastfed babies usually show minimal damage, because breast milk has so many beneficial substances that not only encourage baby growth, but bind up many harmful agents and neutralizes them. If you notice that your baby is sluggish, not doing the things most babies are doing, like following moving objects (people, toys), not interested in "meal times" (nursing), when he used to do those things, then I would advise screening, if it had not been done earlier. Such signs are usually noticed in the first month, and is considered early enough for most problems.

Child Care

All babies, and especially hospital born and those home birth babies that were born posterior, breech, had a tight fit, or a long labor, benefit from Chiropractic care their first week after birth. The adjustment usually is very simple, and requires no x-rays. This prevents "fussy baby syndrome," feeding problems, such as preference to nursing only on one side, wry neck, sleep disorders and other health problems down the road.

Breastfeeding

The most successful breastfeeding mother is one that throws schedules out the door with the trash. Aside from getting up at the proper time in the morning to get breakfast on the table for the rest of the family, so they can go to school or work, and a goal for supper and lunch time, you should not pay any attention to that clock. Breastfeeding babies digest their food much quicker than bottle babies do, so they get hungry quicker. This puts their nursing schedule at about every two to three hours. This does not help Mother get many projects done in one day. Things that once took you only one or two hours to do may take all day. I frequently see a wall hanging that says;

> "Cleaning and scrubbing can wait till tomorrow,
> Babies grow up as I've learned to my sorrow,
> So cobwebs be silent, dust bunnies don't make a peep,
> I'm rocking my baby, and babies don't keep".

There is much good advice in that little rhyme. While rocking your baby, don't forget to support his head. His head weighs $\frac{2}{3}$ his total body weight, so it will be a while before his neck is strong enough to hold his head up.

When putting your baby to the breast, make sure his head is in the angle of your elbow, and his belly towards your waist. With your other hand, drop the flap on your bra, and grasp the breast well behind the brown areola with your thumb and fingers. This is best described as making a "C" with your hand. Resist putting pressure with your fingers by the nipple "so the baby can breathe". Baby will breathe from the sides of his nose, and pressure there on your breast will stop the flow of milk. Now, gently tease your baby by brushing your nipple across baby's lips, in an up-and-down motion. Baby will open his mouth, and when he opens nice and wide, pull him to you, with the arm that is holding baby. At the same time, guide your breast into his mouth, still holding the breast in the "C" hold. Baby should have as much of the brown areola in his mouth as possible.

If he doesn't latch on quite as good as you would like, then slip your finger into his mouth, between his jaws, and he should open up. Slip your nipple out while keeping your finger between his jaws, so he doesn't accidentally bite you. Repeat until he has a good latch. Very large-breasted ladies may need to keep their hand in the "C" position to support the breast. Supporting the breast will give it a little easier shape for the baby to latch onto, and help him breathe out the sides of his nose.

Blisters or cracked nipples are a sign the baby is not latching on correctly, or putting his tongue in the wrong place. The tongue should be visible lying over the front of the lower jaw. To check if the baby's tongue is in the right place, gently pull his lower lip down. The tongue should be visible lying just over the jaw. If it is not, or the baby is making clicking sounds when nursing, *stop*, slip your finger between his jaws, take your nipple out of his mouth, and start all over again. Keep doing this until baby learns how to do it right. If the tongue is curled up to the roof of his mouth, he is really not suckling, he is chewing. The milk will let down, and baby will get enough to satisfy him, but your nipples will be very sore, cracked and may even bleed.

The best investment you can make in your baby is your time. This baby has spent nine months being constantly cuddled, fed and kept warm by mother. The fact that she is born does not end that need. Scripture says, in Leviticus 12:2–5, that we are to give total attention to our girl baby for 80 days after birth. Then we can resume our married life with our husband, and our life is back to normal again. With boy babies, we are to spend only 40 days. Why the difference? Little girls need to learn how to nurture and take care of babies. What better way than from her mother's breast? Little boys need to learn how to nurture also, but God prefers him to primarily learn how to provide for his family and how to protect that family. Ever notice how girls automatically go for the dolls, and boys end up wrestling? It's in the genes that determine whether they will be boys or girls, and that sets the way the boys/girls think, unless someone else messes that up for them.

Much research has been done in recent years concerning what will or will not spoil children. Most mothers know the answer to that in their heart: *spoiling is not giving the child what he needs, but giving him only what he wants.* Picking up a baby because she is crying does not spoil her. She is crying because she feels "left out of the action," she is hungry, needs dry britches, ready for a nap, or she's tired of being where she is (lying on her back, in the infant seat, play pen) and needs a change of scenery, a hug from Mom to let her know Mom is still around. How would you tell people what you need if you could not talk, write, or get around by your self? If the baby cries, she knows you will look for the cause, and then she will be comfortable again. Dying to self, or denying the flesh, will come when she is a little older and personality molding time arrives. . . usually about the time they start to crawl. Discipline in the small child is for their personal safety and teaching them the rudiments of respecting the rights of others. This is done by teaching them what "no" means.

Breastfeeding on demand—that is, *baby's* demand—will assure you of a plentiful supply of milk. This also gives mother an excuse to put her feet up have a glass of water, milk or juice and relax, in the early months after birth. Baby will be on a loose two-to-three-hour schedule by about eight weeks, so you will have about $1\frac{1}{2}$ to $2\frac{1}{2}$ hours between feedings to chase the dust, or hang a load of clothes. With organization and planning, you will work it out.

On days that you plan to do the laundry, or cleaning, you may want to plan an easy, but filling, meal, like a good pot roast, with all the vegetables in the pot with the meat. One-dish meals not only are easy to prepare, they can usually be started early. And you don't have that frantic dash at meal time when you are tired, the family is hungry, and the baby also needs you. Variety will make everyone happy, and they won't mind not having mashed potatoes every day, if they get them two or three times the rest of the week, and it isn't because you want to be lazy. Husbands prefer having a healthy wife to a sickly one, so you need to pace yourself. Working too hard those first few months will dry up your milk. If you do not take care of yourself and allow your body to heal properly now, you will reap what you have sown, with "female" troubles when you get to menopause.

If your baby is fussy, one of the easiest cures is a baby sling, or cuddler. This is a little carrier that holds baby on your chest, leaving your hands free to do what ever needs to be done, from stirring the jelly to washing the clothes. Some babies are frightened to be "alone" in this big outside world, after spending nine months snuggled inside of Mom. Popping them in the carrier beats listening to them cry. Besides crying makes them swallow air, which makes the tummy hurt, which makes them cry, which makes them swallow air, which makes the tummy hurt. . . it just keeps going. Mothers of twins sometimes use a front and a back carrier, until they get bigger. Just remember to trade sides, so each has a turn in front. Those handy sling types would allow a twin on either hip, and you could see what they are doing, and they could see your face too. The baby sling allows for discreet nursing, for those exceptionally busy days.

Other fussy-baby cures that may work, are burping before, during, and after the feeding. A cup of **chamomile tea** for Mother while nursing, or a drop of chamomile tea in baby's mouth, if the baby seems to have colic, and that is very unusual for fed-on-demand breast babies. His adrenal glands may be depleted from the stress of crying, so you may need to get him and you some B complex, especially B_6. Sometimes putting a warm water bottle wrapped in a bath towel in baby's bed with baby on his stomach on top of the water bottle, does the trick (be careful that baby does not get burned). Catnip tea is very good, too. There also are homeopathic colic remedies that work well, and babies like the sweet pills. Or, lie down on the bed with the baby on your chest. Both of you take a nap, and when you wake up, the world will be a better place again. If anyone has a sure cure, I'd be glad to hear of it.

The Scriptures promise that we will have abundant milk in Isaiah 66:11. Often when prosperity is spoken of in the scriptures, it is compared with the abundance of breastmilk. God planned for women to nurse their babies. That's why He put all the proper equipment in place. External size has nothing to do with ability. Size is from the amount of fat under the skin in that particular place. The mammary gland that makes the milk is in the chest wall, in the muscles. I know a lady who was able to supply an intensive care nursery with mother's milk, plus her own baby. She wore a "triple A" cup bra before she birthed and an "A" when she was supplying all that milk!

God knew that if women nursed their babies, lots of good things would happen.

- It is cost-effective. It does not add to the household expenses, because the milk is made from the food mother would eat anyway.
- It is always the right temperature. It never needs to be warmed up.
- It is always available. The supply does not run out after seven feedings a day, and you always have it with you.
- It is always sterile. Harmful substances are neutralized or destroyed.
- (Forgive me for this one) It comes in attractive packages.
- It is full of antibodies to help ward off disease. Most illnesses that mother has been exposed to have caused her to build up antibodies, which are passed on to baby through the milk.
- Nursing your baby encourages her eyes to develop equally, and helps her learn how to focus on close and far away objects.
- It contains a natural laxative, so the baby will not be constipated.
- It contains anti-allergy substances, that will prevent allergies, or minimize their effect.

- It is perfectly designed for your baby, whether he is a premie, handicapped, full term, or a toddler.
- Everyday, they are learning new things about mother's milk, but they cannot reproduce it in the laboratory.
- Family knows they are giving baby the best start possible.

A doctor gave me the first five items on this list a long time ago, and I never forgot them. Science has found 28 substances in human milk that is not found in cow's milk. All the vitamins, minerals a baby needs for health and growth is found in mother's milk. As long as a baby is on total breast milk, all of his nutritional needs for the first year are taken care of. Babies do not digest most solid foods well before the 12th month, and any table foods they eat then, is just because they see the rest of the family eating them. As I started making the list, I kept thinking of more and more, so the list is very incomplete. If you had not thought about breastfeeding your baby, stop and think that God must have thought it very important, or He would have told us about an alternative.

Formula for babies is a very recent thing. Formula as we know it today was not commercially available until the late 1950s. Prior to that, when canned milk became available, it was diluted with water and sweetened. However, the supply was not always dependable. Historically, wet nurses (lactating women who had more milk than their baby needed) were hired, or the baby was fed diluted goat or cow milk. Before canned milk was available, the only time a baby was not breastfed was if mother was extremely ill, had a chronic health problem and the medicine was harmful to the baby, or the child had no mother. Formula companies admit that their product is not as good for babies as breast milk, but they are trying. Formula fed babies have a higher incidence of milk allergies than those breast-fed. They also are sick more often, especially with ear infections, flu, and upper respiratory infections.

All mothers should attend the Le Leche League breastfeeding series, before baby is born and again after baby is born. If there isn't one in your area, write their headquarters: La Leche League International, PO Box 1209, Franklin Park, Illinois, 60131-8209, USA, and ask them to start one. Also ask for a copy of The Womanly Art of Breastfeeding, by LLLI. It sells for $8.95 plus $2.00 shipping and handling. Residents of Illinois and California, please add sales tax. The *The Womanly Art of Breastfeeding* is packed full of information from breast changes during pregnancy to natural weaning, including adding solids. Any woman planning to breastfeed her baby, should have a copy. LLLI is a non-profit organization and donations are tax-deductible, so if you feel led of the Lord, I know they could use help. All LLL leaders have breastfed their children, so you will be talking with women who not only understand, but have experienced and conquered the same problems you have.

The Reluctant Nurser

Most babies are eager to nurse, once they get started, but occasionally a baby will decide to go through the motions until the milk comes in. Then they make up for lost time. Rarely, a baby will refuse the breast completely, but howl for food. This one hasn't caught on to the fact that the cord has been cut and he must work for his supper. If your baby refuses the breast, even after the milk comes in, try pumping your breast and giving the baby breast milk with a bottle. If he refuses breast milk in a bottle, get some Pro-soybee formula. We suggest Pro-soybee, because it has a vegetable base (soybeans) and is less likely to cause milk allergies, but also because it tastes horrid. Breast milk tastes so much better! Ah-haaa. . . now you get the picture (sometimes it pays to be a little sneaky).

Continue pumping your breasts, because we are going to get this baby to nurse and he will like to nurse. You may have to rent an electric breast pump or get a battery operated pump, for efficient pumping. Make sure that you are drinking lots of extra fluids, eating right, and getting plenty of rest between feedings, so you can make lots of milk. Give the baby Pro-soybee formula every four hours the first day. The second day and every day, offer breast milk first at each feeding, if he refuses after tasting it, give him formula. At the end of the second day, start adding breast milk to the formula. One part breast milk, two parts of formula. On day three, slowly increase the amount of breast milk to the formula until it is half and half. Keep it at that dilution through day four. On day five, gradually increase the breast milk ratio to formula until there is more breast than formula, about 3 to 1. Keep it there through day six.

Now remember, you have to keep pumping so your supply will keep up with this demand. On day seven, get some breast milk to bead up on your nipple, and offer the breast to the baby first. You may have to milk your breast and squirt it into his mouth before he latches on. It does require lots of patience and perseverance. Baby Johnny will lick the nipple, and you will have to get another bead of milk on it real quick so he figures out there is a good supply of that good stuff, and latches on for more. Today, you will start limiting the amount of bottle milk and really push the breast. Stop before you and baby are completely frustrated. If "Johnny" is still adamant about not nursing, give him one bottle of formula. Make up as many bottles of breast milk as you can, or get some milk from a lactating mother for this next step. You may need to drip breast milk down your nipple to keep the baby at the breast, until he starts nursing. Sometimes "Johnny" prefers breast milk in the bottle and will refuse the formula. That's okay, we're halfway to the goal. Keep offering the breast and "dripping" milk into his mouth as he mouths the nipple. He will forget that it is not the plastic one, but the real one and suddenly start nursing. Once Johnny latches on and nurses, the war is won.

Now, any time "Johnny" balks at the next step, be persistent, but not at the cost of making baby or you totally frustrated. Remember, you are the adult, your patience is long, and you are smarter than this child. What you want him to do, he will do. . . eventually. If you need to stay at one level an extra day, fine, just keep pumping those breasts. Johnny is getting enough milk if he wets and uses eight to ten cloth diapers a day. This is not a time for disposable diapers, because you can not adequately estimate the amount of fluid output (urine) the baby has. (They contaminate the environment, anyway.)

Breast milk will keep in the freezer above your refrigerator for a couple of weeks, and in the deep freeze at 0°F for three months. Thaw in hot water, swirling the bottle constantly as it thaws quickly. Never put breast milk in the microwave. Microwaves change breast milk; we do not know how seriously, but it is not good.

Pumping is never as efficient as the baby nursing, so your supply will not be quite as good as it would be if he were nursing, but it will get there in 24 hours after he latches on, and discovers the joys of nursing. We know that this works, because a similar regimen is in *The Womanly Art of Breastfeeding*, and we have had the experience with one of our clients. The baby was two weeks old before we started this regimen, but in two weeks he was totally breastfeeding. Once Johnny found out breastfeeding was best, he didn't want to give it up, and was well towards his second birthday before he weaned. La Leche League has a marvelous invention available for about $32.00. It is a small bottle, called the Medela Supplemental Nutrition System that hangs on a cord around mother's neck, between her breasts. There are two thin plastic tubes coming out of the bottom of the bottle, one for each nipple. A valve controls the flow of milk in the bottle until the baby sucks. As the baby nurses, formula/breast milk comes out of the bottle into the tube and into the baby's mouth.

This works for mothers who need to relactate, and even to help adoptive mothers nurse their babies, or help a baby with a sucking problem. If little Johnny-the-reluctant-nurser balks at the breast, this will help him. It gives him just enough encouragement to keep at it, until your milk supply catches up with his demand, and he is willing to keep up the demand. Fortunately, this is a very unusual situation, but if ever faced with it, you won't be as frustrated and bewildered as we were. A very wise doctor (Camilla M. Parham) suggested this program, and we are very glad she did, as the outcome was so very good. Always get help from La Leche League International, for breastfeeding problems. . . they have the answers.

Burping

Most babies burp without any fanfare. Praise the Lord! Then there are others. For these we thank the Lord for with "gritted teeth." Sometimes they swallow air while sleeping, and that bubble is lying there in wait to cause trouble when the milk starts to fill the tummy. Others need to nurse before they get clean britches, because they become so frantic when feeding time is postponed for two whole minutes! You know your baby best, so if your baby has a lot of trouble with gas, check out the burping first.

Some of the more popular methods are with baby peeking over your shoulder, lying on his tummy across your lap, or in a supported sitting position on your lap. All require various pats and rubs on the back to jar the bubble up out of the tummy and out of the mouth. If baby is a spitter the lap lying and supported sitting methods are easiest on the burper. You can direct the wet burp to a "safe" direction and place instead of on your Sunday dress.

If you use the supported sitting position, place one hand on baby's chest, with your thumb and first finger on either side of his chin. Your other hand is free to pat or rub baby's back. It is easier to keep the baby's head up and neck straight to help him burp this way. If he is a spitter, you can direct it into the diaper draped over your hand. If he spits a lot, you can have a bowl ready with your other hand. This makes it easier to estimate the amount baby is losing from his feeding. Some babies burp better this way and do not need a lot of pounding.

After he has burped, the chronic spitter may need to be in a supported semi-sitting position, such as the infant seat provides, to help him keep his feeding down. Fortunately, spitters are not a frequent happening. Some families seem to be more "blessed" with spitters than are others.

Common Questions from Breastfeeding Moms

The following questions and "problems" seem to plague most women who have never breastfed their babies or have not been "successful" and gave it up after the first two or three weeks or months. Breastfeeding your baby is most beneficial if you nurse the baby for nine months or more. Cow's milk is digestible by baby after about one year of age. Goat's milk is slightly better, and formula is very expensive. If Pat has had difficulty nursing her baby beyond the first few months she should get some help here, or go to the Le Leche Meetings.

Fussy, Crying, Cranky Baby

- Is baby hard to burp? Make sure all of the bubbles are out. You may have to interrupt the feeding to keep them from building up and taking up space needed by milk. If baby had a "big burp" offer the breast again.
- Babies need to be cuddled. If yours is unhappy, don't blame your milk. (God made human milk for humans and cow milk for cows.) Look for other reasons: Is baby cold? Bored? Wet? Scared? Lonely? Is it the morning after the family reunion?
- Growth spurts occur around 14 and 21 days, 5–6 weeks and 3 months of age. Babies will nurse almost continuously for 24 to 48 hours as they go through growth

spurts. This answers the law of supply and demand (more baby nurses, the quicker the increased supply will come in). Having a glass of water, juice or milk during these increased nursing times will help increase your supply. (Formula babies need more ounces too, as they grow.) Once the increase is met, the baby will go back to regularly spaced (two to three hours) feedings.

- Mother is eating, taking something that affects the baby: coffee, tea, "no-calorie" drinks, drugs (including over-the-counter remedies for colds, etc.) all have ingredients that may pass through the milk and may affect a sensitive baby. Homeopathic medicines usually do not cause problems, but check with your caregiver anyway.
- Pat may be forcing baby to keep a schedule that does not meet his needs. Be more flexible for a few days and see if he is happier.
- Pat is menstruating. Sometimes the flavor of the milk is affected. Baby can adjust to this. Be patient and persevere.
- Baby is reacting to supplemental formula, a certain "new food" in Pat's diet, or drink. Cut out the suspected item. Pat should drink chamomile, ginger, or saffron tea to calm baby's tummy before or during a feeding.
- Sometimes a colicky baby will have depleted adrenal glands from Pat's diet being deficient in Vitamin B_6. Pat needs to take a balanced B complex vitamin supplement in addition to a balanced diet.

Concern About Not Having Enough Milk
- Not enough stimulation of the breasts. Nurse on both sides at each feeding, making sure the first side is empty before switching. Do not use pacifiers or bottle supplements, and encourage night feedings (sleep with baby in your bed or right next to him so you can scoop him to you for the feeding without waking up too much).
- Baby is going through a growth spurt. Nurse frequently until milk supply increases.
- Started solids too soon. Solids should not be started before 12 months of age. Cut out the solids, nurse frequently until the supply is back.
- Birth control pills, antihistamines (cold or allergy medicines), and diuretics, (tea and coffee affects some

people as a diuretic) may all lower your milk supply, among other side effects.

- Pat is under stress, too busy, or sick. Physical and emotional factors can temporarily affect the milk supply. Relax, drink lots of fluids, and offer the breast frequently. You will weather these temporary "dry" spots.
- Pat is comparing breast milk color with cow's milk. Human milk is "thin" looking, and ranges in color from clear bluish to deep gold. What ever color you have is right for your baby.

Exhausted Mother

- Pat is trying to keep up with all her work and activities she did before baby was born. Slow down! Nursing your baby provides you with a honeymoon. This is the time just for you, baby and your immediate family. A good start means a happier, healthier, more independent baby later on. Extra activities can be worked in after four months. The housework will wait for you. Baby needs you first, so relax. John would rather have a happy wife and baby, than a squeaky clean house and a family that is screaming and falling apart. Take things a little slower. Pace yourself, do one project a day instead of ten and everything will work out.
- Pat needs to rest when the baby takes his big nap.
- Baby sleeping all day, nursing all night and wanting to be entertained. Pat needs to nurse baby more often during the day. Don't put baby off because you are too busy with your housework. Let baby sleep with you at night, so you can sleep more.
- Poor nutrition, lack of fluids. Eat your pregnancy diet while nursing if you have a busy household. Drink 12 glasses of water and juices a day.

Sore Nipples

- Initial soreness is from Pat not used to nursing baby. Make sure baby is latched on correctly. Change baby's position from usual baby carry to the football hold. Massage or effleurage the breast to get milk flowing before baby latches on. As you put baby on breast, take a deep breath and blow it out slowly to the count of 20 as you relax completely to get through the first few seconds of baby's strongest sucking to start let-down. Use an ordinary table lamp two to three times a day as a heat lamp on breasts. A few sips of chamomile tea before each feeding may help. Normal soreness goes away within a week after birth.

- Proper position! Baby's lower arm tucked along Pat's waist like a hug. Baby's tummy against Pat's waist, and mouth open wide to get as much of areola (brown area of nipple) in mouth as possible.
- Frequent feedings before baby gets too hungry (thinks he's starving) and no schedule (!) are easiest on the nipple.
- Nursing too long on each breast the first day or two. Nurse no longer than 15 to 20 minutes after "let-down" on each side the first few days. This ensures both breasts will be equally stimulated at each feeding, and avoids prolonged nursing on the nipple after the milk flow has slowed. When the nipples have become desensitized, the length of feeding is seldom a problem.
- Soap or antiseptic wipes on nipples cause them to dry. The natural oils on the nipples are cleansing and antiseptic. Warm water once a day during your bath or shower is sufficient to keep them clean. If leaking is a problem, wash the breast with a warm washcloth, but *not* the nipples. Washing the nipples more than once a day, even with plain water, can dry out the natural oils and actually cause cracking. Vitamin E can be gently massaged in once or twice a day and does not have to be wiped off for nursing. It is very healing. Exposing the breasts to the warmth and light of sunshine, or an electric light bulb for 10–15 minutes a day can also soothe them.
- Nipples not properly patted dry after nursing. Moist milk left on the nipple can be irritating. Leave your bra flaps down until they are completely dry. Make inexpensive bra pads that can be changed frequently by cutting circles out of receiving blankets, soft cloth diapers, white handkerchiefs or sanitary napkins.
- Bra liners with plastic in them retain moisture. Use them only on rare, special occasions and then only for short periods of time.

- Pat's nutrition is poor, her intake of fluids insufficient. Continue the superior nutrition you had during pregnancy, your vitamins, food supplements such as nutritional yeast (high in B vitamins).
- Rarely, the mother and baby may be passing a yeast infection between them. Persistent, abnormal soreness, a fussy baby who seems to have a sore mouth. White flecks in his mouth which, when scraped off, leave tiny blood spots can tip you off to this possibility. You can nurse through Thrush (yeast infection of mouth) but you and baby must be treated together to avoid reinfecting each other again. Some treatments are vinegar bottom rinses, boric acid wipes, antibiotics or antifungals ordered by doctor, or Homeopathic medicines. Yogurt smeared in baby's mouth helps too. Check with your midwife or doctor for the best thing for you and baby.
- Always wash hands before handling your breasts or feeding baby.
- Leave your bra flaps down and let your blouse or sweater gently rub the nipples.

Baby Has Skin Rash

- Caused by sensitivity to bleach, soap, softener, or fragrances in them. Some fabrics can irritate baby skin. Rinse all laundry well and use natural products whenever possible. Rinsing with vinegar instead of using fabric softeners, then hanging laundry outside helps.
- Reaction to Mother's medication. Check with your midwife or doctor before taking any medication, including prescription and over-the-counter.
- Baby has been fed vitamins, juices or solid foods that he can not digest yet.
- Make sure it isn't heat rash from being too warm, or newborn rash. The latter is from baby's oil glands in his skin not opening or functioning well yet.
- Most newborns have "whiteheads" on their face. These are "milia" and are clogged oil glands. *Do not squeeze or scratch!* They will open up by themselves. Rinse baby's face well with clear water on a cloth. No pressure, please, baby's skin is tender.

Lumps in the Breast

- Fast build-up of milk in the first week or two. Let baby empty them out with frequent, relaxed feedings. Use a hot wash cloth to apply heat to breast and hand express the milk to relieve pressure when you are overfull. You may want to pump the excess and freeze it for future use.
- Bra too tight or pressing against breast, under arms, etc. Get a larger size or go without it temporarily.
- Sleeping in one position all night or in an awkward position that puts pressure on one part of the breast. Change positions more often.
- Going too long between feedings. If you feel you are getting very full, or if you have a let-down, either nurse the baby or take a few minutes to hand express or pump enough milk to be comfortable.

Diapers

I would strongly suggest that you not use disposable diapers if at all possible. Cloth diapers are less expensive in the long run, and there is less chance of toxic shock syndrome. Cloth diapers do not clog up landfills with human waste, causing a potential health problem. The first week, it is a great temptation to use disposables, but you can make your own diaper liners from thick paper towels. These will flush down the toilet, and though the local sanitary district frowns on facial tissue and paper towels finding their way through the sewers, those items will dissolve and process with the other waste. Human excrement will not process out in the landfill when it is wrapped in the paper diaper. The biodegradables are a step in the right direction, but they require direct sun and weather to degrade. . . not a pretty thought with flies, odor, etc. Landfills bury their waste every day, and no one is going to pull your dirty diapers out of the rest of the garbage, so they will degrade faster.

While you are making your diaper liners for the first week (meconium), you might make your own bottom wipes. Using the same thick paper towels (the kind you can clean with, and do not fall apart in your hand), cut each towel in half, fold them to fit a water tight container (Rubbermaid or Tupperware), then pour over them a boric acid solution (the recipe is on the box. Use enough solution to make them damp, but not soggy. Now you have very effective and very inexpensive wipes for your baby. The Boric Acid will prevent diaper rashes. Of course, you want to wash his bottom with soap and water every day, but for the "quick clean up", use the home made wipes. If you like a larger wipe, don't cut the towel. .and you have custom wipes, too.

Pinning the diaper is no longer a problem. There are wonderful clips that hold the diaper securely. They are simple enough for even children to use. A recent item on the market that eliminates pins and clips are diaper covers. They are made of fabrics ranging from all cotton, wool, synthetics and combinations of the above. These either tie on or fasten with velcro! The ones I like best are Bear Bottoms. They are knitted of a waterproof and stainproof yarn. The knit material allows for free exchange of air, but does not allow leakage. . . unless you have half a cup of liquid pooled in that diaper. Bear Bottoms are made at home by a home-birthing, home-schooling Christian mom of seven. Each Bear Bottom is prayed over before shipping to your house, so you and baby will be blessed by the Lord.

Clothing Baby

Of course, baby needs to have diapers, undershirts and some sleepers. The "new" onesies are very nice and double for sleepers in the summer. You need about two dozen diapers a day for the newborn. Usually six dozen is sufficient, because you use some as "burp" cloths. A dozen undershirts or onesies and five or six sleepers will get you from wash day to wash day. Several receiving blankets for light wraps, privacy for nursing in public, and after bath wraps are nice. Two or three warm blankets and/or a bunting for winter, socks, booties and warm hats round out the wardrobe. Beyond that, it's up to you. You can sew a "designer" wardrobe or purchase extras at sales. Whatever you do, you will have fun getting baby's clothes and necessities ready.

The rule of thumb to determine if baby is warm enough is to slip your finger down baby's neck and check the temperature on baby's back. If he is warm there, he is warm everywhere. Baby's hands and feet are usually cold because his circulation isn't working very well yet. Slipping socks over his hands keeps him from scratching his face and will keep them warm. Putting socks on his feet under his sleepers help keep the toes warm too.

Shoes are not necessary until baby is walking outside. Sunday shoes are usually more for show than need. If your floors are cool, you may want to put soft-soled, non-slip shoes on your beginning walker. For your crawler, socks are fine. Keeping those socks on can be a challenge without those handy diaper clips. They will clip socks and slacks together just fine. Little girls may need to wear dark leotards, unless crawling takes place in barefoot season.

Naming Baby

Did you know that the Lord has a name for your child? Revelation tells us that God has a very special name that only He knows about for each of His overcomers. The exciting thing about that is that we will recognize that name when He calls it. I know some folks who have had a special visit from God and when the visit began, God called them by a name they had not heard before, and forgot when the visit was over, but they knew that name was theirs. It was different from the one their parents gave them, but they still recognized it as God's name for them.

The Bible is full of stories that describe God telling parents what to name their child. And that is our example. We are to pray and ask God what the child's name should be. That preparation should begin before the baby is born. One benefit from this is you will know if the baby is a girl or boy. God will not name your boy Sally, or your girl Henry. You may have two names in mind, but the one God wants, is usually the one that you both bear witness to. The other benefit, is *if* you need to call the baby by name at birth, because of an emergency, you will have a name to call. Babies respond to their name at birth. The most often-used reason is to make the baby feel welcomed to the family. Babies have feelings. They hear others being called by a name, except no one calls them by name, so it strikes at their sense of identity. This can delay their early social development.

Some guidelines for those of us who are not sure if we are hearing from the Lord concerning our babies name are:

- Look at the initials. . . do they spell or sound like something that could be used to label a child, such as C.O.W.

for Charles Olsen Wagner. Children can be cruel in their teasing.

- If you have sensitive family members that keep score on who has more babies named after who, you may want to keep your baby's name as generic as you can.
- What does the name mean? Since, biblically, names reflect the child's character you want to name him/her something meaning a promise or blessing. You wouldn't want your child's name to mean thief or sneak.
- Generic names that fit boys *and* girls can be embarrassing or cause the need to repeat the spelling or declare one's gender to every person requesting the child's name. One boy in my grade-school class had to make sure the teacher had the right record for him on the first day of class every year. The new teachers always had him mixed up with a girl in the other class room. That always set off a new round of teasing until he "settled" it. . . again.
- Spelling: keep it simple. Don't try to make a statement of being special with your child's name. They can make their own statement by excelling as a Christian, in their job, etc. You don't want your child to be the last to learn how to write his name, do you?

Jaundice

There are two major types of newborn jaundice. One is **erythroblastosis fetalis**—a pathological, or disease, process. The other is **physiological**—a natural process. The one to be most concerned about is the pathological type, erythroblastosis fetalis. It is a hemolytic anemia of the newborn as a result of maternal-infant blood group incompatibility, specifically involving the Rh factor and the ABO blood groups. It is caused by an antigen-antibody reaction in the bloodstream of the baby resulting from the placental transmission of maternally formed antibodies against the incompatible antigens of the baby's blood.

Erythroblastosis fetalis symptoms are:

- Jaundice occurring within 24 hours of birth,
- Enlargement of the liver and spleen,
- Severe anemia,
- Generalized edema,

- Respiratory distress,
- Cardiac failure,
- Hypoxia,
- Death.

Erythroblastosis fetalis is serious and can cause the baby's death. The disease is thankfully limited to the Rh positive baby born to a Rh negative mother whose blood has been sensitized by either a previous Rh positive pregnancy, or who received Rh positive blood instead of Rh negative. Receiving the wrong blood type in a transfusion is increasingly rare, thank God. It is more likely for a woman to become sensitized from a previous pregnancy. *Always check your client's blood type! Always get client's husband's blood type!*

Some of the more common ways for a pregnant woman to become sensitized to Rh positive blood are:

- Early clamping of the cord
- Miscarriage or spontaneous abortion with vacuum extraction
- Premature partial separation of the placenta
- Pulling on the cord to remove the placenta
- Manual removal of the placenta.
- Spotting during pregnancy
- Cervical capillary bleeding during the pregnancy or labor
- Manual manipulation of cervix during labor.

It is not known why spotting occurs, but some think it may be due to a slight separation of the placenta, which seals over and there are no other symptoms. This could cause some leakage of baby's blood into the mother's bloodstream. Hurrying the placenta to be expelled has also been accused of causing blood exchange between mother and baby. According to current medical knowledge, if RhoGam is not given, and the baby was positive, mother could easily become sensitized. RhoGam is recommended by many physicians in the event of any spontaneous abortion. Many physicians suggest RhoGam to be given at 28 weeks, especially if there has been spotting during the pregnancy. It takes ten weeks for RhoGam to prevent Pat from developing antibodies, so later than 28 weeks prenatally may not give the intended protection (Pat could birth at 37 weeks).

According to the *American Journal of Obstetrics and Gynecology*, Nov. 1984, about 32% of Rh negative pregnant women get sensitized to Rh positive blood.

16%	Sensitized at birth
1½–2%	Sensitized during pregnancy
7%	Sensitized after birth, during third stage
7%	Show sensitization at start of next pregnancy
32%	Total sensitized women

The danger to the baby is not during the pregnancy in which the woman becomes sensitized, it is to any succeeding pregnancies. The next baby that is Rh positive will have the problem, which is the anti-D factor in mother's blood. The anti-D factor transfers across the placenta, and destroys the baby's red blood cells. This can lead to the baby's death if not treated. Treatment may require in utero (if severely sensitized) or post-birth blood exchange for baby. If a baby is severely compromised, he may require a complete blood exchange as a life-saving measure.

Prenatal diagnosis is done by checking the mother's Rh type, Indirect Coombs and antibody titers at the initial visit. If she is Rh negative and her husband is Rh positive, and her Indirect Coombs is negative, Pat should have repeat Indirect Coombs test done every four weeks to check the titer count. If her Indirect Coombs is positive, she is showing antibodies to the baby's blood putting the baby at risk and should be risked out of the home birth service. If it is high, it is confirmed by doing an amniocentesis on Pat and analysis of the baby's bilirubin levels in the amniotic fluid. Higher-than-normal levels result from the breakdown of hemoglobin from the lysed erythrocytes. If her count is extremely high, a transfusion of the baby is attempted, in utero, at a high-risk maternity center. Most often, it is not at the danger level. RhoGam works on the principle that active immunity or antibody formation is suppressed by passive immunity. Once sensitized, RhoGam is useless. The elevated bilirubin levels may not show up until the 37th week. In that event, the L/S Ratio is done with the amniotic fluid sample to see if the baby's lungs are mature enough for birth. If so, and if it is determined that baby can tolerate labor well, Pat's labor is induced, or she will have a caesarean. The baby is monitored for dangerously high bilirubin levels and progress of the hemolytic anemia. If necessary, the baby's blood type can be corrected by doing a complete blood exchange. This is accomplished by simultaneously taking blood out on one side of the baby and putting in new non-sensitized blood in the other.

According to current medical practice, the following women should get RhoGam:

- One who is Rh D and D^u negative;
- One who is not already sensitized and has D antibodies (had a negative Coombs test);
- One whose baby is Rh D and D^u positive;
- One whose baby has a negative direct Coombs test for anti-D (cord blood test).

A crossmatch of her blood and the RhoGam she is to take is done. Then she receives the RhoGam within 72 hours of the birth. Some (Canadian-trained) practitioners are allowing 96 hours, but that is not a usual practice in the United States. RhoGam is made by injecting human volunteers who are Rh negative, with the Rh positive factor, causing antibodies to be formed in their blood. The blood is then drawn and concentrated into a serum for injection. The RhoGam coats any of the Baby's Rh+ blood cells that are in the mother's blood. The RhoGam solution coagulates all the BABY'S Rh-positive antigens so the woman's system does not produce antibodies. These coagulated antigens disappear in about six weeks. No one seems to know where they go or how the body eliminates them. Do they cross the placenta? Do they affect the baby's immune system? No one knows.

The safety of RhoGam is suspect due to the almost total lack of studies designed to answer those questions of safety. RhoGam is a blood product, and subject to contamination. As a wise consumer, it would not be amiss to ask the doctor and the manufacturer what is the AIDS status of this batch of RhoGam. Does this particular batch carry the AIDS antibody? Does it carry the virus itself? What tests have been done to exclude the possibility? Are the tests accurate? The same questions should be raised about serum for infectious hepatitis. Another safety question raised by Paul Hensleigh, MD, of the Department of Obstetrics and Gynecology at Stanford University concerns the potentially damaging effects to the babies in utero. There is some evidence that 4–12-year-old children who were given gamma globulin (RhoGam is a form of human immune globulin), showed some compromise to their immune systems for at least five months. There is reason to suspect a similar effect on the much less mature immune system of a fetus.

Some women become sensitized in spite of having been given RhoGam after delivery. According to the *The British Medical Journal*, April 1987, of 33 deaths from Rh disease in England and Wales in 1985, 8 resulted from sensitization, despite the mother having received RhoGam after previous pregnancies (failure of prophylaxis). In 1984, the failure rate was 9 out of 25.

Some alternative health care people claim that 500 mg of bioflavinoids three times a day will strengthen the walls of the blood vessels sufficiently that they will not "leak" or tear easily, thus lessening the chance of blood transference. Home birth statistics show that home birth mothers have lower transference of blood between mother and baby, resulting in lower incidence of sensitization, because the cord is allowed to stop pulsating before being cut, and the placenta is not rushed in separating by tugging on the cord. *Prevention* of sensitization is the best course in preventing this serious problem in the newborn. However, we cannot be presumptuous!

I recently labor-coached a woman who had had two previous home births with midwives. Pat did not know until I did the routine prenatal profile lab test that she was Rh negative. She knew her husband was positive. At 24 weeks, we found that she had high antibodies (her titer count was rising). She was transferred out of my care to a very good OB/GYN. At 28 weeks, she had her first amniocentesis for fetal well-being. By 36 weeks Pat had had three amnios and on her last amnio the baby was checked for L/S (lung maturity). The titer count was up to a low three. Baby needed to get out! Lungs were mature, and Pat was scheduled for induction. The staff was very supportive and the docs were great. Pat was allowed any position she wanted including walking with the Pit-drip and a portable monitor (new around here). We were in a tertiary care center, too! After the typical hard labor one has with induction, Johnny was born over an intact perineum. He did not have to have transfusion, but he was under two bili-lights and lying on a bili-blanket (has fiber-optic bili-lights woven into the fabric) his first three days, while Pat pumped so Johnny could get her milk in a bottle. Johnny was in the hospital for $2\frac{1}{2}$ weeks and Pat was separated from her other children while she worried over Johnny.

It could have been prevented if the midwives had checked Pat's blood type and taken proper action. There are labs available for midwives, even in illegal states. There are ways to get RhoGam for your clients. If Pat had been able to take the bioflavinoids with her first and second pregnancies, and the midwives had not hurried her dilation, she might have avoided her sensitization. RhoGam would have prevented it, but now she cannot have any more children without risking their lives. She is very highly sensitized and RhoGam cannot be used for her. We were fortunate that we found the problem early, or we could have lost the baby.

Physiological jaundice begins after 24 hours, usually peaking in four to five days. It is caused by the baby breaking down the excess red blood cells that may not have been returned to the placenta before the cord was cut. The good parts of the cells, protein, iron, and minerals, are stored for future use. The rest of the cells are eliminated through the feces, urine, lungs and the skin. While the liver is processing these cells, the extra that are waiting for processing are stored in the fat cells just below the skin surface, causing the skin to become varying shades of yellow. Bilirubin is the yellow or orange coloring of bile, and is a by-product of the processing of the red cells in the liver. The bilirubin usually does not go over 10–12 milligrams per 100 milliliters, and the serum bilirubin usually does not increase at a faster rate than 5 mg/100 ml per day. The conjugated bilirubin (the form the liver changes bilirubin to to help the body excrete it), is less than 1 mg/100 ml. The baby is active, strong, a good nurser and appears to be a happy newborn.

Occasionally the bilirubin continues to climb to 18 or 20 milligrams per 100 milliliters. This usually occurs when mother is taking an aspirin product for post-partum cramping or a cold remedy, caffeine from coffee, tea or soda beverages, sulfa or other drugs that would inhibit the baby's liver from breaking down the bilirubin.

Non-invasive measuring of the bilirubin is using an icterometer. It is a handy little piece of plastic with skin color patches in grades from 1 to 5. This handy gauge shows the comparable serum bilirubin mean and the indirect milligram percent equivalents. The icterometer, about the size of a pocket comb, comes in a soft leather sleeve, that fits nicely inside your Blood pressure cuff bag. It is available from most birth supply folks. You may think it to be expensive, but when you add up the grief and hassle from laboratories, and medical staff that are not supportive of breastfeeding, it is not. This also will be a convincing proof that further evaluation of the baby is necessary, for those who prefer limited allopathic exposure. The National Center for Health has just published a study that states ". . .moderately jaundiced (10–18 mg/dl) pre-term infants do not have any brain damage and should be breastfed and cared for as normal term infants." This means follow the following care plan.

When your baby has physiological jaundice, continue to breastfeed her. It is best to feed the baby every two hours. This gets lots of fluids into the baby and helps her to flush the conjugated bilirubin out of her system. Placing "Patty" near a window in daylight helps too. To take full advantage of the daylight, you want to strip "Patty" down to her diaper, so she has as much skin exposed as possible. The full spectrum of light breaks down the bilirubin stored in the fat cells under the skin quickly.

"Patty" will naturally turn her face away from the sun, so you will not have to blindfold her. If the sun is very bright, you may want to place her back away from the window, or out of direct sun, so she doesn't burn. Cloudy days work, because it is still the full spectrum of light that does the job efficiently. (Sunshine is quicker, but in the northern climes, we take what we can get.) In the winter, protect baby from any drafts from the window, and set lighted, unshaded, non-fluorescent lamps close enough to keep her warm, but not so close she could pull her blanket and topple the lamps on her. If she is just beginning to become slightly yellow, one or two hours will take care of it. If she is more like a lemon, it may take one to three days. You will see a marked difference by the end of the first day in the very jaundiced baby.

The bililights used in the hospital and those available for home use, have a narrow light spectrum, usually the blue spectrum. Some authorities feel the limited light spectrum can have adverse effects on the baby's eyes, liver and DNA. These researchers feel the broad light spectrum such as natural day light or the "full spectrum daylight" fluorescent lights serve the purpose well until more research has been done. Regular fluorescent lights seem to encourage jaundice, so limit your baby's exposure to them the first week, if possible.

Another type of jaundice occurs with **ABO incompatibility**. There is no acceptable way of diagnosing it during pregnancy. This type of jaundice does not seem to cause any problems with the baby. Unlimited breastfeeding is the "cure".

This reminds me of a phenomena called "breast milk jaundice." This is a jaundice that occurs about 14 to 21 days after birth. Occasionally a physician will suggest that you stop breastfeeding, and go on formula, until the jaundice is gone. However, lactation consultants and most midwives concur that only breastfeeding will take care of the jaundice. The baby on formula will learn some bad nursing habits, because it is easier to get formula out of the bottle than milk from Mom. Then you have the problem of relactating. This jaundice goes away in a couple of days anyway, and does not cause any problems to the baby.

Occasionally a baby will have a lot of bruising on the face from a brow or face presentation. This will turn yellow on the second or third day, so you want to watch this baby's chest and eyes for jaundice. The whites of the eyes usually turn yellow at about 12 milligrams per deciliter. I usually compare the chest with the face (brow) when checking for jaundice. If the baby had a tight squeeze through the pelvis, she may show some "hidden" bruising on the face even though she the occiput presented and that "hidden" bruising will show up as jaundice. This usually fades rather quickly.

Circumcision

The next decision new parents need to make is concerning circumcision. It used to be very easy. It was done, because everybody did it and no one thought anything more about it. Now we are becoming aware that that attitude did not make it right. We are beginning to start asking questions about why something is done. Once a client was very offended when I asked if he was considering circumcising his son. "Don't you think God made him according to His own image, that you think it should be changed?" And that is the crux of the matter.

It is human nature to try to improve on everything about us. We color, curl, straighten, and cut our hair, because we don't like it the way it was. When we get bored about rearranging our hair, we start on our nose, or waist, etc. The difference is that all that rearranging of our hair, or nose, only affects our life, not someone else's life permanently. Circumcision is the only time a part of the human body can be amputated without that person's express permission. To amputate anything else without permission of the amputee, is considered medical abuse and malpractice.

The present statistics report that 60% of newborn boys on the east and west coasts are not circumcised. In the midwest, 49% are left intact (uncircumcised). It doesn't take a nuclear scientist to realize that the uncircumcised boy will not feel peculiar in the locker room at school. Yet, that is the most frequent excuse for having it done. Is that why you have your appendix out? The second most frequent is that the boys won't look different from Dad. Do your boys have their tonsils out just because Dad did? Why do we have such a hard time explaining to our children (especially concerning our sexual organs), that some things in the past were done according to available knowledge. We have since learned more about it, and find it not necessary/or needs to be done differently. We are compared to sheep in the Bible, and in many ways we should be like "dumb" sheep. But God does expect us to use the mind He gave us and be wise as the fox.

Not too long ago, it was generally accepted that babies felt no pain, so they did not feel the cut of the knife on their foreskin (even though they cried loudly during the procedure). However, that same baby would squall loud and clear when stuck with the diaper pin or accidentally pinched, and we would apologize for the injury. We believe what we want to believe, and that makes us feel it is all right, no matter what inconvenience it may cause someone else. Babies do feel the pain of circumcision. The reason we always believed they didn't was because we parents were not present when he got circumcised. No one in their right mind would tell the parents that circumcision was very painful, and some babies went into emotional shock from it.

This was of the age that medicine and all its arts was "secret," and only the initiated—the doctors, nurses and their assistants—were able to understand any of it. The "lay" person was not allowed to receive any knowledge without special permission, and then he (the patient) was suspect for wanting to know. Add to this, the average person's lack of knowledge of how his body worked and belief that the doctor knew best. Therefore, what ever he wanted to do or asked if we wanted it done was accepted as a needful thing and no one asked "Why?." Some still adhere to this outdated "ostrich head in the sand" philosophy.

The history and culture of circumcision is well discussed in Rosemary Romberg's book *Circumcision.* She is presently at work on a new book giving the Christian viewpoint of circumcision, that hopefully will be out soon. Since many others have gone into a deep discussion on this subject, I will not. I intend to simply sum up what I feel the Word of God says on this subject.

God instituted circumcision in Genesis 17:10–14, and is proclaimed (if you have not broken the Law of Moses) as a seal of righteousness in Romans 2:25–29. It was to be performed on the eighth day, when the baby's blood level of vitamin K was at its highest, to prevent hemorrhaging (a real and serious complication of circumcision). During the circumcision, the baby also received his name (Luke 1:59). Circumcision was required to participate in Passover (Exodus 12:48), and was a sign of covenant relationship (Romans 4:11). It was necessary as part of the Old Dispensation of law in Genesis 17:10–14.

In the New Dispensation, or the Gospel, circumcision (for the purpose of maintaining a good relationship with God) was abolished Ephesians 2:11–15 and Galatians 5:1–4, because it does not help us concerning salvation, but does force us to keep all of the law, cancelling the redemption of sins through Jesus Christ, and denying the grace of God. The Grace of God has made us (all people) equal in His sight, but circumcision separates and elevates a people above other nations (Colossians 3:11). Circumcision (again, for the purpose of maintaining a good relationship with God) is promoted as a spiritual necessity by false teachers (Acts 15:1), and is a yoke of bondage (Acts 15:10). It was cancelled, repealed and annulled by the Apostles in Acts 15:5-29 and I Corinthians 7:18-19.

Righteousness is a matter of a pure heart and faith in Jesus, not of circumcision (Romans 4:9-15).

"But he is a Jew who is one inwardly, and circumcision is that of the heart in the Spirit, and not in the letter; whose praise is not from men but from God." (Romans 2:29) In verses 25–29 the Apostle Paul scolds the new Jewish Christians for depending on the circumcised flesh to excuse them from the consequences of breaking the law, and lays the case of righteousness by faith in the Lord Jesus Christ, and living a life of submission to God as the way of salvation. In Philippians 3:3 the Christian is described as one who has no confidence in the flesh, but who worships God in the Spirit, and rejoices in Christ Jesus. We "become circumcised with the circumcision made without hands, by putting off the body of the sins of the flesh, by the circumcision of Christ;" that is, submitting to Jesus as He changes our lives from sin to holiness (Colossians 2:11). Today, the Christian is set aside for God by his own dedication, confession of faith and decision for water baptism.

There are few and thankfully rare medical reasons for circumcision. If you teach your children to wash behind their ears, you can teach them to wash the penis, too. Phimosis is a natural condition in the pre-adolescent boy. The foreskin does not need to pull back from the glans until puberty. Washing carefully under the foreskin is all that is needed. While the child is small, gently move the foreskin back only as far as it will go easily, and lather it up well. Rinse off, and any mucus and lint that has accumulated will wash off. While still in diapers, soaking in the bath tub while the rest of his body is getting washed will clear any lint and mucus that might accumulate. *Never force the foreskin back. Never force or use pressure with a Q-tip.* Forcing causes adhesions and scars, requiring circumcision later.

If, after reading all the literature that is available, you still want to circumcise your baby; or your baby is in that very tiny minority that needs circumcision, because the urethra opening is on the side of the shaft instead of at the end, please find a urologist or surgeon that will use local anesthesia. He will still have discomfort immediately after the procedure until the healing is complete, but at least you will have saved him from the excruciating pain of surgery in a very tender place. He can get macho and gutsy when he is emotionally and physically ready by his own decision. Forcing a baby to go through needless pain is considered abuse, if done on any other part of the body.

Immunization

Effective immunization depends on a functioning immune system in the person being immunized. A solution of diluted dead or live disease-causing organisms (protein) is injected into the one to be immunized. The old vaccines were strong enough to give you a mild form of the disease, proving to the provider that you have developed immunity. The modern vaccines, ideally, make you feel "under the weather," and still give you immunity. It is not unusual to have high fevers (over 101°, orally), headache, sleepiness (somnolence), and sometimes sore throat and sniffles.

Complications or reactions from immunization are:

- Occasionally sore or stiff joints
- A very red hard knot over the injection site
- Headache
- Fever over 99°
- Sleepiness
- High pitched crying, or crying that is continuous
- Unusual irritability (the don't-look-at-me-and-if-you-act-like-you-might-touch-me-I'll-scream type of irritability)
- Redness with or without a hard knot or swelling at the injection site   Your child should not receive any more of that vaccine because he is at serious risk of:
  - Convulsions
  - Heart failure
  - Permanent nervous system injury (from seizures to paralysis)
  - Possible death from anaphylactic shock (fatal allergic reaction)
  - Death from central nervous system injury.

There is increasing controversy concerning immunization. The present known vaccines have done marvelously in third-world countries in stopping the cycle of serious epidemics. The danger of most of the diseases that we have vaccines for exist mostly in non-hygienic conditions. Squalor, hunger, and poverty contribute to the severity of the complications. In the well nourished child, with good common sense kind of home nursing care, the complications (in some situations can be serious) are rare. Immunization originally began as protection against life-threatening diseases such as smallpox, diphtheria, and tetanus, but now include most childhood diseases. Ninety percent of children in the United States that do get the common "childhood diseases" do not have complications with them. With improved sanitation, nutrition, and reduced incidence of sweeping epidemics, the risks of having immunizations may outweigh their benefits. There are some diseases, such as **German measles** (3-day measles) that I wanted my daughter and sons to get while they were children. Not because I was particularly mean, but so they would have a lifetime immunity, and would not have to worry about getting them when my grandchildren started coming. The problem I had with that theory was they were too healthy and couldn't contract the disease when they were exposed the first six times. When my daughter and first son finally did get German measles, it was a very light case.

German measles can be very dangerous to the developing baby, especially in the first trimester. If "Pat" should develop German measles then, she is in danger of spontaneous abortion, or a developmental problem in the baby. German measles can cause blindness, deafness or deformity in whatever is being formed at that time. The vaccine lasts for about ten years, so your daughter will need a booster about age 10 and 20. It is not advisable to get a Measles booster if you could be pregnant, or within three months before the pregnancy, because of the danger to the unborn child. The German measles vaccine has been linked with temporary arthritis. Some cases have been reported of the unborn child having contracted the disease with resultant deformity or death when siblings in the family were vaccinated while mother was pregnant.

One of the reasons given for the vaccine is to prevent blindness. Measles does not cause blindness, but a temporary photophobia that mothers used to treat by pulling the shades and darkening the room. This meant no reading and today would mean no television. This photophobia usually ended with no long-lasting effects about three days before the measles rash was gone. The other reason is encephalitis. Excluding the "normal" sleepiness children have as part of the disease, the incidence of true encephalitis in areas of poverty and malnutrition may be about 1:1000. In middle class or upper class children, the incidence is about 1:10,000 or 1:100,000.

The vaccine is associated with encephalitis in 1 per million and with a series of other nasty complications such as subacute sclerosing panencephalitis (a serious inflammation of the brain causing mental deterioration, atrophy, cortical blindness, myoclonus [involuntary contracting of muscles], etc.) and other neurologic and sometimes fatal conditions, i.e., ataxia (inability to coordinate muscle movements), retardation, learning disability or hyperactivity, aseptic meningitis, seizure disorders and hemiparesis (one-sided paralysis). Could the current epidemic of learning disabilities and hyperactivity have anything to do with immunization before the immune system is mature?

The **smallpox** vaccination was discontinued because the complications were worse than the risk of disease. The risk of a person being hospitalized with encephalitis or with eczema vaccinatum and progressive vaccinia was about 10 per million vaccinations. The risk of such serious complications as eczema vaccinatum, accidental implantation of vaccinia on the eye, or superinfection of a variety of skin conditions neared 1,000 cases per million primary vaccinations. It is rare to find smallpox anywhere in the world today.

In 1969 there was an outbreak of **diphtheria** in Chicago, with 16 persons contracting the disease. Of those, four had "complete immunization coverage," and five had completed one or two doses of vaccine. Two of these people had evidence of "full immunity." In another report, one out of three fatalities had been "fully immunized" and 14 of 23 carriers had been "immunized." Sixteen cases of diphtheria out of the entire population of Chicago (3,005,072) does not seem like an epidemic to me. There are about five cases of diphtheria in the United States each year. What it does illustrate is that immunization is not 100% effective and it does have some flaws.

Symptoms are a sore throat with a membrane that develops and covers the back of the throat preventing or making it very difficult to breathe. This membrane can be removed with gauze on the finger, if needed to breathe, but treatment must be directed by a physician and include antibiotics.

Complications are: myocarditis (infection within the heart), and transitory paralysis of the limbs, muscles of respiration (sometimes causing death) or muscles of the throat or eye. Yes, untreated diphtheria can be very serious, even deadly, but we also need to remember that good nutrition and sanitation will prevent most communicable diseases, including the common cold.

The **mumps** vaccine has not yet been proven to last a lifetime, and since the most-feared complication is "sterility" from unilateral (one sided) atrophy of the testicles or infection of the ovaries when contracted in the post puberty teen, it is debatable if pre-teen children should avoid the disease. Orchitis occurs in the post-adolescent male and usually affects only one testis. The other testis will function quite normally and will pose no fertility problems. A tenderness and testicular swelling occurs in 25% of young men, but usually disappears in several weeks with bedrest with no lasting effects. Mump related meningitis occurs in 10% of all mumps cases. Again, three to five times as many males will have meningitis than females.

The **polio** vaccine is very controversial, especially since Dr. Jonas Salk, the developer of the killed-virus vaccine, and other scientists all testified that the few cases of polio since the 1970s were probably caused by the live virus. The live polio virus vaccine is standard practice in the U.S. In Finland and Sweden, there have been no cases of polio in ten years. They use the killed polio virus in their vaccination program. (Maybe we should review our program.) Pregnant women should avoid being in contact, especially changing the diapers of recently vaccinated children. The polio virus can be inhaled and cause problems for the unborn baby.

The effectiveness of **whooping couch (pertussis)** vaccination is only about 50%, and may be the cause of encephalitis and very high fevers after getting the vaccination. This vaccine is regarded as so dangerous that most public health authorities prohibit its use after age six. (Then why are we giving it to our babies?) It is a curious thing that if you have all of the symptoms of whooping cough and you are over nine years of age, you will be treated for bronchitis, or chronic cough.

This happened to a client's family and their babysitter. But the one-year-old was treated for whooping cough, as was the eight-year-old. All three had the very same symptoms and laboratory test results. The difference was age. When inquiry was made, the physician in charge of all three cases said children over nine years of age do not get whooping cough. A second opinion was sought, and that comment was confirmed as "standard thought." However, the "second-opinion physician" disagreed with the opinion of first physician, and put the rest of the family on preventive antibiotics, "because there are a lot of adults running around spreading whooping cough in our area." (We were in the middle of an outbreak in that area at the time.) "Second-opinion physician" also does not believe in routine immunizations, and the first physician does. The vaccine for whooping cough has been around for at least 40 years, because I had it as a child. That means that there are "a lot of adults" that no longer have immunity, because they fall in that 50%. By the way, the baby sitter was immunized about ten years prior to getting the "bronchitis" that gave whooping cough to the one-year-old.

Side effects from the pertussis (whooping cough) vaccine include; high fever, a transient shock-like episode, excessive high pitched screaming, somnolence, convulsions, encephalopathy, and extremely rarely, thrombocytopenia (deficiency of clotting elements in the blood). The side effects can occur up to seven days after receiving the vaccine. According to the 15th meeting of the Panel of Review of Bacterial Vaccines and Toxoids with Standards and Potency, complications of pertussis vaccinations are not regularly reported, because "physicians are not cognizant of the importance of reporting untoward reactions or may be unaware of their clinical features." Considering the litigious society we live in, we can understand why "untoward reactions" are not reported.

Pertussis vaccine has the highest and most severe complications of all vaccines, and has been linked to crib deaths by several studies. You may want to read *DPT: A Shot in the Dark* by Harris L. Coulter and Barbara Loe Fisher, for an in-depth study on the Diphtheria/Pertussis/Tetanus vaccine.

This brings us to **tetanus**. Tetanus needs the intestinal tract of farm animals and manured ground to develop. In other words, pastures and gardens or fields that have been fertilized with barn manure. Horses are used to develop the vaccine. The tetanus organism is injected into the horse, and after a short period of incubation, blood is withdrawn from the horse and the vaccine serum is made. If you are sensitive to the horse serum, another form made from human globulin (Tetanus Immune Globulin, Human). T.I.G. is used for those that have had less than the full series of four injections, and have received a serious wound. It is effective to prevent tetanus, but not able to develop antibodies (no lasting protection). It is the rusty nail from the barn, corral, etc. where farm animals have been in the last ten years, or the farm/barn fresh manure for your garden or lawn that *may* harbor the organism. If you live in a new subdivision (less than ten years old) that was farm land before the houses were put up, then maybe you will want tetanus immunization. If you are around horses daily, or at least frequently, you also will want to have tetanus shots every 10 to 20 years.

It was once thought that a tetanus booster should be given every year. Now most authorities say every 10 years. If you work with farm animals, and because tetanus toxoid has horrid neurological complications, such as loss of use of arms, loss of voice, difficulty in swallowing, dizziness, weakness of legs, staggered walk, and abnormalities in heart function, among other things, I suggest no more often than every 10 years, because the vaccine lasts for 12 years. T.I.G. has not been associated with reactions, but because it is made from human serum it may, but very unlikely, contain infectious material. All globulin products are tested for blood-borne pathogens and are as safe as is humanly possible.

The greatest incidence of tetanus is about 100 cases per year in the United States, since 1976. Less than ten cases are found in those under 30 years of age, and are rarely fatal. Immediate vaccine reactions are usually mild and rarely severe. Long-term side effects are unknown.

First aid for all puncture wounds is hydrogen peroxide. If it bubbles and fizzes, there is infection present. The fizzing usually works dirt and harmful organisms out of the wound. It should be watched, however, for reddening of the area, swelling, heat around the wound, or red lines radiating out from the wound. Antibiotics or antibacterials (goldenseal powder) should be applied after cleaning and a clean dressing kept on the wound. Apis or Ledum are homeopathics specific for puncture wounds or insect bites. If redness, etc., should occur, or the above conditions suggest possible exposure to tetanus please seek a health professional for care or consultation.

Other vaccines that are being pushed today are **varicella** (chicken pox), **acellular pertussis** (whooping cough with fewer side effects than the other vaccine providing immunization is done after two years of age but still dangerous), **pneumococcal** (pneumonia) and **hemophilus influenza, type B** (HIB) for meningitis. Please do some independent reading in the books I have listed in this section and determine your child's vulnerability to these diseases before going to the nearest clinic. Just because it is free or costs a lot, does not make it good. "Good intentions" pave a very well-known and travelled road.

There is a lot of concern that vaccine induced immunization suppresses the immune system when done too early in a child's life. Children that have not been immunized and were breastfed appear to be able to throw off exposure to disease with no more than light cases. Most physicians start "baby shots" at three months of age, because that is a routine well-baby check up, and parents are still a little nervous about knowing if their baby is as healthy as they think he is. If they waited to start the immunizations at six months, the parents would be accustomed to caring for the baby and have the confidence that they know what they are doing and possibly would reject the immunizations. Baby's immune system is not working efficiently until she is six or more months old. And that is where the controversy concerning immune system depression begins. My personal opinion is that we live in an age where we need our immune systems working at top efficiency, and I advise everyone to pray and seek God's wisdom and direction, and to get informed. Read the following publications, pray and then do what your conscience tells you to do. We did not get our 19-year-old immunized, when he was little, and his health has been better than his brother and sister that did get immunized. The only communicable diseases he has had was a very light case of chicken pox (after many deliberate exposures) a few colds and a light case of the flu every two to three years.

Please read *But Doctor, About that Shot* by Dr. Robert Mendelsohn, *DPT, A Shot in the Dark* by Harris L. Coulter and Barbara Loe Fisher, *Immunization: The Truth Behind the Myth* by Walene James, *The Immunization Decision* by Randall Neustaedter and *Vaccination, Social Violence, and Criminality: The Medical Assault on the American Brain* by Harris L. Coulter before getting your (baby shots) vaccinations and immunizations for your children. These books will also give you the information you need about the complications and incidences of the diseases as well as problems with the vaccines and length of immunization. The alternatives to vaccinations and immunizations are also given. Scripture is always a good place to go when needing answers to life's problems. Exodus 8:22–23, Deuteronomy 7:15, Psalm 16:10–11, Luke 10:19, Isaiah 53:6 and I Peter 2:24, and James 5:13–16 deal with illness and God's approach to health. With a little time and patience, you could find lots more. Leviticus 19:28 deals with "cuttings and marks in the flesh" and usually is interpreted as referring to tattoos, but some vaccines are scratched into the skin. Did I mention the definition of immunization? Webster says it is immunity or exemption from something. . . note Deuteronomy 7:15.

Should you choose to immunize, please wait until the baby is at least six to twelve months old to start. The vaccine reactions are not as severe then, and the immunity "takes" better. Your baby is getting antibodies from your breast milk of every disease you have built up immunity for, as long as she is nursing. So that is the logical time to start. Of course, common sense says that you protect your child from others coughing and sneezing on them, or sharing a toy with someone suffering from a sore throat. This is easier said than done when in church or around folks with those symptoms. (Parents are not always aware that junior has a sore throat, either.) If your child is well nourished and gets proper rest and is not in a "run-down" condition, he will be able to overcome the majority of germs that are besetting others.

If you choose not to immunize, you may need to write a letter to the school authorities that it is your conviction not to immunize. Your church does not have to preach against immunization for it to be your religious conviction, in most states. It does not have to be on church stationary, in those states. Some states/school districts may want your letter co-signed by elders or pastors. Some parents have "formed a church" to fulfill the letter of the law. You may want to check your local laws. There may be legal limits as to how few can be in your "church". If you home school, you do not have the problem.

A suggested form is:

```
Date: _____

To Whom It May Concern:
In accordance with the (state statute/Bill
#xx, number yy), under the title  "EXEMPTION
FROM IMMUNIZATION", I hereby declare that I,
as a parent (or guardian) have responsibility
for _____ (child's name),
a minor enrolled in school, I withhold my
consent and request that said minor be exempt
from any and all vaccinations on the grounds
that such is contrary to my beliefs and
convictions.

(Signed)_____
        Parent or Guardian

_____
Address

_____
Telephone
```

I can't emphasize enough that you must do your own research on such important decisions as this. Space does not permit me to go into immunization in great detail, especially when others have done it so well already. Gather your information, read, talk about it with your spouse and pray. Once you have your direction then follow that leading knowing that is the best thing for you to do, at this time of your life, with the information that you have.

MAPLE SYRUP URINE DISEASE is peculiar to Old Order Mennonites and some other Mennonites, especially in Pennsylvanian communities. MSUE can be more serious than PKU, in that irreversible brain damage begins on the third day noted by a high pitch scream. Treatment consists of a protein restricted diet, caloric support, and supportive care in the acute case. For long term care a synthetic diet that is deficient in branch amino acids is given. MSUD is fatal in 1:175,000 newborns. Thank God it is so rare in the general population.

CHAPTER 11

COMPLICATIONS AND CHALLENGES

There are a multitude of "things that can go wrong" during pregnancy, birth, and after birth. Fortunately, they are a small percentage of from 5% to 10% of all pregnancies, depending on your "authority." Even the most alarmist (10%) has to agree that this is not a great number out of all pregnancies, when you include the high risk with the low risk woman or baby. The high-risk woman has the highest percentage of problems, and the normal, low-risk woman has the least number of problems, if any. There's your incentive, ladies, to stay low-risk!

The easiest way to stay low-risk is to be diligent in your prenatal care. Eat the proper foods in the proper amounts, *every day.* You can fool your caregiver the first few months by cheating on your diet, but you cannot fool your baby. Baby needs optimal nourishment *all* of the time, especially in the first trimester when everything is being formed. The brain continues to grow for six months after birth, so if you are going to cheat on your diet, what part of your baby do you want to take chances on? Is the outside more important than the liver, or heart, or brain?

Yes, I too can name many a child that has turned out "all right" when mother had a "rotten" diet. Did it ever occur to you that it was because of God's grace and mercy? Are you brave or foolish enough to be risking the sin of presumption, because you "know" better? Remember, God holds us responsible to live what we know. The Brewer Diet for pregnancy takes into consideration the wide variety of lifestyles and incomes, so you no longer have a valid excuse. And, until I find a better and simpler diet, you will have to listen to me push the "Brewer Diet."

Living a balanced life is the key. This means you must do all you can do in the physical realm of eating "right," monitoring your health and the baby's health, and getting your exercise, and educating yourself in good prenatal care, birth and parenting. The other half is just as important: preparing yourself spiritually—realizing what God desires of you and taking the proper steps to conform to His will in your life. What is God's plan for you in the area of parenting? Are there areas in your life that need improvements? Do you have habits that you do not want your children to develop? Maybe this is the time to overcome these things. Growing closer to Jesus, making Him a living, vital part of your life enables you to make these improvements.

The Blood of Jesus was shed that you might be free of infirmity, disease, and have abundant life both physically and spiritually. We need to appropriate His healing and His abundance in our lives. I Peter 2:24 tells it like it is—Jesus did it all. He died for our sins, gave us His righteousness and shedding His blood from the beating and whipping he bore in Pilate's courtyard and then in His crucifixion, took on all of our illnesses, diseases, infirmities and sin, that we might be healed! Hallelujah!

Have you ever taken note of the past-tense of the word "healed" in I Peter 2:24? That means we were healed 2,000 years ago when Jesus bore all of that for us! What we are experiencing now in our bodies is something the devil is putting on us as a result of sin or stressing our bodies by not eating and resting properly. We should pray first, call for the elders to anoint us with oil, confess our sins, and make sure we didn't open the door inviting Satan in to afflict us (James 5:15–16).

If there is no relief and we need assistance from a physical healer, then by all means, go. "There is therefore now no condemnation to them which are in Christ Jesus, who walk not after the flesh, but after the Spirit. For the law of the Spirit of life in Christ Jesus hath made me free from the law of sin and death (Romans 8:1). It would be wonderful if the Church of

Jesus Christ was at that place where we would all be walking in perfect health and righteousness, but we are not. That day will come when God's people get serious and return to his will. In the meantime, we need to do our best to remain under the Blood covering of Jesus and eliminate those things from our lives that hinder us from being all that we can be.

There are many complications possible. But, when you get right down to it, there are very few true emergencies—please study the charts below. Our own ignorance of how the body works has been used against us because we have put blind trust in the "experts." We have been told that "There are so many unpredictables, and when something happens, it happens so quickly that (without whatever technology they are pushing at the moment), terrible things will happen to Pat or the baby".

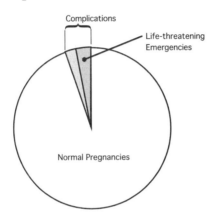

Figure 11-1: A comparison between the incidence of normal labors and those resulting in complications.

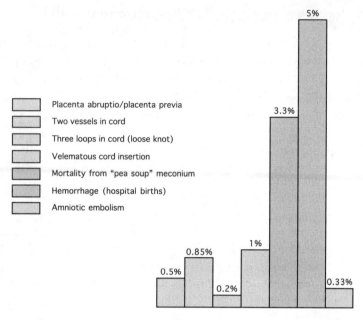

Figure 11-2: A breakdown of the life-threatening emergencies—the 3% in the previous chart. The above percentages are of the life-threatening emergencies only; for example, placenta previa and placenta abruptio occur only 0.5% of 3% of the time. Also note that the above percentages don't add up to 3% because multiple complications can occur simultaneously, and the above chart does not give an exhaustive list of all possible complications, only the most common.

Let's look at those predictable possibilities we have not already covered, and then at the unpredictables. We will only deal with the most common ones, in the time frame that they could possibly occur during the childbearing year. There are many books on the market that specialize in the various complications and anomalies that can occur in women and their babies. If you are a midwife, or live in an area that seems to have more than its share of congenital difficulties, I suggest that you purchase good reference texts covering neonatal and maternal problems. *Williams Obstetrics* by Pritchard and Mac-Donald, probably has the most comprehensive list and percentages of occurrence for both. Please keep in mind all these problems are only—at the *very* most—10% of all pregnancies. With good prenatal care as outlined in this book, your percentage will drop to about 5%.

Metabolic Toxemia of Pregnancy

One of the major predictable complications is otherwise known as **eclampsia** or **toxemia** for short. In Dr. Tom Brewer's book, *Metabolic Toxemia of Late Pregnancy*, a discussion of the myth that MTLP is a disease of late pregnancy, suggests that it really is a liver disease caused by poor nutrition. The liver needs a certain amount of protein to direct the cleansing process of the body. If the liver does not get proper nutrition, it does not release the proper enzymes to the kidneys. The kidneys then do not filter out waste products from the blood. These wastes are then stored in the cells throughout the body, causing edema. This makes the heart work harder, raising the blood pressure. The accumulated wastes begin a toxification process in mother's body and things begin to snowball, leading to convulsions and danger to mother and baby. Untreated, maternal mortality rate is 10% and infant mortality rate is 25%. The symptoms of MTLP, not necessarily in order of progression, are:

- Headache
- Dizziness
- Visual disturbances
- Anorexia or lack of appetite
- Nausea
- Vomiting
- Upper abdominal (epigastric) pain
- Swelling of the face and extremities
- High blood pressure
- Proteinuria
- Hyperactive deep tendon reflexes (clonus)
- Tenderness around kidneys upon percussion
- Decreased levels of Human Placental Lactogen (HPL)

All of the above are also symptoms of liver disease or malfunction. The best treatment is prevention. *If* caught early, strict attention to a high-protein, high-caloric diet will stop or minimize MTLP. If not treated or it has advanced, the only allopathic treatment is magnesium sulfate I.V. during labor to prevent convulsions and keep the blood pressure down. *If* the toxemia is acute, and the magnesium sulfate is not "holding" the blood pressure or the baby is showing distress, Caesarean birth may be mandated.

The "Rollover" blood pressure test is a simple, non-interventive, cost-effective screen to determine if Pat is susceptible to MTLP before these symptoms become frequent or "chronic." Take the blood pressure while Pat sits on the bed or examining table, just before she lies down, and then again as soon as she lies down (in the same arm). If there is as much as 10 millimeters of mercury difference between the two readings, Pat is in danger of developing toxemia (MTLP). If you do this at 28 weeks, you have an accurate predictability rate and plenty of time to correct her diet and get things turned around.

Laboratory tests to confirm toxemia are:

- Serum albumin
- Serial hematocrit
- 24 hour quantitative urinary protein loss
- Human Placental Lactogen

Because of the impaired liver function, placental hormones "pile up" in the liver. Serum estrogen and progesterone levels are higher than normal. High hormone levels frequently cause ripening of the cervix earlier than expected, and very often causes the toxemic woman to go into spontaneous pre-term labor.

The cure is simple and preventive care: *eat protein!* Eat nutritious foods and stay away from the junk foods with high calories but no nutritional value. Follow the Brewer Diet! Use the CCE Diet Cards! They are the easiest ways to get the best nutrition for you and your baby. MTLP is common among first time mothers, but *it is preventable.*

Intra-Uterine Growth Retardation

IUGR is an infrequent, major, but preventable problem. IUGR is abnormally slow or arrested growth in the baby due to Pat not eating properly. She will spill protein in the urine, and the baby will not be growing like it should. Baby should average 1 cm growth per week of pregnancy after 20 weeks. Any baby weighing less than 3000 grams (6 lb, 10 oz.) at birth, is in the risk group with the highest mortality rate. See the fundal height sketch for weekly growth expectation. This lady may be having some serious psychological problems with being pregnant. She doesn't eat because she will get "fat." If she gets "fat", she will no longer "be attractive" and she will not be "popular." Or, she is afraid the baby will be "too big", leading to more fears.

Actually, it is the same as anorexia. She is getting a lot of negative attention (nagging), and needs to learn how to receive attention in positive ways. Most women with these attitudes have a very low self-esteem. The family may have to re-evaluate their treatment of each other, and change their ways for long term improvement in Pat. If forced to eat, she may force herself to vomit. Vomiting can cause dehydration and mess up the electrolyte balance in her body, causing real medical problems in the kidneys, liver, and heart. This compromises the baby even more.

What Pat does not realize, is she is starving her baby and not only is the baby in danger of having serious developmental deformities, congenital defects, central nervous system damage, and or brain damage, but he could die. Babies that survive IUGR are usually mentally retarded. Intense counseling is required in a very short period of time. The trick is to get Pat to show up for that counseling. She may even need spiritual deliverance.

This woman is usually very selfish, and sometimes the only way to get through to her, is to let her know that if she does not change very quickly:

- She cannot have her baby at home,
- She is risking severe maternal complications, i.e., hemorrhage, toxemia, kidney failure,
- She can be prosecuted for child abuse with possible jail time,
- Siblings will be removed from her, requiring court action to get them back,
- Baby could die, be deformed or severely retarded.

The courts have become very interested in the unborn child. They either rule to abort, or prosecute the mother for abuse. In both instances, the court feels that the State has a vested interest in the child (meaning, the child "belongs" to the State). If mother has been found to be "negligent or abusive" she may be required by court order to do any or all of the following:

- "Terminate" the pregnancy (murder the baby by abortion) if she does not want the child and the pregnancy is within time period of legal abortion in the state,

- Take good care of her child until born, or be in contempt of court,
- She may have to serve remainder of pregnancy in jail to ensure compliance to court's decision.

(With the recent 1991–1992 changes in the abortion laws, this mandated abortion/murder may not be a court option in your state.) After birth, the State will remove the baby from the mother's care and place him in foster parent care until the mother relinquishes baby for adoption or mends her ways. The precedent for the above has been set in the courts with drug-abusive women, specifically cocaine and alcohol abusers. If mother has been found negligent with her other children, and they are in court-ordered foster care, you can be assured that she will be scrutinized concerning the care of this baby. If you are dealing with new Christians or in the mission field, you may find yourself in this situation. Women that have had eating disorders are at risk for IUGR.

The other predictable problems were discussed in Chapter 5, Risk Factors. I won't go into them again here.

Unpredictable Challenges

Unpredictable challenges in the first stage of labor include the following:

Lack of progress is usually caused by uterine inertia due to a tired, hungry Momma, or a very distracting birth team. In Isaiah 37:3 the messengers to Hezekiah verbalize what a woman is feeling with contractions that hurt but no progress is being made. Infrequently, lack of progress is caused by dystocia or asynclitism. Both of these conditions have similar cures.

Dystocia is a lack of compatibility between the passenger (baby) and the the passage (pelvis and muscles). If the dystocia is not severe, such as a ten-pound baby and a narrow pelvis, then try to help baby get into the pelvis by opening it up. Squatting; walking up and down the stairs; stepping up and down on simulated stairs; while standing on the floor, place one foot up on the seat of the kitchen chair, or a child's chair; doing pelvic rocks; hands and knees; all these are helpful positions.

Some midwives report success with two people standing on either side of the laboring client and applying pressure to the iliums. With Pat placing her arms across the shoulders of her midwives, each midwife puts her near arm around Pat and pulls the (far) ilium towards her. Or, if more strength or a change of position is needed, she pushes the near ilium away from the midwife towards Pat. This is to open up the mid-plane and the inlet of the true pelvis. It requires stamina and strength. In the same standing position, and pulling the ischial spines open (midwife pulls near ischium towards her-self), can open the outlet of the pelvis. These procedures: squatting, raising one knee or the physical spreading of the bones can open a pelvis from 1 to 2 centimeters! Anytime you apply pressure to the bony parts, expect Pat to be very sore for a few days. (The midwives will be too.) Arnica is helpful for sore muscles.

If you have true dystocia, and baby is unable to enter the pelvis or progress past the mid-pelvis a caesarean may be your only choice. Forceps and vacuum extraction will not bring a baby through a pelvis that is too small.

Fortunately, this is a rare situation unless the couple are from certain different ethnic groups. Asian women, married to non-Asian men have a 95% caesarean rate because non-Asian men have larger bone structure and pass that genetic factor on to their children. Asian women, raised in their native country, generally have a smaller bone structure especially in the pelvis. This is probably due to the higher incidence of malnutrition and/or diet differences. Couples of the same ethnic group rarely have this problem. Afro-American and Anglo combina-tions do not have this difficulty, but African women married to Anglo men do have slightly higher caesarean rate than their Afro-American counterparts. Ethnic Asian women raised in Europe or America, married to Anglo men are less likely to have this problem. This may be a culture problem due to eth-nic intolerance and differences in birthing attitudes. Many subtle culture differences may undermine a woman's self-con-fidence in her daily life, until her confidence in her basic ability to do such an important thing as give birth "in the right way" can be destroyed. This leads to lots of little "failures" leading to the "ultimate failure". . . the caesarean birth. It may also be her way of saying, "I am American. I give birth like modern American women. Please accept me."

Circumcised women may be placed in this category, because the attendant does not know how to help her birth her first baby in America. The majority of female circumcision is done in African countries, but other religious and national peoples may consider it to be a necessary rite of puberty, especially those living in rural areas. The American midwife should exam the potential client with female circumcision, to determine if she is comfortable attending her at home. Female circumcision does cause a lot of scarring, with some altering and removal of the physical landmarks. If she has had children in her home country, the repair may have been what Americans consider unusual. This will require episiotomy to allow the baby to be born. The American midwife will have to determine if that couple desires the "African" type repair or the "American" style that only sews the perineum together, leaving the vagina open for "easy" intercourse. Should they desire the "American" repair, the midwife will need to be prepared to stitch and stop any bleeders or apply hemostatic goldenseal to the raw edges of the labia.

Traditional "African" repair stitches the labia majora closed, leaving a small hole for the urine and menses to exit. The labia minora was excised at the time of circumcision of the clitoris. The husband is to open the vagina for sexual intercourse after postpartum healing, just as he did when they married. Traditionally, a hot knife is used.

Asynclitism is the abnormal attitude or presentation of the parietal aspect of the fetal head to the maternal pelvic inlet in labor. The sagittal suture is parallel to the transverse diameter of the pelvis but anterior or posterior to it. In other words, the baby's head is tilted slightly to one side instead of being in a straight line with his back. He might be "hung up" on one side of the inlet or the other, or he extended his head too soon and got stuck on the pubis.

The asynclitic baby is trying to descend through the pelvis without adjusting his presentation. If the pelvis is already on the narrow side, it may be just enough to keep the baby from descending. Doing one or all of the following will help get labor back on track: pelvic rocks, the "flip-flop" exercise, feeding the laboring couple, giving Pat a massage, darkening the bedroom so she can rest or nap, clearing out the folks that are distracting Pat and "scattering" her birthing strength, or giving her some Pulsatilla homeopathic remedy. If Pat lies on her left side when she rests, the baby will slip into place. However, if the

baby is hung up on Pat's left, she should h
Knee-chest will get a baby off the pubic bon
the vertebrae and helping baby to tuck his chi

Fetal distress is a result of prolonged feta
cord compression (pinched cord), tight cord arou
neck, head compression, maternal distress, hypo
dered maternal and fetal circulation), or poor positi
Stress is caused by something making the baby unco
or react to a strain on his situation. Distress is u. ⸺ oived
stress, and has become an acute, possibly critical situation.
Stress should be resolved before distress develops, because
distress can be life threatening.

If the baby is exhibiting a racing heartbeat, over 160 per
minute, it may be due to a compressed or pinched cord. The
cord may be pinched between the pelvis and the baby's head
(occult or nuchal cord). Pat should be placed in a knee-chest
position so the cord can float out of the way. After ten to fifteen
minutes in the knee-chest position, help Pat to roll either right
or left—in the direction opposite the back of the baby. Check
the heart tones and if they have returned to normal, proceed
with helping Pat get up on her feet. Help Pat get slowly up to
the hand-knees, then slowly up in a standing position. She
may have to stop at the kneeling position if the room seems to
be going in a different direction than standing still. After the
room stops moving, Pat should then walk around for about 30
minutes.

If the heart tones have not changed, go back to the knee-
chest position. Listen to the heartbeat in this position. If the
heart tones do not improve, you should seriously consider
transporting, especially if the baby is not expected to be born in
the next few minutes. Give Pat oxygen at about four to six
liters per minute. If this improves the baby's heartbeat, listen
through one complete cycle (beginning of one contraction to the
beginning of the next), because you want to know how baby
handles the contractions. If baby does well with the oxygen,
your next decision is: how long will your oxygen supply last?
Do you have just enough to transport, or just until the ambulance arrives, or do you have enough for the duration (however
long that may be) of labor? Consider that baby will also need
some oxygen for at least a few minutes after birth, because he
is compromised and will probably need help at first. Unless

...ves are experienced, you have at least two midwives ...t, a doctor willing to come to the birth to help, and/or ...ur protocols (signed by a doctor) allow you to proceed at home, you should transport before birth, because fetal distress is a serious situation.

Isaiah 65:23–24 promises God will hear our prayers and answer them with healthy children. Isaiah 66:7–11 states we will birth our children as soon as we go into labor, and that we will rejoice with our friends concerning the birth. It also promises that our children will receive an abundance of milk from their mother's breasts. This would be a good time to pray and ask God to stand by His Word on behalf of the baby. Calcium tincture and red raspberry tea is of help to the baby and mother.

If baby's heart rate is slow or erratic at 110 or less between contractions and dip even lower with the contraction, baby is in serious distress. You must give mother oxygen, place her on her left side or in a sitting position, whichever the baby prefers, and *transport*. If birth is imminent—in the next two or three contractions, get the baby out as fast as you can. You may have to cut an episiotomy, because this is not the time for an "easy over the perineum" birth.

Bleeding Before, During, and After Birth

God promises in I Timothy 2:15 to save us in childbearing if we continue faithful in Him. Ezekiel 16:6 is a "First Aid" verse. It is applicable to bleeding and to CPR situations. The KJV says God saw us struggling in our own blood, and said "Live!", and we lived. Psalm 139:13–16 describes the care God took when he made us, and how he knew us before anyone else did. These verses imply that, since our God is so concerned about us, He will protect His creation. Especially when we ask Him to.

Spotting of dark red blood is a sign of old blood at any time in your pregnancy. Take it easy for 24 hours. If the spotting stops, return to daily work very slowly, start with doing meals one day, mending and the meals the next, etc. Gradually get back to regular routine in a week. If the spotting changes to bright red, it is a sign of miscarriage (spontaneous abortion) in early pregnancy and premature labor in the second and third trimester.

Sabina 6x is known to stop threatened abortion. In early pregnancy, spotting may also be a sign of partial separation of the placenta. Rest in bed, getting up only to go to the bathroom (don't strain to move your bowels). Sometimes nothing helps and Pat will lose the baby anyway. Then we have to accept that God has called the little one to Himself, go through the grieving process and rely on Jesus for our strength in continuing to live. (Some parents have received comfort by burying the tiny one in a quiet spot in the yard, and having a very private committal service. Babies less than viability are not accepted by a funeral director. Anyone buried in a cemetery must be embalmed, and that is almost impossible with a three-month gestational age baby.) Usually the baby has died sometime before the cramping or spotting began, and is passed along with the clots, unnoticed.

When spotting or greater bleeding occurs in the third trimester, suspect an **abruptio placenta**. If the bleeding is in the last couple of weeks, the client could be effacing, thus disturbing a low-lying placenta or a **placenta previa**. Blood from an effacing cervix will be mixed with mucus and look like menstrual blood, accompanied by a stretching sensation. Placenta blood is bright red, and will be more than cervical blood in quantity.

Abruptio placenta can be occult or frank. If occult, the bleeding will be between the placenta and the uterine wall. This means the center separated, but the margins remained attached. This is good and bad. The good part is the baby is getting some oxygen from Pat where it is attached. The bad news is the baby is possibly bleeding out at the point of separation. Pat is bleeding at the point of separation too! The hidden bleeding is a serious thing, because it can be overlooked. Occult abruptio placenta signs are:

- Pat has noticed spotting when first getting up in morning;
- She has had cramping, varying from mild to severe, followed by spotting;
- Placenta site becomes hard or soft;
- Placenta not heard at attached site (locate placenta as early as you can during prenatals);
- Sonogram confirms separation;
- Fetal heart tones weaker, irregular (danger sign);

- Tenderness in abdomen, especially at site of placenta attachment;
- Pat has a feeling of doom, or something is seriously wrong. Pat may or may not have cramping. If she has cramping, it may be from mild to severe. She may have a tearing or ripping sensation instead, like a Band-Aid being pulled slowly off her arm.

The only occult abruptio I have seen was very atypical, just as the above symptoms show. Pat had been complaining of spotting when she first got up in the morning, for several days. We were unable to find anything wrong. No tenderness of abdomen, etc. One morning she called and said the cramping was getting stronger and the spotting was more than usual today. She came into the office, and I listened to the baby for about five minutes, with Pat lying flat. Suddenly the heartbeat became very fast (about 170) and then after about 30 seconds began to drop very quickly and get faint. Dr. Wonderful was on vacation, and Dr. Backup (to Dr. Wonderful), said come to the office.

Pat sat in the office for $4\frac{1}{2}$ hours, waiting to see Dr. Backup. He decided he wanted to stop the contractions with some Ritodrine HCl (a uterine relaxant). Pat called for my opinion. I agreed, and said she should be in the hospital. Pat agreed. To make a very long story short, the Ritodrine HCl did not stop the contractions, so they sedated her for sleep. In the morning they were going to induce/augment her labor.

Augmentation or **labor induction** is accomplished by starting an I.V. of 5% dextrose in water or 0.9% sodium chloride solution in 1000 cc per bag. Oxytocin (the generic name for Syntocinon, Uteracon or Pitocin) is added at the rate of 1–2 milli units per minute. This may be increased every 15 to 30 minutes, but not to exceed 20 milli units per minute. The goal is to have the contractions at 2–3 minutes apart. Once they reach that level, the Pit-drip is maintained at that dosage, and increased only if the contractions do not last long enough (strong enough) or dilatation is not happening. The Pit-drip is usually stopped after 12 hours, or a caesarean is done, because it stresses the uterus and the baby, and complications such as tetanic contractions are a very real possibility. In a tetanic contraction, the uterus "locks up" into one hard contraction and does not stop—rather like a tetanus of the uterus.

This can lead to uterine rupture and severe anoxia for the baby.

The Pit-drip was started about 7:00 a.m. Thus far, the baby was doing well on the fetal monitor all night and day. About 1700 hrs (5:00 p.m.), 10 hours after the Pit-drip was started, the FHTs quit. At 2100 hrs (9:00 p.m.) an emergency caesarean was done, but not soon enough for little Patty. She was stillborn. The lesson: go with your clients, and get "pushy" if no one responds to your gut feeling of doom. Make them defend their "lack of concern" by explaining to you why your fears are not well founded or why they are following the medical protocols that are in place.

The text book picture of frank **abruptio placenta** is very dramatic and convincing:

- Sudden gush of bright red blood;
- May or may not have a hard sharp pain at onset of gush;
- Pat has sudden fear and near panic for baby (conquer that with prayer);
- FHT will remain good for 35–45 minutes, then may begin to falter;
- Shock.

What to do:

- Pat goes into knee-chest position immediately when she notices the gush;
- Call midwife (she will call doctor to alert hospital for caesarean; you have 45 minutes from onset to get a live baby out).
- Get to hospital as fast as possible. Put your pants on over pajamas (drive yourself if you can get to the hospital in same amount of time it would take ambulance to get to your house. If you need the helicopter because of time crunch and distance, then have the ambulance meet you on way to helicopter pad, or emergency landing pad.
- Call the neighbor over to watch kids, and tell them you can't wait for them to come over, so your kids are not alone for more than a few minutes;
- Leave a note for the neighbor to call your pastor, prayer chain, and the rest of the family
- Pat should be praying and claiming Ezekiel 16:6 while all this is going on, since "all she has to do" is stay in her knee-chest position and stay calm, taking nice deep

breaths for her baby. Pat could do the phone call to the midwife while John is pulling his pants on and getting the car. John will have to carry Pat to the car while she is in the knee-chest position. The safest transport would be by ambulance.

Pat did wake up one night, thinking her water had broken. When she turned on the light, she discovered not water, but blood! She woke John up immediately, and called Doctor Wonderful. He believed her and immediately called the hospital to set up for an immediate caesarean on Pat's arrival. As John put the seat down in the van, Pat called the neighbors to come watch the children. John picked Pat up, keeping her in the knee chest position and carried her out to the car. Just as they were pulling out of the drive, the neighbor (in her pajamas) was running across the yard, wrapping her coat around herself. Thirty minutes after Pat woke up, she was in the operating room getting her caesarean. Little Johnny was alive! and after a whiff of oxygen, did very well. He was born five minutes after Pat arrived in surgery—ten minutes after arriving in the hospital! Surely a new record for caesareans! We praise the Lord that Dr. Wonderful believed Pat, and everyone at the hospital was ready, or Johnny would not have had such an easy start. He could have died just as little Patty did in the previous story.

Placenta Previa

Placentas are usually implanted in the upper third of the uterus. Occasionally they implant in the lower segment, and even more infrequently it will implant across the cervix or very near it. There are three types of previa. The most common are very-low-lying or partial previas. The low-lying placenta is attached to the uterine wall *near* the cervix, but not *on* it. There may be some red blood or a heavy show at the end of labor. Otherwise, there is no problem with the low-lying placenta. Previa does not have a known cause, but it has been suggested that the egg was fertilized at the very end of the fertility cycle resulting in a late implantation. We do know that it occurs approximately 1 in 1500 primiparas and 1 in 20 in grand multiparas (over six children).

When the placenta is partially covering the cervix it is known as a **partial placenta previa** or **marginal placenta previa**. This can cause mild bleeding to hemorrhage during effacement and dilation, depending how much of the placenta is involved and how well the baby's head is applied to the cervix. The risk of hemorrhage is very great and this is not a good risk for home birth. Baby may need resuscitation, at the very least, and Pat may need treatment for hemorrhage, or long-term oxygen during second stage. Neither factor is easily handled in the home.

The only way to differentiate between a very low-lying placenta or placenta previa is by sonogram. A vaginal exam is contraindicated. If it is a previa, and Pat is starting to efface, you could poke your finger through the placenta and cause a severe hemorrhage. This would compromise the baby in a very short time. Placenta previa and placenta abruptio are two mandatory indications for caesarean! The type of incision will depend on the placement of the placenta. If it is anterior, a low transverse is contraindicated because it would go right through the placenta and uterine arteries feeding the placenta, requiring a vertical incision. A posterior previa will permit the low transverse, because the main body of the placenta is out of the way.

Unpredictable Challenges in the Second Stage of Labor

A **prolapsed cord** happens once in 300 births, according to *Williams' Obstetrics*, by Pritchard and MacDonald. It occurs most often when baby's head has not become engaged in the pelvis before the waters break. This increases the potential for the cord becoming pinched between the head and the pelvis as the baby descends during the course of labor. This causes hypovolemia (reduction of blood flow), resulting in impaired oxygen supply to the baby. Remember, whatever compromises the cord, will compromise the baby. The cord is the baby's lifeline.

Anytime the waters break before the baby is well engaged, you need to do a visual or digital vaginal exam and check baby's heartbeat immediately. (Always use a sterile glove when doing a digital exam for prolapsed cord or if membranes may have ruptured.) If the cord has prolapsed into the vagina, you have a choice. You put Pat in a knee-chest position on a firm portable surface such as a tabletop or door, and either reduce the prolapse or brace the cord and transport. Once you start to brace the cord, you cannot remove your hand, so just expect your hand to cramp. The cramp will progress to numbness if you have any distance at all to transport. (This is a temporary situation, but could mean the difference of life and death for the baby. What is most important to you?)

If you are tempted to replace the cord, please pray first. It is a dangerous procedure if you are unskilled. Most doctors no longer do this because of the possibility of fetal distress and maternal hemorrhage or infection. I do not recommend it if you have multiple "occupancy" (twins), or Pat has not dilated to 9 or 10 centimeters, as you need room to work. You of course need to get permission from Pat and John, before you do anything this invasive. Hopefully you have discussed this in class, and they have already talked together about the possibility and made a decision. This is not the time to go into an hour-long discussion about the pros and cons.

Procedures to be done immediately on diagnosis of prolapsed cord:

- Pat assumes the knee-chest position on a plywood board, tabletop or door, for transport.
- Put fresh, sterile glove on the hand that will brace the cord.
- Loosely reinsert cord into the vagina, so it stays warm and functional.
- Without taking hand out of vagina, follow the cord to the cervix.
- Push head up and hold it away from the cord.
- *Transport* (you need strong people to carry Pat out to the car on her board).
- *Do not remove your hand until the baby is born* by caesarean, or the doctor has given you written assumption of responsibility. This states he ordered you to remove the hand bracing the cord, with the date and time, giving the current FHT and overall condition of baby before you remove your hand. It should be co-signed by witnesses.
- Take FHTs every five minutes as you transport. Should you decide to reduce the prolapsed cord by returning it to the uterus, and not transport, do the following:
  - Pat assumes the knee-chest position on the floor or on the bed (not a water bed).

- If Pat feels any distress at the site of the placenta, she should immediately speak up.
- The secondary midwife monitors the baby's heartbeat constantly during the procedure, verbally giving six second variables. (This is when the new dopplers with the tape or LED readouts come in handy.)
- With fresh, sterile, long (sometimes called gauntlet) gloves, gather the cord loop in your dominant hand.
- Push the head up out of the pelvis, check for cord around the neck (if cord around the neck, it must be removed, or baby could strangle himself).
- Bring the cord up into the uterus, and loop it around the leg of baby.
- Release your grasp of the cord and carefully bring your hand out, aligning the head with the pelvis inlet.
- Monitor the baby's heart rate for five minutes for the next hour.
- Assist Pat into the side-lying position, take her vitals, (B/P, pulse) and assess her general condition.
- Carefully assist her into an upright position.
- Listen to the placenta for apparent well being. Baby should engage in the pelvis as Pat becomes upright. Once baby is engaged again, and the heart rate indicates all is well, then resume monitoring as you would in that stage of labor.

Because of the increased possibility of infection, you should give Pat one capsule of goldenseal four times a day for four days, starting now, or Homeopathic Hydrastis 30x potency four tablets sublingually, every four hours the first 24 hours. On day two, every four hours (8:00 a.m. to bedtime) skipping the 4:00 a.m. dose. On day three, take them four times a day, and the fourth day, two times a day, at 8:00 a.m. and 8:00 p.m. Baby should be taking Hydrastis 3x one tablet 15 minutes before nursing, on the same schedule. When placing the tablet in baby's mouth, put it between the cheek and gum, back in the molar area, or he will push it out with his tongue. Tinctures in the same potencies are also available, but may be a bit strong for baby.

Goldenseal is very bitter! If you do not have capsules, then use $\frac{1}{4}$ teaspoon of goldenseal root powder in a glass of unfiltered apple juice. Or, place a small amount of apple sauce on a teaspoon, put the goldenseal in the middle of the apple sauce, and cover with more apple sauce. Swallow without chewing. You will not taste the goldenseal if you swallow it without moving it around in your mouth. The apple cider or sauce will taste like a very "earthy" delicious apple. Goldenseal is not palatable plain.

Cord Around the Neck

While we are talking about the cord, lets discuss the most common event with the umbilical cord. One of every four babies have the cord around the neck. Usually it is only around the neck one time, but can be as much as four or five times. This situation is not a problem, unless it is so snug and short that it prevents the baby from being born, or will put pressure on the baby's throat. A cord so short that it prevents the baby from being born is very rare. Many babies were born with the cord around the neck, and are now very healthy youngsters or adults.

Cord around the neck is thought to be caused by baby turning only in one direction resulting in entanglement. The good news is that the baby has to have enough cord to do this. If the cord was very short, he would not be able to get wrapped in it. I have seen one baby with the cord around the neck four times and three times around body, holding the arms close to baby's sides and wrapped two times around the legs, holding the feet so close together baby had to kick both legs at the same time. Obviously the cord was very long (52 inches) for all of that.

- When the head is born, carefully slip your finger alongside the baby's neck from the ear to the shoulder, and feel for the cord.
- If cord is around the neck, carefully try to get some slack, by a gentle tug on the cord (coming from inside towards the baby's head).
- Slip the slack over one shoulder and then the other.
- Repeat for each loop, if more than one time around the neck.
- If you can not get any slack, you must clamp and cut the cord, especially if it is snug.
- Pat must "blow" through this next contraction, to allow you to cut the cord.

- If the cord is not tight, and baby is coming, slip your index finger between the cord and baby's neck. Anchor your finger on the baby's collar bone. This protects the baby's throat from bruising. The larynx (Adam's Apple) is very soft and easily injured. Holding the cord away from the larynx will protect it from injury.
- Unwind the cord as soon as baby is born.

Occasionally, a baby will be born with a very dark head with cord around the neck. Watch the baby carefully for spontaneous breathing. Once the respirations are established, baby will pink up very quickly. The cord was evidently very tight for a while, causing the peripheral (surface) circulation to be compromised temporarily. A little whiff of oxygen will help baby pink up quicker. If the larynx was damaged, this baby will not swallow well, or cry. It may be difficult to breathe if the larynx was crushed. Laryngeal injuries must be treated by the doctor, immediately! If the cord is very tight against the larynx before you can protect it, the damage may already be done in spite of your best efforts. Thankfully, injuries are very rare.

A **nuchal cord** occurs when a loop of the cord lies alongside the baby's head. This can usually be determined by noticing variable decelerations of the baby's heart rate. Variable decelerations, by definition, are when in response to the uterine contraction, the FHT decelerate to below 100 or as much as 50–60 beats per minute and then returning to normal (baseline) rather quickly with a temporary compensatory elevation in the fetal heart rate. Occasionally they may drop even more. The important factor is the quickness of recovery at the end of the contraction. The deceleration pattern occurs at variable times i.e., at the beginning or at the peak of the contraction.

Meconium staining is a sign of baby stress, either present or past. Staining can come in a variety of colors:

- Straw-colored, there is no problem. The stress was a long time ago and has been resolved, so everything is okay now.
- Brown particles in clear or straw colored water, the stress was more recent but is resolved, and everything is probably okay now.
- The greener and thicker the waters, the more immediate and severe the stress.

"Pea soup" meconium in the waters causes all midwives' hearts to fall into their shoes. Of all the possible problems, this is the one with the worst possibilities. Meconium is soft, slimy, and dissolves in soap water, until air hits it. Then, it takes on the properties of road tar. It becomes sticky and then hard. When meconium is on the skin, or cloth, it can be washed off with hot water. It may stain new diapers, but bleach will take care of that. The problem lies with how are you going to wash it out of the baby's lungs? You can't scrub his lungs with hot water and soap. Should he inhale (aspirate) the meconium, coats the air sacks and prevents them from opening up so he can breathe. In the not-so-distant past, Hyaline Membrane Disease, now renamed **respiratory distress syndrome** was the most frequent killer of newborn infants.

As of this writing, much work has been done on surfactants that will rinse the meconium out of the baby's lungs without damaging them. At this writing, there are two being used on an experimental basis. One seems to be doing better than the other. Once success is consistent, meconium will not be quite as devastating to babies; in the mean time, prevention is our best defense.

Whenever there is meconium staining of any kind, the best prevention is to suction the baby on the perineum with a DeLee mucus trap. As soon as the baby's head is born, tell Pat to stop pushing, insert the sterile tube into baby's mouth and clear it, then proceed to the lungs and stomach and suction in that order. If you get clear fluid from the mouth and lungs, the baby has not aspirated meconium, and your worries are over. If you get meconium or brown back, you must suction until it returns clear. Keep the tube moving, so you do not injure the soft tissues.

If the baby comes so fast that you can't DeLee on the perineum, do so immediately after he is born. As soon as he is born, lift him up to Pat's lap and proceed. Keep the cord warm and moist with the hot compress water and cloths, until baby is out of danger, or the placenta has separated. Occasionally, Pat does not realize how important it is to DeLee baby before she can love him, so you may have to be firm with her. There will be lots of time to love this baby *if* you can get the lungs cleared. Any delay can be fatal.

Many times babies that have aspirated meconium need help getting started. If the baby is pale, warm but not breathing, give Homeopathic Arsenicum 200C or 1M. If asphyxia is present with blue face, twitching in face and gasping for breath, or imperceptible breathing, give one tablet Laurocerasus or Lachesis in the same potency as above. You should see a dramatic change in 30 to 40 seconds. In the meantime, get your oxygen ready, and be ready to initiate CPR. As long as the cord is still functioning, you have time on your side. I have seen Laurocerasus pink up a very dark blue baby with "wet lungs" in five seconds, so learn your homeopathy.

"Pea soup" or thick, bright, grass-green meconium stained waters requires immediate transport and a possible caesarean, depending on baby's condition when you get to the hospital. Continuous electronic monitoring will keep a close watch on the baby's condition. Many times changing Pat's position or the ride to the hospital will cause the baby to change position and resolve the stress. Close monitoring before transport, after changing Pat's position will confirm this. If there is no positive change in 30 minutes, *transport!* Sometimes, all baby needs is a little extra oxygen, but you have to determine if you have enough oxygen for labor and for baby afterwards, should he need it then.

If heart tones are irregular, monitor every five minutes giving Pat oxygen en route to "buy" time for baby.

Once I saw black meconium on the blue pad under a resting mom. I knew the baby was cephalic, so we immediately checked the heart tones and position. The heart tones were in the low normal range, but because she was a first time mom, we transported. The baby showed stress on the monitor, but responded well to oxygen with mom on her left side. Baby was born in the side-lying position with Apgars of 7 and 9. Pat and baby were home three hours after birth.

Breech babies almost always pass meconium during labor, as they descend through the pelvis. This is *normal* for a breech baby. It is caused by the opening of the anus as pressure is applied to the baby's bottom. Remember, in a breech, the baby's bottom is the presenting part that is applied to the cervix. This is not your first sign of stress; the FHT will be your indicator. Some midwives automatically DeLee a breech baby.

Others DeLee only if it is indicated from the baby's attitude and condition at birth.

Developmental disorders in baby are not always emergencies. Sometimes they require a pediatric consultation within 24 hours, but they usually do not affect the birth. Care and treatment is according to symptoms. It is the midwife's responsibility to know what is surgically repairable; for example, a cleft palate and/or harelip. It helps Pat and John to accept the challenges ahead, if the midwife can prepare them mentally, emotionally and spiritually for what is ahead.

The doctor can fill in the details of technique and schedules. The midwife needs to reassure Pat and John that modern medicine can or cannot repair this. Knowing neonatal development can help Pat and John understand at what stage this occurred. If a known contributing factor can be pinpointed, that would be helpful, it sometimes helps to know that. Genetic problems are not avoidable. They happen. Some families have stronger tendencies to certain things, such as Tay-Sachs or Sickle Cell or baldness than others. These are all genetic traits. Some disorders occur because of race; for example, Tay-Sachs or Sickle Cell. Others have no particular genetic reason such as baldness or diabetes.

The only way to avoid genetic problems (and it isn't absolute), is to have genetic counseling and evaluation before you marry. This *may* tell you if you have the same dominant or recessive genetic makeup. This is very expensive and still only gives you the percentiles of possibilities. The bottom line is it is still in God's hands. Are you adult enough to accept God's will in your life and in the life of your child to fulfill His potentialities? Are you spiritually mature enough to be willing to be God's vessel to manifest His glory? Are you spiritually mature enough to be the parent of one of God's special vessels?

We need to realize that just because the majority of children are "normal," the special ones still belong to God. Parents are the caretakers of God's property. Special children need to receive love to grow. They have so much love to give back, I can't imagine not loving them. Sometimes, the nitty-gritty of everyday living can get very wearisome, but God is faithful. He will renew your strength and the end result will be well worth the therapy and time you have spent teaching this special person how to make his own way in this world, until Jesus returns. By the way, special children need the Gospel of Jesus Christ, too. They are very capable of salvation. Even the most severely retarded can grasp the love God has for him or her, and can make a confession of faith.

Shoulder dystocia means that the shoulders are stuck and need to be dislodged from the pubic bone during the birth of the head. It can be mild to severe. *Never twist or pull on the head!* You may decapitate the baby or do severe damage to the spinal cord, resulting in paralysis or death. After clearing the baby's mouth and nose, reduce the body bulk by sweeping the posterior arm across the chest and deliver it. The shoulder girdle is then rotated in to one of the oblique diameters of the pelvis. The anterior shoulder is usually delivered at this point. Usually the corkscrew technique will dislodge the shoulders with birth following.

In a moderately severe shoulder dystocia, quickly turning mother to her hands and knees while the midwife does the corkscrew technique will bring the baby forth. If all else fails, break the baby's clavicle, and apply supra-pubic pressure with the corkscrew techniques. Pat should be pushing *hard*, and the birth team is calling on the Lord to bring deliverance.

You have five minutes to get a healthy baby out! Your assistant should start calling FHTs at 15-second intervals to you as soon as you see the baby's head "suck back in" against the perineum. This is very diagnostic of shoulder dystocia. If your assistant keeps track of how much time you have left, you can determine how interventive you need to be. The longer it takes to get the baby out, the greater risk of death. Death can occur in seven to eight minutes due to cord compression in the pelvis.

Shoulder dystocia occurs at a rate of 0.15% in term deliveries, but if the baby weighs over 4,000 grams (8 lbs, 14 oz), it occurs 1.7%. The larger the baby, the more likely a shoulder dystocia will occur. Pat's pelvic outlet shape and size also are factors. A very angled or flat pubis will be more apt to contribute to dystocia than a pubis that is gently arched.

Unpredictable Challenges During Third Stage

A **retained placenta** is a placenta that does not readily separate from the wall of the uterus. Sometimes a placenta will appear to be retained when it has in fact already separated, and is simply lying across the cervix. Getting Pat into an upright position, or sitting on the commode will usually birth the placenta. This is worth the try as soon as Pat has met her baby, and is showing signs of wanting to get on with life in any position other than what she is in. She usually makes a comment about "When can I have my bath?" or "How long does it take to get the placenta out?". Anything beyond very gentle tugs on the cord will increase the risk of uterine inversion or uterine prolapse!

Gossypium homeopathic is very good for releasing placentas and is in your homeopathic birth kit. You may repeat your dose every 10 minutes, if needed. Licorice, mistletoe, thyme, red raspberry and slippery elm have been used to release retained placentas. Herbals may be repeated every 30 minutes because it takes them longer to work, and they can accumulate. The accumulation can cause reactions to the herb.

In rare cases, the placenta grows into the wall of the uterus. It is then called a **placenta accreta**. Differentiating between accreta and simple retained placenta can be difficult. Usually there is no bleeding with the accreta. However, if the placenta has separated and is lying across the cervix, Pat may be bleeding from the placental "wound" on the uterine wall, because the uterus can not involute, or return to pre-pregnancy size with the placenta in the way. The blood is trapped behind the placenta that is "sealing" the cervix and not allowing the blood to exit the uterus. If you feel the abdomen getting softer, suspect the uterus to be bleeding.

The signs of placental separation are:

- Lengthening of the cord
- Small, short gush of blood
- Pat feels a cramp "I thought my labor was over. . ."

A gentle steady tug on the cord as Pat pushes will then reward you with the placenta. Quickly roll the placenta either clockwise or counter clockwise in your hands as the placenta births. This will wrap the membranes onto themselves, preventing their breaking off inside of Pat. The membranes have similar clinging properties as plastic food wrap. Just as the plastic wrap can tear in unpredictable ways, the membranes will also. If the wrap is stuck on its self, it is very difficult to tear it. The same is true of the membranes. After the membranes are free of Pat's vagina, you can easily examine the placenta and the membranes for completeness.

If you suspect a retained placenta, visual exam of the cervix, will confirm if the placenta is lying across the partially dilated cervix. If you do not see the placenta, it is probably still attached. If you are unsure of using a speculum, you can do a digital exam, but the visual is less invasive. I do not recommend manual removal of the placenta at home. Patience is a virtue in birth, and never more so than when waiting for a placenta. I have heard of midwives waiting 24 hours for the placenta! As long as Pat is not bleeding, patience is worth exercising. Strict cleanliness is required so bacteria do not climb up that cord into her uterus when she goes to the bathroom. For that reason, I would probably choose to exercise caution, and get the placenta out in two hours' time. A uterine infection is a horrible complication of birth, and not really worth the risk, when preventable.

However, if you are trained in manual removal, you do not have any Gossypium, Pat is *bleeding*, and the distance to the hospital is a factor, or the political factors in your area are very dangerous, you may have to try. The *complications of manual removal are severe:* perforation of the uterus, and/or hemorrhage. If Pat is already hemorrhaging and the time crunch has set in, you may have to do it. . . if the Lord, Pat and John agree. When you transport for removal, in a politically dangerous area, just say the baby came quickly before you got to the hospital, but the placenta hasn't come out yet.

- *Do not attempt manual removal if the cervix is less than eight centimeters dilated, and there is no hemorrhage present.*
- Pray for the Lord's guidance, wisdom for the midwife and grace and pain relief for Pat (some chamomile, or valerian may help her relax a little).
- Put on fresh, sterile, long gloves (above the elbow is best).
- Lubricate the gloves with sterile water-soluble lubricant or povidone iodine (povidone is rather harsh on mucus

membrane), or hydrogen peroxide (it foams and can be "messy" but is mild to mucus membrane).
- Gently introduce your hand, finger tips first, into the uterus.
- Follow the cord to the placenta.
- Find the margin of the placenta.
- Try to peel the placenta off the wall by forming a cleavage plain between the placenta and the wall of the uterus, similar to peeling an orange.
- *Do not force separation.* Force means it is probably accreta, and needs a doctor for surgical removal.
- The placenta will peel off easily *only* if it is a retained (slow-to-release) placenta.

In placenta acreta the decidual cells did not develop properly and the placenta has literally grown into the myometrium of the uterus. The myometrium is the layer below the endometrium. The endometrium is what is shed every month during the menstrual cycle and, postpartum, in the lochia. The next severity is **placenta increta**. This is when the placenta penetrates even deeper into the uterine wall. Placenta percreta invades through the entire uterine wall to the serosa layer. Placenta accreta may involve only one or a few cotyledons up to the entire placenta. It is very rare, but until the placenta is birthed in its entirety, cannot be ruled out. Placenta accreta incidence is not known, but is thought by *Williams Obstetrics*, to be one in several thousand. Praise God it is so rare! In order of severity placenta accreta, increta and percreta all require surgical removal and may require emergency hysterectomy.

Suspicion begins when the placenta has not separated after a reasonable time. I have heard of people waiting 24 hours for a normal placenta. The chances of infection increase with a wait this long. Again, the criteria are:
- What is the condition of the mother and baby?
- If baby is nursing well,
- Mother is not bleeding,
- The uterus remains firm
- Temperature and vital signs remain normal. . . watch and wait.

"Hemorrhage" is a word that strikes terror into everyone's heart. By definition, hemorrhage is any blood loss, in the adult, of more than two cups, or 500cc. In the infant, any loss of *one teaspoon* or more is considered very serious. This includes clots. Measurement is best done by catching the blood in a container (pan or bowl), or by weighing the underpads, or by wringing the underpads out and measuring the fluid. This last method has a few flaws, in that you will never get all of the fluid out of the pads, so your measurement will be less than the actual loss, and some of the fluid may be urine or amniotic waters. Weighing the underpads is next best to catching all the birth fluids (waters and blood) in a container. Because Pat may have urinated during second stage, and the after waters following the baby will confuse the amount of blood lost, it is smart to put fresh pads under Pat while waiting for the placenta. Then, if you see bleeding, you will have a more accurate estimate of the blood loss while you search for the cause.

Fortunately, hemorrhage rarely happens at home (less than 1%). It does occur in 10% of all hospital births. The difference is in the comparison between the midwifery emphasis on excellent diet prenatally, coupled with allowing natural processes to function during labor and birth; and the non-midwifery attitude of control leading to mismanagement of first, second and/or third stage of labor in the hospital. The most frequent causes of hemorrhage are:

- A tired uterus from a long labor or extremely fast labor. The uterus "forgets" to involute and does not contract.
- A Pitocin® induction often encourages a uterus to respond only to artificial stimulus.
- The baby is forced out of the uterus with forceps, vacuum extraction, or by people pushing on the fundus.
- Low hemoglobin or hematocrit at the onset of labor.
- Bleeding from the episiotomy/clitorotomy or extension of the episiotomy/clitorotomy into an artery.
- Mismanagement of the placenta by pulling it out before it naturally separates from the uterus. (Pulling on the cord can cause the placenta to tear apart, tear the myometrium (uterine lining), tear the cord, pull the cord off the placenta, or even invert the uterus and cause it to prolapse out of the vagina.)
- Allowing Pat to push before the cervix is completely dilated.
- Deep lacerations severing small arteries.

- Distended (full) bladder
- Pat is exhausted.
- Partial separation of placenta.
- Retained placental or membrane fragments.

There are two types of hemorrhage, **fountain** and **trickle**. The **fountain** hemorrhage is very dramatic and easy to spot, because the blood is flowing very rapidly in great quantity and may even be spurting with the pulse. The best illustration is to compare it with a fully opened water faucet. Pat will bleed out in 45 to 60 minutes, so you must take action immediately.

The **trickle** is a steady flow, but more like a hose that is turned on to water a newly planted tree. Just enough water is coming out of the hose to make a stream, but not enough to dig a hole. The trickle is easy to miss because it looks like Pat is just having a slightly heavy postpartum lochia. The danger is that she will slowly bleed to death in four to five hours. The trickle bleed often stops and starts, which compounds the danger of it.

Management of hemorrhage is straightforward but must be done quickly. The steps you take are determined by when the hemorrhage occurs. If the bleeding is before the placenta is expelled, you must get the placenta out. If, after the placenta is expelled, you direct your efforts to getting the uterus to contract and involute, and/or stop bleeding from any tears present. Go one step at a time, keeping a close eye on Pat's vitals and her mental response to conversation and questions. Keep her talking, even if she has to count or repeat the alphabet backwards. Verbally listing the children by name and birth date, grade in school, special interests etc., will help keep her conscious. If Pat slips away into a "sleep", she is in shock and things are not going well! That is an immediate transport! Having an ambulance stand by during treatment for hemorrhage may be a good idea, depending on your political climate. If things start getting away from what you can do, they can get her to help quicker, and start an intravenous line (if you do not do IVs and they have paramedic certification).

Do the following:

- Determine the source of the bleed:
  - Is it from a partially separated placenta or from a retained piece of placenta or membrane?
  - Is it from a perineal tear?

- Is it vaginal?
- Is it cervical?
- Give Pat "Laborade" to replace fluids at the onset of hemorrhage and keep it coming to prevent shock.
- Speak the Word of God: Ezekiel 16:6; "He saw thee in thy natal blood and said 'Live!' and thou didst live!" and any other scriptures brought to mind.
- In the Name of Jesus, command the bleeding to stop, and the blood vessels to seal over and Pat's body to return to normalcy.
- Use herbs or homeopathics.
- Baby nursing well *or* husband sucking Pat's breast *or* manual stimulation of the breast releases natural oxytocin into blood stream and causes the uterus to contract.
- Massage the uterus firmly but not frantically.
- Administer Pitocin® or ergotrate if you have it.
- Do bimanual compression:

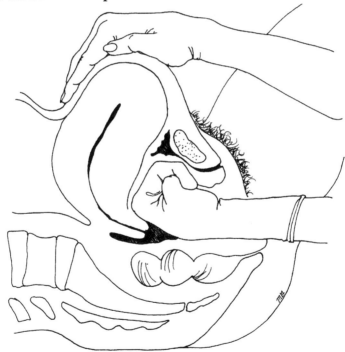

Figure 11-3: Bimanual Compression

- Manual removal of placenta, if partially separated

- **Retained membranes necessitate transport, if they are large sheets**.

Large sheets of retained membranes will adhere to the uterine wall and prevent the uterus from involuting. This requires at least a consultation with Dr. Backup and usually a transport to the hospital. Small pieces of membranes will come out with one goldenseal capsule (size 00) three times a day for two days, then one capsule a day for four days. The homeopathic remedy is four tablets of Cantharis 200 C or 1 M under the tongue, until they melt and are absorbed; this should bring the membranes out right away. Repeat the Cantharis twice, visually check the cervix for membranes at the os. If none is seen and the bleed is continuing, *transport!*

Reaching for the herbs or homeopathics does not negate your faith. God holds us responsible for what we know, not what we do not know. He gave us herbs for the healing and welfare of mankind (Psalm 104:14), as well as His Word. Many times the flow of blood has stopped before I had the tincture in the dropper, but I put it in the juice for Pat to drink anyway. Herbs "work" because they supply something the body needs and is low on, or naturally and gently reminds the body to function. Just as food provides the body with energy to work and repair itself, herbs supply the vitamins, steroids etc., the body needs to maintain itself.

Herbs useful in hemorrhage are usually in the tincture form and can be squirted directly under the tongue or if in a cayenne base, into tomato juice. If Pat is a teetotaler, she needs to be warned that the tincture contains alcohol. Depending on the herb and the formulator, the alcohol could be gin, rum, whiskey or vodka. Women who have abused drugs may be overly sensitive to herbs, especially former cannabis (marijuana) users. Herbs take effect in 20 to 30 minutes.

Single-herb tinctures are:

- White Oak Bark
- Bethroot
- Shepherd's Purse
- Bayberry

Combination tinctures are:

- Bayberry, White Oak Bark and Cayenne (cayenne may not be listed on label)
- Motherwort, Shepherd's Purse, and Bayberry

Homeopathics are very effective, non-alcoholic and work within 10–15 seconds. They are extracted from vegetable, organic and mineral sources, then at a ratio of 1 to 10 parts of diluent (usually water) the mixture is shaken. One part of the first mixture is added to another 10 parts of diluent, shaken again, and that dilution process continues until the dosage level is reached. The more the dilution, the less chemical properties remain, yet the greater medically efficient the remedy. At the desired dosage, it is made into a pellet, tablet, lotion or tincture. Most homeopathics used in the birth bag are herbal based. Some are mineral salts that are commonly found in the human body. The homeopathic remedy addresses the root cause of the problem and stimulates the immune system to correct it. The correct remedy will show improvement within 10–20 seconds. Homeopathic remedies come in tablet, pellet, lotion and tincture form and work by addressing the root cause of the problem and helping the immune system move into rapid action. If a homeopathic remedy you chose is not the correct one, you may try another, until the right one works. If it is the wrong one, it will not cause difficulty. There are very few homeopathics available without prescription that can harm you. The majority of homeopathics are available from the pharmacies that make them as over-the-counter medicines. You are more likely to develop toxicity from an herb than from homeopathics.

Dosage is 4 tablets under the tongue of 200C or 1M potency. If no results are seen in 2–3 minutes, depending on the urgency of the moment, try the next likely, according to symptoms. Homeopathics can be repeated in 15-second intervals in emergencies. The most important guiding symptoms are in bold print.

- *Aconite:* **fear of death, dizzy** on sitting or standing up, active bleeding, fear of moving or turning over.
- *Apis:* Active, dark, profuse, restless, yawning, red spots (like bee stings) on skin, **stinging in ovaries**, symptoms may be brought on by hatred or jealousy, worse with touch or light pressure, tearful.
- *Arnica:* From injury, fatigue, **shock**. Bright red flow with/without clots, sense of soreness, with/without pain, nausea, after long labor, trauma, instrument delivery.

- *Arsenicum Album:* Dark blood, **burning** and lancinating pains.
- *Bryonia:* occurs **with slightest motion (deep breathing, or moving foot)**, dark red blood with headache, common in brunettes.
- *Calcarea Carbonicum:* Profuse red blood, painless.
- *Cantharis:* Expels retained membranes
- *Carbo Vegitabilis:* Passive, continuous, **near collapse, bluish or deathly pale skin.** Rapid, weak pulse, **chilly, wants to be fanned, cold clammy skin as if dead.** No anxiety, difficulty breathing, burning pains in chest and sacrum.
- *Chamomile:* Dark, coagulated and red gushes, irregular flow, **violent pains, ailments from anger, flushed, or one cheek pale, one red**, uterus in small knots, copious, colorless urine.
- *China:* Uterine atony, Much loss of blood, heaviness of head, vertigo, ringing in ears, fainting, fading and loss of senses, gasping for breath, cold, pale, blue face and hands, and delusions when closing eyes. Wants to be fanned.
- *Cimicifuga:* Labor-like pains, ceasing with flow. Passive, dark, coagulated, pains in back extending into limbs.
- *Coffea:* Large black lumps worse with each motion, violent pains in groin, **sexual organs sensitive to any touch** (see *Arnica*, Platina); itching, but too sensitive to scratch.
- *Hamamelis:* Worse by day, stops at night, slow, steady and passive, bright red or dark.
- *Ignatia:* Sinking empty feeling in uterus or stomach. **sadness, sighing, ailments from grief,** obvious or suppressed (grief).
- *Ipecac:* **with or without nausea**, continuous, steady, profuse, cold, shuddering, cold sweat, dizzy, pale, gasping, gushes at each effort to vomit.
- *Kali carbonicum:* **sharp pains from lumbar to buttocks. major remedy for post-partum hemorrhage!**
- *Kreosotum:* worse lying down, stops when standing, dark, acrid blood irritating the body, may stop and start later, **bearing down pains**.

- *Lac Canninum:* Blood hot as fire, stringy, clotting, bearing down pains as if everything would fall out, **ovarian pains alternate sides.**
- *Lachesis:* severe pain in right ovary extending to uterus which increases until relieved by gush of blood.
- *Laurocerasus:* Cold, pale, clammy, from loss of blood, dimness of vision, gasping for breath.
- *Lycopodium:* Profuse, prolonged, part black clots, part red, part serum, worse with stool.
- *Nux Vomica:* With large difficult stools, or **frequent urging with little or no results,** bright red lumpy clots.
- *Phosphorus:* tall, thin women, **copious bleeding** after difficult labor, may be intermittent, cold and weak abdomen, feels worse with touch, sacral pains worse with any motion, flushes of heat moving upwards, **heavy bleeding in nursing women** (this type of hemorrhage may start several days post-partum).
- *Pyrogenum:* Bright red with clots, septic disease, close to *Ipecac,* try one if the other fails.
- *Sabina:* Worse with slightest motion, but better when walking around, pain or discomfort from sacrum to pubes, often with pain in joints, weakness, profuse, offensive, liver-like clots.
- *Secale:* **copious black, offensive discharge,** with black clots, or intermittent with red gushes. Labor-like pains alternate with hemorrhage, tingling all over, better with fresh air or with fanning, passive, worse with motion.
- *Sepia:* congestion with sense of eight, right groin pain, needle-like pain in cervix, wants legs drawn up, **feels bearing down pains as if everything would fall out of uterus, cold with flushes of heat,** constipated, putrid odor of urine.

Breast stimulation causes natural oxytocin to be released into the blood which when it reaches the uterus causes it to contract and release the placenta, if it has not been expelled. Another reason to encourage baby to suckle as soon as possible. Sometimes if Pat is able to squeeze a drop or two of colostrum into baby's mouth, baby will get interested in suckling. If not, manually stimulate the nipple, or have Pat's husband suck her breast.

Manual removal of the placenta is a dangerous procedure. Do not attempt this without prayer or as an absolute life-saving effort. The criteria are:

- Pat is losing lots of blood;
- Nearest hospital or medical care is more than 30 minutes away.

Explain to Pat and John that you "must remove the retained placenta (or large pieces), because it is a life-or-death situation. It is a painful procedure, but you will do your best to do it quickly." Explain what you must do and how you plan to do it.

Procedure:

- Remove soiled gloves and reglove with long (elbow-length is best) sterile gloves.
- Making your hand as small as possible and as gently as possible, insert your dominant hand through the cervix.
- Using the side of your hand as a wedge, slide it along the inside of the uterus until you find the errant placenta. (It should be partially separated since Pat is bleeding.)
- Find the loose edge and keeping the back of your hand against the uterus, palm of your hand toward the placenta slide your hand under the loose edge towards the attached site.
- Gently use your hand as a wedge and peel the placenta away from the uterus.
- *Take care you do not shred the placenta, or leave anything attached.*
- *Do not force the separation; it may be a partial accreta.*
- *Transport immediately, using bimanual compression if partial accreta.*
- Examine placenta for completeness after removal.

Usually, the placenta separates immediately when your hand starts to slide against the attached edge. The uterus should immediately clamp down and involute. If not, do the appropriate action. Examine the placenta immediately on removal for completeness.

Uterine massage irritates the muscles and causes them to contract. Grasp the fundus in both hands and knead like bread dough. If the abdomen in soft and "doughy," be sure you have the fundus in your hands. If the abdomen is very soft, apply enough pressure to the uterus as if you are working with stubborn yeast dough. The vertebrae will give the resistance needed to massage back side of the uterus as you work on the anterior and fundal areas. Your fingers and arms will get sore after a few minutes, unless you work yeast dough often. Check the fundus frequently for spontaneous firmness. You will feel the fundus cramp as you knead/massage. It should be the size and hardness of a croquet ball.

Oxytocic drugs require a prescription from your Dr. Back-up. Dosage is one ampule (1cc) of methergine IM (intramuscular) if the placenta has not been expelled, and one ampule (1cc) of Pitocin IM if the placenta has been expelled. Pitocin closes the cervix, while methergine relaxes it. *In 4th state labor never give either drug intravenous unless diluted in 1000 cc Ringers or NaCl (sodium chloride) solution* through an open line (two hour infusion). If you give "Pit" or methergine in an IV "push" (direct into vein), your client will have hypotension from the "Pit" or hypertension from the methergine. *They do not counteract each other.*

Bi-manual compression (see illustration earlier in the chapter), is used when all else fails and you know the all of the placenta and membranes are expelled. Remove your soiled gloves and on your dominant hand, replace it with a fresh sterile long (elbow length) glove. Slide your freshly gloved dominant hand into the vagina to the anterior fornix, making a fist palmar side up. Your fist must be palmar side up for greatest thrust and strength. Place the other hand on Pat's abdomen, going deeply into the abdomen, grasp the uterus by cupping your palm around the posterior side.

Apply pressure and massage in an in-and-down-ward direction against the posterior wall of the fundus with your "outside hand" and in an up-and-upward direction against the body of the uterus with the "inside hand". Bringing your hands toward each other and squeezing the uterus between them. Continue until the bleeding has stopped. Carefully release the pressure, if hemorrhage continues, or the uterus does not feel contracted, reapply the pressure.

If all has failed, then you must transport maintaining continuous bi-manual compression (your hand will cramp severely, but keep up the pressure for Pat's life's sake), until arrival at the hospital and the doctor has (in writing) assumed the responsibility of caring for her and duly noted that you have done your best according to your skill level, and/or Pat is receiving replacement fluids per IV, and is being actively treated by the physician. This treatment may include hysterotomy to find the source and stop the bleeding.

Oral rehydration therapy is regaining medical favor, according to the latest medical literature, and is a must to treat hemorrhage at home. Pat has lost a lot of body fluids and must replace them or go into shock. There are many electrolyte or sport drinks on the market. If you do not want to make your own, read the labels. You need 100% or at least 75% replacement of electrolytes with few if any, artificial dyes and preservatives in it. Pat's body is in stress already from hemorrhage, she doesn't need her body to have work at getting rid of unnecessary chemicals too. You can start out with natural, unsweetened lemonade, and add the honey, salt and liquid calcium to it. Laborade should be made up for a labor and post labor drink anyway. It is a good idea to have ample supplies for Laborade, just in case you need it in a hurry. The best tasting and quickest fluid replacement is "Laborade."

Laborade Recipe

1 cup lemon juice (5–6 lemons) or concentrate equivalent (or oranges)
$\frac{1}{4}$ teaspoon salt
1 teaspoon liquid calcium, crushed tablets may be used, but do not dissolve well and tend to float on the top
Honey to taste
Water to make a quart

Drink one quart per 10 minutes, until hemorrhage has stopped. Then one quart per 20 minutes until Pat is coherent and able to navigate to the bathroom without help.

Laborade will get Pat on her feet in short order, because it is an electrolyte balanced solution that her body can assimilate quickly to maintain fluid volume, proper blood pressure and prevent shock. (Ice will chill Pat and be counter-productive until she is out of danger of shock.) Shock occurs from lack of fluid volume in the circulatory system. The body will make new blood cells, to compensate for those lost in the hemorrhage, but if her serum/fluid volume is maintained, she will be able to take care of her baby in bed, and get to the bathroom herself.

I have seen Pat drink $2\frac{1}{2}$ quarts of labourade in 30 minutes, thus bringing her blood volume up so quickly, that in 30 minutes after we got the bleeding stopped, she was able to walk to the bathroom without help. She had lost about 1500cc (almost half her total volume) in a fountain bleed. We used massage and 1 amp. Pit to stop the bleeding, and forced the labourade while we were massaging. We wanted to replace fluids as fast as we could, since we were some distance from medical help.

Pat does not remember drinking all that labourade or the massage. This is a peculiarity of hemorrhage. Pat will not be aware of it when it is really flowing. This is why you always look and palpate the fundus for firmness, while you ask Pat and verify if she has or is passing a lot of blood, or clots in the immediate postpartum. If you do not, you may come back later on the first day postpartum to a dead mother at the worst, or a hospitalized mom at best. You never leave a client with a boggy uterus, for any reason. It should firm up within 15 minutes or try to with your steady attention. Keep at it until it stays hard like a croquet ball on its own.

Pat should stay pretty "close to the bed" for a few days, until her body has a chance to replace the red blood cells she lost. Put Pat on a high-iron diet with supplements or my preferences, iron tincture or homeopathic remedy Ferrum Phos, and one quart of fluids (water, juice, milk, laborade, etc) every 3 hours. Take her hemoglobin on the first, fifth and fourteenth days. It should be on the upswing by the the 5th day and close to her nine-month (prenatal) hemoglobin, or better, by the 14th day.

Maternal distress can be caused by physical, emotional and spiritual exhaustion. Physical, emotional and spiritual stress will deteriorate into distress if not dealt with. Please read Chapter 5 for removing the emotional and spiritual stress. Physically, maternal distress can be caused by shock, dehydration, fatigue, and inability to urinate due to dehydration or a bruised bladder.

Shock can be caused from injury to the emotions, spirit, or the body. In childbirth the most frequent cause of shock to the mother is from hemorrhage. If mother receives an emotional shock, healing needs to be implemented immediately, before the enemy builds a stronghold. This stronghold can manifest emotionally or spiritually as mental illness, depression, and anger against God, or physically as a collapse of the major body organs, leading to death. The baby can get shocky from getting overly chilled. This is called hypothermia, and can be very dangerous.

The symptoms of shock are:

- Rapid pulse, may become thready and weak,
- Rapid, shallow respirations,
- Blood pressure may drop slightly *at first,*
- Restlessness,
- Anxiety,
- Weakness,
- Pallor,
- Cool, moist skin,
- Temperature falls as shock increases,
- Difference in the diastolic and systolic pressures narrows in later stages.
- Decrease in urinary output from dehydration,

You treat physical shock by:

- Increase blood volume by oral rehydration, *only if conscious*—she needs to drink 1 quart in 15 minutes;
- If unconscious, start an IV line (law permitting) of 5% D in Normal Saline or lactated Ringers solution;
- Put baby skin to skin to Pat or John;
- Put warm blanket over Pat and baby, with space blanket over and around both (leave air hole for Pat and baby);
- Keep Pat flat in the bed;
- Check vital signs;
- Give herbal teas of brigham tea, dandelion, parsley, cayenne, garlic, ginseng, hawthorn, hyssop or herbals for hemorrhage; or
- Labourade, one quart every 15 minutes for a total of four quarts.
- Homeopathics include the medications for hemorrhage and Rescue Remedy.

Fatigue has many causes, but is unwanted when you go into labor. Get your rest whenever you can, so this nasty doesn't get a hold on you. Learn to live in the Spirit (Ephesians

4:17–24) and pace yourself with your work. There is no law that says you have to do everything in one day. Do something everyday, get your rest everyday. You may have to nap when the children nap in the afternoon, if sleeping at night is difficult or inadequate.

A **full bladder** but you can't urinate, can be caused by pressure of the baby's head, or a bruised bladder from birth. Bruising the bladder most often happens when Pat does not empty her bladder at the end of first stage or during second stage of labor. Sometimes baby's head is large enough to prevent the bladder to empty itself. Cantharis, apis, cimicifuga, bryonia, arsenicum or arnica may be helpful. Some other helps are:

- A drop of Peppermint oil on a gauze square, Kleenex tissue on floor near Pat, or in commode water;
- A dripping faucet;
- Warm water poured over Pat's genitalia, then putting her foot in cool tap water;
- Drink warm fluids, unless the bladder is already excessively full;
- Catheterize Pat.

A full bladder can cause Pat to hemorrhage, so don't ignore it. The bladder will hold the uterus up out of the pelvis. This prevents the uterus from involuting and cramping down. It is advisable for all midwives to learn how to do a urinary bladder catheterization. She may not use it more than two or three times in all the years that she practices, but it saves a transport and a great deal of difficulty for Pat.

Infant distress is usually due to lung or heart difficulties. Some possible reasons are:

- Fluid in the lungs, from aspiration of vaginal mucus or meconium,
- Heart malformations,
- Difficult or prolonged labor,
- Pinched cord in second stage resulting in anoxia.

Stress during labor sometimes escalates into a distressed baby being born. Unless the distress is caused by anomalies, a whiff of oxygen at one or two liters per minute will pink baby up very quickly. Laying the oxygen tubing so the oxygen is blowing past the baby's nose, yet pointing away from the eyes, will do the trick in a minute or two. If baby has heart or lung anomalies, he will need the oxygen to maintain his status quo until you get him to medical help. In that case, attach the neonatal mask to the oxygen tubing and fasten the mask to baby's face with the elastic cord (like a fun mask). Be sure the oxygen does not leak towards the eyes, as that can damage the cornea and cause possible blindness. If you have to maintain the baby with oxygen, purpose to get him to medical care quickly. You may have time for Pat to get a quick herbal bath, and put clean clothes on. But get baby to the doctor within four hours, tops.

Most of these conditions can be prevented by good prenatal care. Frequent changes of the laboring woman's position, allowing her to eat and drink as she wishes, giving lots of attention to her spirit, soul, and body, will eliminate most stress and distress. Studies by Michael Odent and others show that mothers who are allowed to eat, drink and choose their own positions for labor and birth have very favorable outcomes with little or no stress.

Refer to the pie chart earlier in this chapter. Please note that 95% of all pregnancies are normal. That leaves only 5% that are challenges or complications. And only 3% are life threatening; the others can be reversed! Hallelujah! That leaves us with only 3% to really worry about. That 3% is also historically, the reasons for "mandatory" Caesareans.

As the bar chart earlier in this chapter (and repeated for your convenience below) shows, I took the 3% slice and expanded it. There are many situations that fall in that column, and it was too hard to illustrate the tenths and hundreds of percent. How does one divide such small quantities into smaller unit, and still be able to see them? So if you get dismayed, just refer back to the pie chart to get everything in perspective. The categories in the expanded 3% are the most common "problems." Some are life-threatening, some are not. The percentages are the frequency of these problems, according to *Williams Obstetrics*.

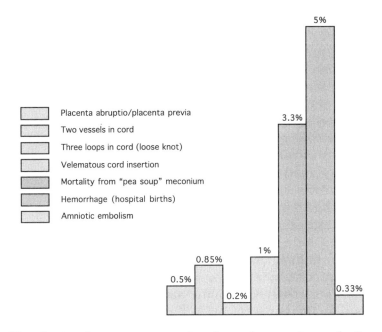

The first column represents placenta previa and abruptio placenta which occur 0.5% of the 3% complications. Next we have the 0.85% incidence of only two blood vessels, instead of three, in the cord. This would indicate possible kidney or liver anomalies (malformation). The third column is not a big problem, unless the loops (loose knot) are pulled tight. Loops occur 0.2% of 3% of the time. Sometimes a false loop occurs when the cord "snags" on its own bumps, but it is not a knot.

A velematous cord insertion looks like a cypress tree in the swamp. The major vessels continue their separation and do not merge into the the three cords of the umbilical cord until they are one to four inches away from the placenta. Often, Wharton's jelly extends from the cord around some of the separated vessels. The danger lies in the possibility, although remote, of the baby getting his foot or hand snagged in the "webbing" of the separated vessels, pulling one or more of them loose causing a fatal fetal hemorrhage. This is not likely, but since all things are possible, it is a possibility. Don't waste your time and energy worrying about this, since you can't do anything about it. You won't even know if it is a velematous insertion until the placenta is birthed, anyway! The velematous insertion and oddly shaped placentas such as heart, oblong, etc., are caused by the baby. When he embeds into the lining of the uterus, he spins. The speed of that spin can polarize that part of the egg sack that will be the placenta and cord. That polarization is thought to cause the above varieties of placenta shapes and velematous cords.

Approximately 3.3% of all complications is "pea-soup" meconium staining. The mortality is caused by the aspiration of the meconium into baby's lungs, preventing oxygenation to occur. Presence of meconium is a result of severe and unresolved stress in baby.

Prolapsed cord mortality is 30% of all prolapsed cords. Fortunately, in the well-nourished woman, prolapsed cord does not occur often because the membranes are very strong and do not break until second stage when the head is passing through the cervix.

Amniotic embolism occurs in about 0.33% maternal mortalities, and occurs most often as a complication of caesarean than from vaginal birth. Some authorities feel that amniotic embolism is the cause of 10% of all maternal deaths, but is usually "hidden" in the statistics as heart or respiratory failure. Amniotic embolism occurs when a bubble of amniotic fluid slips into the mother's blood stream. Amniotic fluid contains waste fetal cells, fetal hair, vernix and fetal waste (urine and meconium, if present). Death occurs when that bubble finds its way into a very tiny capillary, blocking the circulation in the most vital area of the brain. This causes a complete collapse of all the major body organs in about five minutes after onset of the escape into Pat's blood stream. The collapse is so sudden and massive that the doctors cannot reverse it, even if they started treatment the instant the amniotic embolism (bubble) entered Pat's blood stream.

We need to keep all of this in perspective. Even though many of these complications are horrid, they are a very small percentage of the whole. 3% complicated pregnancies compared to 95% normal, uneventful pregnancies, is not often. Complications most often occur when God's laws of natural process are ignored and interfered with. Others are caused from ignoring good health and nutrition habits.

This is not a comprehensive list of challenges, but hopefully we have touched on the more common ones. Remember to not allow fear to get a foothold, because the Lord has given us a sound and sane mind, II Timothy 1:17.

God promises blessings to His people (Deuteronomy 28:1–14). On the other hand, God says that curses come to those who are willfully disobedient (Deuteronomy 28:15–68). God is sovereign. He sends rain on the just and on the unjust (Matthew 5:45). We do what we know is the best for our baby and ourselves, and then we can trust the Lord to send us only what is best for us according to His perfect design in our life. If we have an abundance of "lemons" in our life perhaps we need to make "lemonade," and ask the Lord what He wants us to learn in this situation. Perhaps God is doing a special work in us, that we do not recognize because of the abundance of circumstances surrounding us. We need to seek God's face and yield to His good pleasure in our lives. That is Old English for letting God shape us as the potter shapes the clay to make vessels of honor and beauty or vessels of plainness and utility (dishonor—Isaiah 45:9–11).

If you are not sure about what is happening, pray! Ask God for wisdom (James 1:15) and He will give it to you abundantly. Start evaluating the situation. Do what your skills and knowledge tell you what to do. . . those thoughts just may be the Holy Spirit prompting you. Ask Pat how she feels, if she is concerned or knows that it's going to be all right. Pat will be the first to sense "doom." The Lord promises to bring to our remembrance those things that we have learned, and once you have asked God for help, act on those promptings. God will steer you in the right direction and bless your step of faith. Be sure it is faith and not presumption, or God will curse, not bless, your efforts.

Grief

If you must transport, have a miscarriage/spontaneous abortion, stillborn or a baby with developmental problems, you will have a grieving period. This may be short or long, depending on how well you and those around you handle the loss of your dreams or the loss of your baby.

You have put a lot of time and effort into this "dream birth." Suddenly, or so it seems to you, in the middle of labor the midwife or your husband tells you that it isn't working. The baby is in stress and you have to go to the hospital to birth your baby. It isn't easy to shift gears to "plan B" and be well adjusted in five minutes or less in the midst of labor. After all, it is taking all you have to deal with labor, let alone shifting to "plan B."

Sometime between leaving the house and your six-week check-up, you will have to face the disappointment of not birthing at home. Unless you have a real emergency with the baby, or Pat is in trouble, it's all right to take time out to cry. Tears are very healing. They drain tension out of the body and mind, and empty out anger. Taking five or ten minutes to empty yourself of the disappointment, helps clear your head so you can think about plan B.

Don't hesitate to grieve the loss of your baby, or your home birth. Both were a very important part of your life for a brief time in your life. Friends, family and acquaintances will ask the same questions:

- What happened?
- Tell me the details. . .
- Are you going to do it—home birth, get pregnant, etc.—again?
- Why do you want to do it again?

Whether you lost your baby or your dream birth, reliving the details is painful. But there is healing in that pain. It cuts through the numbness and forces you to start thinking again. The loss of the dream birth is not as severe as losing the baby, even if the hospital birth was the worst experience of your life.

Losing a baby is losing a part of you. There is a cutting off of the family's future. Even when there are other children, there will always be that empty spot. Time has a way of making that spot appear smaller, but it will always be there. The memory of that pregnancy or child will remain as long as you live. The children will have varying levels of memory, depending on their age and ability to grasp what happened.

Don't hesitate to grieve a pregnancy loss. That child was a part of your lives, a real person with all the potential that any full-term living baby would have. Just because her life was shorter than most does not invalidate her being. The stages of grief are:

- Denial: "It couldn't happen to us. This is something that happens to other people. There must be some mistake." or "I wasn't really pregnant. . . the test was wrong."
- Anger: "Why me? Why us?" Lots of crying, yelling and banging around, or silent anger.

- Blame: "It's your fault/my fault." or "If I/they/you hadn't. . ." etc.
- Mourning: Quick to cry, thinking about the loss of the baby and the loss of a dream.
- Healing: Acceptance, looking forward to life continuing on.

Each stage of grief has its own time of healing, if you allow yourself to be healed. As you walk through each step—and they do not have to happen in the above order—you will find yourself growing spiritually and emotionally. This is the positive and constructive side. On the other hand, if you allow this tragedy to become a festering boil in your soul and spirit, it will become a millstone around your neck and cause destruction in your family.

I still remember when we lost our first pregnancy to incomplete spontaneous abortion in 1957. We wanted that baby very, very, very much. After all these years and three succeeding healthy pregnancies, I can still tell you all the details of that day and night. Even to the expression on our puppy's face when he howled at the beginning of each contraction. I always knew when the next contraction was coming, because he would howl very quietly, like a soft moan. Once the baby was passed he stopped howling, and just sighed with each contraction. For months afterwards, it was very hard for me to be around a pregnant woman, especially if I knew her and had to fellowship with her. I was so fearful that I would not be able to carry a child to term, and the spirit of jealousy set up housekeeping. Once I came to terms with that and changed my wrongful attitude towards others, I conceived again and we had a very healthy baby girl. Our joy was complete. Now we knew that not only could we conceive, but we could carry that baby to term, and birth a healthy baby too. We have had two sons since and enjoy all of our children, and now grandchildren. Each birth is remembered as special.

Grief from Miscarriage, Stillbirth, and Developmental Problems

All of this leads us to a subject that many do not like to talk about. We get uncomfortable about it because childbirth is supposed to be happy, not sad. Part of life is death. For the Christian, death is a "change of address" into a "neighborhood" of joy and life, into the presence of God. For the non-Christian it also is a "change of address," but into a "neighborhood" that is worse than the vilest concentration camp, or the most dangerous barrio/slum area of the world. This "neighborhood" is full of torment and agony. Your nearest neighbor will be suffering just as much as you and you have to put up with Satan for eternity.

I personally believe that children (before the age of accountability) even though they have the Adamic nature of sin in them when they are born, return to their Maker, God the Father, if they die before confessing Jesus as Savior. It is our responsibility as parents to teach our children the precious stories from the Bible and the way of salvation from conception on. Many of my clients have read the Psalms or children's' Bible stories out loud during the pregnancy, so the baby would hear the Word of God from before birth. Salvation is not inherited. It is a private thing between God and each individual. But how can they believe, if they have not heard? (Romans 10:14). The thief on the cross did not have a chance to get baptized in water, but Jesus said he would see him in Paradise, because of his confession. Scripture says we must make a public confession of our faith (Romans 10: 9–10), but it is God who searches our hearts and determines if what we say is what we truly believe (Psalm 139:1–12, 23–24). Sad to say, some make a public statement of faith, because it is expected of them by their parents or friends, but the birth of faith in Jesus Christ has not yet happened in the heart (John 3:14–21).

Christian parents should pray daily for their children from conception on. We should pray daily for their proper development: physical, mental and spiritual; and daily put those children in Father God's hands. We need to remember that we are the Lord's caretakers of these children, and He can call them home to Him at any time. It is not selfish to pray that the children have long, happy and successful lives, as long as we are willing to give them back to Father God, should He call for them sooner than we planned.

In our own miscarriage, the years have not diminished our love for the little one we never knew. We know that our little baby is in that cloud of witnesses that will return with Jesus, when He returns (Hebrews 12:1). Then we will have all eternity with her/him, in whatever capacity of fellowship we shall have on that side of glory. If Jesus should tarry, and calls us home before His return, then I am sure we will see our baby then. In the meantime, I am content to know that the baby is with Jesus, and that is all that matters. Anything else is speculation and we are commanded not to do that.

Should the children know about the spontaneous abortion? That really depends on when it happened, how involved they were in the pregnancy and their level of understanding the sovereignty of God. Will they understand what you are telling them and will it will serve a purpose other than to dump your emotions? Use your own judgement based on your family's situation and prayer. Please do not use your children for a dumping ground. They do not know how to handle someone else's grief. They are too busy trying to figure out their own emotions and how they are expected to act now.

I strongly advise parents to receive Christian counsel with an elder, pastor, or other appropriate ministry within the church whenever a pregnancy, or baby is threatened. It should start when the pregnancy becomes threatened and continue until the grieving process is complete. Obviously, counsel and prayer will be needed more often in the beginning than at the end of the grief process.

We live in a society that has grown hardened to the death of the unborn child. Millions die every year from "planned abortion" (murder), with little note taken. We are constantly bombarded with all the reasons why the pregnancy should be "terminated," because a prenatal test didn't have a good report or the baby is of the wrong gender. God will deal with those that cause a child to lose his or her life. Many well-meaning folks do not realize how painful those reasons are to the parents and how much it grieves God when one of His little ones dies. Because we are told that it is silly to get upset over the loss of an unborn child, many parents are cheated out of the proper comfort and support they need at this time. All references in this book to abortion means the common term: miscarriage.

No parent honestly feels that **miscarriage (spontaneous abortion** is the medical term) is for the best, even when undisputed evidence is given that the child could not live without great difficulty and sacrifice on the part of the parents. Parents still feel that it is worth doing what they can for that child. That is love. It can not be measured or erased. Love can be abused, challenged, and ignored, but the only one that can remove it is the one that gives it. In His sovereign wisdom, God has not told anyone His reasons for allowing abortion (miscarriages), developmental problems and stillbirth to happen. Man has tried desperately to make sense and purpose out of it, to take our guilt of sin away and make life perfect. The truth is, we live in an imperfect world because of sin, and imperfect things happen. Everything else is speculation that compounds the grief and inappropriate guilt on the family.

God is too "big" (for lack of a better word) to put in a neat little package that fits our puny understanding. We need to strengthen our faith in a God that loves us and our baby. We need to get to that place where we can trust Him, no matter what comes our way. And you know how far you have to go, after you live for any length of time. Just when you think you trust God for everything, He shows us through circumstances around us, that we haven't even begun to trust Him.

Why does abortion happen? This question is as hard to explain as answering a child's question on the reason for blue eyes. Adults seem to want more explanation than "because God wanted it that way." We want to blame someone or something for losing what we wanted so much. If Pat didn't want her pregnancy to start with, she will carry needless guilt that God was punishing her. I do not believe that God goes around looking for people He can "get back at." My God is too big for that kind of pettiness. That is a trait birthed in sin, straight out of the pit. Pettiness is a trait of the devil. So then, what is the cause? It is only in 51% of miscarriages that a medical reason is even guessed at or known. We have to rely on the faithfulness of God and trust Him to know best. After all, He is in control of life and death.

Medically, there are some known causes. Spontaneous abortion occurs in 10–14 % of all pregnancies. Some authorities say it is higher, because the woman thinks she is having a late period, that is a little heavier than usual. The most common cause (49%) is believed due to "blighted ova." This means that the ova or sperm did not have a nucleus and a baby never started to develop. In 3%, there may be localized anomalies in the uterus (fibroids, hardened uterine lining from using the pill, previous D&Cs, etc.) and in 10% there are placental abnormalities, possible developmental abnormalities in the baby at the earliest stages of growth (while the cells are still dividing), or changes in the baby's environment (hormones, nutrition, or blood) which could be caused by circumstances beyond mother's control. That leaves 38% in the "I don't know" category.

The one thing we do know since the advent of the sonogram, is for whatever the reason, the baby almost always dies before the spontaneous abortion begins. The spontaneous abortion is the body's way to expel the dead baby before it causes infection in the mother. It usually does no good to try to stop the cramping and bleeding, unless you can hear a heartbeat. Some dopplers can pick up a heartbeat at nine weeks. Prior to that, Pat usually thinks she is having a heavy period because she skipped a month. This is also true when the baby is stillborn in the second trimester. Why a woman goes into premature labor in the second trimester is also a mystery. Contributing possibilities or causes for abortion in the second trimester are:

- Maternal disease,
- Hormone imbalance,
- Surgery,
- Abnormalities of the maternal reproductive organs,
- Emotional trauma,
- Physical trauma, or
- Cord accidents such as a tight knot that cuts off the circulation of oxygen to the baby.

Just as often, there is no apparent reason. Death just happens, because the baby is too immature to live. If the baby has a heartbeat, and Pat is in her fifth month, by all means transport Pat to the nearest high-risk maternity hospital. Babies have been known to live weighing only 500 grams (about 1 pound). After 20 weeks, babies have very slim but increasingly better chances to live. The older they are and the more they weigh, the better their chances are. Unfortunately, many of these premies have internal developmental problems that caused their untimely birth. That will compound their struggle for life.

Spontaneous abortion has been categorized into five subgroups:

- Threatened,
- Inevitable,
- Incomplete,

- Missed, and
- Habitual.

Threatened abortion is the one we see most often. Symptoms include bleeding, sometimes mild cramping similar to that of a menstrual period, increasing in strength until it feels like labor, and/or low backache. One in five women will have these symptoms. Of these women with the symptoms, less than half will lose their babies. The bleeding can last from a few days to several weeks. The color varies from fresh bright red mixed with mucus, similar to menstrual period blood, to old blood (dark brown or dark red). Some women have experienced spotting to almost menstrual flow about the time that she would have her period were she not pregnant. This has been compared to a study done on Rhesus monkeys. The monkeys exhibited bleeding from ruptured paraplacental blood vessels and an eroded uterine lining. The bleeding commonly began about 17 days after conception, or $4\frac{1}{2}$ weeks after her last menstrual period.

Some women experience bleeding occasionally from lesions (raw spots) on the cervix, especially after intercourse. Polyps on the external cervical os, or decidual reactions of the cervix, tend to bleed in early pregnancy. Treatment may or may not work. I usually listen for a heartbeat with the stethoscope or the doppler. If I get a heartbeat, I will pray with the couple for God to intervene and protect this new life and then treat with an appropriate homeopathic remedy or herb. If I do not get a heartbeat, I will pray with the couple and commend the baby into God's hands, or treat anyway, if that is their wish. If there is no heartbeat, the baby is already dead and only divine intervention will give them a baby from this pregnancy. This is not easy to accept, especially if the couple has had to wait a long time to conceive. If the bleeding is unrelated to the pregnancy, the bleeding is likely to disappear, regardless of treatment.

Inevitable abortion is signaled by the rupture of the membranes and cervical dilation. Rarely does this not signal the loss of the pregnancy. The fluid may have previously collected between the amnion and the chorion to escape with rupture of the chorion while the amnion is intact. Most often, either uterine contractions begin promptly, resulting in expulsion of the baby, or an infection develops. The placenta and baby are likely to be expelled together.

When **incomplete abortion** occurs before the tenth week, the placenta, in whole or in part, is retained in the uterus and hemorrhage begins sooner or later. This is the main sign of an incomplete abortion. With abortions of pregnancies that are more advanced, bleeding is often profuse and may occasionally be massive to the point of producing profound hypovolemia (abnormally low circulating blood volume). If the placenta is partly attached and partly separated, the retained portion of the placenta acts like a splint and prevents the myometrium (mucosal layer of the uterus that the placenta is attached to) from contracting in that section. The vessels in the denuded area (where the placenta separated) do not contract, because the muscles will not contract until all of the placenta separates. This causes profuse bleeding—hemorrhage.

Missed abortion is defined as the prolonged retention of the placenta and baby after the death of the baby. Typically the early part of the pregnancy is normal, with the usual physical signs of pregnancy: nausea, amenorrhea (no periods), breast changes and growth of the uterus. When the baby dies, there may or may not be vaginal bleeding, or other symptoms warning of a threatened abortion. For a while, the uterus seems to remain stationary in size but usually the breast changes reverse.

Pat is likely to lose a few pounds in weight. Thereafter, careful palpation and measurement of the uterus reveal that it has not only stopped enlarging but is becoming smaller as a result of absorption of the amnionic fluid and maceration of the baby. Many ladies have no symptoms during this period, except amenorrhea (no periods). If the missed abortion terminates spontaneously, and most do, the process of expulsion is quite the same as in other abortions. The baby, if retained several weeks after death, is in a shriveled sack and appears very macerated.

It is not clear why some abortions do not terminate within a few weeks or hours after the baby dies. One study showed that one-third of the women that were treated for threatened abortion with Depo-Prevera retained the dead baby for more than eight weeks.

Occasionally, after prolonged retention of the dead baby, serious coagulation defects develop. Pat may note troublesome bleeding from the nose or gums, and especially from sites of slight trauma. Treatment consists of high doses of Vitamin K, such as shepherd's purse for coagulation and homeopathics for retained placenta with hemorrhage: cimifuga, gossypium, ipecac, sabina, secale, sepia, or pyrogenum. As with all homeopathics, check your manual for the specific remedy in your situation.

Habitual abortion has been defined as three or more spontaneous abortions happening to an individual woman. Forty-nine percent are caused by:

- Malformation of the baby because of malnutrition, genetic or environmental hazards
- Hormone imbalances
- Poor nutrition
- Infection
- Incompatible blood groups between Pat and John resulting in Pat becoming sensitized to all future babies with John's blood type
- Psychiatric
- Anatomic uterine defects
- Incompetent cervix

Steps to prevent spontaneous abortion in future pregnancies include:

- Good nutrition during your childbearing years,
- Exercising your Kegel muscles,
- Adequate Vitamin C and bioflavinoids,
- Prayer,
- Hormone balancing with herbs or physician treatment
- Repair any anatomical malformations through prayer or a physician.

I have seen Kegel exercise strengthen and "heal" an incompetent cervix in just six weeks' time. . . At any rate, when she reached that point in her pregnancy that she needed her cervix sewed up before, it was not needed. The standard of practice by allopaths for incompetent cervix is to apply a purse string suture to the cervix, using the MacDonald or the Schirodkar method. The success rate is about 80% to stop the cycle of abortion.

Treatment for spontaneous abortion is according to symptoms. Progesterone has not been proven effective, and is linked with missed abortion. Ritodrine HCl has had limited success after the 20th week gestation, but must be administered in the hospital in an IV solution. Bleeding and pain together are ominous for the continuation of the pregnancy. Bedrest is recommended. If the bleeding becomes profuse without expelling the baby, hospitalization is required. Usually the bleeding slows down dramatically when the baby and placenta are passed, and hospitalization is usually not required. If the bleeding continues at a steady pace and is like a very heavy menstrual flow in spite of herbs or other remedies, you probably have a trickle hemorrhage, and Pat should go to the hospital for a curettage or suction evacuation.

Herbal tinctures most effective against miscarriage are false unicorn and lobelia when used together. Catnip has also been used with some success. The vitamins E and P can only help the body replace what is in obvious short supply. Homeopathic medicines are very effective. Please check your manual for the specifics. I am only including the most general symptoms. "Fine tuning" the remedy with the situation provides the most effective desired results.

Homeopathics for Miscarriage/Abortion		
Bleeding Present	Pain Present	Bleeding and Pain Present
Cantharis	Cantharis	Arnica
China	Coffea	Bryonia
Hamamelis	Gelsimium	Cantharis
Carbo vegitabilis	Caulophyllum	Cimicifuga
Aconite	Ignatia	Ipecac
Pulsatilla	Ruta graveolens	Kali carbonicum
Pyrogenum	Lycopodium	Kreosotum
	Pulsatilla	Nux vomica
		Phosphorus
		Sabina
		Secale
		Sepia
		Apis
		Belladonna

If miscarriage occurs, but the placenta has been retained, use gossypium, ipecac, sabina, secale, sepia, or pulsatilla.

If bleeding persists and remains heavy, it is usually recommended that a surgical procedure called dilation and curettage (D&C) is done. As a Christian, you will want to be absolutely sure that your baby is dead before submitting to a D&C, or you will be consenting to surgical "therapeutic" abortion. The suction evacuator has replaced the sharp curettage instruments. When used by skilled hands, the suction evacuator leaves fewer scars on the uterine wall and there is less chance of perforating the uterus. Regional or general anesthesia is used to relax the cervix for dilation and protect Pat from the discomfort of the procedure. Once the baby and placenta have been expelled, the bleeding will decrease decidedly to the level of a very mild period for two to three days. It is recommended that you wait six weeks before you conceive again. That will give your body a chance to fully recover and be properly prepared for the next pregnancy with proper hormone levels.

It may take Pat longer to recover psychologically, so each couple must decide individually (as a couple) how soon they want to conceive again. If Pat is overly concerned about pregnancy and self worth, she should get counsel from her pastor or other Christian counselling service available to her.

Stillborn

The child that dies either immediately before birth, at birth, or in the first month of life leaves a family with an enormous void. Shattered dreams, expectations, and empty arms after a pregnancy full of hope, leaves the couple with lots of "Why?" questions. In addition to the emotional pain from the loss, the mother has lots of physical healing to do. She has to contend with breasts that leak and are engorged. A constant reminder of her empty arms.

Pat will need to take medication to help her uterus involute and contract back to pre-pregnancy state, because she doesn't have a nursing baby to help her. The painful contractions from the medication, coupled with her feeling of guilt—false but painful—that she couldn't "make a healthy baby," leaves Pat needing lots of tender loving care. Daddy John is hurting too, but because he is a man in this society, he doesn't show it. He thinks that if he is strong and silent, it will help his wife heal.

The truth is, she needs him to share his grief with her so she doesn't feel guilty about her grief. By sharing with each other, you will grow closer and heal faster. You heal faster because you will minister to one another. One of the biggest problems, post-tragedy, is a lack of communication. This can lead to a hardening of the heart, especially in the more sensitive personality of the couple. Real or imagined hurts and faults will come between them, and this has resulted in added tragedy of divorce and separation.

Sometimes a couple will stay together because they do not want to add divorce to their "sin list." If they are divorced in their minds and hearts, the constant friction of living in the same house or pretending that all is well will be like a carbuncle. Sooner or later the poison will burst out, contaminating all who are around. This is a tragedy worse than the original loss because many will be wounded from this charade, and some wounds will be mortal.

American burial rituals are designed to help the living face reality and give up your loved one with memories of having done the best you could under the circumstances. Because of all the arrangements that have to be made and the shock of it all, the reality of the death is often put off for a week or more. Approximately one week after the funeral, all the friends and most of the family have gone back to their normal routines. This is the worst part of grief. You are now alone, left to think about the loss and shattered dreams. You have to put the baby clothes away, take the crib down, and try to go about daily life as before.

Realize that it will not be like before, but that you can go on. Someday there will be a baby. Not to take the place of this one, but to give you joy and share your love. Until then, or the pain is healed, take one day at a time, looking to God to finish the work He has begun in you.

Another big problem, other than lack of communication with your spouse, is your lack of communication with your Heavenly Father. God is your strength and your source, every day. Don't forget that He is carrying you through the rough spots when you can't walk by yourself. The poem "Footprints in the Sand" should hang on a wall in every home, to keep reminding us of the ever-present mercy, grace, love, and faithfulness of our God.

God understands our pain as no one else can. He gave up His Son for us. He saw His Son become sin for us and die the most shameful and painful death man has ever devised. None of us can ever understand what Jesus gave up to become man and suffer for us, because we are not and never will be gods. We have no point of reference. But, Jesus does. He's been there. Do not forget Him or turn your back on Him; He won't reject you. He will give you the love, peace, understanding, wisdom, healing. . . whatever it is that you need. He will give it to you. The more you turn to Him, the more He will bless you.

Because this child was so real and special for the greatest part of a year to Pat and John, and in varying degrees to the children, Compassionate Friends has suggested a keepsake box or book. This box or book will contain a swatch of baby's hair, foot prints, picture, the blanket that was wrapped around baby when he was born, his knitted hat, etc. Everything that was used or the baby touched, like the tape measure, crib card from the hospital with his weight and statistics on it, his comb. . . Obviously you don't want to keep the ventilator, or other large equipment, but the small personal things that he used or wore his first few hours are special.

After the hustle and bustle of the funeral and packing everything away, and Pat and John have time to sit and remember baby. . . you should get the box out, and look at everything. This is your memory. Sometimes notes from the midwives, nurses and/or doctors are included. We all keep some momento of a departed family member, and think of the good times we had when they were alive. The same is true of this box. "Remember how he looked at us, John." "Remember his sweet little nose? It reminds me of your brother Sam's nose." And the memories go on. Yes, it will be painful, at first. But, as time goes on the pain heals, and you will remember fondly the baby that didn't stay with you for long, but went to be with Jesus early in life.

The memory box also helps the children remember, and gives them an opportunity to ask questions about the here-after. That is another opportunity to tell the story of Calvary and God's plan of salvation for all of us on earth.

Developmentally Disabled. . .
Angels Unaware

Dale Evans wrote a book entitled *Angel Unaware*. It is the story of their child with Downs syndrome. I highly recommend you read it if your child has Downs or other "incurable" problem. It is so easy to write these children off and not expect anything of them. But God gave that child to you. You asked God that nothing interfere with His perfect will in that child's development. Thus, you must believe that God gave this child to you by divine appointment, not to punish you. If you did not have the strength and virtues needed to raise this child in a godly manner, God would not have blessed you with him. God's blessings rarely come out of comfortable and "cushy" circumstances. They come out of the circumstances that make us stretch, reach and sometimes crawl through.

The first thing you must do is find a support group. These parents have found ways of coping and handling the everyday nitty-gritty that is not in the books. In addition, they have done all the research to find local resources. They can tell you which ones are reliable, how to get the best and most useful help, who the local specialists are, and where the best buys are for special equipment and supplies.

Your support group will probably be better informed on your particular challenge (problem) than your doctor. He has to concentrate on many things, while the support group is concerned with one specialty, such as Down's syndrome or other Trisomies. Because of the vested interest of the group, they will keep a closer watch on current research and advances. The national group usually has a newspaper or newsletter, that notes the individual successes of others with the same challenge in life, a feature article about a home-made invention that simplified living for the family, or care of the special person in that family. It is always easier to travel a path when you know there are others walking with you, and can share how to navigate the pot holes and mud puddles along the way.

The best thing this group will do is give you encouragement and hope. Many times, a family has been counseled by well-meaning medical professionals to place the child in an institution, because there was no hope for the child to become self-responsible or able to care for himself. Had many parents listened to this advice and not taken the child home and cared and worked hard at training the child to the highest level that the child could attain, they themselves would have missed many blessings.

I know of a local family that ignored such advice when it was very unusual to have a child with Down's living at home. This particular child was diagnosed as an infant to have no potential of learning. The formal diagnosis was: Down's syndrome with severe retardation, and would need custodial care for her basic needs all of her life, just like a permanent baby in a body that would grow into adulthood.

This family decided this child needed the same chance that everyone else had and began a training schedule. Everyone, including the neighbors, got in on the hard work. They started "tracking," which is a passive exercise method of training the muscles and the child to perform every activity of life that we take for granted; for example, rolling over. For hours and hours they worked, changing shifts when needed, teaching this baby how to roll over, to crawl, walk, talk, feed and dress herself, and all the thousands of things that seem to come automatically for most of us.

What was their reward? She started kindergarten in special education and by the end of the year was in with the "normal" children. She has continued "being average" to this date. A valedictorian, no; she will not be that, but most of us never attain that goal. A contributing member of society? *Yes!* Able to take care of herself and earn a living wage? *Yes!* The children in this family have learned a valuable tool for success. She, her siblings, and her classmates have learned that persistence pays. They have learned that it takes hard determination, persistence and even sacrifice to reach a worth while goal. They have also learned to never, but never, say "I quit." Worthwhile lessons for all of us.

I hope you got my point. There is no substitute for the loving, concerned care that a family can give to a special child. Help your child develop his or her strengths to the fullest. You will find strengths you did not know you possessed, and you will be blessed beyond words.

On the James Dobson radio show, in the spring of 1990, I heard the testimony of a young man who cannot care for himself at all. He has severe cerebral palsy. He is blessed with above average intelligence, but lives imprisoned in a body that does not respond to his will. God has blessed him with a ministry of intercession. When he prays, strongholds are torn down, captives are set free, and God is glorified. Did I mention that this young man cannot speak words that you and I understand? He makes sounds that the powers and principalities yield to because he is praying in the Spirit. . . groanings that cannot be uttered. The Holy Spirit is helping in his weakness (Romans 8:26–27). His parents gave a wonderful testimony of the blessings they receive in being a servant to their son, and of the blessings his siblings and others receive because this young man loves God and communicates with Him.

What if these parents had used the criterion of "If I understand him, then he can learn about Jesus. If he can walk, he is human?" They would have missed out on so much love. They would have missed God! That young man would not have learned about Jesus, nor would he have had the opportunity to believe. No one is foolish enough to say that life has been a bowl of cherries. There have been many hard-rock days, but God has seen them through it. God has given them strength and wisdom. He has blessed them with other children who are quite normal and active in sports and music. All of them are a family. There is no restricting of activities because elder brother will have a hard time getting there in the wheelchair. Elder brother enjoys full status in the family, and they enjoy him.

These examples are extremes, but if it works in the extreme, it will surely work for the rest! God gave this child to you for a blessing. It says so in the Word, Psalm 127:3: our children are God's heritage! If God says this terribly deformed child is His heritage, who are we to dispute with Him?

CHAPTER 12

MIDWIFERY SKILLS. . .
PERFECTION IN AUTHORITY

As Christian midwives, our authority and our skills come from God. He has called us, He has anointed us, and He leads us. Therefore we must be sure that all we do is to His glory, and not ours. It is easy to swell up with pride when we see "our children" walking down the street, or worshipping the Lord at the gathering together of the saints. But we must take pride in what *God* has done, not in what *we* have done. We are His vessels, no more and no less. If God chooses to make one a vessel of honor, that is His business. Remember, that He can also make that vessel of honor a vessel of dishonor also (II Timothy 2:20–26). Praise the Lord.

Paul told Timothy to (diligently) study and show himself approved unto God, a workman that needeth not to be ashamed, rightly dividing the word of truth (II Timothy 2:15). The Lord gave me that scripture in 1967, before I understood that He wanted me to be a midwife. He said I was to study everything I could get my hands on, and sharpen my skills by going to every available workshop I could find, "in the work that I want you to do." I finally understood what He meant in 1977, and proceeded to follow His directions. At the time there was precious little written, and what was written came from the "hippy" culture that I could not relate to. I read it anyway, and gleaned the wheat from the tares. Babies are born the same way to every woman, regardless of the language used. After reading and digesting what I needed to know, I saved the skills sections, herb and supply lists, but destroyed the rest of the books. That continued until I found Joy Young's *Christian Home Birth* book. It is now out of print, but that book was my textbook for years. Before studying, we all need to pray that the Lord will give us the discernment to separate the tares from the wheat, and to guard our minds. Compare the author's philosophies with the Word of God, and discard what does not line up with God's plumbline.

I have been asked by many aspiring midwives what is the best course of study to follow. This depends on how much money they have to spend, whether they are married and have a family, and how God is leading them. In the 1990s, we are blessed with many opportunities, so we need to pray and see what God wants us to do. The majority of opportunities also have strong New Age influences. God may want to use you to convert someone of influence, but be sure *God* is telling you that, and not the flesh. He may have someone else in that place, and wants you to be elsewhere.

There are midwifery clinics/schools in El Paso, Texas, that will give you lots of experience in a short time, and the Midwifery School in Seattle, Washington, enjoys an excellent reputation in academics and experience. The Seattle School of Midwifery course takes about three years, and is the oldest formal school for traditional midwifery students with no medical background in the U.S.

God may have a purpose for you to go to the local junior college for an A.D. R.N. The junior college may not teach traditional midwifery philosophy, but will give you the background courses that some states require before you can apprentice. If there is a commercial herb garden nearby, you may want to take a day and learn what you can about herbs and their traditional uses. Those of you that are blessed with a homeopathic practitioner nearby, do take advantage of that knowledge. Homeopathics do the job much quicker, and are more stable and reliable than raw herbs.

If family obligations are such that you can not "leave home" to go to school, try home school for Mom. Seriously consider Carla Hartley's "Ancient Art Midwifery Institute. A.A.A.M.I. is very comprehensive, and covers *everything* a midwife needs to know from A to Z. Experienced midwives have taken the course after being in practice for some time, and remark how thorough it is and how much additional information they learned from Carla. In addition to following lesson plans, you have homework to mail in on a regular basis. A written acknowledgement will be returned to you with appropriate words of encouragement and direction for further information as needed. Ancient Art takes about three years to complete, and is "New Age free."

There are other correspondence courses, at about one third to one half the cost and time investment of Carla's, but are not as complete in scope or in depth of academics. Midwives Alliance of North America has a direct entry midwife program for "Certified Professional Midwife." North American Registry of midwives has a current registry for any midwife who wishes to be registered for referral. Your state midwifery association may have skills workshops that meet their standards and the requirements of the local law at a fraction of the cost of the national groups.

Going through the state midwifery organization will also help you network with student, apprentice and senior midwives, find a senior to apprentice with, and attend her study group, thus letting your "light" shine. I recommend all student midwives to be active in their state organization. You have the energy and the time to do the necessary work, that the senior does not have because of the intense time demands in her practice. (That does not let the senior out of pulling her own weight in the local and state organizations.) Being active in the nitty-gritty of the organization will help the student learn to organize her life. It also answers the question if she and her family understands what kind of commitment is required.

Being a midwife is like being married. Your commitment to your clients is at their beck and call according to their needs until after the six-week postpartum checkup is past, and sometimes well into baby's first year. (Many times, clients will continue to call back for colds, teething problems, feeding questions, etc.) When that baby decides to birth, you go. That baby is not concerned that it is your baby's first birthday, or your 25th wedding anniversary, or God forbid, your son's or daughter's wedding. Because of that demand on your private time, your family, especially your husband *must* agree that this is *God's plan for you,* and *God's call* on your life. If he is not one hundred percent behind you, your marriage will fail, and so will your midwifery practice. Your children will be totally out of order, and rebellion will be rampant. Such destruction is not from God, but a result of being out of God's order.

It sounds good, and the intention is there, when the wife tells her husband that midwifery is not going to interfere with her duties at home and church, except when births occur, but in real life, it will interfere at some time. The trick is to limit the interference. Everyone understands the midwife has no control over when the baby is going to arrive. They do have a hard time understanding why you are not there to cook meals and keep the laundry up, or why you are sleeping 'til noon. After all, the baby was born at 3:00 a.m. They forgot that you were awake for 36 hours, thanks to your little Johnny being awake from teething the night before, plus the all-night labor. No one realizes the incredible amount of energy a midwife uses at each birth. You get tired when catching babies, especially if you have three births in 16 hours, in three different counties and each one hundred miles from the other. When you come home, you want to crawl between the sheets and be "unconscious" for at least four hours.

Your husband must be willing to grill up hamburgers, or make a pot of chili to feed the crew when you are at births. If he or the kids are running out of clothes, he has to be willing and able to wash a load of clothes; or dig through the clean clothes in the basket and fish out what is needed. If the baby needs clean britches, Daddy must be willing to change diapers. If he is unwilling to do that, then he must be willing to pay for a flexible sitter, preferably an older woman, that will take over when you are gone. You can not fulfill the office of the midwife, while worrying if your children are being kept clean, supervised and fed, while you are gone from home. In addition to all of this physical support, he needs to be interceding with the Heavenly Father on your behalf. His prayers should include protection on the road, going and coming; wisdom; favor from God and man; alert mind and discernment, quick, normal and easy birth, and bind the enemy from interfering in any way. This does not excuse you if you take advantage of your family's support. You need to be an intercessor for your family and your clients. You need to manage your time appropriately, and you need to recognize God's timing in your life. He may not want you to start catching babies until your children are old enough to take care of themselves for short periods of time. If that is so, learn midwifery the slow and steady way. Help the midwife in her office, go to the occasional birth as a helper or birth assistant. Do labor coaching in the hospital and teach childbirth education classes. This will help the midwife immensely, let you "get your feet a little damp," and give you great experience without disrupting your family as full-time midwifery would.

If you are not too discouraged, then you've been called. If you think I'm exaggerating, talk to any midwife, or talk to the husband of a midwife. The divorce rate among midwives is around 85%. Not all husbands can live with a wife who is rarely home for and with him. It takes a lot of hard work, a special man and a lot of help from God to keep a midwife's marriage together. We plan special time about every six months, and no one and nothing is allowed to interfere. That time is for Jim and Betty. If you need a midwife, then call Joan, Jean, Dorothy, Kim, or Barb, but not Betty. She's gone fishing out of state where there is no phone! Our only uninterrupted time may be just that weekend at the half year point, and for two weeks at least once a year. The "big" vacation requires to block out that month from planned births. Somebody always goes over from the previous month, and will go early from the following month, so if I have two weeks birth-free for vacation, I am really blessed.

Setting Up Your Midwifery Practice

Please, do not start a midwifery service without apprenticing first. You need to learn how to take a blood pressure, find fetal heart tones and screen for abnormal fetal heart tones, know how to palpate for a baby, know why you test the urine with those little chemical impregnated strips, know how to draw blood for state-mandated prenatal tests, and also for any other blood tests that may be necessary, know how to determine a pregnancy and estimate due dates. You also need to know how to counsel the client that is fearful, has lots of personal problems and no one to listen to her, how to personalize her nutrition needs, and how to interview and screen potential clients. You need to know what local resources are available, and when to refer your client to them to supplement your prenatal care. Those are basic prenatal skills.

You also need to recognize normal labor patterns and when labor becomes pathogenic, recognizing normal fetal heart tones and abnormal heart tones, knowing how to convert abnormal situations to normal, and, of course, catch the baby in vertex presentation. Know CPR for infants and adults, know how to stop hemorrhage, and stabilize the client until skilled help is obtained.

The minimal postpartum skills include how to care for the newborn, exam and recognize the normal newborn, know how to get breastfeeding established and know how to handle most of the common problems of breastfeeding for the first six weeks. For those breastfeeding problems you do and do not know about, have the La Leche League leader's telephone number handy for your client, so she can get help "from the experts." Take information for the state birth certificate, do the required newborn screening, understand normal postpartum processes, and do the six-week postpartum exam. Another phone number you need to keep handy is your senior/preceptor's number. There will be a thousand questions that come up in your first year alone, that you can't find in your books because the answers have empirical roots. They have been handed down from midwife to midwife for centuries, but no one has put them in book form yet.

You first need to accumulate certain necessities. You have to have a stethoscope, blood pressure cuff, a fetoscope, charts, pen, gloves, lubricant, and a jar of urinalysis sticks, and a "magnificent bag" to put them in. Remember, your bag needs to be large enough to hold your "charts", and other equipment as you accumulate it. Your charts may be of.your own design, or follow guidelines of your state organization, or you can purchase them from Spirit-Led Childbirth, or Kim Perry. You will also want to keep a county and city map in your car for the area you serve.

Your office, to begin with, can be at home. Office at home saves on baby sitters, and the interaction gives your children and your client's children something to do, while you and your client can have a little privacy. Be prepared and keep your sense of humor for those "inopportune" interruptions that are bound to occur. If you prefer not to have your office at home, you may be doing a lot of traveling from your house to clients' homes. This increases costs, both for sitters and upkeep for

your car (gas, oil, tires, etc.). If you are going into a group midwifery service, with a separate office building, like at the "Birth
Center," and *if* your children are well-behaved, then perhaps
they can come with you on the days you are doing prenatals, or
general office work, and no one is in labor. Some midwives
have developed their own "child care center" at the Birth Center. They have hired their own sitters, as employees of the
Birth Center, and have a separate, but adjoining place for the
children to play, sleep, and eat. Close enough to Mom, so Mom
can pop over and nurse the baby, but yet Mom can work without interruptions. Sometimes the clients' children can join in
the fun, especially if the client is in labor, or needs quiet time
with the midwives. These sitters may be available to keep the
client's children occupied or supervised during labor, since
they would be familiar with each other.

Some group practices rotate jobs, so you take turns working the desk, paper work, prenatals, postpartums, taking calls,
etc. Other groups have a secretary/receptionist who does all
the paper work, answers the phone, etc., and the midwives just
take care of the clients. How the practice is set up depends on
how busy the center is, and if the group trains apprentices. If
apprentices receive their training, class time is added to the
midwives' responsibilities, leaving very little time for paperwork. You may even begin your practice in a doctor's office.
This eases you into things, because all you have to worry about
is fitting into the established routine of the office, and honing
your midwifery skills, with experts all around to help. If you
wish to retain your traditional skills, that may be a challenge
unless the doctor also uses traditional midwifery skills at birth.
Often, the observant midwife will see high-risk pregnancy management that will help in her practice. If the doctor has good
manual skills, you could learn additional skills, such as internal and external versions. (You won't want to do high-risk
pregnancy at home.) You can get some good training on setting
up an office in the future, and what to avoid by observing how
this office is run.

Another item that midwives do not like to discuss when first
starting out is *fees*. You need to put all of the expenses of your
education, how much your share of the electricity, heat, use of
the car, costs of disposable supplies and equipment, and
books, xeroxing costs for classes and forms, stationary, tele-

phone, and anything else you may need down on paper, prorating it per client. Then figure out what your time is worth per hour, and how many hours you are going to spend on the average, prenatally and postpartum with the client. Next, add what you think is a reasonable fee for birth. Add that all together. Now what is the average income of your clients? If they are at or just above green card income level, they certainly cannot pay what the the local tycoon can afford. You may decide on a sliding scale with or without barter, with a minimum fee for your low-income families, graduating to a maximum fee for your clients in the upper-income levels. That way, your expenses will be covered eventually, but the low-income people will not still be paying for the last birth when they retire.

The Midwife's Marvelous Bag

There is something wonderful about the midwife's birth bag. It represents mystery and wonder along with reassurance to the client. To the midwife, The Bag represents her ministry. A badge of honor. Her dreams come true. It may even remind her of the client that gave her her Midwife Bag!

Your birth bag may be a custom-designed wonder, a medical bag or a hand-made midwife's bag from a birth supply house. It may even be a bag from the luggage department that caught your eye. Each bag is special to that midwife, and fulfills her own peculiar needs. Where ever you find it, it must be large enough to hold everything, including the "kitchen sink," neatly and in order, so you can find what you need in a hurry. You want to pull the cord clamp or whatever out of the bag without digging through everything at those births when the baby is on the perineum when you arrive. Pockets or built-in trays, as in the medical bag, are an absolute necessity. It must also be light enough when filled to not require a pack mule to haul it for you, yet sturdy enough to withstand all kinds of weather and rough treatment, protect your delicate instruments, and still be attractive.

You may find it more convenient to have a prenatal bag separate from your birth bag. This allows you to keep all of your birthing equipment in one place where it is easy to get to, sterile things will remain sterile, and you don't forget something important, like a fetoscope. Weight is very important. If your bag is heavy when empty, you will need to hire a bag carrier when you get it filled with your equipment! The Sklar feto-scope alone weighs three pounds! If you want to also carry the "necessities" from your purse in the prenatal bag, it will need separated compartments, too.

I'll never forget the late afternoon I went to a home for a pre-natal visit and her tom cat sprayed my prenatal bag while it was open! Everything had to get deodorized and washed. If he had done that to my birth bag, I would not have been ready for the birth that happened at another home that evening! Admittedly that is rare, but there are times when you do not want to expose your sterile supplies unnecessarily. I never forgot to draw the "Blood Line" around my bags again. If your client is struggling with "evicting uninvited critters," you don't want any to hitchhike home with you. Birth bags are full of little hiding places for six- and eight-legged "hitch-hikers" to find. If you are in a home that has "non-paying tenants," in the spirit "draw" a Blood of Jesus "line" around your bag. Those critters will walk up to that Blood line, make a 45-degree turn and walk around your bag without touching it. Even if you acci-dentally placed your bag in their line of march! Praise the Lord! Insects in the house are a curse of Egypt. They are to be treated as such. If you are unfamiliar with this, the scriptural principle is in Daniel 10:13, 20–21, 12:1; Revelation 12:7–9 and Hebrews 1:14. "In the name of Jesus, I place a spiritual hedge of protection about my bag(s), that no insect nor any unauthorized being can enter or defile my bags or any of my goods (midwifery bags, equipment, clothing, car, books, purse, etc.). By the authority Jesus has given me as a believer, I place a guardian angel from Archangel Michael's band to protect me and my 'stuff.'" The Archangel Michael is in charge of the Heavenly Army and "carries" the blood of Jesus, the nuclear arsenal of the believer against the powers of darkness.

The following list is what I carried in my bags. You may find that you can delete some items and you may want to add some others. I found that in the course of a year, I would use everything except the catheter at least once. I usually needed the catheter about every 18 to 24 months. Those items marked with "†" I also carried in my prenatal bag.

- Stethoscope, capable of hearing high, medium and low tones†
- Blood-pressure cuff†

- Fetoscope†
- Sterile and non-sterile exam gloves, singles and pairs†
- Sterile surgical lubricating gel, individual packets or tube†
- Herbal tinctures and/or Homeopathic Midwife Kit†
- Reflex hammer†
- Vaginal speculum (may need two in each bag: one small and one medium or large) †
- Otoscope-ophthalmoscope†
- Flashlight/headlamp (scuba diver's is best)†
- Penlight†
- Hemoglobinometer†
- Urine test strips†
- One accurate scale for mom for prenatals at home (not necessarily in your bag) †
- Band-Aids® for covering venipuncture site, or heel of baby from PKU test†
- One gestation wheel†
- Two thermometers (one oral, one rectal)†
- Handy reference books: herbal, unusual births, homeopathic Materia Medica/Birth Reference Book†
- Alcohol prep pads†
- Lab supplies: Vacutainer™ tubes; grey, red, and lavender tops; pap smear kits, culturettes black and red, Vacutainer™ needles (21g)†
- Lab mailers marked Priority or Express Mail†
- Pens, black and red, one glass-marking pen for Vacutainers™†
- Tourniquet†
- Charts†
- Miscellaneous handouts: mastitis, jaundice, circumcision, candida, increasing your milk supply, postpartum and newborn care, etc.†
- Doppler for those hard-to-hear FHTs
- One sterile urinary catheter
- One Chatillon scale for baby and sling
- Three ammonia inhalants, in case of fainty mom
- One tube of Aquasonic® gel for doppler (surgical lubricant can be substituted)
- One fracture bed pan
- One emesis basin

- Emergency "space blanket"
- Birth certificate work sheets
- One tape measure, in inches and centimeters†
- One suture set (a second set is nice for those back-to-back births):
  - One needle holder
  - One mosquito hemostat, straight or curved
  - One suture scissors
  - One tissue/dressing forceps with teeth
  - Two chromic gut 4-0 suture on $\frac{1}{2}$-inch swaged needle, cutting
  - Two chromic gut 3-0 suture on $\frac{1}{2}$-inch swaged needle, taper point
  - One 5cc vial lidocaine without epinephrine
  - 2 packages of 6 - 8 sterile gauze 4X4's
- Two DeLee Busse bac/shield™ mucus suction traps or similar type
- Two cord setups, one standard plus one extra for surprise twins or back-to-back births. Each cord setup has:
  - One pair of cord scissors
  - Two hemostats
  - One cord clamp or umbilical tape

I kept all sterile supplies in a gallon-sized Zip-lock freezer bag. This protects the wrapping from unnecessary wear and tear and prolongs the sterility of the instruments. All "loose" packages of sterile supplies in your bag should be resterilized every six to eight weeks. The Zip-lock bag keeps the paper wrap from getting torn and wrinkled, extending the "sterile shelf life" in your bag about four to six weeks longer. Paper wraps or bags that are wrinkled have small tears along the creases. That item should be rewrapped before resterilization, especially if it will enter the body; for example, a urinary catheter. Syringes are not okay, even if they have not gotten wet and the protective cap remains on the syringe tip and the plunger has always been inside the barrel. Use it next after noticing the packaging as being weakened, or resterilize it if you have a gas autoclave. Steam autoclaving and oven baking will cloud or melt the plastic, rendering it useless.

Prenatal Skills: Physical Exam

Sooner or later you will have a client who is unable to see a physician for a routine physical exam, or just chooses not to do so for some reason. At her first prenatal, take the time to listen to her heart and lungs, palpate for enlarged lymph glands under the mandible, below the ear, and in the neck. Use your otoscope and look in her ears, your ophthalmoscope to look in her eyes. You are looking for deviations from normal, not a diagnosis. If you find an enlarged lymph gland, but it isn't painful, and Pat hasn't noticed it, keep an eye on it. It may have been busy doing its job and destroying invading bacteria or viruses. It should be back to normal at the next visit. If it gives Pat any pain when you palpate it, do encourage her to go to a physician. It could be very important, or nothing at all. Until you have had training in determining the difference, you best leave it to the "expert." While checking Pat's throat, place your index and second fingers on either side of her larynx (Adam's Apple). Ask Pat to swallow, while you try to palpate her thyroid. It lives right behind the larynx. If you can't feel anything, that's good. It means the thyroid is not swollen or enlarged.

Do a breast exam for lumps and teach Pat how to do her own exam. After visually accessing the breast by looking for dimpling, bruising, inverted nipples (that is, the nipple goes in instead of sticking out), place your fingers alongside the nipple and gently feel for any lumps always moving in a circle and gradually going to the outside of the breast. Pat should have her arm on the side being examined raised and her hand under her head if lying down, or behind her head if sitting up. After examining the breast, palpate the lymph glands in the axilla (armpit), before Pat switches arms. Remember breasts are very tender in early pregnancy and just before a period!

After the breast exam, palpate Pat's abdomen. If she is constipated, she may have some hard lumps that may be felt. Stool will be the shape of the intestines—like a sausage. Tumors are usually irregularly shaped, softer, and do not "move" in the direction of the intestines. Slight tenderness in the lower pelvis is often present especially in a primipara or a very sensitive individual in early pregnancy. Depending on the stage of pregnancy, you may be able to feel the fundus.

Determining Pregnancy

You can stock pregnancy tests, and run them on each new client, or you can have them go to the local crisis pregnancy center for the test. You can also have them stop at a local laboratory for blood hormone levels, which are slightly more accurate if there is a doubt about the pregnancy. Occasionally, and I am finding more frequently, women are spotting in their first trimester. Doing a pregnancy test when Pat comes for her prenatal visit is helpful when she has had medium to heavy spotting. If questions arise, draw blood or send her to the lab for hormone levels. Please review Chapter 11 for discussion on spontaneous abortion. Positive hormone levels are possible for two weeks after spontaneous abortion.

Confirming the probable pregnancy without the use of ultrasound can be done by pelvic exam. After getting Pat's history, and doing the physical exam, you are ready for the pelvic exam. Use a speculum first, according to the following procedure before doing a manual (glove) exam, because the lubricant on your glove will distort or render the pap smear invalid. The midwife uses the vaginal speculum, to look for **Chadwick's Sign**, which is a bluish or purplish coloration of the vaginal and vulva mucosa, and visual exam of the cervix. You do not want to be forceful in your manual exam, as that can start bleeding and possible loss of pregnancy, so be gentle. If the uterus is enlarged, it is a probable pregnancy. Other things besides baby can make a uterus enlarge, such as fibroids or other tumors, late menstrual period, etc. **Hegar's Sign** is the softening and compressibility of the uterine isthmus, causing the uterus to anteflex during the first three months of the pregnancy. When the uterus enlarges enough, it rises out of the pelvis and straightens out. In the meantime, urinary frequency occurs from the fundus pressing on the bladder. **Goodell's Sign** is the softening of the cervix from a firmness similar to your nose to the softness like your lips. Primiparas do not have as dramatic a softening as multigravidas do, but it is present.

Presumptive signs of pregnancy are:

- Abrupt cessation of menstrual period
- Nausea and vomiting (sometimes)
- Tingling, tenseness, enlargement, nodularity of breasts
- Enlargement of nipples

- Darkening of the nipples and areola
- Increased urination
- Fatigue
- Appearance of Montgomery's tubercles or follicles (enlarging of oil glands in the areola)
- Positive pregnancy test
- Continued elevation of basal body temperature in absence of any infection
- Expressing colostrum from nipples
- Excessive salivation
- Chadwick's sign
- Quickening
- Skin pigmentation darkening: linea nigra, vascular spiders, palmar erythema, chloasma, abdominal and breast striae.

Probable signs of pregnancy are:

- Enlargement of the abdomen
- Palpation of the fetal outline
- Ballottement
- Enlargement and irregular uterine shape (**Piskacek's Sign**)
- Hegar's sign
- Goodell's sign
- Chadwick's sign
- Palpation of Braxton-Hick's contractions

Positive signs of pregnancy are:

- Fetal heart tones
- Sonogram (if medically indicated)
- Fetal movement (authorities vary whether it should be positive or probable)

Vaginal Speculum Exam

The speculum can be a plastic disposable, which you can give to Pat for her own use in the future, or a stainless steel sterilizable one. The metal ones are smaller than the disposables, and I think are a little easier to use. But that is a matter of personal preference. I use both. If you are going to take a Pap smear screening for cervical cell changes, or take a culture to determine the reason for the discharge, do not use lubricant on the speculum, because it interferes with the tests.

Before doing the vaginal exam, get the speculum ready by warming it in warm water. The warm water will lubricate the speculum. Swing Pat's hips around to the edge of the bed, and place her feet on the seats of two chairs. You will need to be in a sitting position between Pat's legs either on the floor or on a low stool, so you can look into the speculum to see the cervix and vaginal walls.

Now, with your two fingers inserted to the first joint in the vagina (use water to lubricate), apply gentle downward pressure on the perineum. Take the speculum in your other hand and turn it to the oblique, so the handle is pointing toward eight o'clock or four o'clock. Gently guide it, with the "tongue" closed, along your fingers into the vagina. When you have inserted it three-fourths of the way, turn the speculum so the handle is vertical, while slipping your fingers out of the vagina, and slide the speculum the rest of the way in. Gently spread open the "tongue" by squeezing the handle, maintaining a downward pressure.

Observe the vaginal walls for white spots (candida), or color (Chadwick's sign), bruising, or anything else. The healthy vaginal mucosa is pink. Next by manipulating the speculum slowly upward, look for the cervix. You may have to open the speculum a little more, or close it and, with downward pressure, slide it in deeper. The healthy cervix in a primigravida is pink and looks like a doughnut. There are gradual changes in the shape of the cervix, with succeeding pregnancies, and in the grand-multigravida it is patulous and pink, with the os appearing like a slit. There should not be anything on it or coming out of it. If there is clear fluid coming out of the cervix and Pat is pregnant, check for amniotic fluid with Nitrazine® paper. Always culture any fluid coming out of the cervix. Abnormal discharge from the cervix is symptomatic of pathology, from a simple cervicitis, to a malignancy.

Observing and taking cultures of any fluids coming from the cervix is often preventative to heart break later on. Vaginal infections ranging from simple vaginitis to sexually transmitted disease can be diagnosed from cultures. Warts need to be seen by a physician for accurate diagnosis and screening for hospital birth. Some warts can cause polyps on the baby's vocal cords, plus the added danger of tearing during birth and causing severe hemorrhage.

Sexually transmitted diseases lend their own peculiar complications to a birth, not only to Pat and baby, but are dangerous to the midwife, because she could contract it from the fluids. This is an opportunity to do some labor coaching at the hospital. Pat and John need to have medical care, or they will keep passing this thing back and forth.

Sexually Transmitted Diseases

During your initial interview or at the initial prenatal visit while doing the initial screening blood draw, *always* inquire about Pat or John ever having a STD such as chlamydia, gonorrhea, syphilis, hepatitis B, trichomonas vaginalis, herpes, HIV, or Pelvic Inflammatory Disease (PID). All of them can cause serious problems from scarring of the reproductive tract to neonatal fatality. It is wisdom to risk out women with active STD. Doctors and hospitals are better equipped for the attendant complications.

Herpes can be treated safely with Herp Elim herbal tincture or HRPZ homeopathic formula to induce remission during the pregnancy. Pat may have home birth if there are no herpes lesions present in the vagina or on the labia at time of labor.

Candida Albicans (yeast) infection can be treated with yogurt applied liberally in the vagina, homeopathic Yeast Guard or over-the-counter (OTC) Monostat or Gyne-Lotrim. If the yeast is resistant to this treatment, physician consult is mandatory because it is beyond home care and the baby could be involved with serious consequences.

Bacterial infections such as streptococcus or staphylococcus can have serious consequences such as death for the baby. Always refer to a physician for treatment. It is better to be safe than sorry for the rest of your life.

Pap Smear

"Pap" is an abbreviation for "Papanicolaou," named after the 19th century American physician George Papanicolaou, is a simple smear method of examining exfoliated cells. Exam of the smear is by microscope at a licensed lab. The most common site is from the cervix, but it can be used for tissue specimens from any organ. It allows early detection of cervical cancer, before symptoms are noticed by Pat. Results of the test are reported by classes: Class I means only normal cells are seen; Class II indicates atypical cells consistent with inflammation; Class III is mild dysplasia; Class IV is severe dysplasia, suspicious cells; and Class V shows visible carcinoma cells.

If Pat has not had a Pap smear in a few years, this is a good time to do it. You cannot do an accurate Pap smear if there are too many organisms present from an infection such as *Trichomonas vaginalis* or *Candida albicans*, etc. If you are not sure what the cause of the fluid is and suspect something other than "bacteria," do the Pap smear anyway; just gently wipe the fluid away with gauze (not a cotton ball; it will confuse the reading on the slide). If there are growths on the cervix, like warts or polyps, be careful that you do not cause them to bleed, but include that area in the smear. If there is a problem, it most likely will be in that area. The other area that is the most common site of cervical cancer is at the squamocolumnar junction (where the cervix and uterine lining meet). Be sure that is also included in your smear. If you follow the directions included with your Pap kit, you will get the areas you need. Always get smears from spots with different coloring or appearance in the area directed. If there are areas that do not look normal on the vaginal wall or fornix, take a smear from there and put the smear on a separate slide. Be sure to note on your lab slip where you took the smear. It is wise to recheck a positive Pap smear. Sometimes cells will look like a cancer cell under the microscope, but with a second check, all cells are normal. This could be an answer to prayer, or the body is functioning the way God intended and destroyed the abnormal cells. Lab error can also be a factor. Double-checking a class III to V report by sending the second Pap smear to a different lab may prevent unnecessary suffering.

Use a pencil to write Pat's name and any other information the lab needs on the slide before you begin the exam. There is a one-inch area at one end of the slide for this. When you apply your specimen to the slide, *roll* the cotton swab across the indicated area; do not "paint" the swab back and forth. When collecting with a wooden spatula, place the flat surface against the slide and stroke it once across the slide in a "spreading butter" motion. Do not stir the specimen or slide the spatula back across the cells already on the slide. If the specimen is too thick, then slide the edge of the spatula with a single light stroke down the slide and remove the excess. "Stirring and mixing" the specimens will break and destroy the cells, which causes the smear to be useless, and will need to be repeated. Always collect the specimen on the labeled side.

Calculating the Due Date

Estimating the due date is just that. . . *estimating.* The figure you come up with is merely a ball-park figure. The variable is your client's menstrual cycle. If she has 35–40 days between periods, she will probably go over her date at least two weeks, and possibly three weeks. If her cycle is every 21 days, she will likely be early. The calculators are based on a 28-day cycle because that is the mean, or average, cycle. Even then, there is a built-in variance of five to seven days, plus or minus.

Naegele's Rule for calculating birth day is: Add seven days to the first date of the last menstrual period and subtract three months. For example, if the first date of the last period was January 1, add seven days, giving you January 8. Now subtract three months and you will come up with October 7 or 8. Don't forget to use the actual days in the month, so if you hit February, you will have either 28 or 29 days, and four months have 30 days while the rest have 31. An easier calculation is using the wheel. These little marvels are obtained from birth supply houses, prenatal vitamin companies (pharmaceutical salesmen), and occasionally promos at conventions. Besides telling you the due date (give or take five to seven days), they tell you how many weeks your client is pregnant, the approximate date of conception (information for birth certificate, and helpful if menses date is doubtful), approximate weight and length of the average baby at any time of the pregnancy, and when a positive urine test for pregnancy could first be had.

The other variables are accuracy in recalling the first day of last menstrual period (LMP). Occasionally a special event occurs about ovulation time, and the conception date is firmly implanted in her mind. This date is usually 14 days before her next period, and the calculator makes it easy to determine birth day. If the following variables occur, you cannot calculate birth day with Naegele's rule, because Naegele's rule requires the first day of the last menstrual period. The following variables require different criteria for calculation:

- Irregular menstrual cycle with one or more amenorrheic months;
- Conception occurring during breastfeeding while Pat is ovulating, but not having her period;
- Conception occurring before normal menstrual cycle is established after the last pregnancy or discontinuation of oral contraceptive pills.

When these factors are present, you have to depend on clinical findings such as fundal height, first kicks and a decision on having a sonogram between 18 and 28 weeks. Your clients have to live with their decision concerning the sonogram. This is also dependent on your back-up giving the order for one. The results will be sent to him unless you have staff privileges. If you have privileges, then you can order the sono and will receive the results directly. Generally the fundal height is the same as the weeks pregnant, give or take two centimeters, starting at the 20th week.

Blood Pressure

Taking the blood pressure is a simple procedure but requires practice to coordinate doing three things at once. Practice taking blood pressures on your friends and family until you feel exercised sufficiently to start on clients.

- If the shirt sleeve will slide easily, pull the sleeve above Pat's elbow higher than the width of the cuff.
- If the material is heavy or tight, ask Pat to slip her arm out of the sleeve. If the material is very thin and light weight, you can hear the arterial pulse (duh, duh, duh,) through it, but get experience first. Material causes friction sounds that are confusing to the unpracticed ear.
- Wrap the cuff around the upper arm in a snug (not tight), neat (no wrinkles) manner. A good cuff will have a velcro closure. You want the cuff to overlap sufficiently so the cuff will maintain pressure on the arm.

- If the cuff is too loosely applied, the bladder in the cuff will inflate, but no pressure will be applied to the arm. Release the air, rewrap the cuff (make sure the cuff is deflated) and check the closure. If Pat's arm is very small, you may have to use a child's cuff to get an accurate reading. If her arm is large, you may need a large adult cuff. Most cuffs require a minimum of $\frac{3}{4}$ to 1 inch of velcro to catch and still get a good reading.
- Determine the exact placement of the stethoscope, by palpating the artery with your finger tips. It will be found along or just below the crease, and usually is in the center. Many cuffs have arrows pointing to the artery. It does not matter where the arrow points, as long as the tubing is out of your way.
- Inflate the cuff to about 180 and listen. If you hear the pulse, go up 10 milliliters of mercury (10 ml Hg) more. If you cannot hear the pulse, carefully and slowly let the air out of the cuff. Mark when you first heard the pulse and when you last heard the pulse.
- Write down what you heard. The "first" number (**systolic**), is how much pressure is exerted against the artery walls by the blood with each heart beat. The "last" number (**diastolic**), is the amount of pressure against the artery walls when the heart is at rest between beats.

Normal values are below 140/90. If Pat is very petite and very laid-back, she may not have a B/P over 90/60. The average pressure for a young adult is approximately 120 systolic and 70 diastolic. Hypertension is consistent B/P of 140/90 or more over several visits. It may also be a "normal" value for a lady with 10 children under the age of 11, who just ran up the stairs because she was late for her appointment! Whenever a reading is on the high side, take it over at the end of the appointment. Many times you will get a high reading, due to Pat rushing to get to the office through heavy traffic. After Pat has had a chance to relax and rest a bit, it will be back to normal. Some ladies are so relaxed at the midwife's office that it never is over 90/50 (hypotension)! Take that same lady within the hour to the doctor's office, and it is 130/80! This is due to a nervousness/anxiety that is commonly called "White Coat

Anxiety Syndrome." Pat may even experience it on her first visit to the midwife.

Anxiety will raise the blood pressure. That is why I always make a point to talk with my clients for a few minutes before taking the B/P. Even when rushed, I try to say something to make them giggle or laugh, so the reading will be close to normal. If your client has an elevated B/P, she may have something "eating" at her. Fish around until you get her to talk. She may need some techniques to shake worries off of her and on to Jesus who is able to handle them. See Chapter 5.

Roll-Over Test

At 28 weeks, it is time to do the "roll-over test", to screen for the potential pre-eclamptic woman. The test was named when we used to take the first reading after Pat was lying flat on her back on the bed for five minutes, then we would have her roll over on to her left side and take it immediately. Allowing her to sit on the edge of the bed and then lie down is just as accurate and easier to remember to do.

The first blood pressure reading is taken on the right arm, while she is sitting on the edge of the bed. Leaving the cuff on the right arm, the second reading is taken immediately after she lies down on the bed. If the lady is not eating enough protein, her blood pressure will vary 10 milliliters of mercury from the two readings. She may also be consistently spilling a +1 or more in her urine. The protein spill and epigastric pain are usually warning signs, but she may not spill on her appointment day, if she is cheating on her diet every day except the preceding two or three days.

This is a simple, non-invasive test. If there was a rise of 10 milliliters of mercury (Hg), counsel her to boost her protein and repeat the roll-over test in a week. On the repeat visit, you will see a marked difference. The rise in B/P will not be more than 5 milliliters of Hg, and she will remark how much better she feels. Continue to encourage her to continue improving her diet, and recheck the roll-over test next week at her regular, scheduled time. It should be normal then. If there was no rise, Pat is doing well, and no need to be concerned of toxemia at this time. Encourage her to keep eating adequate protein, drink 8–10 glasses of water a day, get her exercise and plenty of rest.

Palpation

Palpation is a skill that will serve you as well as a sonogram, once you have mastered it. By definition, it is a skill or technique used in physical examination in which the examiner feels the texture, size, consistency, and location of certain parts of the body with the hands. A midwife skilled in palpating the uterus and unborn baby is said to have "eyes in her fingertips." The only way to become skilled is to practice, practice, practice.

Borrow a doll from your daughter, grand-daughter, niece, or your neighbor's daughter. Better yet, purchase one from a supply house such as Childbirth Graphics, and you will have your baby for your classes. Place a soft pillow over the doll. Now try to palpate dolly through the pillow. Once you can figure out the difference between the head and the feet, or feet and hands, have someone secretly change dolly's position. Change the thickness of pillows. Once you can accurately tell where the bottom and head are through a thick polyester pillow, you are ready for a client. The real Pat will help you, because she can tell you where her baby has been kicking. This immediately tells you where the feet are. If the feet are kicking Pat's ribs, the head must be at the other end. Hallelujah!

The **first Leopold's maneuver** in palpation is to stand or sit next to her legs, facing her face and place your (hopefully warm) hands on her tummy with the fingertips of each hand touching and pointing toward her ribs. Using the flat of the palms of your hands and fingers, move the parts you feel back and forth between your hands. Move your hands apart enough to keep the baby between them, but also draw in your mind what you are feeling. Is it round, smooth and firm, or is it bulgy and firm? Does it move away from, or towards your fingers? Smooth and firm (hard) is the head. Bulgy but firm and does not move away from or towards you is the buttocks. If it moves, it is probably an extremity like the arm or leg. Legs usually kick back, and arms or hands pull away from your hands. If in doubt, "walk" your fingers by moving them up and down while scooting them along the area you are feeling. If you are "exploring" the baby's hip or buttocks, you will find a "long" appendage that resembles a fat sausage and "disappears" suddenly out of reach into the uterus. If you hit a reflex spot at the knee, the lower leg will flex and kick back at you. Sometimes you can palpate the leg down to the foot. A hand will move away, but the foot cannot bend away at the ankle like the hand can at the wrist.

The **second Leopold's maneuver** is to slide your hands from the fundus toward the public bone, again very lightly "bouncing" the baby back and forth between your hands, while continuing to look at her face. You are "looking" with your fingers for a long, straight firm line. One hand will feel this flat firm area, and the other one will feel lumps that keep disappearing. The "lumpy side" is the front of the baby and the long, firm, smooth side is the back. The "lumps" are the hands, arms, legs and feet curled up in front of the baby. Continue to walk your hands down towards Pat's pubic bone. You should feel a round hard object. That is the baby' head.

The **third Leopold's maneuver** is also known as **Pawlik's maneuver**. Grasp the contents of the lower abdomen with your thumb and first two fingers of your outstretched dominant hand on either side and wiggle it back and forth. If the "head" is all that wiggles, then it truly is the head. If the rest of the baby wiggles too, then it probably is a breech and you need to recheck the fundus for "parts." An additional procedure is to grasp the fundus with your other hand as you grasp the baby with your dominant hand. This will give you a better idea of the fetal lie and presentation when in doubt.

For the **fourth Leopold maneuver**, ask Pat to bend her knees while you position yourself to face her feet. If Pat does not bend her knees, she will experience pain with this procedure, but it will give exact information about presentation and adequacy of the pelvic inlet when there is any doubt. Place the palms of your hands on either side of her abdomen just below the umbilicus with your fingers pointing toward the symphysis pubis. Now press deeply with your fingertips and move them into the lower abdomen toward the pelvic inlet. If the head is the presenting part, one of two things will happen. If one of your hands makes contact with a hard round mass, but the other continues on in the direction of the pelvis, you have found the cephalic prominence. If the cephalic prominence is on the same side of the woman as is the fetal back, you have a face presentation because the head is extended. If the cephalic prominence is on the same side as the arms and legs (small parts) it is the **sinciput** (forehead) and the baby is in a **vertex** presentation with a well flexed head. Praise the Lord! If both hands simultaneously encounter a small hard mass which is equally prominent on both sides, baby is in a military or sincipital presentation. You are feeling the occiput and the sinciput at the same time. If your hands are able to continue their movement toward the pelvic inlet after palpating the cephalic prominence, the head is not engaged. In a breech presentation, the mass will have a feeling of give along with the trunk of the baby. If your hands seem to diverge away from the presenting part and the abdominal midline, the presenting part is either engaged or "dipping." Dipping (or "diving") is when the presenting part has not descended enough to engage, but has entered the pelvic inlet.

If your right hand felt the back, the baby is in the Left Occiput Anterior position. If both hands felt basically a straight line with mirror bulges and the head is down, then the baby is in the Occiput Anterior Position. Possible cephalic (occiput) positions are recorded as: L.O.A., R.O.A., R.O.T., L.O.T., or O.A. depending on the anterior/posterior diameter of baby's head in relationship to the pelvis. This is described as Anterior, Posterior, or Transverse, Right or Left Occiput.

The breech position is described as Sacral for the sacral bone that is presenting, and is described as: R.S.A., R.S.P., L.S.A., L.S.P., L.S.T., or R.S.T.

When the face is presenting instead of the occiput (back of the head), it is described as **mentum**. It will be Right or Left Mentum Posterior. The baby will have to be born in the posterior or her head will become impacted and a Cesarean will be necessary. This is because the neck is extended and the length of the neck is much shorter than the sacrum. Approximately 0.5% of all posterior babies engage in a face presentation. This baby will be born chin first, then mouth, nose, eyes, brow, anterior fontanel, posterior fontanel, and finally the occiput as the head flexes. The body follows as it would in the occiput birth. Face-presentation babies always have very bruised faces for the first 12 to 24 hours. The eyes of course are very swollen too, so the midwife will have to be very careful when she examines the eyes. She may have to wait for a few days. Observe very carefully for drainage and at the first sign of red, yellow or green drainage, have the pediatrician check the eyes for damage. Goldenseal eye wash is a good preventive. Wipe baby's eyes gently with a cotton ball soaked in goldenseal eye wash at every diaper change or feeding. This will rinse out any vaginal bacteria and mucus that could cause problems and help reduce the swelling and bruising of the eyes from birth. If there is any of the above drainage in spite of the eye wash and prayer, do not hesitate to seek medical advice.

Equipment

Because equipment is expensive, and the student or apprentice midwife can get very confused when reading the catalogs, I've been asked to include a short discussion on my preferences and what my experience has been with fetoscopes, dopplers and oxygen supplies. You will find that I have definite opinions about them. If you have the opportunity to borrow someone's equipment, or at least try it out, I would recommend you do so. Every midwife has her own preferences. What works best for you, is what you should use.

Fetoscopes

Fetoscopes are a variety of the stethoscope used for listening to chest, lung and abdominal sounds and for taking blood pressures. The advantage over the stethoscope is that it is acoustically superior for hearing FHTs.

My personal preference is the **Sklar-Leff**. It has many advantages. Because of the long tubing, Pat can hear her baby's heart beat. The Sklar will pick the FHTs up as early as nine weeks. This is nice if there is a question about viability after spotting. The bell is detachable for warming, and weighs three pounds. The bell is autoclavable. Heart tones are easily heard behind the pubic bone, after the waters have ruptured, right up to birth. The midwife can easily hear the FHT while sitting next to Pat on the bed without bending or straining her back. Because of the long tubing, FHTs are easy to take (without the midwife imitating a pretzel) when Pat is in a kneeling, hands-and-knees, or knee-chest position, or if the baby is in a posterior lie. It is also easier to pick up the "underlying" twin. The disadvantages are the weight of the bell, and needing to break scrub if you are alone at a birth. A sterile wash cloth over your glove solves that problem. The biggest disadvantage is the cost, about $185.00.

The second best fetoscope, in my opinion, is the **DeLee-Hillis**. The DeLee-Hillis has the advantage over other similar types in that the head band allows hands-free listening without breaking sterile technique. Sometimes the midwife must isolate the baby with her hands to make sure she is listening to Baby A while her hands are corralling Baby B. Depending on baby's lie and position, FHTs can be heard from 14 weeks gestation through much of second stage. FHTs are difficult to hear when baby's back is behind the pubic bone in second stage. That can be a critical time for some babies, especially if they are there for a while. It is also very dependent on baby's good position, i.e., back is anterior. Sometimes the DeLee-Hillis does not do well after membranes have ruptured or if baby is in a posterior lie.

Other varieties of the DeLee-Hillis do not have the head band for hands-free convenience. The basic fetoscope is the **Allen**. It has a pad for the forehead. Hearing is facilitated by the amount of pressure given by the head against the fetoscope on Pat's belly over the baby's back. Pat cannot hear her baby's heartbeat because the tubing is too short.

The **Series 10** has an amplification chamber in the head-piece, which is padded. This scope is better than the Allen, but has a disadvantage in that you must use one hand to steady it, and Pat cannot listen to her baby's heart beat. The price is the same as the Allen. The Allen, Series Ten, and the DeLee-Hillis require the midwife to bend over Pat to get the FHTs.—a decided disadvantage for long hours in the office or a long labor, in terms of the midwife's aching back.

The only thing that wears out on a fetoscope would be the tubing, if you mistreat it by using harsh chemicals, alcohol, heat, soap without rinsing well. The tubing is rubber, and will crack and rot if mistreated. I had my original DeLee-Hillis for 15 years and the tubing was still good. The only "repair" needed was improving the padding for my forehead on the head-piece. My Sklar is still going strong after years of constant use. Replacement tubing is available by the inch from many surgical supply houses, and is relatively inexpensive.

Dopplers are probably the most confusing to purchase. They come with or without internal speakers. External speakers mean a separate piece to keep track of on the end of a very fine and delicate wire. If the doppler does not have an internal speaker, you must have an external speaker or a hcadset that looks like someone took half of a stethoscope and attached a thin wire to it. If you are going to use a doppler, you really want to hear those heart tones because you can't with a fetoscope. Pat and John's frame of mind will be better if they can hear them, too. There is a new doppler out that on command prints out the FHTs on a graph, just like the "real" monitors. It also has a digital display. Others have the digital display without the printout. Dopplers for obstetrics start at the 2 MHz frequency of ultrasound. This allows you to pick up FHT at nine weeks gestation. The 3 MHz doppler will give more ultrasound exposure.

Questions you need to ask yourself are:

- What is the ultrasound output (MHz)?
- How many weeks gestation is it possible to first hear FHT?
- Is the speaker internal, external, or a separate purchase?
- Does a headset come with it for privacy? Is it available?
- What is the power source? If battery, are they easy to replace or special order? Is it rechargeable?
- What is the warranty and what does it cover?
- What is the FHR range of accuracy?
- Does it have a digital display?
- Does it have a print-out mode?
- Does it have a carrying case?
- What does it cost?
- Is it connectable to a tape recorder? Is the connecting cable included with the doppler?
- Does gel come with it?
- Does the transducer attach to the doppler? Or does it dangle from the connecting wire?

Make a chart of all the brands you are considering, with column headings of all your questions. This chart will help you see clearly how they do compare. The next is to consider the cost outlay for something you probably won't use very much. You want the best for the least. There is nothing more frightening/frustrating than to need a doppler because you can't pick up the heart tones and not have one in 150 miles.

The specifications for my idea of a perfect doppler would register FHR from 40 to 200 bpm, have an internal speaker, connects to a tape recorder (and includes its own connecting cable), has a headset and prints out the FHR, has an autoclavable sheath that slips over the transducer (to protect your sterile field), has a flashing red "idiot light" to warn of low battery power, and automatically turns off three minutes after last signal. The transducer is attached to the doppler by a tangle-free cord and mounts on the doppler when not in use. The cost would be $600.00.

The rationale for the 40 to 200 bpm would cover the most dangerous low and high ranges. Any baby that has 200 bpm is going into heart failure, if not already by the time you read it. The advantage is that although difficult, it is possible to count to 180, but above 180, you need the readout, especially while transporting. The extremely low range will tell you if the baby "bottoms out," but comes back up to respectable levels and how long is he "in the basement" with the slow bpm? This is critical information.

Umbilical Clamps

Another confusing decision is the cord clamp. This is not an expensive piece of equipment, unless you are considering the **Auerbach bander**. The bander looks a lot like a hemostat, but has a spring-like gizmo that holds the elastic band on the bander until ready to apply the band to the cord. Advantages are:

- Easily sterilized with other birth instruments
- No plastic to discard
- Does not catch on diapers and clothing
- No need to remove
- Doesn't tug on cord stump
- Is cost-effective per birth: the bander costs $24.00 (includes 150 bands).

The **plastic cord clamp** is, in my opinion, bulky and can be hard to use with gloves on. When the cord is dry, it requires a special scissors to cut the hinge to remove it for comfort's sake. It does catch on diapers and clothing. Sometimes it hinders drying, if Pat is lax about the goldenseal.

The **Hesseltine** is a metal clamp. It resembles a bobby pin with a catch at the open end. The Hesseltine does not catch as much on clothing and diapers as the bulkier plastic clamp does. It is reusable after washing and sterilizing. It is sterilizable with birth instruments.

The traditional cord care is tie a knot in the **cord tape**. The knot must be a tight square knot, or it will come loose. Tape is $1.20 for two 18-inch strands, $15.00 for a 20-yard spool, and $20.75 for a 100-yard spool. Sometimes tape will hinder the cord from drying quickly, but must remain until the cord falls off.

Again, what is your preference? Experience says use the easiest and the quickest method. There are times you need to clamp and cut the cord really fast. Hemostats do the job quickly until you have the time later, but if it is a transport, you take the chance of losing your hemostat.

Care and Cleaning of Your Instruments

There are several rules about instruments, that really are just common sense:

- Don't use them for anything but what they are made for;
- Keep them clean and lubricated;
- Don't step on them;
- Don't throw them around.

The economy-priced instruments will last long enough until your birth volume increases so you can afford the professional ones. The difference is in quality of workmanship, the metal used and the hinges. The economy quality usually is plated with chrome or a thin coat of stainless steel. After a while this will crack and peel. Once there is a break in the "coating," it is a trap for bacteria, blood and rust. That is the end of your instrument. It is better to purchase the professional quality right from the start, even if you can only buy one set. That's okay; you just have to be more diligent about sterilization immediately so you are ready for the next birth. Most of us start out slowly, so there is plenty of time between clients to get ready for the next birth.

After each birth, using universal precautions of eye protection, mask and gloves, (according to OSHA guidelines):

- Wash your instruments thoroughly with instrument cleaner or a pH-neutral solution; not soap and never povidone iodine. Use an instrument brush to get into all the surfaces of your hemostats, and do the hinges. Instrument brushes have long, high-quality nylon bristles to get in those hard-to-reach places. Rinse very well.
- Use instrument stain remover, *not baking soda or cleanser*, to remove tarnish and stain. Abrasives will harm the metal and eventually ruin your instruments.
- Instrument milk inhibits rust and lubricates, thus ensuring a long life for your instruments. It comes in a concentrated liquid for soaking, or a spray for quick jobs.

It is worth taking care of your investment. While cleaning your instruments, look carefully for any nicks on the cutting surfaces. Sharpen them frequently. After sharpening, wash and rinse them again. A sharp umbilical scissor is a blessing. Dull ones macerate the cord and increase the risk of infection.

After your instruments have soaked in the instrument milk, shake off the excess and pat dry. Do not rinse. Wrap your instruments immediately even if your next birth is three months away. The wrap will protect them.

There are three different materials to wrap your instruments with. All do the job nicely.

- **Chex-All Sterilization Pouch:**
  - Self sealing;
  - Plastic face for easy viewing of what's inside;
  - Indicators inside and out (gas or steam), show if contents are sterile;
  - They come in a handy 5″×10″ size (as well as other sizes, depending on your supplier);
  - The backside is paper, so it can be torn accidentally in your bag (place them in zip-lock-type bags for storing safely in your bag). Sold by the box of 250.
- **Sterilization wrap** is a blend of paper and fiber:
  - Need sterilization tape for closure and sterile status;
  - Label/date it with a laundry pen to identify contents;
  - It comes in ready-cut sheets 15″×15″ or 20″×20″;
- Do-it-yourself **muslin:**

- Muslin easily available at any fabric store, and is safe for baking-, steam- or gas sterilization.
- Preshrink the muslin before cutting and sewing.
- For a 15″×15″ square for instruments (double thickness), sew all around, leaving two inches to turn the square right side out.
- Sew all around $\frac{1}{4}$ inch from the edge;
- Sew on the diagonal from lower left corner to upper right corner, then on the diagonal from lower right corner to upper left corner.
- Slip-stitch closed.
- You need to use sterilization tape for closure and sterilization status.
- Label for contents and date of sterilization.

The muslin wrap is environmentally friendly because it is reusable for decades, whereas the others are used one time only. Another advantage with the muslin wrap is that you have as many as you need, and don't need a lot of storage space. The muslin wrap (30″×30″) is wonderful for sterilizing your fracture pan, too. Any scraps from making wraps can be made into recyclable pouches for your comfrey compresses, or sitz bath herbs (bias tape or soutache braid makes good durable drawstrings). Remember to add one cup of chlorine bleach to the soap water when washing your birth linens. Muslin holds up well to bleach washings. Always wash your birth stuff separate from your other clothes.

Laundering your birth clothes and linens:

- Run through pre-wash first.
- Add one cup of bleach.
- Add soap according to manufacturer's directions.
- Use hot water in the "heavy soil" cycle.
- Dry in your dryer, set on the cotton, high-heat cycle or hang out in the sunshine if sun is available. If the sunshine has missed birth laundry day for several washings, you may want to iron the linens when they are almost line dry, for sanitation reasons.

As soon as your instruments, fracture pan and linens (including your universal-precautions apron, etc.) are washed and dried, they should be wrapped in whatever you choose to use. Either the Chex-All pouches, paper wrap or the muslin wrap. Unless you are not expecting any births for three months, it is a good idea to sterilize right away. That way you won't be caught unprepared. If you do three births or more a month, you should have a second set always sterile and ready.

Sterilizing Instruments and Linens

Sterilizing your instruments can be done in several ways. The most easily available is the kitchen oven.

- Pre-heat the oven to 250 degrees.
- Place a cake pan with one inch of water in the oven between the heat source and the instrument/linen packs (the water prevents scorching).
- Bake for one hour.
- Let the packs cool completely (for several hours), out of any drafts. If the packs cool too quickly, the contents may not dry, causing instruments to rust and towels to mildew. The packs can cool in the oven, after the heat is turned off, if you take the water pan out of the oven and leave the door slightly ajar.
- Sterilize 100% cotton goods *only;* man-made fabric blends tend to scorch or melt!

While the oven is preheating, wrap your instruments, fracture pan, and anything else you plan on sterilizing. Write the date on the tape using the hash bars as the dividers between your numbers; for example, "4/6/93." The bars on the tape will turn dark grey or black when the pack is sterile.

A large pressure cooker works great. In fact, the hospital sterilizers work on the same principle as a pressure cooker. Of course, they are much bigger and some also are "gas" sterilizers, but for most things, they use steam. Gas sterilizers are used for sharps, because the gas does not dull the edge as fast as steam. Unfortunately, gas sterilizers are outside of the average midwife's budget. Cold sterilization of your scissors is available with cold sterilization solutions, but carrying a jar of solution and instruments to births or in the trunk of your car for weeks on end is not practical. Cold sterilization is for use straight out of the solution. You cannot wrap it in a cloth and expect it to be sterile, unless you heat-sterilize it.

For steam sterilization:

- You need 15 pounds of pressure for 25 minutes to do the instruments, linens and fracture pan.
- The tape will turn black to show it is sterile.
- Set out on cake racks, out of any drafts, to cool.
- If you want to sterilize water, do it separately from your other packs:
  - Use small canning jars, half-pint or less.
  - Seal as for canning, snug up, then release one quarter turn.
  - Bring to 10 pounds of pressure for 15 minutes.
  - Let the water jars cool in the cooker until they are no longer boiling.
  - Set the jars out to cool.
  - Seal by tightening the lids.

The shelf life for water is one year if not opened.

The shelf life of oven-sterilized instruments and linens is six weeks. The shelf life of pressure-cooker-sterilized instruments and linens is eight weeks. Once things are cooled, they should be bagged in a strong plastic bag such as lines the 40-pound boxes of detergent and placed on the shelf, or with your birth bag. The plastic will keep it clean, and possibly extend the sterility a few days. Unfortunately, they do not (yet) have indicators for expiration of sterility. That is why you must date each package. Always rotate your sterile supplies, or you will find something six months old when you need something sterile. If you have not used it before the shelf life is past, remove the old date tape and replace it with a new date tape and re-sterilize. It is a good idea to dry your instruments and linen packs away from drafts, or they will retain moisture in the center and will rust or mildew. . I failed to do that once, and opened up "sterile," but mildewed towels. Needless to say, we couldn't use them, and it took lots of bleach to get them in usable shape again. After that, I dried my linens in the oven, set at 200 degrees, for 30 minutes.

If you have a birth center and do lots of births, you may want to invest in a "real" sterilizer. These are very expensive, and very impractical unless you need to do three setups a day or up to five a week.

Things that "unsterilize" your packs:

- Opening them;
- Getting them wet;
- Dropping them on the floor or ground;
- An expired shelf life;
- Spilling powder, sand or dirt on them;
- A male animal spraying them;
- Any pressurized spray, insecticide or not, sprayed at it.

When any of those things happen to your pack, you must resterilize it.

Non-Interventive Pelvimetry

In an excellent but out-of print book, *Stepping Stones to Labor Ward Diagnosis*, I read how to determine the obstetric type without doing an internal exam. The author was a practicing obstetrician-gynecologist in Australia in the 1950s and into the 1970s. During that time a link between bone cancer in pre-adolescent males and routine x-ray for fetal position, size and pelvic compatibility during the ninth month gestation was done. (Sound familiar for sonogram exam today?) Further research of x-ray exposure during pregnancy produced other links to fetal anomalies and led to warnings against such exposure during pregnancy. During the late 50s and into the 60s, Dr. R. H. Hamblin began his research to find an accurate, but non-threatening method to determine pelvic (passage) and baby (passenger) compatibility. As his research progressed, he found he could predict labor patterns and reasonably predict labor time and even if a woman would have easy or difficult births. To verify his findings he had three groups. One group had the traditional x-ray and digital pelvimetry, one group had the x-ray, digital pelvimetry and the non-interventive pelvimetry and the third group had only the non-interventive pelvimetry. He found the third group to be as predictable as the others, with two major differences. Client satisfaction and relaxation was greater in the third group, during the initial prenatal visit, with greater confidence in their ability to birth naturally. Vaginal exam for the curvature of the sacrum and the mobility of the coccyx can still be done *if* there is any question because of the medical history.

Just as you notice if your prospective client is middle-aged, young, slim, or obese, you can tell if she is android, anthropoid, gynecoid, or platypelloid. Because certain pelvic types produce certain labor patterns, you can predict when you need to be at Pat's, and how her labor will progress. This is great for prenatal counselling. If Pat's pelvis is a little narrow at the inlet, she will have a longer first stage. If she has a nice, open inlet, but narrows slightly at the midplane, you know that her labor will take longer between 4 and 7 or 8 cm. Pat may want to build up her stamina for squatting, or know ahead of time that there will be a time during labor when she will want to walk up and down stairs, or stand alternating with one leg on a stool, stork style (also known as the **Parker maneuver**). She may need to know that at one time, her labor will slow down so she can take a nap, but when the contractions wake her up the baby will come very quickly. When you are proven right, Pat and John will think you surely are a prophet, but it is simply a matter of "reading" the body build and thus "reading" the corresponding pelvis.

Dr. Hamblin's book is rather lengthy, but I will try to summarize his research into useable nuggets. Remember! God's people have a lot of variety. Pelves are not always textbook clear. Most of the time, unless your client comes from stock that has never married outside of her "tribe"—for example, the same town in Europe, Africa or Asia, etc., or religious community with common ethnic ancestry, like the Amish—her pelvis will probably have some minor deviations.

I always made a practice to evaluate Pat when I met her for the first time. She never knew before hand that I was "reading" her pelvis, so she was relaxed, and not trying to "look good." When doing the initial physical exam at the first prenatal, I explained to Pat how I evaluated her pelvis and then would try to guess how her previous labors had been. She could correct me, and I would learn another variable. Over the course of the pregnancy, I would observe and try to determine the reason for the variance. Most of the time it was because Pat didn't know she had a narrow spot, and instinctively did something, like stayed home until after her labor slowed down and then started to pick up again. Because few nurses have seen active labor contractions slow way down after being five minutes or less apart, they do not count what has gone on earlier that day as active labor. Had they examined Pat, she would have had her labor augmented when it slowed down and she would have been diagnosed as having dysfunctional labor, instead of normal for Pat.

The following descriptions will give you, the midwife, general parameters to categorize the individual pelvis that is before you. Each pelvis type has its own peculiarities that the midwife will appreciate and learn to associate with certain labor patterns. This will be of great benefit to her and her clients.

The shoulders of a **gynecoid** woman are not square; they slope laterally. The average length of her forearm and hand is exactly that recorded in the Bible, one cubit or 18–20 inches. Her forearms are always longer than a span or nine inches, and her fingers are long and tapering. Because her bones generally are light, the transverse diameter across the metacarpus (back of her hand) is not broad. The "carrying-angle" at the elbow of a gynecoid woman is set widely to allow her arms to swing easily past her hips, which are wider than her shoulders. Although her legs narrow symmetrically from prominent hips down to her feet, the inner aspects of the thighs and knees of this type of woman do not touch when the ankles are approximated (side by side). A probable sign of adequate or wide transverse diameter of the pelvic outlet.

Babies have no real difficulty making the passage in the gynecoid pelvis, as long as they follow he rule of entering the passage way straight on, either anteriorly or posteriorly, and not shoulder first. Should the baby decide to enter on the oblique, he will have difficulty getting through the midplane, because that area is the narrowest part of the pelvis, but widest in the anterior to posterior plane. This is why palpation is such an important skill. Your fingers need to develop "eyes" so you can "read" what is going on in this uterus. If mother is blessed with plenty of room for this baby, the labor will probably take just a little longer until the baby is through the midplane, or baby will turn his head into the curve. The gynecoid pelvis allows breech, compound and facial presentations with little difficulty, mechanically speaking. I have even seen babies presenting obliquely throughout the passage with little mechanical difficulty. However, Pat would have preferred not having such a long and painful labor. This pelvis type is most common at 41–42%.

Android women are a complete contrast in appearance and obstetric behavior. They are heavy-jowled, thick set and square-bodied at the shoulders, waist and hips. Their masculine thighs run straight down to thick ankles. The bones of the android woman appear heavy and massive. It is by their hands and feet that it is sometimes possible to recognize them. They are broad across the metacarpals and metatarsals (instep) and the fingers and toes are short, straight and square. Masculine characteristics predominate in other respects in android women so that they are mentally ill-equipped for the feminine task of childbirth and their contractions often prove to be unsatisfactory, colicky, inert and inefficient. She has to work harder at her labor, and take full advantage of the "stops" to nap and relax. Her labor will probably be lengthy and the stop-and-start pattern is typical. The midwife needs to encourage the team to rest as much as possible. Pat's nutrition and liquid intake is very important. The midwife needs to be alert for positions that will encourage baby's passage, and prevent Pat from becoming exhausted. The hardest point is at the outlet. Baby does need to be small.

The android pelvis is often called the male pelvis because it is found in more men than women. It does occur in about 32.5% of white women and 15.7% of non-white women. Because of its "heart" shape, it encourages the baby to enter the inlet in a posterior position. It is short and narrow in all of its planes, allowing little maneuvering space for the baby. This pelvis has the highest incidence of cesarean birth, stillbirth, and forceps births of all the pelvic types. If baby is on the small side, under seven pounds, he has the best chance of birthing vaginally. These babies usually have a lot of molding in order to pass through this narrow pelvis. Squatting during the difficult second stage, standing or squat "thrusts" with the push may be needed.

The hands of the **anthropoid** woman may also help to identify her. They are long and narrow and the hypothenar eminences (fleshy elevation on ulnar side of the palm of the hand) have characteristic straight-edged medial borders. The anthropoid woman is tall and slender and dolicho-cephalic (long head). The rami of the mandibles (upward angle of the lower jaw) are long and her shoulders are wider than her hips. Her body will remind you of a triangle. Not to be disrespectful, but this woman will have strong ape-like characteristics. She will have a very uneventful labor, especially if baby addresses the pelvis in the posterior. If baby is "floating" above the inlet beyond "due date," review dates. If dates are correct, palpate for position of the presenting part. If baby is presenting transverse or in the oblique, Pat could try the knee-chest position during the Braxton-Hicks contractions. Lying on her left side when sleeping or taking an appropriate homeopathic medicine will usually move the baby into the pelvis.

The anthropoid pelvis is very common in non-white women, 40.5%, compared to 23.5% in white women, and encourages the posterior position. As long as the pelvis is on the large side there will be no problem, and as long as baby follows the curve in the posterior. This pelvis is the deepest of all the types due to the long sacrum.

There is very little in the general appearance of a woman with a flat or **platypelloid** pelvis to suggest that type of abnormality exists. It only occurs in 3% of all women, which is a real Praise the Lord! She may be of very short stature and her hands and feet of less than average length. This pelvis will be wide enough but not deep enough to birth a baby. Her profile (from the side) will appear to be very narrow compared to her width.

Women whose pelves have been deformed by spondylotheses, congenital dislocation of the hips, polio or tuberculosis, disease of the spine, the diagnosis is frequently suggested by obvious external signs, such as lumbar lordosis, scoliosis, pendulous abdomen, or she may walk or lie in an abnormal manner.

With a platypelloid pelvis, transverse cephalic position appears to be the easiest for baby to birth, but really is not easy to birth vaginally. This pelvis is like a gynecoid that has been flattened in the anterior-posterior plane. Baby can not birth cephalic anterior/posterior through the shallow sacral curve, unless the head is on the small side. Baby must turn to cephalic if presenting breech. Baby does not have enough room to maneuver through this short but shallow area in the breech.

As a rule, babies like to keep their spines in a straight line with their heads. In order to negotiate the platypelloid, baby must look over one shoulder when entering the sacral curve. If there is enough room to rotate to the anterior position, baby will probably make it through all right. The danger of overextending the muscles on the side of the neck causing Bell's palsy is very real. Generally, chiropractic manipulation can correct this, if treated in the first few weeks after birth. This labor will probably move along quite well until transition and second stage. Then it will be very painful and slow, if successful. Most women with platypelloid pelvis have cesareans.

A common problem with a Platypelloid pelvis is a persistent transverse lie. Baby is so comfortable in his cradle he forgets to get into birthing position. To correct this, the midwife needs to confirm the position of the placenta is not low lying or a previa, a common problem with transverse lies. Baby will begin labor in the cephalic-transverse, but must rotate to vertex to pass through the midplane of the pelvis.

Pat's labor may be long if the baby is reluctant to "drop" into the midplane. Side lying or vertical positions may help. If the midplane of the pelvis is too shallow or constricted, Baby will not be able to adjust, and a cesarean may be necessary. To change from transition to vertex with the side lying attempt, Pat needs to be lying on the side opposite the head, to get the head off the pelvic crest. That should show Baby which way to go and going into the vertical: walking up and down stairs, squatting, even squat thrusts, should get baby into the midplane into birthing position. Please keep a close monitor on Baby and be alert for any sign of distress, which would mandate transport. If Baby refuses to enter the midplane, or descend, Pat will have to have a cesarean.

If the midplane and the outlet is adequate size for the baby, another option may be a podauc version. After the midwife scrubs, she puts a long (elbow length) sterile glove on. Gently, fingers first, insert your hand into the uterus, reaching for baby's feet. Grasping both feet securely, gently pull baby's feet through the cervix. Pat will want to push, so let her birth the baby as a regular breech from this point on. FHTs should be monitored constantly during the entire procedure as well as the placenta.

Few Americans can claim ancestry from a single nation. The United States is a melting pot of many nationalities, and when couples fall in love and marry, we rarely limit their eligibility to same ethnic origins. Someone with Scottish ancestry is likely to marry someone with Italian ancestry, etc. This causes combination pelves in the offspring, and why American women have "atypical" labor from her German or Swiss or Indian sister who never married outside of her ethnic group. Because of this varied ancestry most American women have combination pelves. Do not despair. This can be simplified by simply looking for the following:

- Feminine feet, ankles, hands and wrists;
- Space between the knees when standing straight, but relaxed.

These two areas tell you that the mid-pelvis is gynecoid:

- Able to "carry" two one-gallon buckets without banging her knees while allowing her arms to hang naturally indicates a gynecoid outlet;
- The cubit forearm (includes the hand) describes the gynecoid inlet.

Any variation may encourage you to check the lower two-thirds of the sacral curve and the shape of the coccyx. If Pat is shorter than 5 feet 3 inches and has a forearm measurement of 16 inches, she is still in the gynecoid type if all the other factors are the same. I have seen women with very light feminine bone structure between 4'8" and 5'1" height birth easily and only had a 15- or 16-inch forearm. Dr. Hamblin based his findings on the 5-foot, 6-inch, to 5-foot, 8-inch woman.

Most women really appreciate this method, as it saves them from getting poked and prodded. Many midwives have short fingers and it is very difficult to get accurate measurements without putting a lot of pressure on tender tissues. What I like best, is that it works every time! Hallelujah!

Traditional Pelvimetry

Before doing a traditional pelvic exam, you need to know what your hand measures from your middle (tall) finger to the base of your thumb at the web. A minimum of 12cm is needed to measure the **diagonal conjugate**. Knowing that your finger to base of thumb measures the minimum and you can't reach the sacral promontory you know that there is probably enough room for the baby to come through. Next measure the width of your knuckles at the base of your fingers. Include your thumb, bending it nail towards finger knuckle (if necessary) to measure 10cm. Be considerate and tell Pat that you will not hurt her, but that she will feel some pressure. Remember to give her the same courtesy and respect that you wish others would give you. Allow Pat as much modesty as is possible. Visual access is not necessary for pelvimetry, so a small sheet as a modesty drape helps her relax.

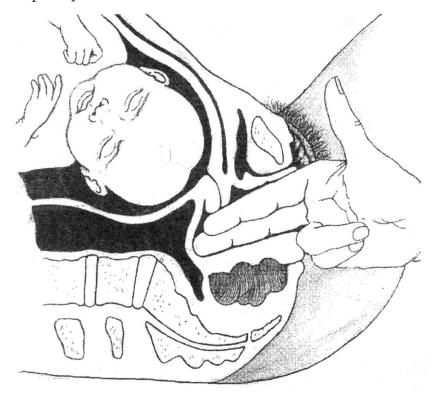

Figure 12-1: Pelvic Exam

After gloving, after the Pap smear has been done, insert the lubricated, first two fingers of your dominant hand palm side up, into the vagina. Check the arch of the pubic bone by separating your two fingers slightly to protect the urethra and gently palpate the shape and thickness of the pubic bone. The arch needs to be at least 90 degrees, and will allow both fingers to gently fit in the arch. A thick and flat pubis may not give the baby enough room to go through the midplane.

As you sweep your fingers down the side walls, note the firmness and the shape that you are feeling. Are the walls hard as "steel" or simply good, firm muscle? Are they rounded or steep?

Follow the vagina to the posterior fornix (behind the cervix) until your finger tips touch a firm hard bone that seems to "poke" towards you. That is the sacral promontory. (On the outside of your back, it is where the back bone makes a sharp turn "in" at the top of the crease of your buttocks.) As you "reach" for the sacral promontory, take care that you do not pinch the labia or the clitoris with your thumb. Pinching can be avoided if you put most of the pressure of the "reach" on the perineum with your third and fourth fingers, keeping your thumb relaxed and to the side (pointing over your third and fourth fingers). Mark on your examining hand where the pubis ends, until you know from experience what the distance would be. This should measure from 11.5 to 13 cm. The average is 12.5. This measurement is for the **diagonal conjugate**. It is the only clinical measurement of the inlet possible without sonogram or x-ray.

The **midplane** is measured by sliding your fingers down along the sacral curve to the coccyx. Again, measure the distance to the pubis by marking your examining hand. Next to the inlet, this is the most important measurement for the midwife to have. This measures the **antero-posterior diameter** of the midplane, or the narrowest part of the pelvis. If Pat's inlet and outlet are gynecoid, but this is contracted, she will have a very long midstage of labor. If the baby is average to large and insists on going through the midplane cephalic anterior or posterior, he will not make it through. The head will have to come through transverse, and baby will have to be on the small side, less than seven pounds. If the midplane is contracted more than 9.5, baby will not be able to come through. The average measurement is 11.5cm.

While your fingers are at the coccyx, slide your other hand under Pat, following the sacral curve to a point just above the rectum. (This feels weird to Pat, so tell her you are *not* going to go into the rectum and explain what you are doing.) Now move the coccyx back and forth between your fingers. Does it move easily? Does it deviate from front to back and tend to go side ways? Side movements are not helpful, and could cause the baby to hang up. The coccyx needs to "bend" back out of the way of the head, side movements do not open up the space for the head, and may cause the coccyx to fracture.

Locate the **ischial spines** by sweeping your fingers from side to side passing in front of the coccyx. (Your confirming landmark will be a slight reflexive twitch or a jump and an "ouch" from Pat when you put pressure on a small, bumpy bone at three o'clock and nine o'clock. This is where the sciatic nerve passes over the pelvis to the legs from the spine.) Once you have found the ischial spines, determine if they are blunt and rounded or pointed and very noticeable. (Pointy or prominent ischials can catch and hold a baby back from descending, causing a lot of low-back pain.) Prominent ischial spines may take up valuable passage space. When you find the ischials, sweep your fingers from one ischial spine to the other. Sweeping your fingers between the spines gives you an idea of the width of the pelvis, and similar to determining ten centimeters dilation. You will want to have the same distance between the ischials. Gently slip your fingers out of the vagina and make a fist. Place the knuckles of your hand and thumb if needed against Pat's perineum between the **ischial tuberosities**. This measurement will confirm what you felt when you swept your fingers between the ischials. It is easy to confuse the tuberosities with the spines. The spines are what you sit on and curve up to the pubic bone and frame the baby's head at the outlet.

Once the exam is over, gently wipe Pat's genitalia with a baby wipe, to remove the excess lubricant, then pat-dry with a tissue. When removing your gloves, make a fist and carefully pull the cuff over the hand and around the curled fingers towards your palm. This keeps whatever fluids may be on your glove from splattering and contaminating your room, by keeping everything on the inside of the glove. If you do this over the waste basket, you will have less chance of splattering Pat and yourself with mucus and lubricant.

Study the following drawings of the different pelves. Familiarize yourself with the landmarks. Most midwifery exams have questions on the bones and measurements and how to identify the various pelves. You need to understand every inch of the road the baby must travel on the road to birth. Make a pelvis model your best friend until you are confident that you know every twist and turn of the baby and every "curve in the road" as well as the back of your hand. Then, when a hitch occurs in labor, you will be able to "see" where the baby is and what position he should be in. That will be the clue as to what you need to do to facilitate the baby to get in that position that will help him birth.

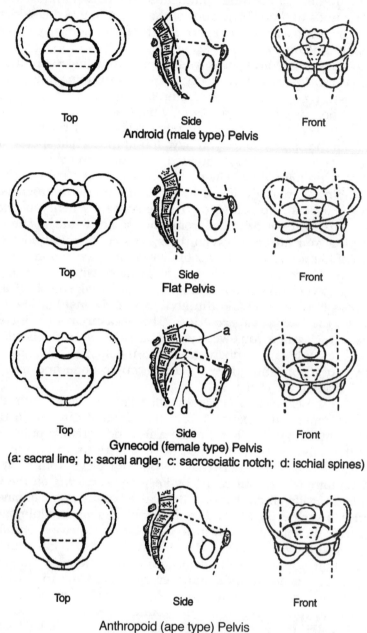

Top   Side   Front

Android (male type) Pelvis

Top   Side   Front

Flat Pelvis

Top   Side   Front

Gynecoid (female type) Pelvis

(a: sacral line; b: sacral angle; c: sacrosciatic notch; d: ischial spines)

Top   Side   Front

Anthropoid (ape type) Pelvis

Figure 12-2: Pelvic Types

Fetal Heart Tones

The ability to hear the baby's heartbeat before 16 weeks will be determined by baby's position, the tenseness of the abdominal wall (athletic women with strong abdominal muscles make it the hardest to hear), the amount of abdominal fat, and the amount of amniotic waters. All of these factors will bear on the ease of hearing the heart tones throughout the pregnancy. In the first trimester, one additional factor comes to mind: how sensitive is your hearing? Listening in the right spot helps considerably.

Generally speaking, the baby will be out of the pelvis and easier to hear after 16 weeks. After palpating and locating the baby, mentally draw a line from the diaphragm to the pubic bone. Then, mentally draw another line from one hip bone to the other with the two lines bisecting at the umbilicus (belly button). You have just "divided" the abdomen into four quadrants; the Right Upper Quadrant (RUQ), the Left Upper Quadrant (LUQ), the Left Lower Quadrant (LLQ) and the Right Lower Quadrant (RLQ). Remember, whenever directions are used concerning the baby's or Pat's position, right and left is the same as *Pat's* right and left, not *yours!*

If the baby is in the breech position, the heart tones will be heard above the umbilicus, in either the left or right upper quadrant. The posterior baby's heart tones will be heard well to the side. A guideline that can be used is to mentally draw two roughly parallel straight lines from Pat's nipples to the middle of her thighs. Any heart tone heard to the outside of those lines is in the posterior position, whether right or left. Heart tones heard between those lines means the baby's position is anterior. If you hear the heart tones best along the horizontal line you "drew," baby is in the transverse. Palpation will have told you the position, but the FHT will confirm what your hands told you.

Normal heart tones are between 120 and 160 beats per minute (bpm). The rhythm should be steady when the baby is resting. If baby is kicking, there should be an increase of frequency during the movement, perhaps as much as 15 or 20 beats per minute. Kicking or hand movements against the stethoscope sound like books dropping on a carpeted floor. The heartbeat sounds more like a muffled clock ticking. The cord has a swish and a beat attached to the swish, while the placenta sounds like a washing machine swooshing the water and clothes about. The smaller the baby, the smaller the heart. The normal-sized heart of a human is about the size of his fist. Listen accordingly. Don't expect an adult sound coming from a twenty-five-week unborn baby. Baby should sound like a wind-up Timex under four thick feather pillows at 14 weeks: very faint. Baby's heart is about $\frac{3}{8}$ inch across, so it won't sound like a bass drum! When taking FHTs early in pregnancy, you may want to have your finger on Pat's pulse. That will help you differentiate from an abdominal "echo" of her pulse and the little baby.

If you have pets and children, listen to their heartbeats. Dogs and cats have rapid beats and slightly different rhythm than humans. I don't recommend using a stethoscope on a bird, as they may think it is a snake and have a heart attack! Another exercise, if you are not in a practice with a lot of opportunity to listen to unborn heartbeats, is to listen to a newborn's heart through blankets. That will help sharpen your ears. The "older" or larger the unborn baby is, the easier to hear the heartbeat.

If the baby's heart rate does not react by speeding up with baby's movements, suspect any of the following:

- An immature or compromised central nervous system;
- A baby that is so stressed out, his adrenaline is depleted, thus preventing the heart from increasing in speed; or
- A possible congenital heart problem and for baby's sake the heart does not speed up.

Try stimulating the baby by palpation, patting at the baby's feet, and generally trying to "wake him up." Listen to the heart rate when baby is kicking or turning. It should increase during the movement, and slow down quickly after the movement is over. If it doesn't react to your stimulation, ask the parents when is the baby most active. That is the time you will want to listen again. You may have to make a trip to their home, if activity time is when Pat lies down to sleep at night. If activity is vague and sporadic, add to your suspicions concerning central nervous system problems. You will have to voice your suspicions with the clients, and suggest a sonogram or consult with Dr. Wonderful. Dr. Very-Nice-But-Distant should be consulted, if Dr. Wonderful is not available.

Pat's baby had heart tones as steady as a clock. They never varied, and baby was also very quiet and seldom moved when we had our visits. Pat assured me baby moved at least 10 times every day, so we decided baby just enjoyed the quietness at the office. Pat did remark that when two-year-old brother was too rambunctious on her lap, baby would ease away and to the side when possible, instead of kicking back like her other children did. We joked about how easy-going this baby was, and passed it off. This is her story.

Pat was seeing an obstetrician throughout her pregnancy. During the seventh month, she decided on a home birth. Her physician had offered the AFP test and sonogram at 16 weeks, but Pat had refused. She "wanted to have happy thoughts about my baby, instead of worrying about any 'serious nervous system' maybes. Besides, I can't abort my baby. It is against my religious beliefs!" I questioned her about her doctor suspecting anything, and giggling, she replied, "He never says anything good, just negative "might bes" and "maybes" because I've had four children, and my age. He's always been that way, just a worry wart." After a difficult labor, for Pat, and difficulty in my determining what the presenting part was, little Johnny was born. . . anencephalic. After a short time of grieving, and letting the children hold baby briefly, we prepared Pat, John and baby Johnny for transport to the hospital. The area was not friendly to midwives and homebirth couples. Her obstetrician was one of the least friendly. In the emergency room, the pediatrician and the anesthesiologist (who intubated Johnny for labored and slow, 20, respirations) wanted to transport him to a tertiary care center that also was an organ transplant facility. Pat and John refused transport and chose to let Johnny die in their arms nine hours later in a private room with family and close friends present.

A "peer review" was held and I was censured for not getting the proper screening done and causing this obstetrical event! I told my backup that Pat was not my client until the last trimester (7th month) and in fact was seeing her OB, a prominent physician and professor at a nearby medical school, through out her pregnancy. I also told Dr. Backup that she had refused the AFP and sonogram, according to the copy I had of her records. It seems that Pat's doctor had accused me of preventing such screening and that he "had no control over me, but something should be done about that midwife!" Had I told my backup about the situation, as soon as it had occurred, he could have taken a copy of Pat's doctor's records and my records to the committee, saving himself embarrassment and I wouldn't have received a nasty letter. They would have decided "the event" was just one of those things that happen in a busy doctor's office, and would have recommended "stronger encouragement for having the tests done."

It is hard for most obstetricians to realize there are people that will not abort for any reason! The peer review committee may either direct the hospital or committee chairperson to:

- Write a letter of correction or restraint to you.
- If you are licensed by the state in any capacity, a letter of complaint to the proper licensing agency. This could result in loss of licensure.

This can open the door for state prosecution and end your career as a midwife and possible jail time! Please, keep communication open between you and your backup. Talk or write him about each of your cases, so he has an idea of how many normal pregnancies you are seeing. You do not need to go into detail, but at least let him know that you have a case load of 30 clients, and of those you have some questions concerning one. Go on from there and express your concern. He may want to see the chart or only the client, after hearing what you have done to rule out the "whatevers" you have been concerned about. He may have a suggestion that is very simple, or may reassure you that at this time he thinks all is well.

Fortunately, most of the time, baby responds well to being palpated and poked at with a good heart-rate increase, returning to baseline when the movement ends. Your chart should show variations of counts from visit to visit and as long as you don't have the same number, but a variation of 10 or so, baby is normal.

When monitoring FHT during labor, be sure to listen during a complete contraction cycle at least every hour, especially during a long labor. Listening to FHTs only between contractions will not give you the best understanding of baby's tolerance to labor. Baby should react to the peak of the contraction the same as he would to a major movement. Pat will tolerate the pressure of the fetoscope better during a contraction if she knows that it is to monitor how the baby is doing.

Normal Fetal Heart Action

Usually baby does very well. The normal response is to increase the heart rate 10–20 beats as the contraction reaches the peak with recovery to normal before the end of the contraction. It would look like this if you graphed it.

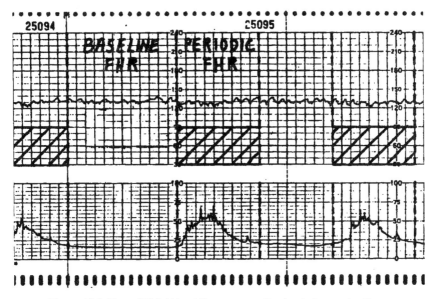

Figure 12-3: Normal Fetal Heart Trace responding to uterine contractions

This increase is baby's normal response to a momentary decrease in oxygen through the placenta during the peak of the contraction. As the uterine muscle contracts, it squeezes the blood vessels that feed the placenta. Baby's heart responds by beating faster to circulate what oxygen there is through his vital organs. This only lasts 15 to 20 seconds, and usually is of no pathological consequence.

Problems can arise if this acceleration is over 160 bpm and increases during the contraction, but is slow to return to base of 150 or less. This would indicate fetal distress due to uneven pressure on the head. Position change for Pat is mandatory. Usually this takes care of things. This pattern can occur in the last few minutes of second stage. If so, do what you can to facilitate the birth. A few whiffs of oxygen may be helpful.

Tachycardia and Bradycardia

Tachycardia is a condition in which the baseline FHT is between 161 and 180 bpm. Tachycardia may indicate:

- Immaturity of the automatic nervous system in a premature baby
- Maternal fever resulting from amnionitis or chorioamnionitis
- Mild fetal hypoxia (low oxygen level in baby) and may warn of upcoming fetal distress
- Drug reaction of baby to drugs (Ritodrine, Apresoline/ hydrolazine) or herbs (lobelia, blue cohosh) given to mother. Tachycardia, combined with late decelerations or prolonged variable decelerations, with or without meconium, does indicate fetal distress! Tachycardia, meconium and maternal fever are particularly serious!

Bradycardia is a condition in which the FHTs are less than 120 bpm. Moderate bradycardia is a baseline level of 100 to 119. Marked bradycardia is a baseline below 100 bpm. When bradycardia occurs during variability of FHT, it is not necessarily a warning sign, but do assess the duration of the severe bradycardia, time left before birth, and if other signs of fetal distress are present. It is not unusual to have bradycardia when the fetal head descends rapidly into the pelvis. A common occurrence with precipitous births. If the baby has a bradycardia baseline during the pregnancy it is probably due to maternal drug effect (reaction to mom's medications), maternal hypoglycemia, or baby has congenital heart problems. Cesarean birth is not necessarily indicated, but I would suggest close consultation with Dr. Wonderful during the pregnancy.

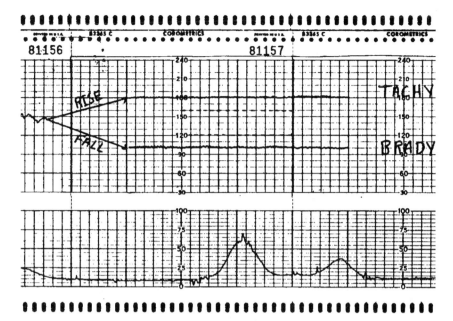

Figure 12-4: Tachycardia and Bradycardia with minimum variability

Minimal/absent variability indicates:

- Immature autonomic nervous system
- Congenital anomalies
- Medication given to Pat
- Fetal anoxia
- Fetal acidosis

This may be your first indicator of approaching fetal distress. If minimal or absent variability is combined with late deceleration, serious and acute fetal distress is present. If it is combined with late deceleration and tachycardia baby is in big trouble. You have fetal distress at its worst!

Marked variability by itself is not abnormal and as long as the FHT rate does not change, it is in normal limits. The deviation from normal occurs when the FHT rate changes too. A pattern of marked variability preceding minimal or absent variability is ominous! In other words, as long as the baseline is in the 140s with marked variability going to 170 during the contraction and then returning to the baseline, baby is okay, but bears watching. When the baseline changes from the 120s to the 130s to the 120s to the 140s, and accompanied by marked variability of 30–40 bpm with the contractions, I would start praying and putting "Plan B" into effect immediately. Don't wait for the tachycardia. If baby will birth before you could get to the hospital, have the oxygen at the ready, and notify Dr. Wonderful Backup of the situation. Be ready to resuscitate. Hopefully when baby is born the Apgars will be 6 and 10, and you can give Dr. Wonderful Backup an immediate good report of situation. He will probably want to see baby anyway, but if baby is doing well, you won't have to pretend to be an ambulance driver.

Deceleration Patterns

Deceleration patterns are periodic FHR changes associated with uterine contractions and are described by three patterns; early, late and variable.

Early deceleration is generally thought to be caused by head compression. It rarely dips below 100 bpm and it follows the pattern of the contraction, thus it is called a "uniform-shape pattern." It begins with the onset of the contraction and ends with the end of the contraction. It lasts only as long as the contraction, about 90 seconds. This is considered a normal reaction to contractions, as long as it is clearly differentiated from a late decel pattern. This is a Type I dip.

Late deceleration reflects the shape of the contraction, so it too is a uniform–shape pattern. Instead of starting at the beginning of the contraction, it starts either during the peak or shortly after the peak of the contraction and lasts about 90 seconds. Because it started late, it will carry over into the rest between contractions. If you only listened between contractions, you would not pick this one up as something to pay attention to. The dip may be within normal FHR range, shallow (10 bpm below baseline), or pronounced. **The *amount* is not dangerous; the fact that late decels are *present* is dangerous!** Late decels are due to utero-placental deficiency. Baby's lifeline is compromised! It is a **Type II Dip**, and a life threatening situation. Immediately do the following:

- Notify Dr. Wonderful Backup;
- Have Pat lie on her left side in the car;
- Give Pat oxygen by mask at 6 liters per minute;
- Get to the hospital as soon as you can, praying all the way (pick up your stuff after the birth and everyone is stabilized).

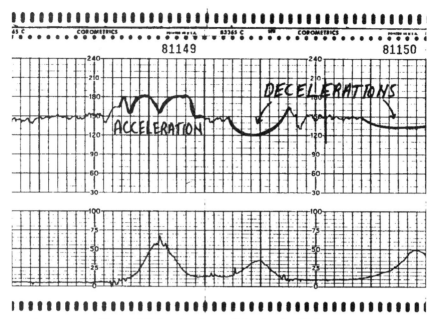

Figure 12-5: Acceleration and Deceleration Patterns

Causes of Type II Dips are:

- Hypertonic uterine contractions from oxytocin induction or stimulation;
- Markedly infarcted placenta;
- Maternal supine hypotension syndrome (Valsalva syndrome);
- Placenta previa;
- Abruptio placenta;
- Hypertensive disorders of pregnancy;
- Intrauterine growth retardation;
- Any other condition that may interfere with placental circulation.

Obviously, any of the causes could occur at home. Stimulating contractions with herbs can cause hypertonic contractions, just as Pitocin® can. Placenta previa could be missed if it was a marginal previa, abruptios have no respect for anyone and could happen at any birth place, maternal supine hypotension syndrome or the Valsalva syndrome is preventable. If you keep Pat off her back, and keep changing her position every two hours, this will not be a problem. A placenta with infarcts (scars) in it could happen anywhere. Pat needed to eat more greens, or keep away from butting animals and lap-bouncing children. She may have had some slight separations (minor abruptions) with spotting during the pregnancy that could have caused the infarcts. Infarcts look like white or yellow gristle. Intrauterine growth retardation is from malnutrition (need I say more?). Certain prescription drugs could narrow Pat's blood vessels, or she could have decreased blood flow from plaque in her arteries, and thus compromise the amount of nutrients and oxygen the placenta would receive.

Variable decelerations do not reflect the shape of the contractions, thus they have variable shape on the graph. They also vary in shape from one occurrence to another, in duration and also relative to the onset of the contraction. The decel may occur at any time during the contraction. You may see Type I, II, or III Dips if you graphed the pattern out. The important element in variable decelerations is that the FHR returns to normal quickly. Note the following:

- Slow recovery or an absence of variability indicates a more seriously compromised baby and Dr. Backup should be notified.
- Transport should be considered if birth is not imminent.
- Variable decels with quick recovery and a compensatory elevation in FHR as it returns to baseline indicates a nuchal cord.
- It is common during descent.
- Shallow variable decels with a quick return to baseline and good variability usually do not indicate acidosis.
- Frequent occurrence of this type should be reported to your backup.
- It is common in second stage with OP position.

What to do:

- Change maternal position
- Give oxygen to Pat by mask at 6 liters per minute (lpm)
- Do a vaginal exam to determine:
  - Whether or not there is a prolapsed cord;
  - Rapid descent of the head against an incompletely dilated cervix (rim or anterior lip);
  - Presentation and position (occiput posterior and face presentations often have variable decels).
- Notify Dr. Wonderful Backup.

Again, whether you transport or not will depend on what Dr. Backup says and your level of experience. It is better to transport and have healthy baby and mom and maybe look silly because everything turned out okay, than to stay at home and wish you hadn't. Transports can be learning situations, if you want them to be.

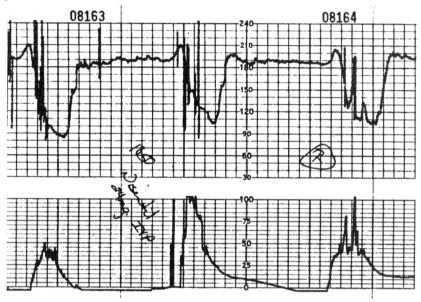

Figure 12-6: Variable Decelerations

Acceleration Patterns

Acceleration patterns are periodic increases of FHR in response to the contractions and indicate an intact cardiovascular system in the baby. They are often seen in breech presentations during vaginal exams and in response to sound. There are two types: uniform accelerations and variable accelerations.

Uniform accelerations reflect the pattern of the related uterine contraction. It might be a reflection of stress on the baby. As long as the FHR remain in normal limits and return to the baseline rate after the peak of the contraction is over and before the end of the contraction it is considered normal.

Variable acceleration does not reflect the pattern of the contraction because it increases faster than the intensity of the contraction and it varies in relation to the onset of the contraction. It is caused by baby's movements or stimulation of the baby by vaginal exam, scalp electrode, and is a normal response. We consider variable acceleration as a sign of baby's well-being in a non-compromised baby.

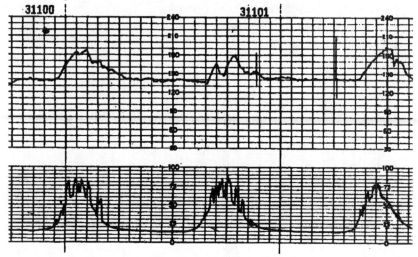

Figure 12-7: Accelerations

The Sinusoidal Pattern

The sinusoidal pattern has an undulating, repetitive and uniform pattern with an equal variance of no more than 5 beats above and below the baseline. This pattern does not respond to any external stimulus, contractions, or baby's movement. The cycle is two to six per minute. The sinusoidal pattern is the most dangerous FHR pattern, and requires immediate physician consultation. It can be due to fetal anemia from placenta abruptio, placenta previa, erythroblastosis, or severe fetal distress. Oxygen and immediate transport are your only options, while you pray that God will be merciful and grant these parents a healthy baby. We did have such a birth. As long as Pat stayed on her left side and had oxygen by mask at 6 lpm for her two-hour labor in the hospital, the baby responded to the contractions well. The FHTs were never completely out of the sinusoidal pattern, but during the contractions he fluctuated 10 bpm.

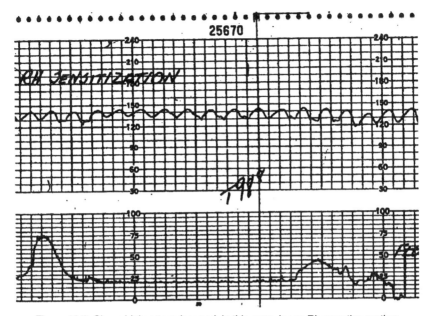

Figure 12-8: Sinusoidal pattern (caused, in this case, by an Rh-negative mother having been sensitized to her baby).

Fetal Distress

Fetal distress means the well-being of baby has been compromised. It may be chronic with onset during pregnancy, or acute beginning in labor, or both. Chronic fetal distress is usually secondary to uteroplacental insufficiency during the antenatal period. This may be due to intrauterine growth retardation and postmaturity syndrome. Late decels with or without variability, are your clue. The onset of labor usually precipitates the acute distress. Acute fetal distress can also be caused by cord compression, prolapsed cord, nuchal cord, or true knot in the cord.

Variable decels are the most common pattern with cord compression or OP in second stage and rapid descent through the pelvis of the fetal head during second stage. This is best illustrated by a drop from 0 station to birth in five seconds. In the home situation, you would not get a chance to hear the dip in FHR during this time unless you were listening with the fetoscope, a doppler, or a fetal monitor was in use. This is not always acute distress. Cord compression may lead to acute distress, if you cannot change baby's position by changing Pat's position, and trying the flip-flop, or knee-chest position.

What to do depends if the following are present:

- Maternal complications such as diabetes, preeclampsia, hypertension, all increase the risk of uteroplacental insufficiency;
- Fetal complications e.g., postdates, intrauterine growth retardation;
- Presence of meconium;
- Stage of labor in which the abnormal FHR occurred.

If baby has been compromised by the above, he will have few if any reserves to handle the stress of birth. Remember, baby is working as hard as Pat is, and he needs to have something to work with. This necessitates immediate transfer. **I strongly suggest that you transport if the baby is having abnormal heart rate patterns**, especially in legally difficult places. It is better to transport and have the problem corrected from baby changing position en route, than to have a compromised baby with limited resources at home. Hospitals are equipped and trained for the emergent situation. They excel with the abnormal. It is the *normal* they have trouble with. We are trained for normal, so we need to keep that in mind when faced with these unusual situations.

Occasionally during the prenatal visits you will have a baby that delights in playing "hide and seek" with the midwife! This child will grow up with a well-developed sense of humor. Ha! You may have to get the FHTs when the baby is least expecting it. I have seen babies actually roll away from the fetoscope and turn bottom end or head toward the "scope." Once I told a baby, "If you don't let me listen to your heartbeat, I will get the doppler and you will have to have ultra-sound radiation. You won't like that, Little One, so you'd best cooperate." I thought it was worth the try, and it did make Pat giggle, and relieved her tension. (I had been trying for 10 or 15 minutes to hear baby's heart rate.) Anyway, it worked, and the baby rolled right back so I could hear the heart tones. I thanked the baby for being so cooperative and added, "that wasn't so bad now, was it?" At the next visit, I told the baby to "be patient with me, and you won't have to put up with my messing around (palpation and auscultation) for long." Baby was still during the FHTs and then rolled over!

Dr. Thomas Verny and Jack Kelly wrote *The Secret Life of the Unborn*, and detailed their research on the awareness of the unborn child to the extra-uterine environment around mother. I found it very good, as it documented everything that I felt in my heart when carrying my babies. My babies reacted to what was going on about me. One child hated my shopping at a nationwide discount store, but enjoyed immensely the prayer meeting or Bible study. I could tell by the way he kicked and made me so uncomfortable in the former, that he would prefer not to be there. He was almost four years old before he could go in that store without complaining. I like Dr. Verny's book. Some folks took exception to one paragraph on abortion. When read in context, I felt that it was a sarcastic comment on the current mindset of some folks. If that paragraph is offensive to you, cross it out, and study the rest.

Version: Changing the Position of the Baby

If the baby is in the transverse position, it is for the convenience of the baby. Mother is more comfortable too, because she can breathe easier and move around without baby "getting in the way." The baby is either in the process of turning from breech to cephalic, or mother has been doing a lot of bending over in the garden, and it is much more comfortable for baby. Baby doesn't get as "squished" in transverse as in a vertical position when mother bends over. Remember, baby is in breech position for most of the first two trimesters. Some time in the sixth or seventh month, baby turns to cephalic, and in the process may be transverse for a time.

Occasionally, baby will decide that transverse is more comfortable than vertical. After all, the pelvis acts like a cradle, and baby can get real comfy. If the baby is still transverse when he should be thinking about getting ready to engage, you have to turn him. Start with lying on the side opposite from the head when resting/sleeping, and doing pelvic rocks three times a day when up and about. If the pelvic rocks and side lying don't seem to get the message across, try the knee-chest position. This means Pat's chest is on the floor or mattress and her "bottom" is sticking up in the air, because she is on her knees and her legs are at at right angle to the floor.

A thin pillow may make it more comfortable for her head. Pat should stay in this position for about 15 minutes. After 15 minutes, she can get up on her hands and knees until her head clears, then she must stand up and walk around for about 30 minutes. Often Pat will feel the baby's head slide into the pelvis when she stands up. This will be so "quick" and "strange" to her that she may even cry out slightly or complain of a momentary pain when the baby "lands" in the right position in the pelvis.

Breech Tilt

Your next "trick" out of your bag is the breech tilt. This is for the breech as well as the transverse baby. In this exercise, like the knee-chest exercise, you are trying to get gravity to pull the head off the iliac bone in the transverse lie, or the baby's bottom out of the pelvis in the breech position. When Pat rolls to her side, hopefully the head will go to that side because it is the heaviest part of the baby and will answer the call of gravity. As she stands up, the head is suppose to slip into the pelvis. Then while she walks for the prescribed 30 minutes, the head will settle into the pelvis, ready to come out on birth day. Occasionally, it takes the breech baby two tries on the breech tilt. The first try to go into the transverse position, the second to slip into the pelvis in cephalic presentation. Rarely, a baby is determined to be born breech, even after these exercises. If baby insists on being breech, expect baby to be entangled in the cord, or at least have multiple loops around his body. The majority of such instances are uneventful births, because baby just slides through the loops and is born in the breech position. Rarely, the cord is so tightly wrapped that baby does not descend and requires a cesarean.

The breech tilt is done two different ways. Both require Pat to recline with her hips 18 inches above her head. She may stack pillows up, sit on them and have someone help her lean back until her shoulders and head are on the mattress/floor, or Pat may lean her ironing board against the seat of the couch. Again with help, Pat needs to straddle the ironing board (or any other sturdy board at least 12–18 inches wide and 1–2 inches thick by 4–5 feet long), then sit on it and lean back until she is lying on the board with her head below her hips. She can "prop" her legs up on the couch, or on the board, for comfort's sake. Pat must remain in this position, with her hips elevated 18 inches above her head, for 15 minutes. Then with help (because she may feel like the room is spinning a bit) Pat rolls off the board in the same direction the baby is facing, to a hands and knees position on the floor. This should encourage the baby to tuck her head, which causes the head to slide into the pelvis! Praise the Lord! After getting her bearings, Pat should stand up by walking her hands up her legs, just like the toddlers do, or crawl to the couch and use the couch to assist her to stand. Once she is on her feet, Pat is to walk for 30 minutes and get the baby settled into the pelvis. Check baby's heart tones and rate while Pat is getting her bearings while on her hands and knees and again when she stands up. If Pat needs to lie down on her side, when she gets off the board, then check the FHT's then.

The "Flip-Flop"

Another exercise that is helpful when the baby seems to be "stuck" in a poor position for birth is the "flip-flop." This exercise will, not so gently, jar the baby out of the pelvic cradle, or off the pubic bone and enable Johnny to tuck his chin for a more synclitic position in labor.

You need a minimum of two people to help Pat, and a soft place such as sofa cushions on the floor, or a bed that is accessible from both sides. When you flip or flop Pat, please do it quickly, but also break her fall to the side, by staying in control of her body movements. Pat must not try to do the movements herself, because that will tighten her abdominal muscles and prevent the baby from moving. The baby needs to move out of the pelvis, so he can tuck his chin and get realigned to a better or best position.

This is the procedure:

1. Person A is at Pat's head and will stabilize her head, as she flips Pat at the shoulders.
2. Person B is at her hips and will flip her from the hips.
3. All movements must be done between contractions!
4. Assist Pat to the knee-chest position on the prepared area.
5. Wait 15 minutes.
6. Pat remains relaxed while the two people positioning Pat do *all* the work.
7. After the "last" contraction, on the count of three: A and B, in coordinated effort, keeping Pat's spine straight, flip Pat from the knee-chest position to the side the baby is facing, or to her left side.
8. Pat remains on her side for 15 minutes.
9. After the "last" contraction, positions are taken again, and before the next contraction begins, Pat is flopped back to her knee-chest position.
10. After 15 minutes and her last contraction, Pat is helped to her feet and allowed to walk for 15 to 30 minutes.

This is very effective to turn a posterior or a face (mentum) presentation to anterior or occiput position during labor. Of course, it is best to do it early in labor (you have more time to do the flip-flop between contractions in early labor), but can be done in transition. Sometimes the baby slips out of his asynclitic position and immediately into a synclitic one so fast, that when Pat stands up to walk, baby engages and drops to a +2 or +3 station. Be near Pat's birthing spot, if you are doing the flip-flop during transition, because Baby may decide to make his appearance very quickly.

Always palpate the baby and during labor, confirm your palpation with a vaginal exam to determine baby's position before trying to change the position. Sometimes the baby will flip on her own between birth day and the last visit. This will often happen during the night while Pat is sleeping on her left side. Be sure to thank God for His mercy and the baby for being so obedient and kind when she does turn.

Version by Massage

Many times, if Pat would just get herself comfy in a recliner, or make a recliner with a comfy chair and foot stool, she can massage her baby into turning. At the last visit with the midwife, she learned how to tell where the head and back are, so now she locates them. Pat gets comfy in the chair and starts to gently massage her tummy.

- Massage in a circular motion in the direction you want baby to turn.
- Apply gentle pressure at the back of baby's head, moving toward face, and simultaneously
- Apply gentle pressure at baby's bottom, to encourage baby into a forward roll (somersault).

Baby has become accustomed to Pat's voice, but this time Pat is going to talk to baby and tell her, "Baby, I love you, and I want the best for you. Today, the best for you is toss turn upside down, so your head is down. That is where the 'door' is for you to come out. It is easier on you and on me if you go out the 'door' head first. Baby, please follow my guidance and turn. Thank you." Then, "lift" the baby's bottom up out of the pelvis and give the head firm downward pressure so the baby will do a forward roll into the pelvis. Pat should try this about two or three times a day for at least a week before the external version is attempted. It may be worth the midwife's time to check Pat's technique before external version is considered. The technique may need to be corrected and Baby will respond to the corrected technique.

This exercise is not as interventive as the external version, and baby is not as apt to become compromised. Pat will not do anything that is hurting her, and has the advantage of being able to sense if the baby seems to be getting into trouble. The amount of pressure is slightly more than Pat already uses when she rubs her tummy. Often, the baby will turn during the night while Pat sleeps on her left side, after a massage session.

- If the massage hurts, she is applying too much pressure and should stop the procedure.
- If the baby is reacting in a negative way, she should stop.
- Do not repeat if Baby has turned, or Pat is uncomfortable, or baby objects to the procedure.

- Listen to fetal heartbeats after each massage session.

Pelvic rocks, squatting, breech-tilt and sleeping on your left side, all help turn a baby that is not yet engaged in the pelvis. Pulsatilla 200 C and other homeopathics are also very helpful in turning a baby. These methods are the least invasive and the safest ways to turn a baby. A sonogram can monitor baby's direction and movement, if you feel the risk of sonogram is worthwhile. Don't forget to thank God for His mercies, and baby for cooperating when she turns.

External Version

External version is a procedure that should not be done before 38 weeks or after the baby has engaged, and only if there is at least two skilled midwives and one apprentice present. This is a very interventive procedure, and should be done only as a last resort.

The risks are:

- *Cord entanglement, and*
- *Premature separation of the placenta, with its attendant complications.*

External version should not be attempted unless:

- *You have three midwives or two midwives and at least one apprentice;*
- *You have faithfully tried the breech-tilt twice a day for at least two weeks;*
- Pat has tried to massage her baby into cephalic position for two weeks, prior to and between the breech tilt exercises;
- *God said to do it after praying about it.*
- Pat has at least an average amount of waters. If she has a small amount (oligohydramnios), the danger of entanglement of the cord and tearing of the membranes is too great. If she has an abundance of waters, (polyhydramnios), you can't get a good feel of the baby, but baby will respond to pelvic rocks and side lying very quickly.

This is a last-resort procedure, and the clients need to know the risks. If the midwives are not comfortable with doing the external version, it is better to consider doing the breech birth, if the baby is of average size, or having a doctor attended birth. If the baby is large, you want to evaluate the pelvis very carefully, before attempting the version. If the baby is large and the pelvis is marginal, the baby may be trying to tell you something. You would be better off shopping around for a doctor that will do a breech birth, if you are not confident about a breech birth, even if you have to do some travelling. It beats the risks of being in an emergency situation beyond your skills and equipment. I'd rather have a cesarean than a compromised baby.

What you need for an external version:

- Skilled midwives or doctor trained in the procedure.
- The birth kit, in case labor starts.
- A doppler.
- Child care for Pat's other children.
- At least one apprentice to chart, minute by minute, heart tones and exact steps of procedure.
- Allow at least two hours of uninterrupted time.
- Either unplug the phone or have someone sitting at the muffled phone ready to answer it.
- For best results we need a very relaxed Mother.
  - In the hospital, Pat may receive a light relaxant.
  - At home, a cup of chamomile or valerian tea, may be nice if Pat is nervous.

The procedure:

- Position Pat in a somewhat reclined position, about 10 degrees. She needs to feel comfortable; low enough to have the maximum amount of room for the baby to move, yet up enough to prevent supine hypertensive syndrome.
- Palpate and make sure the baby has not turned on its own. Double check with a vaginal exam.
- Take heart tones with a fetoscope or doppler for a base line.
- Pray for baby to turn quickly, easily, and safely, and ask the Lord to give the midwives wisdom and skill.
- Locate heart tones and monitor constantly. One midwife has full responsibility of giving the heart tone count every six seconds. If the tone quality changes, she should notify the midwife attempting the version immediately. The procedure stops, until the baby is stabilized.
- The other midwife starts to turn the baby in a somersault motion, with downward pressure to the head, and

upward pressure to the baby's bottom. The head must remained flexed at all times, or it will become a face presentation. (Knee-chest or Flip-Flop might convert a face to occiput presentation.)

- The apprentice records the FHT, and progress of the version as orally reported by the midwives.
- When baby has turned to cephalic, mother then is helped up, and she walks to get the baby settled in. (Another 30 minutes).
- Listen to the baby's heart beat every five minutes for a full minute for 30 minutes, to make sure everything is remaining within normal limits.
- Leave a fetoscope, if you have an extra. It gives the parents confidence, should they wish to check the baby during the next few days. If you don't leave a scope, you should check heart rate every 15–30 minutes for four hours after the procedure, and daily until birth or you are confident baby is doing well.
- Mother should keep track of the baby's movements for the next week. There should be no less than six to ten movements per day.

Counting Movements

The healthy term unborn has about ten major movements a day. That means that he has a group of kicks, which is counted as one major movement, then again in a few minutes will do the same thing. That is another movement. When the baby rolls from side to side, that is another movement. If the baby kicks with his feet, then "bangs" with his arms/hands, they are counted as two movements.

This is often done when the baby is suspected of being post-due, as well as after a version. As long as the baby has six to ten major movements a day, it is considered healthy. Sometimes the baby will have a lot of movement for about 30 minutes or an hour and then will be quiet for four or five hours. As long as the movement is smooth and regular, baby is okay. If the movements become frantic and spasmodic or jerky, the baby should be monitored immediately. If the heart tones have changed from what has been "normal" perhaps a sonogram or consult with your back up is in order. The cord may be getting pinched, or there may be some entanglement, or the very rare placental "failure" from over-calcification.

Oligohydramnios and Polydramnios

Oligohydramnios is an abnormally small amount of amniotic fluid. This condition is linked with kidney abnormalities and other congenital abnormalities, IUGR (intra-uterine growth retardation), early rupture of membranes at 24 to 26 weeks, and postmature syndrome. Lung hypoplasia and limb deformities have also been linked to oligodramnios. The limb deformities come from the loose membranes wrapping around a limb and cutting off the circulation.

Warning signs are:

- "Molding" of the uterus around the baby;
- Baby easily outlined, even the small parts are easily identifiable; and
- Baby is not ballotable when palpating.

I have had limited success in improving this by encouraging the client to drink lots of water and other fluids and salting their food. I have not seen anyone get waterlogged, but it has improved over what it was when we started, to just below normal. Normal amount of amniotic waters at term is about two cups or 480cc. Pat of course is receiving lots of compliments from family that she doesn't look pregnant, and how "lucky" she is that she is not "big." The midwife has to work hard to show Pat that is wrong thinking, and how hazardous it is for the baby not to have enough water.

It is easier to prevent by encouraging Pat to drink 8–10 twelve ounce glasses of liquids every day. Salting food to taste is very important in pregnancy, and will prevent oligodramnios and other problems caused by a low salt intake. If Pat has a problem salting her food, because of past advice, then encourage her to eat some salty food everyday: for example, pickles, potato chips, etc.

Polydramnios (hydramnios) is the opposite. This lady has an abundance of water. So much so, that it is hard to palpate the baby through the tightly stretched abdomen. It is also difficult to hear the FHTs with the fetoscope. Things to look for with hydramnios are:

- Multiple pregnancy (especially monozygotic twins);
- Diabetes;

- Erythroblastosis;
- Fetal malformations of the gastro-intestinal tract or central nervous system.

Complications can include:

- Malpresentations that could complicate birth;
- Abruptio placenta;
- Uterine dysfunction during labor, due to "over distention;"
- Immediate postpartum hemorrhage from uterine atony caused by the over distention;
- Cord prolapse from the baby not engaging well (floats in the water).

Many women have polydramnios every time they get pregnant, and have normal healthy babies, but it is good to keep your eyes open. This lady will be very large early in her pregnancy and will be getting all sorts of flack about her size, from her friends. She needs a lot of encouragement, because she physically feels pretty miserable in her last two months. Her "ninth month miseries" are multiplied, because they start in the seventh month.

Urine Testing

Usually, midwives are mostly interested in the protein and glucose values, to monitor Pat's diet. But there are other stories told by the urine test strip that will help monitor Pat's continuing good health. I prefer using the ten-chemical strips, because it gives me a better indication of how Pat's liver and kidneys are working. Understanding what the different categories can tell you about her health will relieve your mind of a lot of questions, such as is this a bladder or yeast infection, or protein from the mucus plug melting.

The **pH** indicates the acidity or alkalinity of the urine, which reflects the acid-base balance in the body. Normally the urine is slightly acidic at 6. It can range as low as 4.6 or as high (alkaline) as 8. The pH reflects how well the lungs and the kidneys are doing their jobs of regulating the acid-base balance in the body. If there is severe kidney or lung dysfunction, blood and tissue pH will be disturbed and show up in the urine.

Leukocytes in urine are detected by the presence of granulocytic leukocytes. When the chemicals on the strip react with the leukocytes the color purple emerges. Granulocytic leukocytes are present if any inflammatory (infection) condition exists. A melting mucus plug or mucus from intercourse in the last 24 hours will register 2+.

Nitrite is present if Pat has an urinary infection, and shows as a red-violet indicator. Bacteria in the bladder will give off nitrites as quickly as four hours after the colony develops. This is early enough that Pat will not have any symptoms of infection. Usually this early in the game, flushing with one quart of liquids, especially cranberry or tomato or citrus juices every hour, alternated with water will flush the bacteria out of the bladder. If Pat develops a full bladder infection, Cantharis 6x or 3x will give instant relief and cure the infection when taken every 3 to 4 hours. More often if the bladder infection is very acute. If antibiotics are taken, be sure to eat yogurt and take vitamin B and K supplements to replace the intestinal flora (which produce these vitamins) that the antibiotics destroy.

Pregnant women, school children (especially girls), diabetic patients, elderly men and women and newly married women are "high risk" for nitrites in the urine.

Protein reacts in the green spectra. If Pat is spilling protein, I know that she: a) isn't eating enough proteins or, b) is eating incomplete proteins. In either case, the body is unable to utilize what she is eating, so throws it away as unusable. If her diet is good, persistent proteinuria may indicate her kidneys, thyroid or heart needs checking out, in the worst-case scenario. Some people normally throw protein off during the day when they are active. Proteinuria is also present with fever, emotional stress and strenuous muscular exercise, toxemia of pregnancy, and kidney infection.

Glucose reacts from yellow to green. A "penny" sucker will give a green reaction, as will a ripe pear if eaten less than two hours before the test. A high carbohydrate meal (burger meal) will also cause glucosuria in the well-nourished pregnant woman. Please check with Pat to see if she has had any sweets recently; it may have been a rare sweet treat. If it is unexplainable, and she throws one gram of sugar again, then see *Gestational Diabetes* in Chapter 11.

Ketones color changes are from beige to violet. They are present if Pat is not eating enough calories, and her body reserves (fatty acids) are being used up. Those reserves are what Pat will need for labor and the first six weeks after birth.

If there is insufficient production of insulin by the liver, Pat will also throw ketones in the urine (she will also have 2+ or more glucose, if diabetic). Other reasons are: frequent vomiting, diarrhea, digestive disturbances, exposure to cold or severe physical exertion.

Urobilinogen is the by-product of broken down red blood cells by bacteria in the intestinal tract. Most normal urines will show some in the pink range. Positive readings go to red. If you are getting red readings, and your client is also anemic, you may have some detective work to do. Elevated urine urobilinogens almost always indicate pre-hepatic jaundice. Hemolytic anemia, pernicious anemia and sickle cell disease need to be eliminated if the bilirubin is normal, but the urobilinogens are persistently elevated. Antibiotics will reduce (true) urobilinogen levels.

Bilirubin is a product of degenerated heme from the hemoglobin of old red blood cells. The globin is a protein that is recycled in the body along with the iron the red cell was carrying. Antibiotics will give false positive results. Elevated bilirubin in the urine always indicates liver cell disease and or biliary obstruction. Bilirubinuria indicates liver disease before any clinical signs are usually evident.

Blood, as one usually thinks of blood, is not what is measured on the urine sticks. It is instead free hemoglobin that is being released from red blood cells due to their breakdown or hemolysis, somewhere in the body. The hemoglobin is filtered out of the blood into the urine by the kidneys. (Hematuria is the presence of intact red cells in the urine, and must be detected by microscopic examination.) When hemoglobin appears in blood, it is a sign of disease, and the urine will be colored from clear red, clear red-brown to clear dark-brown. The Bio-Dynamics test strips claim to measure both intact red cells and free hemoglobin, as number of red cells per microliter (one-millionth of a liter) of urine.

Hemoglobin in the urine may be caused by:

- An irritation from harsh toilet paper, or
- Intercourse in the last 48 hours.

It can also mean:

- There is an infection such as candida or cystitis;
- Possible uterine bleeding or melting of the mucus plug;
- Bladder or kidney infection (see *Nitrite*);

- Severe or extensive burns;
- Eating or drinking certain poisons such as mushrooms, acids, or certain drugs (sulfonamides, arsenic or anticoagulants);
- Strenuous, unaccustomed exercise (such as running on a hard surface; jogging barefoot causes trauma to the cells passing through the feet);
- Exposure to excessive cold;
- Respiratory acidosis (resulting from sleep in some people in their 30s and 40s);
- False positives from tetracycline or similar antibiotics that use ascorbic acid as a preservative, or taking large doses of Vitamin C; or
- False positives from menstruation.

Generally speaking, hemoglobinuria usually indicates some form of kidney or urinary tract disease or disorder. While discussing the "pretty colors" on Pat's urine stick, you can personalize her nutrition needs, and how to solve them with her budget. If she needs to address infection, you can give her some alternative choices to antibiotics, such as vitamins, herbals or homeopathics, hopefully before allopathic care is necessary.

Venipuncture: Drawing Blood

It is best to learn this at a workshop, so we will consider this a review of what you already know. You may want to practice on some cooked macaroni before attempting this procedure on a client, especially if it has been a while since you did a venipuncture. If you worked where a phlebotomist or the lab gathered the samples, you may have to practice a couple of times. This is a skill that is very helpful when you work with a lab.

First you want to assemble all the Vacutainers™ that you will need for the tests you want done, plus the needle, collar (adaptor), gloves, tourniquet and the alcohol preps. Some folks use povidone iodine swabs for preparing the site. A small towel for Pat to lay her arm on is a comfort measure for her. Assemble the needle on the collar (adaptor), and slide the first Vacutainer™ in to the line. You do not want to puncture the rubber stopper completely or the vacuum will escape. The negative pressure is what draws the blood.

Because of the epidemic levels of Hepatitis B and HIV, among other blood-borne contagious disease, it is a good idea to use universal precautions when drawing blood. This means that you wear gloves when drawing or handling anything that has blood from your clients on it. Your medical insurance company can back out of any medical bills you may incur if you do not use universal precautions. Homosexuals and bisexuals are not the only ones running around with these diseases. The heterosexual community is contracting HIV and hepatitis faster than the homosexual community, according to the National Public Health Department's Center of Communicable Diseases, Atlanta, Ga., in their 1990 report.

The easiest sites to draw blood are in the forearm, either at the antecubital fossa (middle of the bend in the elbow) or about midway down the forearm. These veins are near the surface of the skin and are large. If using the velcro type of tourniquet, apply it tightly without pinching. If using the rubber type, lay the arm over the tourniquet. Bring the ends up (one on each side of the arm), holding tightly to the tourniquet, stretch one end out from the arm while crossing it over and tucking a half loop under the steadied end. Lower the tourniquet to the arm, checking that it is tight enough, but not pinching Pat. Scrub the area well with the alcohol preps. This will raise the veins for better visibility. Asking Pat to open and close her hand will also enlarge the vein. Gentle slapping, or a warm towel will also bring the vein up for better visibility, and ease in inserting the needle. Procedure:

- If you are using povidone swabs, now is when you wipe the area.
- Pick up the Vacutainer™ that is assembled in the adaptor.
- Steady the vein with your non-dominant hand below the chosen insertion site.
- While keeping tension on the skin, insert the needle into the vein with your dominant hand.
- Slip the needle inside the vein at least half its length to reduce the risk of pulling it out when manipulating the Vacutainers™.
- Steady the needle with your non-dominant hand so it will not move in the vein.

- With your dominant hand, steady the collar and seat the Vacutainer™ so the blood enters the tube. Have the next tube handy.
- Carefully remove the first tube and insert the second tube without moving the needle.
- Continue as many times as you need samples.
- Release the tourniquet before you remove the needle so Pat will not get a big bruise.
- Apply pressure on the needle where it enters the skin, as you withdraw it, with a dry 2"×2" gauze square.
- Have Pat bend her arm tightly against the gauze for a few minutes until the bleeding has stopped.
- Apply a Band-Aid® tightly over the site, to prevent any blood leakage until the clot is formed at the vein, and to protect Pat's clothes.
- Label the tubes with your client's name and any other information the lab requires.
- Complete the Lab form including insurance information, if applicable and send it to the lab.

Occasionally, the puncture site will start to bleed about 15 minutes after Pat leaves the office. A Band-Aid® seems to prevent that, or at least stems the flow until you can get a pressure bandage on it.

If working with a lab some distance from you, you may want to Federal Express it for overnight delivery. Priority Mail will get your samples within 48 hours for one third the cost of Federal Express, in those areas that Federal Express can not deliver within 24 hours. The U.S. Postal Service is not picky about blood samples like some delivery services are. UPS will not handle blood or other body fluid samples. Most laboratories have a start-up kit that includes the supplies that you need for the most common lab tests including request forms and foam mailers. Fees and postage are about the same between labs, but get bids for the best deal. Working with a local laboratory often has the advantage of using their pick-up service. Some labs will even supply a centrifuge and microscope (handy to tell if Pat has a leaky bag of waters). Certified Nurse Midwives, Nurse Practitioners or Physician Assistants may be of help in finding a lab.

Finger Puncture for Hemoglobin

The purpose of taking a hemoglobin test is to measure the oxygen- and carbon-dioxide-carrying ability of the blood. Changes in plasma volume are more accurately reflected by the Hgb concentration. This is a "back door" way of looking at the iron-carrying ability (hematocrit) of the blood. If the hemoglobin is down, the hematocrit and plasma volume will also be down. Doing the hematocrit requires a centrifuge, which is not easily portable, usually expensive, and hard to come by, unless working with a laboratory that will furnish one, thus an impractical piece of equipment for most traditional midwives.

As a courtesy, ask if Pat is right- or left-handed, and if she has a preferred finger. The finger you would have used may be sore already. Once the finger has been chosen, have her hold her finger down, so the blood will run into the finger. If she holds her finger up the blood will drain back into her hand. This is a good time to set out the lancet, hemolysis stick, slides, clip, alcohol sponge and hemoglobinometer.

- Cleanse the ball of the finger with the alcohol sponge, and let it dry. Fanning it will speed it up some (alcohol makes it sting).
- Stick the site with the lancet in a quick, firm manner.
- Fill the slide with the two drops of blood, and time how long it takes for Pat to stop bleeding, while you stir the slide with the hemolysis stick. Do not wipe or put pressure on the finger.
- Carefully place the cover on the slide so it doesn't splatter, and put it in the clip.
- Pat should have stopped bleeding by now; this usually takes about 30 to 60 seconds. Let her wipe her finger with the alcohol sponge.
- Slip the clip into the hemoglobinometer, and match the colors.

You want to take the initial hemoglobin at three months, if you did not draw blood for a complete blood count. This would approximate the pre-pregnancy value of the hemoglobin. The blood volume has been "diluted" as much as it is going to be, and you will be able to tell if Pat needs more red cells. Walking and other aerobic exercise is great, but do not depend on exercise to do all the blood cell increase needed. Diet is much more reliable. Counselling on what foods are high in iron, and how to fix them to get maximum benefit is very helpful. Remember, calcium binds with iron and makes it unusable, but taking vitamin C with iron between meals increases its absorption.

I usually take the second hemoglobin at six months to see how things are going. The baby starts storing iron from Pat at six months, so if she is low, it will get lower unless turned around now. If Pat's third reading is 11 or less at the beginning of the ninth month, she needs to take iron blend tincture at 10 drops with a glass of juice (preferably citrus) three times a day for a week. That should get her Hgb up to 12, if she started at 10. One week of the tincture will raise the Hgb 2 grams/deciliter (g/dl). I consider 11 on the low side, and 10 the absolute limit for home birth. Anything below 11 will run the risk of hemorrhage, and Pat will have to take Shepherd's Purse tincture and chlorophyll for the high vitamin K content, if there is no time to raise her hemoglobin before birth day.

Variations or interfering factors to the Hgb count are:

- Slight Hgb decreases normally occur during pregnancy because of the expanded blood volume;
- Living in high-altitude areas causes high Hgb values;
- Drugs that may cause increased levels include gentamicin (sulfate antibiotic) and methyldopa (Aldomet, an antihypertensive);
- Drugs that may cause decreased levels include antibiotics, antineoplastic (anti-tumor) drugs, aspirin, indomethacin (Indocin), rifampin, and sulfonamides;
- Blood dilution from over-hydration decreases Hgb;
- Dehydration causes an artificially high value;
- Persistent decreased values may indicate any one of the anemias, lupus, spleen disease, cancer, or a blood disease. Or, Pat isn't getting enough iron from her foods and needs vitamin or herbal supplements.

Intrapartal Skills: Labor

The one thing the midwife needs to keep foremost in her mind is to allow her clients to progress at the client's own rate. If Pat is allowed to labor according to her own rhythm, everything will be fine. This requires patience, patience, patience. Trying to hurry things along when it is not warranted, causes the same interference that results in arrested labor at home and Cesarean birth in hospitals. On the other hand, you do not want to ignore warning signals. Vigilance to maintain normal natural processes is the greatest service the midwife can do for her clients. With this in mind, I will address the more common forms of the normal labor, and give you some guidelines as to when to determine if the normal is deviating towards the not normal.

Classic Labor

It is so tempting to call this one "normal," but all of these patterns are normal for the women that experience them as the usual way they have babies. The classic pattern most women experience lasts from 4 to 14 hours, the contractions build gradually from easy, light, and mild to very strong and hard. This labor usually starts with contractions 10–15 minutes apart, lasting 15 to 30 seconds and may have a predictable pattern. Usually Pat can finish up whatever is most pressing before she has to concentrate on working with her contractions at the 5 cm "mark." At the start, she feels an ache in her lower back with the contractions, that gradually extends around to below the pubic bone and spreads upward to the fundus as the contractions get stronger. Second stage lasts from one to two contractions to about two hours.

Maintaining her nutrition and hydration seems like an unnecessary interruption to Pat, but is necessary to keep up her energy and the pH balance in the baby. Labor coaching depends on how well she is handling her contractions. The midwife should be ready to give Pat massage, help Pat breathe easy and natural so she doesn't hyperventilate. Rotating duties with the birth team and John concerning massage and coaching, keeps everyone fresh, if it doesn't upset with Pat's flowing with the rhythm of her labor.

Don't neglect monitoring the heart tones every hour in early labor and every 15 to 30 minutes, for a full minute, as labor progresses. Once the waters break, you want to take them at the time of the break and every five minutes thereafter. If the break is early in labor, I usually listened every five minutes for the first hour and then every 10 to 15 minutes until labor became more active. I usually did a vaginal exam on arrival, if Pat seemed to be concentrating on her contractions and not again until she started to get "grunty." If she developed a worrisome pattern, I would recheck for dilation, presentation and descent more frequently. If waters are ruptured, minimize your vaginal exams to barest necessity and always use sterile technique, squirting povidone iodine over genitalia and glove rather than surgical lubricant.

Start-and-Stop

The start-and-stop pattern tempts the attendant to "get things going," because you start feeling like a fireman going to a bunch of false alarms. Tension can begin to build up in the midwife, if she so very carefully scheduled the births on the calendar, and Pat is starting to go into the "space reserved" for Mary. This is why you must pray and trust God to be in control of your client's lives as well as yours. When John calls, you don't know if this is the "big one," so you don't want to roll over and go back to sleep when called. If it is a practice run, find a horizontal place and finish out the night at Pat and John's. The final call will usually resemble a form of the precipitous labor, because so much preparatory work has been done, so don't waste time responding.

One cause of start-and-stop is the "White Coat Syndrome." This is so named because it is nervousness or anxiety around "medical professionals." W.C.S. may result from an unfamiliar apprentice or assistant being present. Personality clashes may have a great bearing on stop-and-start. If the laboring woman is nervous or uncomfortable with the place or the attendants, she will not feel like she can birth well with them. Her body is saying "Let's have birth day," but her mind and emotions are saying "Later." She may be so worried about her midwife not arriving in time, that she stops her labor with her worry. So get things settled early on, so she can labor and not stop before the baby comes.

Malpresentation can also cause start-and-stop, as well as the slow and steady pattern. Using the pelvic rock, knee-chest if waters are intact, and the flip-flop, may correct a cephalic malpresentation. If baby is not engaged, and presenting in a breech position, you may want to consider external version, *if* you have the confidence and the skills needed. Pulsatilla or other homeopathic medication, given according to the manual is very helpful in turning or changing malpresentations. Some report good results with homeopathics even after baby was engaged.

Stop-and-start may be caused by Pat being very sensitive to Braxton-Hicks contractions. Braxton-Hicks can be very strong and feel like early labor.

With my second child, I exercised my doctor's patience to the very last strand. First, I was overdue. Steve finally arrived four weeks post due date! Secondly, between his birth day and the EDD I was either in the office at least once (other than my scheduled appointment), or in the emergency room (to rule out labor) every week. He did admit me once for overnight observation. What precipitated all this "attention" was my Braxton-Hicks contractions. They came every day, at different hours, but always lasted two hours. That in itself was not much, but they started out two minutes apart! Our daughter was born in two hours and 15 minutes with a labor that started with contractions two minutes apart! We were always taught in Obstetrics that the second baby usually, if not always, took half the time of the first!

When Steve finally came, I was admitted at 5cm and in the delivery room 30 minutes later. If the doctor had not decided to stop in OB before making his surgical rounds, he would have missed it, because he didn't believe me when I called. "You said that yesterday, when you called, Betty." "But, this is different. I'm going in, anyway." Pat usually knows when it is birth day. If she isn't sure, and has had a lot of stop-and-start, go anyway. On one of those trips home, you may find a short cut that will cut some valuable minutes off your response time.

Slow-and-Steady

Slow-and-steady requires the attendants and coach to work hard at keeping Pat relaxed, rested, hydrated and nourished. This rhythm allows nap times early on, and should be taken advantage of by all. Sometimes a slow labor will develop into a precipitous pattern after 5 or 6 cm and will skip transition altogether. Strong massage with a kneading, rubbing motion, keeping your strokes long to medium in length helps Pat relax.

In transition, she may need help to prevent hyperventilating. Maintain face-to-face and eye-to-eye contact, while bringing her to a slower and deeper rhythm, if she is breathing too fast.

If she needs to breathe fast during the peak of her contractions, help her do shallow but equal exchange of inhaling and exhaling, with slow, deep, breaths as soon as the peak is over. Give her lots of encouragement and praise on how well she is working to have her baby. Fetal heart tones need to be monitored the same as in all other patterns, unless Pat is sleeping; then, take them when she awakens for a contraction.

Deciding when the midwife should stay and when should she give the laboring couple space to labor alone and privately, is a judgement call. You must pray and do what you and your clients are comfortable with. If you have prenatals you could be doing, and Pat has not reached 5 cm yet, you could do them, providing you give the phone numbers or have a pager so you could be reached, and you don't have far to go. If John has to go some distance to get to a phone, and Pat suddenly decides to really perk along, how practical is your leaving? What if Pat leaps from 4 to 9 cm ten minutes after you leave? I had a client that could get about four hours of sleep between her first three hours of labor and birth, because of a "stop" in her labor. If I was not there when labor started up again, too bad. Three contractions and the baby was there! John got exercised as a substitute midwife several times!

Often Pat will start out slow, and if given positive encouragement, labor will move right along. I covered a large geographic area, and on occasion I would be over a hundred miles from a client that started into labor. One particular time Pat's husband called saying Pat was having five-minute contractions. My family and I were at a first birthday party for one of "my" babies, and at least one hundred miles away on congested two-lane roads from Pat! Fortunately, my house was on the way to Pat's. We flew across the countryside, taking the back roads to avoid traffic. My husband put my birthing stuff in the car, while I changed my clothes. I continued on to Pat's, expecting to find a baby when I arrived. Pat was rocking by the fire place, enjoying quiet and warmth, munching popcorn and sipping juice, with contractions still at five minutes apart and mild to moderate in strength. Knowing Pat, I checked FHT, checked dilation (4 cm), timed the contractions, set out my supplies, and got the paperwork started. About 45 minutes after I arrived, Pat asked me to check her again, "just to see how far she had progressed." She was at 9 cm and +3 station! Just enough time to go to the bathroom one more time while I prepared the birthing stool. Five minutes after getting on the stool, she had a sweet baby girl. I was in the house about 1 hour, and it was $3\frac{1}{2}$ hours since she paged me.

As I was leaving to go home after the four-hour postpartum watch, my pager went off again. Since I was at the outer limits of my pager, the voice was not real clear, and all I heard was "two to three minutes apart, please hurry!"

I knew that one of the four due within three weeks had just birthed, so that left me with three to call. You guessed it. I woke up my husband and all three before I found out who it was. Fortunately I was only 40 miles away. I arrived, and Pat was 4 cm, with mild to moderate contractions. The birth team was there but the labor had stopped and would not restart, even with herbs. By this time it was close to noon and I was getting very weary. Instead of curling up in a corner some- where, I chose to drive 45 miles home to sleep. About 45 min- utes into my nap, John calls close to panic, "Hurry, please hurry, the baby is on its way!" I dash back, turn into the drive on two wheels. John greets me with a proud look on his face, but still somewhat concerned. I run into the house, and find Pat nursing her baby. John had caught his first son, after a string of girls! Everyone was fine, with no tears or skids.

Sometimes the slow and steady labor stays slow until birth, about 20 hours after onset. This is normal as long as progress is being made. Progress is determined by descent of the baby, effacement, and dilation is taking place. Sometimes it is one or the other, as opposed to all at once, but progress is progress. Rome was not built in a day, and neither are some births. Vaginal exams every hour or two only irritate the vaginal mucosa and get Pat nervous. That combination can stop labor real quick. It also starts the clock going on possible infection, and you don't want that to get started!

Once Pat has reached 4 or 5 cm, I suggest that you plan to stay for the duration of the labor. Keeping some crocheting, knitting or a book that is not related to midwifery in the car for such occasions is handy. You do have to avoid giving the impression that you as a midwife are bored, and that the clients are taking up your valuable time. Playing a board game with Pat, John and whomever else is there can relax Pat so well that her labor really gets going. Once Pat relaxes and forgets about "performing" for the midwife, her dilatation and descent can progress at about 1 cm every $1\frac{1}{2}$ to 2 hours.

Major factors in this kind of labor are:
- A narrow inlet or midpelvis;
- Posterior presentation (especially with back pain);
- Nuchal hand or hands;
- Face (mentum) presentation; or
- Breech (sacral) presentation (especially if baby is not yet engaged).

The rules for a slow labor are:
- *Sleep* while Pat, John, and you can before the contractions get hard;
- Maintain hydration, nutrition and relaxation;
- Help Pat pace herself, alternating between upright and side-lying positions and not working hard too soon;
- *Patience* to all! If Pat and baby are doing well, all is well!
- Encourage Pat to sleep as much as she can before and after contractions, and after birth.

Precipitous

Some ladies are blessed with fast labor. A precipitous labor is two hours or less from start to finish, starts out with very few, if any, five-minute contractions. The contractions usually start at two or three minutes apart and 45 seconds long, moderate to strong in strength and moving very quickly to two minutes apart, lasting 90 seconds and very strong in strength. Second stage is usually over in two or three contractions. Pat needs very concentrated coaching to keep her relaxed and hydrated. A sip or swallow of any liquid between contractions is about all she can handle.

Monitoring the baby very closely is needful, because the stress of such a fast but hard labor can affect the baby. The problem with that theory, is most midwives walk into the room just in time to catch the baby, and Pat and John are glad you made it. This baby will not let you take your coat off or glove your hands first. These are the births that occur in the taxi cab or elevator when a hospital birth was planned.

One major advantage is Pat doesn't have time to get all worn out, and is on an adrenaline high for about four hours after the placenta is expelled. Another advantage is baby seldom has trouble coming out with this fast labor; it would be slower if there was any dystocia. Baby may be small, but don't count on it. My first baby weighed 8 lbs 15 oz, and it was all over, including the placenta, two hours and fifteen minutes after my first contraction.

Be alert for hemorrhage! Pat could hemorrhage any time in the first four hours. Her uterus has worked so hard in such a short period of time, that once the placenta is out it just wants to rest, instead of contracting and start to involute. Make sure it gets and stays firm. Do what you must do to keep it firm until the baby latches on. The baby is apt to be a little slow to start, so have the oxygen as handy as you can. A little free-flow oxygen usually is all baby needs. He's just as surprised and glad as Pat that it is over. He just doesn't know what to do about it. The immediate first four hours postpartum can be as hectic as the labor and birth, so stay alert! Most of the time Pat precips, nurses her squalling baby (who is complaining about the "rude" expulsion from his comfy quarters) and everything is wonderful. Precipitous births usually are so fast and clean, you don't need most of your supplies. If Pat has had support on her perineum, or birthed in an optimum position she probably won't have any tears. Instead of pushing, she breathed her baby out, hoping the midwife would arrive in time or to help her husband, as he caught this slippery young 'un.

Expect a precip, if she has had lots of prelabor episodes. Prelabor gets a lot of the preliminary things out of the way, like ripening, effacement, getting the cervix nice and stretchy in the multip and even sometimes dilation up to 4 cm before active labor begins. I always left a copy of Dr. Gregory White's *Emergency Childbirth* with the couple if Pat had a history of fast labor, or we had more than one practice run. John was supposed to read it and have it handy "just in case." One husband that attended his wife while waiting for the midwife to arrive said, "Everything happened so fast, I didn't have time to read before it happened." After saying that he realized he should have read it ahead of time! All was well, praise the Lord! His wife had a one-hour labor and baby was doing well. This is the time I remind the couples that this is what the midwives in

Exodus 1 were referring to when they said "the Hcbrew women. . .are lively."

These variations of normal labor patterns can cause Pat to have more pain than with the classic "normal" labor. Sometimes the labor pattern will cause the baby to react with unusual FHT patterns. Usually, changing Pat's position helps the baby and Pat. Position change for Pat or the baby can ease the pain for Pat and the stress for baby, and may even convert an unusual pattern to normal.

If the baby is in a good cephalic position, but the FHTs are showing some stress, there may be a pinched cord. Pelvic rocks and the knee-chest position usually help the cord float out of the way when the head shifts even the tiniest bit. The FHT will respond immediately. If position changes do not help, try putting Pat on her left side, give her some oxygen by mask at about 3 or 4 liters per minute. (Eight liters is better, but if you have only one tank, you may need to conserve so you have some for the baby if needed after birth.) If there is a change, see if the baby will tolerate Pat breathing room air. If not, then you will have to transport to prevent a very stressed baby at birth.

Valsalva Maneuver

This is defined in Mosby's *Medical, Nursing and Allied Health Dictionary* as "any forced expiratory effort against a closed airway, as when an individual holds the breath and tightens the muscles in a concerted, strenuous effort to move a heavy object or to change position in bed." This is the technique Labor and Delivery Nurses teach women for pushing the baby out. It is very effective in an emergency because it will multiply the force of the contraction 20 to 30 times. The complications, however, can be severe. The least severe, but still troublesome, is the bursting of Pat's facial capillaries because she kept the strength of the pushing in her head instead of directing it to the baby.

Most women are dehydrated to some extent in second stage, even if the IV has been running. This dehydration causes the blood to thicken from lack of plasma volume. This viscosity increases the risk of blood clotting. If Pat has varicose veins, that can be tragic with already depressed circulation in the legs becoming even more depressed with clots forming. The blood clotting can cause vascular accidents of the brain (strokes). When relaxing after each pushing effort with held breath, the Pat's blood rushes to the heart, and can overload the cardiac system, causing cardiac arrest.

Now, concerning the baby: when Pat holds her breath, baby does not get any oxygen, only carbon dioxide. Baby needs oxygen. To compensate for the low oxygen level in the placental blood, his heart beats faster. This shows as fetal distress on the monitor and when auscultating the FHTs. If Pat takes good deep breaths between contractions, baby can tolerate the low oxygen levels during the contractions (for an hour or so), providing Pat has not been getting glucose (sugar) in her liquids orally or IV. Glucose decreases baby's labor tolerance to normal situations and eliminates his tolerance for abnormal situations. Fruit juice is okay.

Another type of Valsalva Maneuver is caused by Pat lying flat on her back during labor. The weight of baby compresses Pat's aorta and vena cava, reducing the circulation to and from the uterus. This is often called supine hypotensive syndrome. Results are the same as above.

Perineal Massage

Perineal massage should be started about six weeks before estimated due date, for most people. If Pat is very small and tight, she should start earlier. I have had clients that started at six months gestation, because Pat was congenitally undeveloped externally, and birthed a nine-pound baby with no tears, or skid marks. Sometimes this little exercise leads to "more interesting" things, so Pat and John will want to set aside a time that will give them as much uninterrupted time as they will need. Any cold pressed oil, such as olive or the very expensive Vitamin E oil works very well. Some couples have used almond oil, because of the nice aroma. Vitamin E capsules can be punctured with a clean needle and used instead of bottled oil. Two or more capsules are sufficient per massage, according to your needs. This is less expensive than the bottled oil, yet will nourished the tissues too. You only need a small bottle.

This is how you do it. Be gentle, John. This is not a race. This is a time for gentleness. If Pat does not like the exercise, it is because John is working too hard and too fast, so she gets all tense to protect herself. This causes pain and increases the anxiety about tearing "wide open" when the baby is born. The purpose is for Pat to learn how to relax against the pressure of the baby's head, so he will ease out as he is born.

Here is the procedure:

- John washes his hands thoroughly and removes all residue of resin, paint, grease, etc., from around the fingernails (these substances can cause Pat a severe irritation or infection).
- Pat makes herself comfortable in bed.
- Pour a little oil into a small clean bowl, or "pop" a capsule and squeeze the oil onto his fingers. Cap the bottle, so it doesn't spill. Once oil is poured out, do not pour it back in. The remainder will be used on birth day, and must stay clean.
- John, dip two fingers into the oil. Gently and lovingly slip your oiled fingers into Pat's vagina.
- Thinking of the numbers on the face of a clock, with 6 o'clock at the center of the vagina (under your hand), slowly and gently slide your fingers from 6:00 to 4:00, then back to 6:00 and over to 8:00 o'clock several times.
- Once the oil has been well distributed, dip into the oil again to get more if needed. Pat needs to feel quite moist and oily.
- Slide the length of your fingers into the vagina, or as deep as is comfortable for Pat.
- At 6:00 o'clock, slowly apply pressure down (evenly along the length of your fingers) against the floor of the vagina. Increase the pressure until Pat tells you to stop.
- Hold the pressure steady, then when Pat tells you "okay," increase the pressure again until she says "stop."
- Hold the pressure steady again. When she says "okay" again, this time *slowly* release the pressure until the pressure is gone. Slowly slip your fingers out of her vagina. Exercise is over.
- Next time repeat the same steps.

Gradually increase numbers of fingers, two at a time and pressure over a period of days and weeks until you can stretch Pat open $3\frac{1}{2}$ inches. Take your time, sometimes it takes several days between increases of pressure or stretch, for Pat to relax well at that level of pressure. Once Pat has learned how to relax against this pressure, she will do very well on birth day.

Some folks have thought this to be a real "hokey" exercise and thought they would like to be excused from it. I always asked Pat if she was at all concerned about tearing, or was she confident that she could relax against the pressure. If she had any hesitancy at all, I encouraged their participation. You see, our culture has developed a fear about the natural processes of life, especially birth, and replaced the trust we should have with fear. Until women in North America look on birth as normal and have confidence that God knew what he was doing when He made female bodies, we shall continue to do apparently "hokey" exercises, to develop that trust again.

Universal Precautions

"Why scrub? Why take 'universal' precautions? My clients are clean. I don't have to worry about catching anything from them." Yes, that's what I always said too, but I wonder if I wasn't stretching the grace of God just a little thin. Are all of your clients equally safe from you? Can you document that they are absolutely free from AIDS? Have you personally done AIDS screening on them weekly for the last 15 years? Have you personally been with that person 24 hours a day for the last 15 years, and know that person has never:

- Kissed nor had sex with anyone other than their monogamous spouse (who is also pure),
- Had a blood product medication or therapy (for example, RhoGam or a transfusion),
- Borrowed a used hypodermic needle,
- Had a tattoo,
- Pierced her ears,
- Cut his/her teeth on a shared toy that was wet with another's saliva (as a baby),
- Has had dental treatment or care,
- Has shared a tooth brush,
- Sat on a public toilet?

These are known means of contagion other than human breast milk. Can they ask you the above questions and get the right answers?

None of us are truly safe, *if* we depend on the arm of flesh. Psalm 91 tells us that we are free from the deadly pestilence. If you take time to cross reference that, you will find a multitude of verses that promise deliverance from deadly plagues. The string attached to that promise is to live in righteousness and holiness before God. He expects us to do that according to our knowledge of what that is. If we have a great understanding, then He expects us to live according to our best ability. If we barely know or understand, His grace will help us to grow in that area.

Meanwhile, He expects us to do what we do know. That includes the natural as well as the spiritual. If we apply good common sense to our actions and scrub up to limit the introduction of foreign bacteria and viruses to Pat and the baby, God will take care of the rest. If we use common sense to protect ourself from unknown bacteria and viruses Pat may be carrying, God will take care of the rest. This is not limiting God. It is limiting our tendency toward presumptuousness.

We use universal precautions for drawing blood, doing finger sticks for hemoglobin, examining the placenta, matching the urine stick, or any time you are in contact with anything with a body fluid on it. Pass the waste basket to dispose of a facial tissue. Don't take the tissue from them and throw it in the basket. If Pat or John are offended because you are wearing gloves, explain to them that you are in contact with so many people, that just washing your hands does not remove all of the viruses and bacteria that may be hiding under your nails or in a paper cut, so you are protecting them from any possible "unfriendlies" that may be lurking about. That usually takes care of it.

For all of the above, you do not need to use sterile gloves, because you are looking for a barrier and non-sterile gloves will serve the purpose. Now the kicker to all of this: *viruses are much smaller than sperm.* Sperm have been known to sneak through apparently intact condoms. (So how can condoms protect from AIDS?) Latex surgical gloves are slightly thicker than condoms. In spite of using universal precautions, you are not guaranteed to be protected from any virus, fungus or bacteria. Healthy, unbroken skin combined with gloves, protective clothing, and protective glasses will protect you from contaminated fluids saturating your clothing and standing on your skin, but they are not a guarantee to protect you from any viruses.

Doing lab work, you only need the glasses and the gloves. Now at a birth, it is easy to explain that you always get in the way of the birthing fluids, and you are trying to keep yourself from being "drowned." No one will fault you for that. Fortunately they have attractive barrier aprons, or scrubs if you want to go that far, so you don't look like the hospital. Whatever you wear, it should be washable and chlorine-bleachable. So far chlorine bleach seems to destroy the HIV virus, as well as the other nasties. When you have finished the procedure or cleaned up the birth area and are ready to take your protectives off, be sure to wash with soap and water your arms, hands, and face as well as any other parts of your body that were exposed to birth fluids, as part of your own protection.

Dispose of all "sharps" and syringes in proper containers. The lab will supply you with one, and then will properly dispose of the contents when you send the full one back. Anything that is not paper, has body fluid in it or has been used to "invade" the human body, can or did puncture, has the ability to poke and possibly injure the eye or skin, and cannot be resterilized, should go in that container. Obvious examples besides syringes and needles, are amnihooks or amnigloves, hemoglobin lancets, and "wasted" Vacutainers™. The illustration on the container will give you simplified reminders. You can get unsterile disposable single gloves quite cheaply. Save the sterile, paired gloves for birth and sterile singles gloves for vaginal exams. Disposable paper and soiled material should be burned. If burning laws prevent that, double-bag them and put them in the trash. The placenta may be frozen and used in a future childbirth class, or must be buried at least 12 inches deep to prevent animals from digging it up.

One of the hardest things to learn is not to touch anything with your hands after "scrubbing up." We are so used to using our hands for everything, that to consider what looks clean as being "dirty" is hard to program into the brain. If you have access to a good, non-toy microscope, look at ordinary things around the house through the various magnifications. You will see things "growing" that you never imagined possible. . . just don't get paranoid about it. God has made our bodies so fearfully and wonderfully that we need some of those uglies to maintain our health. In fact, if you looked at and cultured cells from your skin you would wonder how all the viruses, bacteria and fungi could possibly live on your clean skin and you survive that apparent onslaught without being sick all the time.

We can if they remain in balance. They are balanced by each other, and a healthy, non-traumatized body is able to rally the army of white blood cells and lymphocytes and all the antibodies we have developed over our lifetimes to kill and destroy the invaders. When that mechanism is compromised by poor diet, not enough rest, injury or overwhelming numbers of invaders, we get sick. A major and common factor in compromising the healthy body is to abuse it by not eating properly and not getting enough sleep. This will compromise the immune system (white blood cells and lymphocytes, etc.) and the adrenal gland. The usual result is a cold. A chilling thought for you; *white blood cells also act as host to the AIDS virus.* However, one must be exposed first.

In the real world of the 1990s, we have additional problems. We are all aware of the spread of AIDS, and we either get paranoid or presume that the Blood of Jesus will protect us. I know and believe in the power of the Blood, but I also know that presumption is its own curse. I have known monogamous, Blood-bought Christians that have picked up herpes from public toilet seats. I no longer assume the public toilet seat is "clean" just because it is dry. I carry disposable paper seat covers, and make sure my clothing does not come in contact with the commode or the floor. (Shoe soles are always considered dirty.) It is recommended that you dispose of the first five inches of tissue on the roll or whatever is exposed on the big rolls, use tissue between your hand and the handle to flush and toss all the "barrier" paper into the bowl, so it is removed with the waste. Viruses can live on a dry toilet seat for 14 hours! The AIDS virus can live out of the body in a dry glass dish for four days! Please do not think that I have developed a fixation about "getting something," because I haven't. I just believe that while we claim the promises of God, we also do not walk down the freeway during rush hour and declare that the trucks and cars cannot touch us! We must use the common sense that God has given us. Our trust is not in gloves and barrier towels or clothing! Our trust is in God! But we must not tempt the enemy and give him opportunity that he need not have.

If you read alternative health information about AIDS or HIV (Human Immune Virus, meaning it is immune to human immune system defenses), you will soon find experts that scoff at the public view that contagion is spread only by blood, sex and shared needles. Many alternative health advocates and a few bold mainstream types are suggesting we put all AIDS (Acquired Immune Deficiency Syndrome) and Hepatitis B victims in colonies or specialized hospitals, as we did the lepers and tuberculosis patients before we had effective medication to counter those diseases. Please read Dr. (MD) Lorraine Day's books and watch her videos on AIDS. They are revolutionary but well-documented. Dr. Day has been severely criticized for sharing her information, but as a Christian she felt she has no other choice. See the bibliography for her list of books.

Revelation, chapters 6 through 9, warns God's people of the plagues of the end times. According to a report from Dr. John Ward, chief of AIDS surveillance for the Centers for Disease Control and Prevention there was an increase of 35,000, or 204%, of new cases of AIDS between January 1, 1993 and March 31, 1993. We are surely in the time of the opening of the sixth seal and maybe even entering the sounding of the sixth trumpet! AIDS, of course, is not the only criteria. Matthew 24, Daniel chapters 7–9, Mark 13, and Luke 21 also discuss the times we are living in. Our only hope is to hide in the Rock and surrender our body, soul, and spirit to Jesus, making Him the Lord of every thing we think, do, and say. Making Him our all and all. Each of us must intimately know Him and hear His voice so well one can have a two-way conversation with Him. That is dwelling in the secret place of the Most High (Psalm 91). It is the only way to be in the "right spot" at the "right time" for your deliverance from the destruction that the enemy plans for you. (He doesn't want to go into the abyss by himself, and he is taking as many "sleeping," unaware Christians as he can with him.)

We Christians must daily read the Bible, meditate on what was read and pray constantly for God's wisdom, protection and Blood covering. Do not allow the combination of "busy-ness" in your practice and/or your multitude of duties for and with your family to rob you of daily quiet time with Jesus. That is your only safety in these perilous times.

Another serious problem, but not as deadly, is Hepatitis B. That is spread by body fluids, especially blood and contaminated needles, *just like AIDS*. Hepatitis B affects the liver. In advanced liver damage, transplants are possible. However, the good news is that Hepatitis B has been around for a very long time and allopathics and homeopathics know how to treat it. Yes, it is contagious and you will be in isolation, but you can get relief. One of the first signs is malaise, sometimes nausea and vomiting, just like the flu. Jaundice, and pain in the liver usually shows up as it progresses without treatment. When people turn yellow like lemons, even their eyes, they generally seek medical help, so Hepatitis B can be very advanced before treatment begins. The vaccination is only 50% effective.

The Alan Guttmacher Institute (also known as the research arm of Planned Parenthood) announced on March 31, 1993, a study that claims more than 1 out of 5 Americans are infected with a viral sexually transmitted disease like herpes or hepatitis B. Such viruses can be controlled, but not cured, and often recur. The study also projected that even more Americans are likely to contract a sexually transmitted disease sometime in their life, with the greatest effect on women and people under the age of 25. The plagues of Revelations are upon us. We *must* hide in the Rock, Jesus, and be under His protection and covering, or we too will be subject to the plagues of Egypt. Now is the time to pray that God will protect His children, as He did the children of Goshen before the Exodus, or we will not survive.

Surgical Scrub

The last thing you will do after getting Pat's "nest" ready for her to birth, is scrub. As we already discussed, you have touched lots of things that are not sterile, including Pat's cat and dog. When speaking of sterility, there are several levels. The highest and strictest form would be found in the surgical suite where organ transplants are done, on down to scrubbed, but not gloved which is called surgically clean. That is what your clothes are when the dryer turns off. Washed, dried and untouched by anything that has not been washed and heated to 160 degrees F. Your hands are not heated to 160 degrees, but the friction from the scrubbing removed many of the germs from their hiding places.

Almost every surface has germs of all varieties. When they are in their own environment, and not in contact with an open wound, most of these "buggies" are pretty harmless. This changes drastically when blood, warmth, and darkness are present. They multiply faster than mice and gerbels, causing infection and disease. Some organisms are wonderful to have around, such as those that make the flowers and veggies grow in the garden. Get those same organisms around a new mother and she has a bad infection.

There are two basic surgical scrub solutions. One is povidone iodine and is impregnated in the surgical brushes, the other is Hibiclens for those who are sensitive to iodine. Hibiclens does come on brushes, but you have to search them out. Set out your supplies, brushes, sterile towels (open the pack, but do not take towels out of wrap) to dry your "sterile" hands on, and running water, if you have it. If not, you need someone to pour fresh water over your hands to rinse.

- Put on any clean, non-sterile protective clothing; for example, apron, glasses, etc.
- Wet your hands and arms to the elbow, under running water. Do not turn water off until procedure is over.
- Pick up your brush and wet it. Do not put brush down again until scrub is over and you are ready to rinse.
- Scrub with your brush in a circular motion starting at your fingertips, moving up your hand, wrist, and arm up to the elbow. Do the same with the other arm, after rinsing the brush, taking two minutes per arm and hand (about eight minutes total). Do not put the brush down while cleaning your nails.
- With the plastic nail cleaner provided with the brush hopefully still stuck into the foam backing, clean under your nails. Rinse the nail cleaner under the water after each pass under the nail. When the nails are clean, drop the cleaner into the waste basket, or stick it back into the foam backing.
- Resume scrubbing, giving particular attention to the hands and lower half of the forearm. Pass the brush through the running water as often as needed to keep a nice lather going.

- When two minutes have passed (total of ten minutes scrubbing), rinse well, dry with the sterile towel and put the sterile gloves on.

You are ready to catch the baby. From this point on, the only things you can touch without contaminating yourself are your sterile supplies, the underpads from the birth kit, Pat and baby. The underpads (the side that has not touched the floor), Pat and the baby are not sterile, but they are clean. Should you touch anything else with your gloves, you have to put fresh sterile gloves on; your gloves are contaminated.

If you don't have ten minutes to scrub before baby arrives, scrub hard and fast. Do as thorough a job as you can in the time that you have. When you arrive at Pat's and do not have time to scrub, put sterile gloves on, and you will be considered surgically clean. That is much better than bare hands that have opened the trunk (cars are not surgically clean with all that road dirt on them), picked up the dropped car keys in the barnyard, etc.

During a start-and-stop labor or slow first stage, but you think once Pat gets over a certain hump, things will really get going, you can do your ten-minute scrub early and dry with a non-sterile, but clean towel. Don't glove up yet. When Pat does get moving and is close to birthing, all you need to do is put your barrier garment and glasses on, do a fast two- to five-minute scrub, dry with the sterile towel and glove up then.

Gloving Up

Putting sterile gloves on requires concentration and practice. Most people need at least five practice sessions before they feel somewhat comfortable and skilled at not contaminating the sterile part of the glove and getting the gloves on in a reasonably quick manner. The only part of the glove you can touch is the part that will be against the skin of your hand. You will note that each glove has a cuff on it.

- *The fold end of the cuff and inside the glove are the only areas you can touch with your bare hand.*
- Have glove package open so the inner wrap is unfolded. The cuff end or thumb should be labeled. Open the inner wrap so the glove is exposed. It does not matter which hand to glove first. I usually glove my dominant hand first.

- Carefully pick up the glove (for the other hand) at the fold of the cuff, allowing it to drop open for your other hand to slide in.
- Firmly holding the glove by the top of the fold end of the cuff, locate the thumb side of the glove. Slide your dry hand into the cuff, guiding your fingers into the proper finger spaces.
- Pull the glove on sufficiently to get the other glove on your other hand. Avoid touching the "raw" edge of the cuff with your bare hand.
- With the ungloved hand, open the other side of the glove wrap.
- Slide your *gloved* fingers *under* the cuff on the palm side of the glove and pick the glove up. You may steady the glove with your gloved thumb on the "raw" or edge end of the cuff.
- *Carefully* insert your hand into the glove without your bare hand touching your gloved hand, guiding your fingers into the right places.
- Pull the cuffs up, taking care not to touch any part of the glove that has touched bare skin. Smooth the glove over your fingers so you do not have little bubbles sticking out at the ends. They will be in your way, keeping you from picking up the cord clamp, etc., if you don't.
- Do not touch anything that is not sterile with your gloves or you will have to reglove before touching a sterile field.

Ruptured Membranes

At the end of the pregnancy, Pat will experience an increase in mucus discharge. It can be thick and irritating or a copious liquid discharge. Because of the amount, Pat may question if her membranes (bag of waters) are ruptured. A panty liner, changed every time she goes to the bathroom, will help her feel more comfortable. Pat should never use "feminine deodorants" or douches for "feeling fresh." They change the acid base of the vagina making Pat susceptible to vaginal infections and other problems. A daily bath or shower is sufficient for health and freshness.

There are three "kinds" of ruptured membranes:

- Premature: membranes rupture spontaneously (unaided) before the onset of labor, by hours or weeks
- Spontaneous: membranes rupture by themselves, usually just before birth but can be at the onset or any time during labor.
- Surgical or Artificial: membranes are purposely ruptured with an amnihook or amnicot by the birth attendant.

Sometimes Pat will report hearing or feeling a "pop" and wonder if her waters were broken. As long as Pat is ready to start labor, or is *in* labor, this is not a problem. The problem comes when the membranes rupture prematurely, or early. That is, before any signs that labor has started.

Usually the waters break with an obviously big gush. Other times there is a small leak up high, and because it is a dribble at most, it is difficult for Pat to determine on her own if it is the waters or the baby putting pressure on her bladder causing an involuntary leak of urine. Since normal waters are clear, and in small amounts do not give off the tell-tale odor of "salty, slippery, water," visual exam (looking at it) is not adequate. The quickest and surest test is the Nitrazine® test.

Procedure:

- Using sterile technique, put sterile gloves on.
- Insert a sterile vaginal speculum (lubricate only with water or the paper will not indicate accurately).
- Using dry, sterile glove, tear off four inches of nitrazine paper and keep the strip dry.
- Get a sterile cotton-tipped applicator (a long sterile Q-tip)
- Touch the discharge coming out of the cervix with the sterile applicator.
- Be careful not to touch anything but the cervical os.
- Touch applicator to nitrazine paper
- Match the color on the test strip with the color chart on the nitrazine case. If the waters have broken, the strip will be dark blue or greenish blue.
- Gently close the speculum and slide it out.
- Take gloves off carefully so you don't splatter mucus on anyone.
- Dispose of the nitrazine strip, applicator, and gloves appropriately.

Once it is proven, or even *suspected*, that Pat's waters are broken, *nothing* can enter her vagina that is not sterile. To violate that rule is to run the risk of amnionitis, chorionitis, or endometritis (puerperal fever). All of the above will not only endanger Pat, but just as importantly and seriously put Baby in danger! These infections are so dangerous because of the great blood supply to Pat's uterus. When infection is present in the membranes or the uterine lining in a parturient women, she has puerperal fever (childbed fever) and is at high risk of developing systemic bacterial sepsis, or septicemia. Septicemia can and will kill if not contained and dealt with quickly. The only treatment is massive doses of parenteral (IV) antibiotics before bacterial sepsis or septicemia develops.

Baby can get septicemia also through the placenta and when cutting the cord, the bacteria will enter baby's blood. You can't sterilize the cord before cutting it. Wiping with alcohol doesn't do it. You need pressurized heat to get these bacterial nasties. Both Pat and baby will have to be hospitalized and on heavy antibiotic therapy to overcome this one unless the Lord intervenes.

Puerperal fever was unknown until hospital birth became common early in the 19th century. It has always been considered a disease contracted from hospitals and doctors, not from midwives. Puerperal fever is still common in hospitals, especially after cesarean or forceps births. It is much easier to prevent infection than to stop it. So we will concentrate on prevention.

If Pat's waters break at the onset or during labor, keep vaginal exams to the barest minimum. If it is absolutely necessary to do a vaginal exam, use a sterile glove and povidone iodine for lubricant. Pour povidone iodine over Pat's genitalia and your glove, while holding your hand close to the clitoral area. Be sure you have absorbent, disposable pads under Pat to protect her bedding! (Peroxide takes blood out of cloth, including rugs, but does not do as well on povidone iodine). It will serve you well to learn how to assess Pat's progress by feeling the strength of the contractions with your hands, determining baby's descent by location of the FHTs, and how Pat is reacting to her contractions.

Premature Rupture of Membranes

By definition, Premature Rupture of Membranes (PROM) occurs before the onset of labor, this can be days or hours. In planned hospital births, PROM is considered a high-risk situation. The standard of practice for physician attended PROM, is to induce labor with Pitocin® in IV. The dosage is increased until Pat has and maintains contractions at the rate of three contractions per ten minutes. Because of the high risk of infection in hospital births, Pat must have her baby 12 hours after the membranes rupture.

There are some complications other than infection when the waters break. If the baby has not "dropped" or become engaged before the waters break, there is a chance the cord could get washed down in front of the presenting part, a prolapsed cord. This could cause cord compression, and newborn distress. When Pat calls and says her water broke, ask her for the following information:

- What color was it? Clear? Yellow? Dark green? Light green?
- Wash your hands Pat, and feel inside the vagina for a "rope." (It may be very high, at or in the cervix)
- Is/was there an odor?

It is a good idea for the midwife to check Pat and confirm that all is well with Baby and Pat as soon as possible. If the waters are not clear, the midwife needs to determine what the cause is.

- Yellow waters reveal past (perhaps a month ago) but resolved/corrected stress, all is well now.
- Light green waters reveal present and early, or mild stress.
- Any particles of stool in waters?
- Dark green waters reveal recent "intense" stress, baby needs help! Thick "pea soup" particulates are very dangerous and require immediate transport.
- Shades of brown reveal strong, recent, but resolved stress, maybe last week.
- Any odor other than a wet earthy (plowed ground after rain), slightly salty odor should be treated as though infection is present. Stained waters with or without an odor require serious evaluation:

- Is Pat in labor?
- If green, how soon until birth?
- If PROM or early in labor, transport after notifying your backup.
- If birth is imminent, notify your backup and prepare to transport Baby, or follow protocols.
- Monitor FHT every five minutes until admitted to hospital.
- If not in labor, transport; baby is in stress/distress and needs help

Home care of PROM is basically: eyes and ears open, and keep your hands out! Labor usually begins within 12 hours. If you keep your hands and everything else out of the vagina, the risk of infection will be minimized. If Pat does the following, she should be fine:

- Drink one quart of liquids every two hours.
- Continue eating from the diet cards and get your rest. Birth day is coming!
- Increase your Vitamin C to 500 mg more than what you have been taking, three times a day.
- Check Pat's temperature three to four times per day. (Make sure Pat hasn't eaten or had anything to drink for at least 20 minutes before taking her temperature, or it will not be accurate.)
- Do not do any lifting; sit on the couch and let "big sister or brother" crawl up to Pat.
- Stay squeaky clean; rinse the genitalia with povidone iodine (one finger-width in peri-bottle of warm water) every time you go to the bathroom.
- Wash the perineum with soap and water after each bowel movement.
- *Light housekeeping only.* No floor scrubbing, no wood chopping, no garden tilling, no mowing the yard, no moving furniture. Let grandma or aunty do those things while they wait for the baby to come.
- No tub baths, shower only. If no shower, clean tub with comet and rinse with chlorine bleach, rinse tub well again with hot water,
    - Kneel in tub. Do not sit in the bath water!
    - Pour water over body to rinse.

- *No sex to stimulate labor;* the penis is not sterile and infection could result
- Enjoy the children, read lots of stories to them, do puzzles, take walks through the garden, yard or on your side of the block.
- Stay away from public areas like malls, parks, etc., to prevent contamination from public toilets

About the second year of my midwifery practice, Pat's waters broke on Monday night at midnight. The waters were clear and had no odor. She still had no contractions Tuesday morning. I did the only vaginal exam (until labor was well established on Friday), and found baby's head was applied nicely to the cervix. The heart tones were good and we waited for labor to begin. Pat followed the above instructions. We monitored Pat's vital signs and Baby's FHTs three or four times a day and occasionally she would have some mild contractions, but that was all. By Thursday, Pat decided to check with her backup, who wanted to evaluate her in the hospital. An external monitor was applied to assess baby for two hours. No problems! Cultures were done on the waters and from the vagina which came back negative. Dr. Very Nice then gave them three choices:

- Stay in the hospital, get induced and have baby *tonight;*
- Stay in the hospital and wait for labor to start, and have baby in hospital; or
- Go home, wait and have baby at home, when baby is ready to come.

Pat and John chose to go home and wait. They were very relieved with the confirmation that all was normal. They had a good night's sleep, and started labor about 8:00 Friday morning. By 1:00 pm a healthy baby girl was born over an intact perineum, with Pat in the supported standing position, because of slight shoulder dystocia. Postpartum was uneventful.

If the cord is prolapsed, you must immediately decide what you are able/going to do. Your choices are:

- To brace the cord while pushing the head back during immediate transport, or
- To reduce the prolapse, monitor baby and Pat, and wait for birth.

The standard of practice for most midwives is bracing the cord and transporting.

- Monitor FHTs every five minutes until admitted to hospital and doctor assumes responsibility.
- Insert sterile gloved hand into vagina.
- Locate cord.
- Place index and middle finger tips on baby's head with cord lying between.
- Exert enough force against head to relieve pressure on cord.
- Hold that position until you arrive at hospital.
- Pat is carried out to car or van (preferred) with midwife bracing cord!
- Pat must remain in hands and knees or side lying during transport.
- Maintain bracing until doctor assumes responsibility, in *writing*, for baby and Pat.

Surgical Breaking of the Waters: Amniotomy

There are now two ways to surgically break the waters. One is the **amnihook**, the other is a small plastic "hook" on the tip of one finger on a special glove, called the **amnicot**.

It is rare that one needs to break the waters in a home birth. Reasons for surgical (artificial) rupture of the membranes are:

- It may help the baby address the cervix, if forewaters are holding the baby's head away from the cervix;
- A need to stimulate labor if hypotonic uterine dysfunction is present;
- To facilitate fetal descent before pushing breaks the water, allowing cord prolapse.

Undesirable possibilities of surgically breaking the waters:

- Cord compression,
- Asynclitic head position,
- Cord prolapse problems.

Reducing the prolapsed cord requires a skill level at least on the senior level, after much experience. Do pray before attempting this procedure, because infection, and cord entanglement or cord strain at the umbilicus are possible complications.

To reduce the prolapsed cord:

- Check FHTs.
- Put Pat in the knee-chest position until midwife is scrubbed and gloved.
- Put a long sterile glove on dominant hand.
- Gather the prolapsed loop in hand.
- Push the baby's head back away from cervix (the head must not be well engaged, or at least must be easily disengaged).
- Bring the cord past the head (on the face side, if possible).
- Find a foot and loop the cord in your hand around the foot.
- Bring your hand out.
- Check FHTs every five minutes for one hour, or until birthed.

Catching the Vertex Baby

Warm comfrey compresses (I grow my own comfrey) feel so nice to the perineum as the mother is pushing. It gives her a place to focus her pushing, and also increases circulation so the muscles relax and stretch at their optimum level. It also lets Pat know that you are paying attention and helping her. Sometimes you have to do a little perineal massage, if the baby is slow in descent, is on the large side, or it is Pat's first baby.

As the caput begins to show, some warm olive oil to the vagina near the baby's head helps natural lubrication. A quiet, steady hand on the compresses is very reassuring to Pat. If your compress hand is constantly moving, it is very distracting to her. If baby is quite slow, massage the vaginal muscles, paying attention with circular massage on the tense ones. Sometimes steady pressure is tolerated by Pat more than the moving massage.

While applying pressure to that tense spot, ask Pat to relax that spot for you. When she does, you can feel the baby wanting to move down to that spot. Holding that muscle until the next contraction usually allows the baby to slip down to that spot with the contraction. Continue to massage as needed. Make sure the compresses do not get too cold, or too hot, because either way, they cause tension instead of relaxation.

Occasionally the baby goes from a full crown and then is born to the brow in less time that it takes to say or read it, you can slow down the speed a little by slipping the palm of your hand or warm comfrey compress over the occiput and gently "resist" the baby's outward flow. Not too strongly, you may put too much pressure on the cervical (neck) vertebrae. You want just enough pressure to keep the baby from "shooting" out as from a cannon. While you are controlling the speed of a precipitous birth, Pat should be ha-ha-ha-ha-ha-le-lu-jah-ing her way through the contraction. Her body is exerting 40 pounds of pressure against the baby to get him out. When Pat pushes, she is multiplying that by at least three times.

Always keep your compress hand flat against the perineum, in a "C" shape with the web of the thumb at the introitus. I used old, soft wash cloths for my compresses. I also found that because my dominant hand was so busy, the non-dominant hand should be used for the compresses. If the perineum or labia starts getting very white, *gently* "pull" some of the side tissues toward the perineum or labia by using a *slight* pinching movement, cupping your hand as the perineum bulges out around the head. As the baby eases his head over the perineum, keep the head flexed, by applying a downward and outward pressure on the back of the occiput. This protects the tender anterior tissue, like the clitoris and urethra. Watch for the "newborn Heimlich" maneuver.

While supporting the baby's head with your non-dominant hand/wrist, check for cord around the neck or a nuchal hand with your dominant hand. The baby will be wanting to start turning to the right or left. Sometimes the shoulder will birth as the baby turns, depending on Pat's pushing. Usually the anterior shoulder will be born first. Allow the head to move slightly up or down opposite the birthing shoulder, to give it room to come out. Then, sliding your non-dominant hand under the baby towards the mother, lift the posterior shoulder out. These babies are like little greased piggies, so hold on tight to an arm while supporting the head with your non-dominant hand. Keep your dominant hand close to Pat, and catch the rest of the baby as it comes sliding out. The body usually follows the shoulders very quickly with a gush of waters. Occasionally, the body is born one contraction at a time. This is nice for your first catch or if you've had a long or a very short labor, because the uterus has a chance to contract down around the baby as the baby is born, thus eliminating the possibility of a heavy bleed.

Immediately after the feet are birthed, put the baby on Pat's tummy or chest if the cord is long enough. Dry the baby and then cover him and Pat with warm, dry towels and blankets. Listen for breathing and heart rate with the stethoscope, unless the baby is screaming and a bright pink. If baby's respirations are 30 to 60 and heart rate is over 100, sit back and let John and Pat get acquainted with their baby. I always let Pat and John discover the sex of their baby, even if I know what it is. They have had to wait the longest to see what God has given them. If baby had the Heimlich maneuver on the perineum, you only have to adjust the cord, to make sure there is no tension on it. If there is tension, pull the slack from the placental side of the cord. Be gentle! If there is resistance, do not force the issue. If baby has mucus in the mouth, use the bulb syringe to get the mucus out of the mouth, back of the mouth, and then the nose. Do not touch the back of the throat, or you could delay the breathing and heartbeat by triggering the vagal response.

Catching the Breech Baby

Breech presentation occurs only 3% of all pregnancies. Praise the Lord! Fortunately, the **complete breech** is the most common. Labor will be very much like the posterior labor. There will be a lot of pressure in her back, and Pat will be more "comfortable" standing or walking. Dilation may be slower because the buttocks are softer than the head and do not put as much pressure on the cervix.

Figure 12-9: Breech Positions

Pat will have the urge to push earlier with a footling or frank breech presentation, because the buttocks or feet can slide through a 5- to 7-cm dilated cervix easier than the head could. Pushing before the cervix is fully dilated, can cause the after-coming head to become entrapped, and the baby to breathe prematurely. Pat will need intense coaching to help her during transition, because the presenting part will be pressing on the expulsion reflex nerve. This is the smallest part of the baby, so it can slip thru before she is completely dilated.

The hands-and-knees position for Pat will relieve premature expulsion reflex, so she can breathe through the contractions until fully dilated. She will probably be more comfortable birthing in the hands-and-knees position, or on the birthing stool. For your first breech, pray that it is hands-and-knees, because it is easier for the midwife to see and maneuver. These directions are for hands and knees. To catch in a lithotomy position or on a birthing stool, reverse the directions from down to up, etc. Hands and knees birthing looks like a sacral posterior position to the baby catcher, but is really sacral anterior.

Second stage labor is usually slower because the buttocks are soft and the heavy head is "on top" and does not respond to gravity as easily as in the vertex presentation. Be absolutely sure that Pat is fully dilated before you allow her to push, whether she agrees with you or not.

Some experienced midwives do not want Pat to push until the baby is born to the umbilicus or nipple line, and then push constantly until baby is born. Others say once the cervix is fully dilated, push when you feel like pushing. I've tried them both and prefer the latter. It seems more natural for the mother, and baby seems to progress better. You will want to go over in your mind many, many times the technique of catching the breech baby, so it will seem natural to you when it does occur.

Meconium is a normal part of breech birth, because of the stretching of baby's rectum, as he comes down the birth canal. Use comfrey compresses and perineal massage as usual.

Complete Breech

A complete breech is when baby is sitting tailor-fashion in pelvis:

- Allow the hips and legs to birth over the perineum as a unit.
- When baby is birthed to the waist, pull on the cord to get as much slack as possible without applying pressure.

Birthing the arms, shoulders and head follows the Frank Breech.

Single Footling

This presentation often has the other foot with the ankle resting across the presenting leg's thigh. It can also be sticking up, as in the frank breech position, with his ankle by his ear! Pat needs lots of coaching, because she may be only 4 cm dilated when that foot slipped out! Once she is 10 cm, and the hips are at the perineum, you can see where the second foot is. If baby is doing a "high kick," reduce the second leg. Use the same technique as in the complete breech, except you may have to rotate the upper and lower leg some to bring the foot across the abdomen. Practice this movement on yourself by noticing how your leg moves when you cross your legs at the knee. Now bring your thigh up close to your abdomen while doing the same movement with your lower leg. Same movements with the baby. Reduce the legs using the Pinard maneuver:

- Insert your dominant hand into the vagina.
- Follow the leg from the thigh to the top of the knee.
- Slide the lower leg across the chest, while bending it downward at the knee towards the heel.
- Applying gentle pressure at the thigh, just above the knee, guide the leg down across the body and out the vagina.
- As the leg crosses the abdomen, slide your hand down to the calf of the leg.
- Gripping the lower leg firmly and with your index finger pointing up over the kneecap, bring the leg out the vagina, following the direction of the heel.

Frank Breech

Both legs are alongside of baby's ears. This is handled just like the single footling, but you do it twice. Because of space constraints, you will probably have to change hands to reduce the second leg. In the haste of the moment, please be sure to have a good grip on the baby before inserting your other hand to reduce the second leg. Next to the complete breech, this is the next most common breech. Thankfully, the frank breech and the footling breech are very infrequent variants of the breech birth. Remember, Pat is in hands and knees position.

Now that the legs are born, we can go on with the breech birth. With the next contraction, the baby will be born to the waist:

- Gently tug on the cord for slack, so baby has reserve oxygenated blood in the cord while the head compresses the cord as the head passes under the pubic bone.
- Keep baby's body lying on your non-dominant arm, while your dominant hand is doing the maneuvering.

After the next contraction, you will know if the hands are up "praising the Lord, or if they are folded across his chest. If this child is already praising the Lord, you will need to interrupt him long enough to **reduce extended arms**:

- With dominant hand, find one arm, apply downward pressure at the inside of the elbow, causing it to bend;
- Grasp the elbow and with your fingers along baby's forearm, and point the hand to the opposite arm;
- Sweep the arm across the abdomen and down at the side;
- Repeat with the other arm.

So far, the baby is in the sacral anterior position, but he will want to rotate for the shoulders as soon as those arms are out of the way. Keep both hands on the baby as soon as the arms are free, because when he rotates for the shoulders, he could slide right off your arm.

- Wrap the baby in a warm towel or blanket as soon as the body is exposed for better grip on the baby, and to prevent premature breathing. If the baby slips off your arm, it can cause sudden pressure on the neck, which can develop into a wry neck.

- Be very sensitive to the way the baby wants to turn. Do not prevent his natural restitution, or try to force him in a different direction.
- When the baby rotates, allow him to sag slightly downward, allowing the posterior shoulder to be born first.
- Lift and straighten the baby out and the anterior shoulder will follow.
- Now, comes the tricky part: the *head.* The head must be out within five minutes after the cord is exposed to prevent premature breathing of the baby. The head must rotate to 45 or 90 degrees bringing the sagittal suture from the oblique or transverse respectively, into the sacral anterior position.
- You can monitor what the baby is doing by watching his back. It will be lined up with his head.
- *After-coming heads cannot be born in the sacral posterior position because the human neck is not long enough to pass between the sacral promontory and the pubic bone in the breech presentation.* If the baby decided to rotate to a posterior, then you must rotate him to the anterior position, by reversing him. This area requires a tucked chin for posterior birth, not military attitude as the head is in breech presentation at this point. The chin will catch on the pubic bone if in posterior sacral position. The pubic bone will roll the head into a tucked chin position if presenting sacral anterior.

After-coming heads *usually do not need help.*

- Keep the baby "sandwiched" between your hands and forearms.
- Bring the baby up until the hairline on the back of the head (sub-occipital) is visible under the pubis.
- Lower the baby without extending the neck past normal, so chin, mouth, nose, eyes, brow, anterior fontanel, posterior fontanel and occiput can be born in sequence.
- Usually the baby will slide out in the proper sequence as you lower the head, allowing the occiput to be the last over the perineum.
- Do not allow the head to pop out too fast, as this can cause intracranial damage.
- Too-slow delivery of the head can cause hypoxia.

- Allow the baby to "sag" while still supporting most of the weight, so the head will follow the curve of Carus (sacral curve).
- First the chin, then mouth, nose, eyes, brow, anterior fontanel, posterior fontanel and finally the occiput is born.
- Control the speed, so it is not too fast nor too slow
- If head requires flexing, use the Mauriceau-Smellie-Veit maneuver:
  - Slip the back of your second (tall) finger in and against the roof of the baby's mouth to birth the head over the perineum.
  - Place your first and third fingers on the cheek bone below either eye.
  - Be careful you do not let your fingers slip into the eye orbits or you'll damage baby's eyes.
  - Avoid traction/pressure on baby's lower jaw or base of tongue.
  - Baby's body is astride your non-dominant arm and hand.
  - Hook your index and middle finger over both shoulders (with the neck between).
  - Take care not to put pressure on the brachial or cervical nerve plexus. This is the hand that will apply traction.
  - Grasp the shoulders with rest of fingers and thumb.
  - "Bring your three fingers together" with upper jaw between them and tuck the head by bringing chin towards baby's chest.
  - Move the outside hand (on the shoulder) towards the elbow (outward and upward motion) until sub-occipital hairline is visible under the pubis.
- If the head resists flexing, the second midwife should apply supra-pubic pressure on the baby's head, while first midwife applies the traction to the shoulders.

Often a breech baby will be a little slow to start, but some free-flow oxygen by his nose will perk him up very quickly. Some midwives and home-birth doctors routinely give a few whiffs of oxygen to breech babies. As long as the eyes are protected from the oxygen, no harm is done and it will compensate for the possible periods of anoxia from cord compression. Cord compression is a common risk/complication with breech babies, so keep the oxygen handy at the birth. Baby's bottom will be bruised for a few days. It wasn't made for opening "birth doors." The head is usually nice and round because the bottom did all the work. Just don't let Aunty Worry Wart see his bottom for a few days and everything will be pink and rosy by the time she gets around to changing baby's britches.

Examination of the Placenta

Since examination of the placenta has already been discussed, I won't go in much detail here concerning the normal placenta. That is well covered in Chapter 7. Some unusual and (thankfully) rare things to look for are the succinturate placenta, ruptured cord vessels, and aneurysm of the cord vessels.

The **succinturate** placenta have "extra" or small satellite placentas in the membranes, but separate from the main placenta. The connecting blood vessels run along the surface of the membranes, or between the amnion and chorion layers of the membranes. These "satellites" are not always distinct like the main placenta. They may look like a clot or they may be like a miniature placenta. The most important thing to remember about placentas is not to force them to separate. If you do force a slowly separating placenta that happens to be succinturate, you could leave the small one behind to cause you and Pat trouble later in the first 24 hours. Succinturates are the leading reason why you exam the membranes and make sure you have all of them out of the uterus, before going home. Goldenseal helps expel slow placentas as do the following homeopathic medicines according to the following symptoms:

China: atony of uterus, hemorrhage, heaviness of head, vertigo, ringing in ears, fainting, fading or loss of senses, gasping for breath, cold, pale, blue face and hands, delusions when closing eyes, wants to be fanned.

Cimicifuga: severe tearing pains, uterine inactivity, headache, brain feels like it will burst. Rheumatic clients.

Gossypium: after premature birth, will not loosen not matter what you do (squatting, sitting on commode, etc.).

Pulsatilla: uterine inertia, redness and soreness of hypogastrium, worse with touch, retention of urine, tearful and "mild" women, often blondes.

Sabina: intense pains, pain or uneasiness from sacrum to pubes, fluid blood and clots in equal parts with each pain.

Secale: constant, strong sensation of bearing down, yet ineffectual pains, hourglass contractions, too relaxed for uterine action, chilly but colder with covering or warmth.

Sepia: congestion with sense of weight, pain in right groin, and/or needle-like pains in cervix, draws legs up, feels bearing-down pains as if everything would fall out of uterus, cold with flushes of heat, constipated, putrid smell of urine.

Ruptured Cord Vessels

Ruptured cord vessels do not happen often, according to the textbooks. Even less often than a succinturate placenta! Thank God. However, one midwife reports having two incidents in 30 births. Your first clue is there suddenly is a lot of red blood. If the baby is crying, it may be a pulsing flow. It usually occurs as the baby is birthed, and can be anywhere along the cord. It is usually caused by the cord getting pinched and stretched by the baby's head as it goes under the pubic bone. Whenever you have bright red blood suddenly appearing as the baby is born, check the cord. Should the blood be coming from a ruptured vessel in the cord, clamp both sides immediately and cut between the clamps. The baby circulates his blood through the placenta, so if the cord or placenta is bleeding, it really is the baby that is bleeding. He cannot afford to lose very much blood, because he only has between 125 ml (4.2 oz) and 150 ml (5 oz) at birth (the average teacup is 6 oz!). Nursing will help him get his volume back up, but do not waste time before clamping. Even a teaspoon of blood is a lot for that newborn to lose. You do not want the baby to go into shock! Of course, if the bleeding is not coming from the cord, check the vagina, cervix and/or perineum for tears.

The above symptoms are what the textbooks say. Now you can read what a midwife actually experienced with two occurrences of ruptured cord vessels. As usual, the real-life picture can vary from the "classic picture" in the books.

"The first rupture was on the visible portion of the cord, and was clamped on the placental side. The cord was immediately clamped and cut on the baby's side of the rupture. I didn't wait for the pulsing to stop!

"The second time, I didn't discover the rupture until I examined the placenta. The Lord was protecting the baby and me, because the Wharton's Jelly did its job to shut down the bleeding! Some vaginal bleeding had been apparent, but resembled the separation 'gush.' It stopped shortly after I saw it, so it didn't occur to me what had happened. The baby's head had been bloody at birth. Baby was born blue, hypotonic and needed free oxygen. The heart rate and cry were normal.

"Baby does have Down's Syndrome, which accounts for some of the hypotonia at birth. Thank the Lord, He knows what to do, and His ways are above our (puny) ways (Isaiah 55:8–9). This baby was meant to live, even with my not realizing the cause of her problem." This midwife also had a succenturate placenta with velametous cord insertion in the same group of 30 births. She said "I guess statistics don't care who gets them. Ha, Ha." My experience with the unusual, is they occur in groups of three, and then you do not have a repeat for a long time. So, if an unusual occurrence happens, be alert for more of the same in the next six months.

Frequently one sees an area in the cord where the vessel seems to be suddenly very big. On close examination the vessel wall is quite thin and ballooning out compared to the rest of the cord. This is an **aneurism of the cord**. A very appropriate response is to thank God for his protection of the baby and mother. Had that ruptured in utero, baby would have hemorrhaged to death and Pat may have had some problems, too. But as in the velematous cord insertion, what might have been did not, and for that we are grateful to the Lord who is Lord over all.

Lacerations, Episiotomy/Clitorotomy and Suturing

Some midwives are redefining the word episiotomy and renaming the procedure as clitorotomy. This is based on the understanding that the muscle being incised is continuous with the muscle supporting the clitoris. Therefore the "perineal" area is not defined finely enough and needs a more precise definition. Because you will see the term "clitorotomy" in newer literature, I am including it next to the term "episiotomy." Do not confuse clitorotomy with female circumcision, clitorectomy. The suffix "ectomy" means "removal of" and the suffix "otomy" means "incision of."

Episiotomy/clitorotomy is not done in the usual home situation. It should be used only as a life-saving situation, and if the perineum is that tight, it will tear anyway. It is commonly thought that episiotomy/clitorotomy saves two to five minutes of time (one to two contractions). There are a few situations in which that might be life-saving, such as fetal distress. Shoulder dystocia is a condition where the baby is stuck in the pelvis by the pubic bone. Soft-tissue incision will not have that much value, when you need to reduce the amount of passenger due to the lesser space in the passage way (pelvis). Thankfully, I have never had to do an episiotomy/clitorotomy. Not that I wasn't tempted, but baby slipped through on the next contraction, and I could put the scissors down.

Anne Frye has written an excellent 260-page manual on suturing with a companion video so you can see the "how to" and compare your practice stitches with the video. Anne also covers the legal issues, the anatomy, types of needles and sutures, etc., in great depth, but in an easily understood manner. It is the only complete manual on suturing on the market today. There is no way I could condense the depth of her writing in this book, so buy hers. I will simply tell you enough to make you want to know more, or to review what you already know. To do well in suturing, you need to attend a workshop, or invest in Anne's manual and video at a fraction of the cost.

At the interview, you need to establish with Pat and John your usual procedure with tears or when you would do an episiotomy/clitorotomy. This is when you determine if Pat is allergic to anesthetics. If so, is she willing to have the repair without anesthesia? There are different classes of local anesthetics. Anesthetics from one class can be used in case of allergy to another class, in most cases. Unless you have a large practice, you may not want two different classes of anesthetics open. I probably used two vials (20 cc) total in one year and I was very generous with my dosages. Always double-check with Pat concerning allergies, before you inject any anesthetic. She may have developed one or remembered one since the interview. Expiration dates need to be considered, too. If the date is the same as the month or the month previous to when you wish to use it, it is no good. Example: December 1992 or January 1993 is no good January 15, 1993. At the least it will not give any anesthesia and at the worst, Pat could have a serious reaction from the chemical changes in the anesthetic.

If you absolutely have to—life-or-death situation for baby—need to do an episiotomy/clitorotomy, do it when Pat pushes, and she will not feel the cut as much:

- Slip the index- and middle fingers of your non-dominant hand between the baby's head and the perineum.
- Slide the sterile scissor blade between your fingers and cut. The perineum is tough, so make sure you have sharp scissors.
- Cut no more than $\frac{1}{4}$ inch to the side of the midline of the perineum, aimed at 5:00 or 7:00 o'clock, or the midline at 6:00 o'clock.
- Just a little nick will cause the perineum to tear enough to let the baby out. All episiotomies/clitorotomies extend—they tear farther than was incised—so keep the cut to a nick.
- Support your incision, so it will not extend too far!
- After the baby is born, stuff two or three gauze 4×4s into the incision and apply pressure to minimize bleeding until you are ready to repair.
- Stabilizing mother and baby and expelling the placenta take priority over repairs unless Pat is bleeding from a severed artery!
- Repairs can wait up to six hours after birth.

Previous episiotomy/clitorotomy is not a deterrent to birthing over an intact perineum in succeeding births. John and Pat will just have to do the perineal exercise a little more diligently, and the midwife will have to be diligent with the warm olive-oil massage and comfrey compresses. Most tearing at births is along the scar from the old episiotomy/clitorotomy. Scar tissue does not stretch like normal tissue, so special attention must be given it at succeeding births.

Sometimes a woman will tear a little bit at birth. Unnoticed nuchal hands that slip by without getting reduced are the leading causes. Skid marks are slight splits in the first layer of skin or mucus membrane. They heal much better if left alone than if they are stitched. The trauma of injecting an anesthetic and pulling the needle and thread through the surrounding tissue is greater than the original injury. It's similar to putting a stitch in a paper cut: it's a minor but painful injury and will heal in just a few days without a lot of attention other than keeping it clean.

A tear deeper than $\frac{1}{2}$ inch in the vagina and $\frac{1}{4}$ inch on the perineum should be stitched together. The alternative is for Pat to not climb stairs, and keep her knees together all the time for two to three weeks, until the tear has healed. Allowing her knees to separate except for washing and perineal care will pull the healing tissue apart, lengthening the healing time.

Purposes of suturing are:

- To prevent infection from contamination by urine and stool;
- Restores the structure of the perineal muscles;
- Prevents fistulas from forming due to incomplete healing in the deeper muscles; and
- Promote self-esteem for cosmetic reasons.

A properly repaired laceration should bring all the muscles, mucosa, and skin together without puckers, stretches or gaps, and the final scar should be as thin as a hair, and as hard to find. Pat should not have any continuing pain, after the healing is complete, and it should not interfere with Pat's and John's marital relations. In short, her genital area should be "as good as before."

To limit trauma to already-traumatized tissue, use a round, non-cutting needle on muscle and a round, cutting needle for the skin. The round needle gets its name from looking like part of a circle. . . round, as in the illustration. A straight needle, such as you use when you sew buttons on your blouse, is very awkward when trying to make a circular movement. In suturing, your needle goes in and down on one side of the tear, crosses over through the muscle to the other side of the tear, and up to the surface. When you tie the knot, the suture (thread) has actually made a continuous circle—impossible with a straight needle. Straight needles are for flat surfaces, not the "V" found in perineal tissue repair.

The non-cutting needle is like a ball-point needle for sewing knits on your sewing machine. It slips between the muscle fibers, lessening the trauma and limiting the needed healing to the tear, while adding support to the injured tissue. Skin cells are flat and layered like a stone or brick wall, requiring a sharp cutting point and edge to cut through the cells. It is the "armor" of the body.

Using needles with the suture "swaged" or fused into the end of the needle helps prevent added trauma. You can purchase eyed needles and separate suture, but you are constantly threading your needle, and have to pull the "bump" (where the suture goes through the eye of the needle) through the tissue. Muscle is not too bad, but skin is tougher, and the drag causes the needle hole to open wider, adding to the trauma.

Suture size is determined by the surface (place) to be stitched, the tension on the muscle to be repaired, and delicacy of the area. The smaller the suture, the more zeroes. Suture for the eye is much finer than perineal muscle. Generally, because the perineum takes a lot of pressure when we sit or walk up stairs, 2-0 or 3-0 is used. Skin suture is 3-0 or 4-0. 3-0 suture is a little thick for skin, but acceptable for perineal repairs.

Most folks do not like to get stitches removed, although it is generally painless. Today's sutures will dissolve about the time the healing is completed, so suture removal is not necessary, unless Pat is allergic to common suture, and in that case, Doctor Wonderful or his colleague Dr. Convenient should do the repair with one of the special suture materials available, but too expensive for the traditional midwife to keep on hand.

Chromic gut or the new synthetics will dissolve in about 10–40 days and they retain their strength for two to three weeks, until the healing has taken place in the deep muscles. Plain gut will dissolve in one week and lose its strength in about three days. It also has more allergic reactions than the chromic coated or the synthetics. Pat will have to limit her herbal bath "soaks" to ten minutes at a time, or the water will dissolve her stitches prematurely.

Equipment needed for your suture kit:

- 4- or 6-inch hemostat, curved or straight;
- 4- or 6-inch needle holder;
- 1 suture scissors;
- 2 packages of suture with round needle, 2-0 or 3-0;
- 2 packages of suture with cutting needle, 3-0 or 4-0;
- 4–6 sterile gauze 4×4s.

The needle holder and scissors can be a single combination instrument. This ingenious invention has the needle holder at the point and the scissor part just behind it. This can be handy since it shortens the steps and hand movements. Your dominant hand always has the right instrument for sewing or cutting.

In a separate package, have:

- One vial of local anesthetic (1%);
- One 5cc syringe with $1\frac{1}{2}$ inch 23g needle; and
- One pair of sterile gloves.

The most important thing to learn about suturing, other than matching "what goes where," is how to tie the knot. If you do not tie a secure knot, the stitch will not hold and all of your efforts will be for nothing. The knot can be practiced with a 36-inch shoestring or 36-inch length of colored yarn or string. Some workshops suggest clothesline. Please do not use your delicate instruments to practice with if you use clothesline. Use kitchen tongs or locking pliers, instead. Abusing your instruments will cause the hinge to spring or break, and then they will not hold the small diameter of suture or crimp a bleeding artery or vein when you need it.

The procedure is as follows:

- Clip your needle holder on one end and the hemostat on the other end of the string.
- Stick your big toe in the "U" end. Your toe is the "muscle" you just made a "stitch" in.
- Adjust the string, so the needle holder end is about half as long as the other.
- Take the needle holder off the long string and replace it with the hemostat.
- With your dominant hand, hold the short end taut.
- Pass the needle holder over and then under the (long) end, close to the toe.
- Grab the tip of the short end with the needle holder and pull it through the loop.
- Tighten the knot by crossing your non-dominant hand over your dominant hand (still holding the string) and pull it snug.
- Repeat twice, passing the needle holder over and then under the long string, grabbing the short end with the needle holder and pulling it through the loop. Tighten the knot each time.

Winding your suture around before the knots keeps you from making your knots so tight that they pull during the healing process. When injured tissue heals, it swells and this gives the knot the slack it needs to keep everything together, but still allows for the swelling. Three knots per stitch reminds us that a three-fold cord is not quickly broken (Ecclesiastes 4:12).

If the sutures come out before the tear has healed in the first couple of days, you can restitch. First, you need to remove any sealed tissue by rubbing it with a sterile gauze square. If the surface is red and raw looking, it has not started to heal yet. Simply restitch as before, making sure the knots are secure and you do not cut closer than $\frac{1}{4}$ inch in to the knot. Remind Pat to come out of the herbal bath before ten minutes, not soak in her tub bath, and keep her perineum dry.

You can practice suturing on a chicken (the winged variety), a beef heart, or on foam, as Anne suggests in her book. She even has patterns to make your own models, so you can recognize your landmarks when it is time to do the real thing. Chicken muscle and skin have about the same texture as human muscle and skin, so when you have practiced on the foam, you can stitch the roasting hen together. Use a sharp knife or scissors to make your practice "tears." As your skill increases, get creative in making your "tears", so when the "bad" tears come, you have the confidence to repair them, especially in politically difficult areas.

Now to practice. With a 2cc syringe, inject water ("Lidocaine") vertically along the edge of the tear from the skin into the muscle. Dribble a few drops on the skin before the needle goes in to help numb the area so "Henny Penny" chicken won't jump away from you. Always pull back on the plunger before injecting to see if you accidentally punctured a blood vessel (never inject Lidocaine or any other local anesthetic into a blood vessel; it can cause Pat to go into bradycardia or shock and lead to serious complications). Inject the anesthetic as you pull the needle out. Once "Henny Penny" chicken is anesthetized, you may sew her up.

There are four basic suture stitches (see illustration below):

- **Blanket** stitch or **Continuous Locked** stitch: Used on the floor of the vagina;
- **Interrupted**: Each stitch is knotted and suture is cut between knots, usually used on muscle layer below the skin or on the skin itself.

- **Continuous**: The first stitch is knotted and basting or looping stitches continue to the last stitch which is knotted. This is best for the deep muscle layer, or very shallow tear.
- **Running** stitch or **Hidden Hem** stitch on the skin or deep labial tear (longer or deeper than $\frac{1}{4}$ inch).

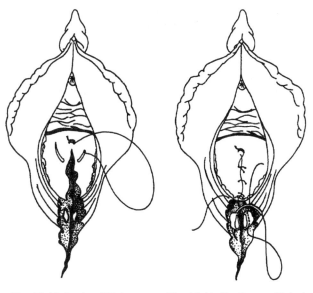

Fig. 12-10. Anchor Stitch

Fig. 12-11. Continuous Unlocked
Stitch and Crown Stitch

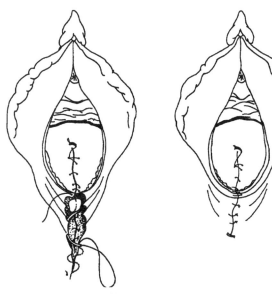

Fig. 12-12. Deep Interrupted Mattress
(Hem) Stitch

Fig. 12-13. Interrupted Stitch

Your goal in suturing, is to return Pat to the same appearance as before she tore. Neatness counts.

Start at the deepest and the farthest point from you, as illustrated. The vagina (unless deeper than one inch) and deep muscle can be repaired with the continuous basting stitches. Be sure to keep tension even between the stitches, but not enough to pucker, just enough to bring the edges together. Take no more than $1/4$-inch "bites" with the needle and place a stitch every $1/4$ inch in the deep muscle, with each layer $1/4$ inch deep. This will prevent fistulas and pockets from forming.

Complete the deepest layer in the vagina first, working your way up to the surface. Then start at the deepest layer in the perineum, even if it is only one stitch. Then go to the next layer, until you get to the skin. At the introitus, you bring your suture up through the hymenal ring and hand-tie a $1\frac{1}{2}$ square knot with the "tail" of the suture from the vaginal floor. Now you take the 4-0 suture and repair the skin starting at the point farthest away from the introitus. For the skin you may use the interrupted stitch or the hidden hem stitch. Pat will appreciate the hidden hem stitch when she wipes with the tissue, because she won't have any stitches to snag the tissue paper during perineal care.

If you get to the skin layer, and Pat has a tag that does not fit, it is alright to clip it off, as long as it is a small one that would not allow blood flow. It is best if you can "piece" everything back together, because it did fit before. However, if you have to fit something in like an extra puzzle piece, it is better to clip it, because it will not heal well. Long tags need only to be stitched in place, around the outside edges with a basting or running mattress (hidden hem) stitch. Sometimes tags happen when the previous repair was too tight, or the present edges were incorrectly aligned.

Labial tears do not happen often. They do require anesthesia because of the many nerve endings. If it is a skid mark and less than $1/2$ inch long, don't mess with it. If it is deeper, a stitch will hold the edges together and eliminate the burning sensation labial tears have. If it goes all the way through like a cut, use a running stitch back and forth, ending on the outer edge with the knot. Care must be taken to prevent puckering on labial tears. If they do not heal smooth as God made the labia, Pat will have discomfort all of her life, especially during intercourse. The fewer the knots, the better on labia, so stick to the running type of stitches with labial repairs.

This is so brief, you cannot call it adequate, but it is a review if you have not had to suture for a while. That is the beauty of Anne Fry's video and manual. You can review and reference the rare and unusual as well as get a good, complete discussion on the more common situations.

Herbal Bath

The herbal bath after the placenta is expelled makes Pat feel wonderful. It is relaxing, smells good and cleansing. It also helps baby relax, plus it helps dry up the cord stump and soothe his skin. Baby is used to being is water, and he relaxes very quickly in the warm bath. The herbs promote healing of those tender, bruised tissues, and if there are any small skid marks or lacerations the herbs take the sting and swelling down. Pat can take the bath 2–3 times a day, and baby will enjoy it, too, at least once a day.

During labor make a strong "tea" of the herbs and add it to the bath water after birth. The water needs to warm, but not real hot, about the same as the inside of your elbow. Pat can add more hot water, if she prefers, but it's best not to start out too hot. The herbal bath can be purchased from the birth supply company with the birth kit, or you can buy them in bulk from Frontier Herb Co. or Mari Mann Herb Farm and make up your own packets using small muslin bags.

Herbal Bath Recipe

1/4 cup sea salt	1/2 - 1 oz shepherd's purse
1 ox ura ursi	1 large bulb garlic, peeled & separated
1-2 oz comfrey	Lavendar, sage, or other aromatic herbs
	Can be added as an option

Simmer the tea until water is very dark. Strain the tea as you pour it into the tub of bath water. Pat, you and baby will not smell like garlic... I promise.

Patti Fitzgerald

The birth of Allison Kathleen, born April 26, 1986:

"My birth experience didn't just happen in one day. I had made an appointment to see an obstetrician, but another hospital birth wasn't what I really wanted. I called La Leche League to find out if there was anyone in the area that helped with home birth. Luckily, one member had given birth at home, and recommended Betty. Jerry was surprised when I told him, but he agreed to go along with a home birth. We met Betty, and attended childbirth classes. I wish every woman could have these classes. We were given so much information on nutrition, how to prepare for a home birth, and with discussion of how we all felt about birth. I felt that I had found an inner strength, an earth-mother quality that could get me through this pregnancy with ease.

"Allison was born on April 26th. She had been "ready" for two weeks, so when contractions started at about 4:00 a.m., I knew that it was real labor. I called my mom and sister first, as they had to come from out of town. I then called my friend Laurel. As it turned out, my daughter Desiree had stayed overnight at Laurel's house. This worked out well because she was able to get Desiree, my daughter, dressed and awake. Jerry had called Betty. While we were waiting for everyone to arrive, we made sure that everything was ready. Soon everyone was here. There was an excitement in the air. We were really going to have a home birth! Everyone ate some breakfast together. At this time my contractions were coming hard enough that I decided to lie in bed.

"Jerry and Betty stayed with me the whole time. It was great having Jerry there. He helped me work through each contraction, and I felt that I could transfer some of the pain to him. In the meantime, everyone else was keeping things running smoothly. There was either some juice or a familiar face when I needed it, and Desiree was being taken care of. Desiree, who is five, came in several times to see me, but each time I was in the middle of a long, hard contraction, and she was told not to distract me. I really felt bad about this, because I wanted to hold her. These last five hours would be the end of our special relationship. After all, she wouldn't be an only child anymore.

"My labor seemed to be very hard, and I was wishing it would be over soon. Each time that I went to the bathroom, I could feel Allison moving down. It certainly felt better to labor in a sitting position. Finally, while I was sitting, the water broke. I thought that my insides were falling out, and I was so glad that Jerry was there to grab on to. Betty said to squat by the bed, because the baby was going to be born now. I thought 'How am I supposed to squat when I am in so much pain?' I did it though, and to help me, my Mom laid across the bed and held my arms. I did a lot of yelling and pleading during the pushing. I was worried that Desiree would be scared, as she was watching. However, it didn't bother her.

"On the fourth pushing contraction, Allison's head was born. At the next contraction, Betty got her arm and shoulders out. Jerry finished delivering her. I couldn't believe that this little person had come out of me. I was so glad that she was all right. Betty put Allison on my lap. She was completely alert and looking around. She didn't want to eat, but kept looking around toward voices. Allison was quiet and didn't cry. After the placenta was delivered, Jerry cut the cord. Allison and I took a bath together, then went to bed for some bonding time. Desiree quickly checked her out, and then left. Jerry and I spent a lot of time just looking at her and touching her. I had the great birth that I had been hoping for. I was able to labor in a completely natural way. Most importantly, I was able to enjoy my baby for as long as I wanted. I am really thankful for women like Betty that make home birth possible."

Gerald Fitzgerald

"I came home for lunch and Pat said, 'My doctor appointment is at one. Do you want to have the birth at home?' She said that is what she wanted, so I went along, although I was apprehensive. We went to classes every Saturday for three weeks and we discussed everything from nutrition to umbilical cord. The more I learned, the more I realized that the birth experience wasn't something that needed happen in a hospital. It seemed to me, the more relaxed the mother, the easier the birth. If she is in a secure environment, one that she is comfortable in, and one where she has the people she wants and needs, then the birth has to be easier.

"I worried the last week of Pat's pregnancy, because Betty would be out of town on Saturday, and I just knew Pat would go into labor on that day. So, I started going over everything. As it turned out, Pat went into labor Saturday morning at around 4:00. I called Betty and the people who were to be there: Pat's Mom, sister and a good friend, Laurel P.

"The contractions became harder and harder as time went by. Betty and I massaged Pat and gave support as needed. I didn't have too much trouble until the last hour. It was very hard to stand by while Pat was in hard labor. There was a real feeling of helplessness and inadequacy.

"The actual birth was incredible. When the baby crowned I was ready. But when the head emerged I was overwhelmed. To me the head was so large, that I just stared. There was a small problem because Allison's hand was bunched up by her head, and wouldn't allow he body through. Betty disengaged it and out she came. Betty pulled my hand under Allison, so that I could brag that I had caught the baby.

"Little bubbles were coming from her mouth. It's something very hard for me to explain. She really didn't cry but kind of looked around. Betty was busy with the bulb [syringe] although the mucous was minimal.

"I was glad it was over for several reasons: One was that Pat wasn't in pain anymore. Another was, we had been up a long time, although it had only been around five or six hours.

"Betty was a real anchor. Her experience and beside manner were a Godsend. She was very good for my peace of mind."

Midwife's Notes

Allison had a nuchal hand that required a little extra help from me. Once the arm was delivered, the shoulders were quick to follow. The placenta came before we were ready for it, because I was so busy with the bulb syringe getting the mucus in her mouth. We didn't clamp and cut the cord until the placenta was birthed. That was a potentially difficult situation. If the placenta was sitting at the cervix for any length of time, Allison could have been pumping her own blood out through the placenta. The separation in this case was from a low implantation, and the placenta was expelled very quickly. Blood loss from Allison was minimal, if any.

Jeff Carr

"7:45 p.m., Friday, April 18, 1986. Baby daughter! I can't help thinking about the verse, 'We see in a mirror dimly now, but then face to face;' as transition neared, I felt this about our baby but at the same time I'm thinking this is the heart of God saying to His children on earth that have been 'born' into heaven: 'I can't wait to be right with you and you right with me, face to face, without this separation between us.' (Mark 10:26)

"On the rush of feelings as Betty put the baby on Julie's tummy, I cried as I thought how easy it's been for me but how hard for Julie. I was thinking it's got to be the same when I get to heaven. How easy for me. How hard for Jesus. He did all the work. He still does.

"Several people have asked 'Do you feel like a father?' or 'Do you feel different?' I know I don't *feel* any different but yet I *know* something is different. At least a new dimension. Now I am a son, a husband, a father. Only an inkling of God's Trinity relationally (at least). I know from now on, whatever I read, see, experience, etc., will touch on or relate to my mind and heart the 'revelation' of this birth.

"There are so many correlations between the whole 'process' of birth, labor, gestation, etc., and spiritual birth into heaven, spiritual regeneration, nurturing, maturity. . . Like how a healthy baby has a three-vessel umbilical cord, and a healthy (true) Christian is spiritually connected to the Father, Son and Holy Spirit through man's heart or spirit. How 'neat' that I couldn't have conceived of a way to love Julie and our child, yet now my heart is easily shared with two. That shows me that I can 'love my neighbor' if I want to and how God can easily share his heart with the whole world. It shows me how the baby emerges from relative 'darkness into the light;' from a one-dimensional world, from a binding, restricted, pressurized world to a free, open moving world, to have the thought 'Oh, now I can really see, hear, feel and sense, instead of just vague awareness.'

"The unknown becomes captivating with 'What have I done to Julie?' I thought, 'What if it's 10 or 20 more hours, or if like some women, this baby literally kills her? That unseen thing that no one knew and they could both be gone. She's not my wife, Lord, not mine, but yours, shared with me for however long. It's breaking my heart now nearly literally as I'm torn between Job's wife's 'Curse God and die,' and Jesus' 'Thy will be done.' It must be the latter to 'entrust' our soul to a living faithful Creator (I Peter 4:19b). I can't change Julie's pain or condition any easier than I could change any or all of my bad habits. I questioned how a simplistic moment in the blink of an eye, I 'caused' Julie this much anguish and pain. 'My fault.' If I could have destroyed myself in some way to save Julie from this, I would not have hesitated. But I was (am) powerless, impotent, feeble in my own strength to help her or the baby, let alone myself.

"But that wasn't what caused the knot in my stomach and throat, or tears in my eyes. Julie is so trusting of Me! Not me alone, but she responded to my most gentle word or caress. As if she thought I would be able to take care of anything that might happen. Oh, she called on the Lord and cried as I imagined. Probably more than (my) worst (imaginations), but she held my hand gently but firmly as if all she had to do was just squeeze a little and I could stop it! If I asked her to relax as I lightly rubbed her knitted brow. . . in a blink she did it! Against all reality she did as I asked, almost immediately without complaint, though possibly everything in her rebels at me, in a sense she trusts. Her cries even now ring in my ears and 24 hours later I cry—an uncontrollable response that I desire to fight but realize that if I do I will be callous to God's own heart.

"I don't remember this rending of my soul, except when Lassie died when I was a child, and maybe close when I found myself away from home, in my own house trailer in an almost foreign land. Those days seem to pass, but this may stay forever. I have to realize my impotence before God and hand Julie, 'my' baby, and myself, back to Him even as Julie is now doing. But then the head of our baby is being birthed, and Julie cried gently, 'I want to see our baby, help me Jesus.' I cried the same thing for different reasons I think, even as I do now. What seemed like hours, but in reality was moments, pass quickly and now the head the head is crowning. It is soon now. As the Tin Man in *Wizard of Oz* said, 'I know what a heart is like when it's breaking', or something like that. Now Julie's gentle cries between hard pushes come with a smile and a joy I can feel! I still feel it!

"As I try to speak there is concrete in my throat. I don't feel much below that, yet what is it for Julie? How about the baby. . . oh, poor pitiful me. Ha! 'Moments', someone said 'are like a quarter spinning on edge, between heads and tails; a moments' passing, to blink, is to miss one or two.' But in that much time, Betty put our baby on Julie's tummy. I can't imagine how 'it' got here. I was just mustering strength for another heart-wrenching contraction, wondering about Julie. . . she's working so well! Loving, trusting, crying, laughing? She is laughing! And that is our baby, not ours but the Lord's, but ours!

"'It's a girl,' Mom said with almost a question, a hint of surprise, and Marti echoed with a 'coo' in her voice, but Julie? She's smiling and crying too. I don't know what to do myself, but I wonder if I really did anything at all. But I know I did. I 'helped', I think. I rubbed out cramps, I spoke tenderly, though I felt like screaming inside, I rubbed and stroked; like I said, I didn't do anything. Julie did it all.

"Now she's smiling, talking gently to our baby, who's gently cooing back, gurgling a sweet 'sentence.' I must be really weak, 'cause I cry deep inside again, but it's all mixed up. I am so happy for Julie and baby and I realize this is what it is all about! Julie has known all along, but now it's hitting home for me. I have spent hours thinking about how to help Julie since early this morning, but in the last 10 to 20 minutes, I actually entered the picture—-who am I? I know better who God is now.

"Julie and baby are in a herbal bath, just cooing and gurgling. Baby just goes 'limp.' She is so at home and relaxed. Julie is in love with someone else, and I am so happy. I'm thinking now of songs that played on our tapes and how they apply. Julie and Jesus have done so much for me, all the work. How can I even begin to repay that love? Matthew 26:39; Mark 12:28-31.

Julie Carr

(The following was written after finding out we had a girl.)
"April 18: Woke up around 3:15 a.m. with some cramping. Got up and went to living room to eat cereal. Around 5:00 went back to bed. Slept in 'til 9:00.

"Woke up and still had cramping. For some strange reason I felt like I should call Marti and ask about the signs of how she knew it was the real thing. Since Braxtons weren't letting up and I had cramps, I called Betty and asked if she would do an exam. She took a shower and came around 10:30. She told me that I had dilated to 3 cm. From discussions, we knew it was a good probability baby would be born before midnight, on Sue's birthday, April 18.

"The day was sunny even though rain had ben predicted. The first warm day after a week of cold spell. I felt good and even got things done around the house while Betty ran a few errands. She would return around 1:00 to see how I was progressing. Jeff had gone on to work for a short while since they were short-handed and trucks needed loading. The Lord really answered a prayer when he had his truck loaded by 1:30: a feat rarely able to be accomplished before evening. I was anxious for him to come home. He was here by 2:00, and Betty had re-examined and concluded that I was now dilated to 7 cm. I felt so many prayers being answered. For one thing, I had been praying and thinking about the way labor would feel like all week long. I asked the Lord to give me strength. I'd heard so many stories, and I so wanted the birth to go without complications. Especially with a home birth. Contractions were really mild at first. So mild in fact, that I could feel free to talk and joke with the birth team: Betty, Marti, Mitzi, Jeff and I. Marti, with Mitzi, had arrived shortly after Jeff. So everyone was present around 2:30.

"Each contraction was dealt with fairly easily with deep breathing in and out. I felt best on my side, though. When I did need to urinate, contractions became quite strong when sitting up. So much so that I needed to go limp and fall against whoever was with me—mostly my sweetheart, Jeffers. I remember how he was there for me. I really was comforted by his presence and was so grateful for having the opportunity of having a home birth. We could feel complete freedom to draw strength from each other. God's grace was so real. The last leg of the journey was the longest and hardest. I've read that labor is described as the hardest work a woman may do in her life. It takes over your total consciousness even though there was a spell during hard labor where I felt 'out-of-body.' I felt the intense pain of strong contractions, but also witnessed them.

This is where a strong support team is critical. Again, I was blessed with excellent backup.

"I remember during one very hard contraction, having severe leg cramps start up. The minute I yelled out in distraction over the problem, everyone on both sides started quick massaging of every muscle point of both legs. My next distraction came with 'back labor.' Again, everyone did everything in their power to apply pressure or massage. I was most amazed by everyone's undaunted loyalty during my pushing. At first I was almost afraid to push, but when contractions got harder, pushing was almost merciful. No matter how little or great I pushed, everyone encouraged me: stating how I was being 'a good mom,' and I was 'going to see the baby soon.' This was overwhelming! That is what the whole thing was about! Seeing that life in your face, face to face. The reality of the whole reason for pregnancy, labor, change of life-style, etc. Granted, there were moments in thought that seemed to scream out 'God, am I going to die? So, this is travail! This is the only time we will have a child. I could never go through this again.' Now I see how quickly that can change. That is, now that I have seen our little girl.

"With baby in the birth canal, the pushing was an extremely strong urge. I remember sounding very guttural, almost like a football player. I'd go from heavy-duty grunt to crying to breathing. It was a blur and I kept my eyes closed until after the water broke and crowning was announced, she was almost there. Then the tiny life within emerged! Another prayer answered: no tears! I remember everyone's amazement at 'It's a girl!' All of Jeff's side, including myself, had felt it would be a boy. All of my side of the family felt it would be a girl. I loved her instantly! She was so beautiful and pink and so wonderful to see.

"My whole thoughts of pain were being erased and replaced with an avalanche of joy for this fantastic bundle of life. I remember Jeff being at my side. His eyes said it all: 'I'm proud of you, I love our little girl. Isn't she beautiful!' He had tears in his eyes. A moment that makes life worth living!

"We were on a new road now. Early in the labor I remember Jeff saying, 'Can you believe this is happening?' referring to being parents and seeing our baby. I replied that it was something how it seemed like yesterday when I had just re-met him at the skating rink. The beginning point of our relationship. Now we were at a new horizon in our life. That of raising our daughter and possible children of the future. Since God made our perfect little daughter, Jessica, we'd now need Him to teach us how to raise her. He is true in His love for His children and we now have stepped out in faith."

APPENDIX

STERILE SUPPLIES SETUP

Everyone develops their own placement of supplies at births. Once you have decided how you want things set up, always set up the same way every time. This is very helpful when you need something in a hurry and must send someone for something, and you can say: "Bring the sterile wrap from the right rear corner of the dresser", or, "Please bring the blood pressure cuff and stethoscope. It is on the left and near the front of the dresser".

I always put the items needed for labor farthest from Pat's nest for birthing, with second- and third-stage items closest to where Pat planned to birth. The sketch below is how I had everything set up. If you are just beginning, you may want to try and see how this works for you. You may want to try several different set ups before you find one that works for you. I found that all I needed was an area about 14 inches by 18 inches for all the equipment needed. My oxygen tank was usually placed off to the side, usually next to the dresser, or by the closet door. Just so it was handy yet out of the way.

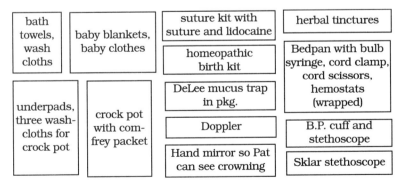

bath towels, wash cloths	baby blankets, baby clothes	suture kit with suture and lidocaine	herbal tinctures
		homeopathic birth kit	Bedpan with bulb syringe, cord clamp, cord scissors, hemostats (wrapped)
underpads, three washcloths for crock pot	crock pot with comfrey packet	DeLee mucus trap in pkg.	
		Doppler	B.P. cuff and stethoscope
		Hand mirror so Pat can see crowning	Sklar stethoscope

Equipment/Supplies Provided by Parents

1 Birthing Kit: I had a custom kit set up by the birth supply companies, that Pat and John would order by name. This ensured me that the right number of blue pads, the Hesseltine cord clamp, povidone iodine, scrub brushes, gloves, sterile lubricant jelly, bulb syringe, plastic backed sheets, peri bottle and baby's cap were in the kit. (Occasionally they would purchase a different kit, and the very thing I depended on being in the kit and did not carry in my bag would be missing. . . that required some inventiveness and ingenuity.)

1 Kleenex or new roll of toilet paper, or new roll of soft paper towels

1 Box winged night-time/super sanitary pads. (the wings are helpful to keep the panties from soiling the first week postpartum)

3–6 clean towels and wash cloths

Baby clothes, diapers and blankets

2 Plastic drop cloths or old vinyl table cloths (one for floor and 1 for waterproofing the mattress

2–3 trash bags or 2 five gallon plastic buckets

Snacks and juices for Pat, John, midwife and helpers.

1 casserole in freezer for first meal after birth

Place for helpers and midwife to bed down during a long labor, or early labor during night.

I often just stayed the night if Pat birthed after 9 p.m., and then got up early the next morning to go home, otherwise I wouldn't start home until 1:30 a.m. and would only get 2-3 hours of sleep. This way I'd get 4-6 hours of sleep, and would save me a trip back the next day.

Herbal Bath Recipe

1 oz. Sage   1 large clove Garlic   1 ox. Comfrey leaves
1/4 c Sea Salt   1/2 oz. Shepherds Purse

Place herbs in recycleable muslin bag. Make a strong tea in non-metalic pan. Add tea to bath water. If you do not use a bag, use a plastic strainer to strain tea. Water will turn brown when you add the tea. Herbs can be used for 2baths before discarding in the garden compost pile.

APPENDIX B

VAGINITIS

For those of you that are doing well-woman care, you may on occasion have a lady with vaginitis. The following has been taken from an out-of-print book written by a Dr. Nelson. You can purchase a microscope from the local school district when they auction off "excess or old" equipment. Another source is the local toy store, for an inexpensive one. Be sure the highest magnification is at least 1000× magnification, for it to be of use to you.

You can use your microscope to check for leaking membranes in threatened abortion or late pregnancy. Using sterile technique, swab the cervical os with a sterile swab (long Q-tip), and roll the wet swab across the clean slide. If amniotic fluid is present, you will see a fern pattern on the slide. The nitrazine paper will also show dark blue to dark green.

Major Categories of Vaginitis

	Candida	Gardnerella	Trichomonas	Atrophy
Complaint	Pruritus	Fishy Odor	Discharge	Bleeding
pH	4–5	5–6	5–7	6–7
Discharge	Thick, Cheesy	Scant, Creamy	Thin, Copious	Scant, Purulent
Wet Smear	Hypae	Clue Cells	Motile Protozoa	WBC, Parabasals

1. Insert small strip of nitrazine paper in anterior or lateral fornix for pH reading
2. Small amount of representative discharge on slide mixed with few drops of saline.
3. Small amount of representative discharge on slide mixed with few drops of KOH.
4. Read slides on low and high magnification; close down iris diaphragm of microscope to diminish light intensity for greater contrast.

Medicated Douche Solutions

Ingredient	Indication
Normal Saline	General Use
White Vinegar	General Use
Alkaline Powder	Mucolytic
Potassium Sorbate	Anti-Fungal
(Over-the-Counter, Medicated)	
Hydrogen Peroxide	Anti-Gardnerella
20% Saline	Anti-Trichomonas
Sweet Acidophillus Milk, Yogurt, Lactobacillus Solution	Recolonization, Restoration of Normal Flora
Buttermilk	Elimination of Odor from Vaginal Fistulae

Douche Recipes

White Vinegar: 1 Tablespoon white vinegar to 1 quart water.

Normal Saline: 1–2 teaspoons table salt per quart water.

20% Saline: 20 parts salt per 100 parts water.

Trichomonas: 1 cup table salt stirred vigorously into 4 cups water (salt solution is lethal to trichomonas). Follow with yogurt applied to vagina with clean fingers (gloves).

Herpes II: 10% povidone iodine painted on cervix and vaginal walls with douching with same strength, b.i.d., inactivates virus (*not a cure*), or:

    Herp Elim tincture: 10 drops q.i.d. under the tongue;

    Herp Elim Ointment to lesion q.i.d., or;

    Hrpz homeopathic combination tablets q. 4 hours until relieved

The Correct Way to Douche

Observe the following procedure when douching:

1. With the tubing clamped off, insert the douche tip to the cervix, using slight downward pressure, until the juncture of the tubing and the tip is at the introitus.
2. Gently but firmly, hold the labia together, squeezing the vagina closed around the douche tip and preventing the egress of fluid.
3. The other hand opens the valve, with the bag suspended at about shoulder height.
4. When a sensation of fullness is felt, at about the one-half-pint mark, close the valve and hold labia closed for one minute, leaving the tip inside the vagina.
5. Allow the solution to run out, then repeat until the bag is empty.

Douching should not be done routinely, nor should a pregnant woman douche. However, there are extenuating circumstances. If a woman is pregnant, and has contracted trichomonas or has an resistant form of candida (yeast), you may want to pray before considering a medicated douche. You have to decide which is worse, the antibiotic cure or the douche. With the availability of over-the-counter medications, that until recently were by prescription only, douching should be a very last resort. If your client is pregnant, and the homeopathic, herbals and over-the-counter medications have not helped, she should see a physician immediately, and be transferred out of your service. You are dealing with a severe infection, and it is out of your league.

APPENDIX C

SCRIPTURE LIST BY CHAPTER

Introduction

Isaiah 44:2–4, 24
Job 31:15, 33:4
Psalm 119:73
Psalm 68:5
Psalm 139:13–16
Ecclesiastes 11:5
I Thessalonians 5:23
II Timothy 2:15
Mark 16:16
II Timothy 1:7 (Amp)
I John 4:16
Proverbs 14:18
I Corinthians 3:16

Chapter 1: *Nutrition. . . The Beginning*

Genesis 1:29
Leviticus 11:3,9,21–22
Deuteronomy 14:1–20
Genesis 9:2–4
Acts 10:15
James 4:7

    God created food to sustain life in the "eater". Just because a food is there and "legal" according to scripture, does not mean we are to overindulge in it. Self-control is a fruit of the

Holy Spirit; a virtue we are to practice all the time. While pregnant, please use your diet cards and you will find that the cravings will go away, and you will not be binging.

Chapter 2: *Infant Development. . . The Breath of Life*

Deuteronomy 28:1–14
John 3:16
Galatians 3:13, 5:9
Proverbs 11:1
Jeremiah 17:5
Psalms 109:17–19, 139:13–16, 119:73, 121:7
Genesis 1:27
Romans 8:9–10
Ecclesiastes 12:7
James 2:26
Isaiah 44:2–4, 24
Job 31:15, 33:4
Ecclesiastes 11:5
Isaiah 40:11, 49:1, 5, 15
Ezekiel 16:4–6, 9
Ephesians 4:23–32
II Timothy 1:8–9

Chapter 3: *Prenatal Care. . . Parenting Begins*

James 2:22
II Timothy 3:7
I Peter 5:5, 7, 2:24
Ephesians 6:1–4, 11–18, 5:15–17, 22–31
Romans 8:1–9, 13:13–14
Acts 3:19
I Thessalonians 5:17
Colossians 3:18–21
II Peter 3:1–12
I Corinthians 6:19–20
Galatians 3:13–14
Isaiah 53:3–6, 55:8–9

Chapter 4: *Tests and Technology. . . The Wonders of Modern Medicine*

John 14:13–14
Numbers 23:19–20
Psalm 36:6
I Peter 2:24
Genesis 49:24, 2:7
Psalm 34:20, 63:5, 31:24, 42:11, 37:4, 84:11–12, 119:73.
   68:5, 139:13–16
Isaiah 44:2–4, 24
Acts 10:15
Job 31:15, 33:4, 1:21–22
I Samuel 1:18–21
Matthew 6:33
Ecclesiastes 11:5
Philippians 4:8–9
I Thessalonians 5:23
II Timothy 2:15
I John 4:16
Proverbs 14:18
I Corinthians 3:16
Numbers 23:19–20

Chapter 5: *Risk Factors, Emotional Issues and Guidelines*

James 4:7–11, 17, 5:16
Matthew 6:25–34, 12:30, 36–37,
II Timothy 1:7–9, 17,
Philippians 1:6, 4:8–9, and chapter 6
I Thessalonians 5:8–11, 14–18, 24
Ephesians 3:14–21, 6:1–4, 10–18, 4:23–32, 5:15–17, 23–31
Colossians 3:14–21
Galatians 3:13–14, 5:1, 9
John 10:28–29, 8:44, 3:16
Proverbs 31:10–31, 18:21, 11:1
Isaiah 54:13, 63:9, 65:22–23, 53:3–6, 55:8–9
Deuteronomy 11:26–28, 7:7–19, 28:1–68
Exodus 1:15–22
Mark 11:23
Acts 23:12–14

Luke 9:50
Judges 5:23
Jeremiah 48:10, 17:5
Psalm 109:17–19
Romans 8:1–9, 13:13–14
Acts 3:19
I Peter 5:5, 1:3–25, 2:1–12, 24, 3:1–12
I Corinthians 7:12–16, 6:19–20
Job 1:21–22

Chapter 6: *Choosing Your Midwife, Helpers, and Physician*

Matthew 7:6
James 2:17–18
II Timothy 2:15
Ephesians 6:13–20
John 3:16–21
I Timothy 2:15
Leviticus 18:1–18

Chapter 7: *Labor and Birth. . . In the Fullness of Time*

Romans 3:23, 5:12, 6:1–23
Ephesians 2:8–9
Isaiah 61:9
Genesis 3:15–17, (and vs.6)
Galatians 3:13

Chapter 8: *Natural Birth After Cesarean. . . New Beginnings*

Psalm 127:2
Proverbs 3:24
Hebrews 1:14, 4:12
I Timothy 2:15
Genesis 1:31 (Amp)

Chapter 9: *Midwifery and the Law. . . Judgment*

Exodus 1:17
Ephesians 5:22–25, 6:13
Romans 8:31, 37
Isaiah 43:2
Proverbs 3:26
Psalms 27:1–3
Colossians 4:5
Matthew 5:13, 33–37, 10:16
I Thessalonians 5:16–22
James 5:12
II Corinthians 3:1–6

Chapter 10: *The Newborn. . . The Heritage of the Lord*

Psalm 139:13–16
Ecclesiastes 11:5
Leviticus 12:2–5
Isaiah 55:11
Genesis 17:10–13
Romans 2: 25–29
Luke 1:59
Exodus 12:48
Romans 4:11
Ephesians 2:11–15
Galatians 5:1–4
Colossians 2:11, 3:11
Acts 15:1, 10, 15–29
I Corinthians 7:18–19
Romans 2:25–29, 4: 9–15
Philippians 3:3

Chapter 11: *Complications and Challenges*

Isaiah 37:3, 65:23–34, 66:7–11, 44:3–4, 9–11
I Timothy 2:15
Ezekiel 16:6
Psalm 139:1–16, 23–34, 127:3
Jeremiah 1:12

I Thessalonians 5:24
Job 33:4
II Timothy 1:17
Deuteronomy 28:1–68
Matthew 5:45
James 1:15
Romans 8:26–27, 10:9–10
John 3:14–21
Hebrews 12:1

Chapter 12: *Midwifery Skills—Perfection in Authority*

II Timothy 2;25, 20–26
Daniel 7–9, 10:13, 20–21; 12;1
Revelation 6–9, 12:7–9,
Hebrews 1:14
Matthew 24, 26:39
Mark 13, 10:26, 12:28–31
Luke 21
Psalm 91
Ecclesiastes 4:12
I Peter 4:19b

There are many more scriptures that could apply. Please feel free to add them to this list. Commit them to memory, so they will be available at all times, not just when you have this book with you.

> O how love I thy law! It is my meditation all the day. Thou through thy commandments has made me wiser than mine enemies; for they are ever with me. I have more understanding than all my teachers: for thy testimonies are my meditation. I understand more than the ancients, because I keep thy precepts. I have refrained my feet from every evil way, that I might keep thy word. I have not departed from thy judgments: for thou hast taught me. How sweet are thy words unto my taste! yea, sweeter than honey to my mouth. Through thy precepts I get understanding: therefore I hate every false way. Thy Word is a lamp unto my feet and a light unto my path. I have sworn, and I will perform it, that I will keep thy righteous judgments.

—Psalm 119:97–106

APPENDIX D

BIBLIOGRAPHY

Introduction

1. *Holy Bible*, King James Version, Zondervan Publishing Co. Grand Rapids, Mi.
2. *Normal Christian Life*, Watchman Nee, translated from Chinese, Christian Fellowship Publishers Inc. N.Y., N.Y.

Chapter 1: *Nutrition. . . The Beginning*

1. *Holy Bible*, KJV
2. *What Every Woman Should Know—The Truth About Diets and Drugs In Pregnancy*, Gail S. Brewer and Tom Brewer, M.D. Medical Consultant, Penguin Books, 1985
3. *Let's Have Healthy Children*, Adelle Davis, A Signet Book, New American Library, 1981
4. *Nourishing Your Unborn Child*, Phyllis S. Williams, R.N. Avon Books, Div. the Hearst Corp., 1982
5. *The Supermarket Handbook*, Nikki and David Goldbeck, Signet Books, New American Library, 1976
6. *Diet for a Small Planet*, Francis Lappé, Balantine, New York, NY, 1971
7. *Public Health Reports, Journal of the U.S. Public Health Service*, Vol. 105, No. 1 (Jan.–Feb. 1990)
8. *The Vitamin Bible*, Earl Mindell, Warner Books, Ed. Raawson Wade Publishers, Inc., 1981
9. *Back to Eden*, Jethro Kloss, Back to Eden Books, P.O. Box 1439, Loma Linda, CA 92354, 1982

Chapter 2: *Infant Development. . . The Breath of Life*

1. *King James Bible*, Zondervan Publishing House, Grand Rapids, MI
2. *Life Unto Life*, Fetal Growth and Development, Childbirth Graphics Ltd., Rochester, N.Y., 1988
3. *The First Nine Months*, Geraldine Lux Flanagan, Simon and Schuster, Rockefeller Center, 630 Fifth Ave., N.Y., N.Y. 10020

Chapter 3: *Prenatal Care. . . Parenting Begins*

1. *King James Bible*
2. *Medical Diet for Normal and High-Risk Pregnancy*, Gail S. Brewer, Tom Brewer M.D., Medical Consultant, Fireside Books, Simon and Schuster, N.Y., N.Y.
3. *None of These Diseases*, S.I. McMillan M.D., A Spire Book, Pyramid Publications for Fleming H. Revell Co., 1977
4. *Back to Eden*, Jethro Kloss
5. *The Vitamin Bible*, Earl Mindell
6. *Public Health Reports, Journal of United States Public Health Service*, Vol. 105, No.1
7. *Metabolic Toxemia of Late Pregnancy*, Tom Brewer, M.D., 1982
8. *Essential Exercise for the Childbearing Year*, Elizabeth Noble, R.P.T., Houghton Mifflin Co., Boston, 1982
9. *Exercises for Birth*, Veronica WAgner

Chapter 4: *Tests and Technology. . . The Wonders of Modern Medicine*

1. *Normal Christian Life*, Watchman Nee
2. *Birth Reborn*, Michel Odent, M.D. A Plume Book, New American Library, N.Y., N.Y.
3. *The Brewer Medical Diet for Normal and High-Risk Pregnancy*, Gail S. Brewer and Tom Brewer M.D.
4. *The Herb Book*, John Lust, N.D., D.B.M., dist. by Nutri-Books Corp., Box 5793, Denver, CO 80217
5. *Back to Eden*, Jethro Kloss

6. *Herbally Yours*, Penny C. Royal, Sound Nutrition, 1449 W. 10300 S., Payson, Utah 84651, (801)423-2657, 1984
7. *The Brewer Medical Diet for Normal and High-Risk Pregnancy*, Tom Brewer

Chapter 5: *Risk Factors, Emotional Issues and Guidelines*

1. *King James Bible*
2. *Amplified Bible*, Zondervan Bible Publishers, Grand Rapids, Mi.
3. *Webster's New Dictionary and Thesaurus*, Geddes & Grosset, Windsor Ct., N.Y., N.Y., 1990
4. *Christian Home Birth*, Joy Young, out of print
5. *Childbirth Without Fear*, Grantly Dick-Read, Helen Wessel and Harlan F. Ellis, M.D., Perennial Library Harper & Row, Pub. N.Y., 4th ed.
6. *Husband-Coached Childbirth*, Robert Bradley, M.D.
7. *The Brewer Medical Diet for Normal and High-Risk Pregnancy*, Gail S. Brewer & Tom Brewer, M.D.
8. *Taber's Cyclopedic Medical Dictionary*, 16th ed. F.A. Davis Co., Phila. PA
9. *Williams Obstetrics*, Jack A. Pritchard, M.D. and Paul C. MacDonald, M.D., Appleton-Centur-Crofts, N.Y., 15th ed.
10. *Compassionate Friends*, see your local chapter
11. *Illinois Alliance of Midwives Standards of Care and Risk Factors*, 1990

Chapter 6: *Choosing Your Midwife, Helpers, and Physician*

1. *Birth and Bonding of the Family*, Anna Smith, order from The Fraley Family, 6 Cheval Dr., Oak Brook, IL 60521
2. *Holy Bible*, KJV
3. InterNational Association of Parents and Professionals for Safe Alternatives in Childbirth, (NAPSAC), Rt. 1, Box 646, Marble Hill, MO 63764
4. La Leche League, International (LLLI), P.O. Box 1209, Franklin Park, IL 60131-8209
5. Crisis Pregnancy Centers
6. *Children at Birth*, Marjie and Jay Hathaway, AAHCC

7. Midwives' Alliance of North America (MANA), Signe Rogers, Sec. P.O. Box 175, Newton, KS 67114, (316) 283-4543
8. American College of Nurse-Midwives, 1522 K Street, Suite 1120 Washington, DC 20005
9. *Raising Them Chaste*, Richard C. Durfield, Ph.D., and Renee Durfield, Bethany Publishers
10. *Mom and Dad and I Are Having a Baby*, Maleki

Videos

1. *Andrew's Birth*, American Academy of Husband-Coached Childbirth
2. *Children at Birth*, American Academy of Husband-Coached Childbirth
3. *Children at Birth*, Penny Simkin

Chapter 7: *Labor and Birth. . . In the Fullness of Time*

1. *Holy Bible*, KJV
2. *Entering the World*, Michel Odent, M.D., A Plume Book, New American Library, N.Y.
3. *Childbirth Without Fear*, Grantly Dick-Read, M.D. and Helen Wessel
4. *Christian Home Birth*, Joy Young
5. *Husband-Coached Childbirth*, Robert A. Bradley, M.D.
6. *The Biological Specificity of Milk*, W.G. Whittle-Stone, DSc., pres.at LLLI, 4th annual Breastfeeding Seminar for Physicians, San Francisco, CA, March 13, 1976
7. Illinois Department of Public Health, Div. of Lab. P.O. Box 19435, 825 N. Rutledge St., Springfield, IL, 62794-9435
8. *Nurse Midwifery*, second ed. Helen Varney, Blackwell Scientific Pub. Boston, Ma., Blackwell Mosby Book Dist. 11830 Westline Indust. Dr., St., Louis, MO 63146
9. *Homeopathics for Birthing*, Jana Shiloh, M.A., dist. by Homeopathic Educational Service, 2124 Kitteredge St. Berkeley, CA 94704, $10.95
10. The Accoucheur's Emergency Manual, W. A. Yinling, Moonflower Birthing Supply, 2810 Wilderness Place, #D, Boulder, CO 80301

11. Guide to Homeopathic Remedies for the Birth Bag, 2nd Ed., Patty Brennan and Pat Kramer, Moonflower Birthing Supply

Chapter 8: *Natural Birth After Cesarean. . . New Beginnings*

1. American Academy of Husband-Coached Childbirth, (Bradley Method)
2. International Cesarean Awareness Network, P.O. Box 152, Syracuse, N.Y. 13210, (315) 424-1942
3. Apple Tree Family Ministries, P.O. Box 9883, Fresno, CA 93795
4. *Silent Knife*, Nancy Wainer Cohen and Lois J. Estner, Bergin & Garvey Pub., Inc., Granberry, MA
5. *Open Season*, Nancy Wainer Cohen, Bergin & Garvey Pub., Inc., Granberry, MA, 1991
6. *Holy Bible*, KJV
7. Institute in Basic Life Principles, Box One, Oak Brook, IL 60522-3001
8. *Heart and Hands, A Guide to Midwifery*, Elizabeth Davis, John Muir Pub., New Mexico, 1981
9. Childbirth Without Fear, Dick Grantly-Read, M.D. and Helen Wessel
10. *Husband-Coached Childbirth*, Robert Bradley, M.D.

Chapter 9: *Midwifery and the Law. . . Judgment*

1. *Holy Bible*, KJV
2. *Safe Alternatives in Childbirth*, NAPSAC
3. *Compulsory Hospitalization or Freedom of Choice, Vol. 1–3*, NAPSAC
4. *The Five Standards of Safe Childbearing*, NAPSAC
5. *The Childbirth Activist's Handbook*, NAPSAC
6. *21st Century Obstetrics Now! Vol. 1–2*, NAPSAC
7. *Divided Legacy: A History of the Schism in Medical Thought, Vol. 1–3*, Harris Coulter, Ph.D., Homeopathic Educational Services, 2124 Kitteredge St., Berkeley, CA 94704
8. *Regulating Birth: Midwives, Medicine and the Law*, Raymond DeVries, 1985

9. *Midwifery and the Law*, Mothering mag. special ed. 1982
10. "State Laws and the Practice of Lay Midwifery," Irene Butter and Bonnie Kay, *American Journal of Public Health*, 78(9):1161-1169, September 1988
11. *The American Midwife Debate, A Sourcebook on Its Modern Origins*, Judy Barrett Litoff, 1978
12. "The Statistical Case for the Elimination of the Midwife: Fact Versus Prejudice," *Women and Health*, 4(1):81–96 and 4(2):169–186, 1979
13. *The Practice of Nurse-Midwifery in the United States*, U.S. Dept. Human Health Services, Children's Bureau, Margaret W. Thomas, 1965
14. The Rutherford Institute, Post Office 7482, Charlottesville, Virginia 22906-7482

Chapter 10: *The Newborn. . .*
The Heritage of the Lord

1. *Holy Bible*, King James Version
2. *The People's Doctor Newsletter*, Robert Mendelsohn, M.D. Vol. 9. No. 1
3. *The Womanly Art of Breastfeeding*, LLLI
4. *American Journal of Obstetrics and Gynecology*, Nov. 1984
5. *The British Medical Journal*, April 1987
6. *The Immunization Decision*, Randall Neustaedtler, OMD, L. Ac. pub. North Atlantic Books, 2800 Woolsey Street, Berkeley, CA 94705
7. *Immunization: The Truth Behind the Myth*, Walene James, Bergin & Garvey pub. Granberry, MA 1988
8. *DPT: A Shot in the Dark*, H.L. Coulter and B.L. Fisher, Harcourt, Brace, Jovanovich Pub. Orlando, FL 1985
9. *But Doctor, About that Shot*, Robert Mendelsohn, M.D. Contemporary Books, Chicago, 1987
10. *Vaccination, Sociopathy and Criminality: the Medical Assault on the American Brain*, Harris Coulter, North Atlantic Books, Pub. Berkeley, CA, 1990
11. *Webster's New Dictionary and Thesaurus*
12. *National Center for Health*, United States Public Health Service, Washington, D.C.

13. Panel of Review of Bacterial Vaccines and Toxoids with Standards and Potency, 15th meeting
14. *Estimation of Gestational Age by Maturity Rating*, chart, Mead-Johnson and Co., Evansville, IN 47721
15. *Vaccinations and Immune Malfunction*, Harold E. Buttram, M.D. and John Chris Hoffman, pub. The Randolph Society Inc. Quakertown, PA 18951, 1987; Library of Congress Card Catalog Number 84-081956

Chapter 11: *Complications and Challenges*

1. *Holy Bible*, KJV
2. *The Accoucheur's Emergency Manual*, W. A. Yingling
3. *Guide to Homeopathic Remedies for the Birth Bag*, 2nd Ed., Patty Brennan and Pat Kramer
4. *Williams Obstetrics*, Pritchard and MacDonald
5. *Homeopathy for Birthing*, Jana Shiloh
6. *Angels Unaware*, Dale Evans

Chapter 12: *Midwifery Skills. . . Perfection in Authority*

1. *Holy Bible*, KJV
2. *Christian Home Birth*, Joy Young
3. *Secret Life of the Unborn*, Thomas Verney, M.D., and Jack Kelly
4. *Steppingstones to Labor Ward Diagnosis*, R.H. Hamblin (out of print)
5. *Nurse Midwifery*, Second Edition, Helen Varney
6. *Understanding Lab Work in the Childbearing Year*, 4th ed. Anne Frye,
7. *Homeopathic Medicines for Pregnancy and Childbirth*, Richard Moscowitz, M.D., Pub. Homeopathic Educational Service, 2124 Kitteredge St., Berkeley, CA 94704, $14.95
8. *Accoucheur's Emergency Manual*, Y. A. Yingling
9. *Homeopathy for Birthing*, Jana Shiloh, M.A.
10. *Guide to Physical Exam*
11. *Healing Passage: A Suturing Guide for Midwives*, Anne Frye
12. *Suturing Technique*, the video companion for *Healing Passage*, Anne Frye

13. *Mosby's Medical, Nursing and Allied Health Dictionary,* 3rd ed., pub. C.V. Mosby Co., 11830 Westline Industrial Dr., St. Louis, MO 63146

APPENDIX  E

RESOURCES

I advocate birthing at home with a midwife or a doctor. However, I also realize that sometimes you cannot find a midwife or a doctor, because there are none in your area that will attend home birth, or none in your area with like philosophies of birth and sanctity of life. If, after prayer, spiritual discernment, and examination of conscience, with full awareness of the responsibilities given to you as parents by the Lord, you still choose to birth at home without trained attendant(s) present, the following resources will be of benefit.

NAPSAC
Rt. 4, Box 646
Marble Hill, MO 63764
www.napsac.org

Quarterly newsletter on childbirth alternatives, extensive mail-order bookstore on birth, breastfeeding and parenting. Will provide telephone counseling and information on husband-assisted home birth.

Emergency Childbirth
by Gregory White, M.D.

Required reading for all planning husband-assisted birth. Written by a home-birth physician with over 40 years of experience, this book was designed for policemen and firemen who assist births in the field. Don't just read it, *memorize* it. Available from NAPSAC at the above address. .

New Nativity
P.O. Box 6223
Leawook, KS 66206

Birth and the Dialogue of Love, by Marilyn Moran; philosophy and rationale of husband-assisted home birth.

Happy Birth Days, by Marilyn Moran; an anthology of birth stories with a wide variety of situations.

Love-Making During Labor, Marilyn Moran; pamphlet, beneficial effects of loving husband-wife intimacy during labor.

Two Attune
Box 12-A/SP
Harborside, ME, 04642

Quarterly newsletter with articles and birth stories. Husband assisted home-birth information and support by mail.

La Leche League International
9616 Minneapolis Ave.
Franklin Park, IL 60131
(708) 455-7730

Mother's milk best for baby and home birth. Breast feeding support, advice, pumps, etc. League groups and leaders location, and more on web site. www:lalecheleague.org.

International Cesarean
Awareness Network (ICAN Inc)
1304 Kingsdale Ave
Redondo Beach CA 90278

Before and After cesarean advice and counseling. Childbirth Educator training, workshops and conferences. Referrals. Call (310) 542-6400, Toll Free (877) ASK-ICAN for support. www.Ican-online.org

Midwifery Resources

Seattle Midwifery School
2524 16th Avenue South
Room 300
Seattle, WA 98144
(206) 322-8834

Midwifery academics and skill training for people without medical background.

North American Registry
of Midwives (NARM)
Phone: (888) 84-BIRTH
E Mail: Iowamama@aol.com

Education advocacy, midwife referral. Information you need to become a CPM.

Ancient Art Midwifery Institute (Formerly Apprentice Academics) P.O. Box 788 Claremore, OK 74018-0788

Home school for Mom. Everything you need to know academically to be a midwife. Excellent for practicing midwives too.

Birth With Love Midwifery Supplies 513 - 27th Street North Great Falls MT 59401 (800) 454-4915

Ollie Hamilton has what ever you need for your bag, or for your parents need for baby. Also has bargains—used but good instruments available. www.birthwithlove.com

Midwifery Education and Accreditation Council 220 W Birch Flagstaff AZ 86001 (520) 214-0997 AMABAUL@ aol.com

Recommends curriculum and accredits midwifery schools and education opportunities for midwives. Maintains current listing of accredited midwifery schools in the United States. Only agency of multiple avenues of education approved by the United States Department of Education.

Kim Perry, RN, CPM 11607 E 1700 St Cambridge IL 61238 (309) 937-1138 e-mail: kimrncpm@inter.com

Kim designed wonderful forms that are specifically for the home birthing midwife on a computer disc. The forms are: Physical and Obstetrical history, Prenatal Care, Labor and Birth, and Postpartum and Newborn exam. This is a real bargain. You can customize your form on the disc and your form is always available. No waiting for the copy shop or delivery truck. $12.00 S&H incl.

Midwifery Institute of America Mary Burleson PO Box 2 Welmer TN 38375 (901) 934-4696

Resident and correspondence school. Housing costs included in tuition. Kitchen facilities available. Christian emphasis. Write or phone for class schedule.

Christian Childbirth Education Betty Peckmann 03 Robert Drive Normal, IL 61761 (309) 452-4182

Brewer Diet Cards; easiest way to do the Brewer Diet or get 2500 calories of *good* quality food for pregnancy and during lactation (breastfeeding). $8.00 plus $2.00 S&H. State meat or vegetarian; $10.00 plus $2.00 S&H for both.

Yalad Birthing Supply PO Box 8111 Canton OH 44711-8111

Midwife owned birth supply with Christian view. Write for free catalog.

Spirit-Led Childbirth
PO Box 1225
Oakhurst CA 93644
(888) 683-2678

Very complete Christian birth supply house. Books, midwifery supplies, parenting supplies, everything you need. Web site: www.efn.org/~djz/birth/spiritled E-mail: birth@siercatel.com

Anna Marie and Richard Fahey
Christian Homesteading Movement
Rd. #2 N
Oxford, New York 13830

Homesteading, midwifery/homebirth skills, herbology, taught in appropriate week long intensives with Christian emphasis. Hands on, and theory. Write for schedule and costs.

MANA Information
Signe Rogers, Secretary
PO Box 175
Newton KS 67114
manainfo@aol.com

Midwife referral, information, newsletter, regional and national conferences.

Childbirth Graphics
Div. WRS Group, Inc.
Waco, TX 76702-1207
voice: (800) 299-3366 ext. 287
fax: (817) 751-0221

Wonderful visual aids for classes; charts, models, suture model for practice videos, books, multi-cultural and ethnic styles, Hispanic/ English, teens etc. Secular view. Visual aides appropriate for home and hospital birth classes.

Arrowroot Natural Pharmacy
83 E. Lancaster Ave
Paoli, PA 19301
(800) 234-8879
FAX: (800) 296-8998
Homeonet: Arrowroot

Remedies in single and combinations, pellets, tablets, ointments, dilutions or tinctures. Professional discount to midwives, nurses, etc., homeopathic birthkit source late 1996.

Homeopathic Educational Svcs
2124 Kitteredge St.
Berkeley, CA 94794
(800) 359-9051 (orders only
FAX: (510) 649-1955

Books, homeopathic kits, remedies, study courses, videos, seminars, reference books, software, general information.

Frontier Herb Coop
2000 Frontier
Norway IA 52318
(800) 729-5422

Organically grown herbs, spices, extracts, tinctures. Will sell bulk amounts. Check out the web site for full description of their products: www.frontiercoop.com

Cascade Healthcare Products, Inc. Supplies, instruments, books, etc.
141 Commercial St. NE
Salem, Oregon 97301
(800) 462-4784

Supplies, instruments, books, etc. Everything you need for your practice from "A" to "Z", wide spectrum of philosophy. Bought out Moonflower.

Health Center for Better Living
6189 Taylor Rd.
Naples, FL 33942
voice: (813) 566-2611
fax: (813) 566-9508

Herbals from Christian store. Best variety I have ever seen in catalog. Bulk, capsules, tinctures and tea bags. Write for catalog.

Mari Mann Herb Co.
1615 St. Louis Bridge Rd.
Decatur, IL 62526
(217) 423-6012

Organically grown (not wild crafted) herbs on own farm, non-toxic room deodorants, potpourri, etc., bulk herbs. Christian view, right to life. Write for catalog.

Faith Gibson; runs a couple of organizations, mostly over the internet:
1. Mennonite Order of Maternal Services, 760 San Clemente, Mountain View, CA 94043. Wrote an article: *How Religious Practice Can Help Us Preserve Community-based Midwifery.*
2. American College of Domiciliary Midwives, 285 Church St., Mountain View CA 94901. Write for information packet.

APPENDIX F

AFTERTHOUGHTS ON LEGAL ISSUES

In November of 1988, my apprentice and I attended a still-birth. Heart tones were fine until five minutes before birth, when they suddenly started to drop. We called 911 when the baby did not respond to CPR, and the local EMTs responded with the police. Mother, baby and I were all transported to the hospital in separate vehicles. I thought that I would be able to be with Pat to continue to support her, but instead they put me in a room for interrogation. Fortunately, I remembered:

Rule Number 1: do not talk to anyone about the case, no matter how sympathetic and kind they may be. What you say may and will be held against you. You may talk about the weather, sports, ladies fashions, etc., but not the case.

Rule Number 2: refer all questions regarding the case to your lawyer, even if you do no have one yet. Simply say you do not have his card with you at this time, and will not answer any questions unless he is present. This includes the police, coroner, press, physician(s), nurses, friends, and insurance companies.

I had heard of a lawyer in a neighboring city that specialized in alternative health defense, so he was the first lawyer I thought of when I was arrested over the phone seven days later. After the Grand Jury met (we were waiting in the hall outside of the jury room), I was booked (had a mug shot and got fingerprinted) and released on bail. The sheriff and staff were taught special procedures by the Department of Professional Regulation while the Grand Jury met, because they were treading on such thin circumstances, on how to proceed in my booking. After some negotiations, we plea-bargained with the Christian County prosecutor. The deal was that they would drop the felony charges of practicing medicine without a license (Class X: 3–4 years in prison and $10,000.00 fine) and we would sue the State of Illinois Department of Professional Regulation, Department of Public Health, the Illinois Secretary of State and the Governor. This would be a class-action suit, seeking to establish the right to practice midwifery, the right to obtain the education and apprenticeship necessary to become a midwife, and the right of the consumer to choose the services of a midwife. My lawyer explained to me that it was a perfect opportunity to establish the legality of midwifery in Illinois and perhaps nationally. He compared our case with the start of the civil rights movement; when a little black boy wanted to ride an empty bus that passed his home and school on its way to pick up white students. It sounded very noble and altruistic, so I agreed.

In 1992, after three years of writing briefs and two Federal preliminary hearings with extremely high legal fees charged by my lawyer, and enormous mental stress and the pressure of needing to practice exemplary midwifery, without ever having a court "trial" where testimony would be given and a decision would be made, I buckled and had a breakdown. I had lost the support of my family, church and friends. Only my friends in midwifery were still encouraging me, but they were all out of town, had no money or political clout, and I felt very alone. About this time my lawyer started putting pressure on me for large sums of money, "since he had given up his practice to work on my case." His attitude was perceived by me as not being friendly, so in order to stop increasing the debt, I dropped the suit. The statue of limitations had run out a year before, but because of my "high profile" (otherwise called "hutzpah") suit, it was suggested by my attorney that I would be watched very carefully, and I should stop practice.

That was a very difficult decision for me. I know God called me to be a midwife, and His calling and anointing is without repentance. I put in a lot of time praying about my "disappointing God, and disobeying His charge to me." This is when the Body of Christ began praying and fasting for me. We started attending an expression of the Body of Christ, about 50 miles from us, and through their ministry received deliverance and encouragement in the Lord. I have been restored to complete health and now teach in the fellowship as the Spirit leads.

At the time of my resignation, I had 30–40 clients and was attending 6–8 births a month, solo. This heavy workload was to try to pay my legal fees. I averaged about three hours sleep a night, when I got any, and put about 500 miles a week on my car. I was pretty stressed out, so it is no wonder I became ill. My spare time is now spent in quilting and sewing, and other family endeavors that had to take a back seat while attending to my midwifery practice.

As of September 1995, I became a Certified Professional Midwife. We believe CPM should be the national entry level of midwifery because it maintains the same skill and knowledge/education level as put forth in this book, thus, presenting to the midwifery client a useable standard on which to base her decision for care giver

ꟼNDEX

A

C

D

E

G

H

J

K

L

M

O

P

S

T

U

V

W